PRAISE FOR
LIFE, ON THE LINE

"This is an autobiography that rises above both [the food and cancer] genres. Achatz's story is a compelling tale of artistic genius that will make you cry and, if you are in the Chicago area, perhaps shell out $200 a person to eat his food."
—Associated Press

"[*Life, on the Line*] may be the best, most inspiring chef memoir ever written."
—*American Way*

"[*Life, on the Line*] is full of energy and without pretense."
—*Chicago Tribune*

"The next great food memoir."
—*Details*

"Perhaps knowing how the story ends—genius chef from a small Midwestern town survives advanced cancer of the tongue (the tongue!) to achieve every accolade known to his profession by the age of 36—is what makes the candid new memoir by Grant Achatz so compulsively readable. You want to know who this guy is, and *Life, on the Line* delivers."
—*Chicago* magazine

"This is not the cancer story in which the disease makes the guy realize he needs to stop focusing on his work and finally spend time with his two young sons, see his parents more, and reconnect with his former sweetheart. No, this is the cancer story that makes a man realize that his screaming ambition was right the whole time and that if he had only a month to live, he'd better get some stuff done."
—Joel Stein, *Time*

"This must-read for the culinary crowd is the literary equivalent of caviar and Krug. Foodies will marvel at Achatz's thought process on his molecular creations, while Kokonas provides a detailed glimpse of the artistic vision and creation of modern fine dining."

—*Booklist*

"Writing with the panache of professionals, Achatz, chef and owner of Chicago's Alinea, and his business partner, Kokonas, relate the story of Achatz's life and work in a memoir that lives up to its expansive subtitle. . . . Achatz and Kokonas share an engaging, well-written, and informative description of what it's like to work in commercial kitchens along with the stirring story of Achatz's fight for his life."

—*Library Journal*

"Much like sitting down to eat at his groundbreaking restaurant Alinea, reading the story behind Grant Achatz's life will take you places you never imagined. From his upbringing in a small family restaurant to staring death in the face while winning the title of Best Chef in the United States, his is a truly inspiring story—not only as a chef but as a person." —Eric Ripert, chef/co-owner, Le Bernardin

"What is amazing to me, a writer who's been covering this industry since about the time Grant arrived at The French Laundry, is the honesty and jarring frankness with which Grant and Nick write, from every angle—personal, emotional, even financial. Grant's career, the opening of Alinea, his beating cancer—it's a hell of a story." —Michael Ruhlman, author of *Ratio* and *The Soul of a Chef*

"As readers and booksellers, we're always delighted when a book affects us in one overarching way, but when it does so in three or four ways it's something to behold. *Life, on the Line* pinned me to my chair. Grant Achatz and Nick Kokonas's book is intense, what I can only think of as the literary equivalent of Grant's food—surprising and unique. . . . Ultimately, the book is a candid testament to a phenomenal creative drive joined with a phenomenal will to live. This *Life* is stunning."—Sheryl Cotleur, Book Passage, Corte Madera, CA

"When I first picked up the book I thought it was another self-promotion by a well-known chef. I was mistaken; it is the story of a man who rose to the top of his chosen profession by working incredibly long hours and paying meticulous attention to detail to produce food in the best way he could. He pushed the boundaries of how food was cooked and presented and won many fans and accolades as he did so. Grant Achatz was backed by Nick Kokonas financially, as a mentor and as a partner; his part of the book gives the reader a very good idea of what it to takes to set up and run a high-end restaurant. The kicker comes in the last few chapters where we learn that Grant had a particularly insidious form of cancer that could destroy his career or possibly end his life; the reader will then fully understand the title of the book. We can all get inspiration and hope from the way Grant battled the cancer and won."

> —Douglas Westgate, Octavia Books; New Orleans, LA

"*Life, on the Line* is easily one of my favorite food memoirs of all time. It's honest and powerful. For those of us in the book industry, the lessons they teach about the perfection possible in ceaseless change that's solidly grounded in hard work are essential."

> —Michael Barnard, Rakestraw Books, Danville, CA

LARA KASTNER

Grant Achatz is the multiple award-winning chef and owner of Alinea, Next, and The Aviary in Chicago. He has written for *Gourmet* and *The New York Times* Diner's Journal and is a columnist for *The Atlantic's* Food Channel. He lives in Chicago with his girlfriend and two sons, Kaden and Keller.

Nick Kokonas, since 2005, has partnered with Achatz to develop Alinea, Next, and The Aviary, where he is actively engaged in strategy, marketing, and planning. He lives with his wife and two sons in Chicago.

LIFE, ON THE LINE

A CHEF'S STORY OF CHASING GREATNESS, FACING DEATH, AND REDEFINING THE WAY WE EAT

GRANT ACHATZ
AND NICK KOKONAS

GOTHAM
BOOKS

GOTHAM BOOKS
Published by Penguin Group (USA) Inc.
375 Hudson Street, New York, New York 10014, U.S.A.

Penguin Group (Canada), 90 Eglinton Avenue East, Suite 700, Toronto, Ontario M4P 2Y3, Canada (a division of Pearson Penguin Canada Inc.) • Penguin Books Ltd, 80 Strand, London WC2R 0RL, England • Penguin Ireland, 25 St Stephen's Green, Dublin 2, Ireland (a division of Penguin Books Ltd) • Penguin Group (Australia), 250 Camberwell Road, Camberwell, Victoria 3124, Australia (a division of Pearson Australia Group Pty Ltd) • Penguin Books India Pvt Ltd, 11 Community Centre, Panchsheel Park, New Delhi–110 017, India • Penguin Group (NZ), 67 Apollo Drive, Rosedale, Auckland 0632, New Zealand (a division of Pearson New Zealand Ltd) • Penguin Books (South Africa) (Pty) Ltd, 24 Sturdee Avenue, Rosebank, Johannesburg 2196, South Africa

Penguin Books Ltd, Registered Offices: 80 Strand, London WC2R 0RL, England

Published by Gotham Books, a member of Penguin Group (USA) Inc.

Previously published as a Gotham Books hardcover edition

First trade paperback printing, March 2012

10 9 8 7 6 5 4 3 2 1

Gotham Books and the skyscraper logo are trademarks of Penguin Group (USA) Inc.

Chicago Tribune article on pages 376–378 reprinted with special permission of the Chicago Tribune; copyright Chicago Tribune; all rights reserved.

The images on pages 234, 235, 237, and 238 are courtesy of Grant Kessler. All other images within the text are courtesy of the author

The Library of Congress has cataloged the hardcover edition of this book as follows:

Achatz, Grant.
    Life, on the line : a chef's story of chasing greatness, facing death, and redefining the way we eat / Grant Achatz and Nick Kokonas.
      p. cm.
    ISBN 978-1-59240-601-2 (hardcover) 978-1-59240-697-5 (paperback)
1. Achatz, Grant.   2. Cooks—United States—Biography.   3. Cancer—Patients—United States—Biography.
I. Kokonas, Nick. II. Title.
    TX649.A25A3 2011
    641.5092—dc22
    [B]   2011004317

Printed in the United States of America
Set in Apollo MT and Gill Sans • Designed by Elke Sigal

While the author has made every effort to provide accurate telephone numbers and Internet addresses at the time of publication, neither the publisher nor the author assumes any responsibility for errors, or for changes that occur after publication. Further, the publisher does not have any control over and does not assume any responsibility for author or third-party Web sites or their content.

---

*Penguin is committed to publishing works of quality and integrity.
In that spirit, we are proud to offer this book to our readers;
however, the story, the experiences, and the words
are the author's alone.*

 LIFE, ON THE LINE

On June 8, 2008, I flew to New York to attend the James Beard Foundation Awards. I was nominated for the Outstanding Chef Award. It is the ultimate recognition a chef can get at the Beard Foundation, and arguably the ultimate recognition for an American chef, period. I wanted to win.

I just didn't want to be there when I won.

Five months earlier I had finished a brutal course of chemotherapy and radiation treatment for stage IVb squamous cell carcinoma. There is no stage V or even a IVc. The cancer was located primarily in my tongue and was a tumor that took up more than 50 percent of the visible part. According to the scans, it had also metastasized to my lymph system, located primarily on the left side of my neck. Everyone certainly *hoped* it had not spread below my collarbones. If it had, well—time to "get your affairs in order."

The chemotherapy had left me bald, pimpled, scaled, and sore. The radiation had burned my tongue and face from the inside out. The lining of my esophagus would shed like a snakeskin and I was forced to peel it out of my throat while choking and vomiting. I started the treatment at 172 pounds. By the end I weighed 127.

I couldn't taste a thing. Nothing. Food was cardboard and salt was just sand in my mouth, dissolving oddly and slowly with no purpose. Eating was a horrific and painful ordeal to be tolerated three or four times a day. Cooking at Alinea became a gauntlet to run every night: wonderful smells that you can't taste, food you used to love that you can't eat.

By the time the Beard Awards arrived, I had begun to recover from the treatment. I was in remission and apparently cancer-free. But the healing process would take time, and now I had to show up at Lincoln Center in New York, greet the other chefs, the restaurateurs, and the press.

I wanted to run away. I looked terrible. I had a scraggly goatee because I was unable to shave without peeling away my skin. My hair had started to grow back, but the back of my head was still bald—I looked like a sixteenth-century monk. My legs were sticks and the skin over my rib cage was sunken in. The tuxedo draped over my shoulders like it would on a hanger.

But what really concerned me was that I could barely talk. My tongue was half the size it used to be—it was nearly all tumors, and now those tumors had been vaporized by radiation. It was peeled, red, white, and sore, and the muscles that control it had been atrophied by the radiation. Part of my neck and most of my lymph nodes had been removed, leaving nerve damage under my chin. My lips didn't always go where I intended them to, and my speech sounded slurred and distorted. Like eating, speaking was arduous.

None of this was a good setup for a public appearance. And it got off to an awkward start. When I arrived at Lincoln Center, many of the country's great chefs tried to avoid me. No one approached me to say hello. I walked through the crowd and felt like a leper. At that time it did not occur to me that they were trying to "act normal," to not have to ask, "How are you doing?"

The only good news at this point was that I was reasonably certain I would not win. Nick Kokonas, my business partner, put my chances as only a good friend could: "You have no chance of winning. Dan Barber is going to kick your scrawny ass. He is a great chef, he's been at it longer, and he is from New York. That is a killer combo. And he cooks real food. You're screwed." We had a good laugh at that, but it was exactly what we both thought.

I grabbed a glass of champagne as a prop and stood in a corner with my girlfriend, Heather. Although I considered leaving, she convinced me to go inside and sit down. I slumped down in my seat and the awards began. These ceremonies tend to drag on, and Outstanding Chef was the very last award to be given.

Finally, Kim Cattrall slinked onstage to announce the last award of the evening. I perked up momentarily, smiled when my name was read as a nominee, and settled back into my chair. Then the announcement: "The Outstanding Chef in America for 2008 is . . . Grant Achatz." I was stunned. Suddenly I was onstage and the crowd stood, cheering. The words, unprepared, tumbled out of me:

"Rather than thank specific people who obviously I need to, but in fact, probably know who they are, I want to tell a quick story instead, if I could. In 1996, I started at The French Laundry as a commis. I was twenty-two years old, and I was in awe. I walked into that restaurant, and I saw a gentleman that ultimately would become my mentor and, at this point, even though it feels a little awkward to say, a great friend. What struck me about the restaurant was 'the push.' I had never seen it before in my life. I had never experienced the discipline, the dedication, the intensity, the tenacity, and the drive that both the chef and all of the cooks possessed. I pulled that in, thinking it was going to make me a good cook and ultimately, a great chef. What I didn't know was that it was actually going to save my life. That drive, that tenacity, that dedication that I took in at that restaurant . . . it became a part of who I am, ten years later, twelve years later. It helped me get through a pretty ridiculous battle.

"I think that everybody in the room can be proud of that, because everybody can relate to how cooking, in one way or another, has not only influenced their professional career, but also their lives. Also, I need to thank everybody in this room for the tremendous amount of support that I received in this last year. I had e-mails, countless phone calls, letters, packages, offers from chefs that I consider mentors, friends, colleagues, and visionaries to help in any way that they possibly could at a time when I needed it. I didn't let any of them come to the restaurant and cook like they suggested. I couldn't do that to the [Alinea] cooks. But the support that I received was critical at a time when I needed it and again, I think we can all be very proud of that. I know that it really helped me push through. That's really it. I'm kind of in awe. I think that it's an amazing honor, and I really appreciate it, and I thank you all. Thank you."

The award is fantastic for any chef to win, but for me it was a new beginning.

The news of my cancer was on the front page of the *Chicago Tribune* and covered prominently by the *Wall Street Journal* and the *New York Times*, but the news of my recovery was less publicized. Business at Alinea, for the first time ever, began to wane—patrons thought I was still sick, or worse—dead—and I was worried that while I had beaten cancer, I had not won the fight for the restaurant I loved. But that award made all the difference. Customers came back. I saw things more clearly and became more focused.

I returned to Alinea the next day, stepped into the kitchen, and worked with a vigor I had never felt before.

PART 1

STANDING ON THE MILK CRATE

My mom pulled a dining room chair over to the stove and turned a milk crate upside down on the seat so I could stir the cherry Jell-O into the hot water. I watched as the powder dissolved like magic, knowing that when it cooled, it would turn into a strange, jiggly solid. At five years old, it was my introduction to cooking.

My mom worked weekends for Grandma Achatz at her restaurant in the riverside town of Marine City, Michigan. A village of four thousand, Marine City sat just across the border from Ontario, Canada. Mom baked pies and cooked short-order breakfasts while I was given a few dishes to "wash." The Achatz Café was tiny. The whole place was basically just eight bar stools and a kitchen, which wasn't much aside from a tabletop griddle for the hash browns, bacon, and sausage links; a few small residential refrigerators; and a beat-up stove. The design was Americana, circa 1965.

My dad's sisters Liz and Patty cooked while Aunt Cathy waited tables. They would do their work while giving me small tasks to keep me occupied and out of the way.

I never got a toy Easy-Bake oven or a play kitchen. I played every day at the Achatz Café surrounded by my family and a town full of people who knew my name.

As I grew a bit older I graduated from pot washer to vegetable peeler and eventually to chief egg cracker. The egg station, two portable electric burners with not much more power than a coffee warmer, was situated at the front of the restaurant in front of a few large windows overlooking Main Street.

There was a lot of foot traffic on Main during the warmer months, and people peeked in to see me sitting on the counter next to my grandmother, cracking eggs into the pans for her.

"We got an 'over hard,' Grant, you're up!" she would call out. I would then run over to crack a few eggs. With the over-hards it didn't matter if the yolks broke. But through time I broke fewer and fewer, and one day my grandmother called me over and said, "This one's over easy." I cracked carefully, aware that the customers were watching. A bit of pride welled up in me. I was the little kid who could cook—I was at the top of the egg-station now, doing the over-easies.

In February 1980, when I was seven, my parents borrowed $5,000 from my grandmother to open their own restaurant.

Mickey's Dutch Treat was an ice-cream parlor right next to the train tracks that divided the small community of Richmond, Michigan. My grandmother's sister had heard that the owner wanted out and mentioned it suggestively to my father. Dad was hanging drywall at the time, but he had worked in restaurants off and on since he was sixteen. The dream of self-employment was something he always fostered, and cooking seemed as logical a choice as any other for a business.

The new restaurant was given a quick once-over, and the Achatz Depot was born. It was open for breakfast, lunch, and dinner seven days a week—and my dad didn't skip a day that first year.

From the start the Depot was busy. The Achatz name was synonymous with food in the area. There was of course my grandmother's place in Marine City, and ten miles to the east in Armanda, Dave Achatz—my dad's first cousin—owned a very successful diner. Irene's Catering, my great-uncle's business, had been feeding people at weddings, graduations, and funerals for years. The Achatz family fed the community, cradle to grave.

Achatz Depot grossed nearly $200,000 its first year, all the while paying the enormous rent of $300 per month. That is good money now, and in 1980 it was a huge success. Dad worked eighteen hours a day then, but he didn't seem to mind it. Success has a way of making the work seem less like, well, work.

Much like his mother's place, the general hiring strategy was to find the closest family members and put them to work. My mom was there while I was at school. Two of my dad's brothers, a couple of sisters, a cousin, and my mom's brother also worked there. The Achatz Depot was more like the Achatz Family Reunion with a shifting cast of characters, depending on the day and time. And like before, I came in whenever I could during the week and all day on the weekends.

It felt like home.

"Just take the burger blanket, stick three or four fries in the middle, and wrap that sucker up like a taco and eat it." Burger blankets were thin-cut, half-dollar-sized pickles that we put on nearly every sandwich.

Uncle Norm demonstrated the process of eating his creation with exaggerated gusto. He tilted his head to the side and looked like Ozzy biting the head off a bat, complete with growling sound effects. These kinds of things can leave an impression on a young boy.

Norm, my dad's youngest brother, was baby-faced, but big. Tall, thick-boned, and bordering on rotund, he was the archetypal mean uncle. He was the relative who would wrestle a bit too hard and hit you on the shoulder when you weren't looking, leaving a serious mark. A headlock followed by some *SNL* noogies were standard protocol every chance he got. "This will toughen you up, you spoiled brat."

Norm was my godfather. He was also a surrogate big brother, a sibling that I never had. I loved him a lot despite, or perhaps because of, the tough love. Like most of my extended family, Norm worked at the Depot as a line cook between his own drywalling jobs. He was definitely rough around the edges—he had a raspy voice from years of drinking and cigarettes, callused hands from hanging drywall and cooking most of his life, and a fading, crappy tattoo on his forearm that read simply, NORM. Occasionally, when there were a few moments to spare and Norm and my dad shared a beer or two, they would spin tales of pool games and bar fights, and to my eight-year-old ears it seemed that Norm was indeed a good coach for learning to get tough. He lived alone and spent much of his free time hunting and fishing. Norm basically lived a Hank Williams Jr. song, and whenever possible, I tried to tag along.

"Grant, you just try it. Trust me, it's good," he chuckled in the way that usually meant anything but "trust me."

I was pretty sure this was a mean prank to gross me out. I backed away slowly, out of arm's length, and bought some time to see if he made himself another of these strange concoctions. He did, over and over. He genuinely seemed to be enjoying them. Eventually I got curious enough to try it.

I took the first bite carefully and braced myself for a putrid taste. But somehow it was good. No, it was really, really delicious. I reached for another.

"I told you. See, you should listen to your uncle Norm more often. I have a few things I can teach you."

"It's so weird, though, right?"

"Not really—you put ketchup on your fries, right?"

"Yep."

"Well, what's in ketchup, Grant?" He said this with a swooping voice, emphasizing that he was stating the obvious.

"I don't know, tomatoes?"

"Well, yeah, but what else? There's a ton of shit in there, right?" He walked over to the shelf and grabbed a bottle of Heinz. "Here, read the label, little man."

"Tomatoes, corn syrup, vinegar, salt, sugar . . ."

He cut me off, "Right. And what is in pickles?"

He grabbed the five-gallon bucket of "burger blanket–style" pickles and put it down on the stainless-steel counter with a wallop for emphasis.

"Okay. Now read these ingredients to me."

I started, "Cucumbers, water, vinegar, salt, sugar . . . hey, what is that?" I pointed to the calcium chloride.

"No idea! Come on. See what I'm getting at? All the same stuff in there. They just swapped out the mashed-up tomatoes for some cucumbers, and bam, you get a pickle. In London they shake vinegar on their fries."

"Really? Gross. But this tastes good!"

"Of course it does!" he bellowed as he flipped his side towel off his shoulder, twirled it up, and snapped me in the thigh.

By the time I was nine the Achatz Depot had settled into a steady and more predictable pace, and my dad put the systems in place that allowed him some free time. He was still working eighty hours a week, but he found time to spend with me outside the restaurant.

He enrolled me in karate, and every Tuesday night we'd go together to the dojo.

We'd strap on our helmets and I'd jump on the back of his Honda V65 Magna, wrap my arms around his torso with a death grip, and we'd shoot down St. Clair Highway. He would yell over the noise from the air whizzing by our heads about how to improve my form or the strategy needed for an upcoming sparring session.

One night he was explaining how you don't have to hit someone hard to take them down.

"Aim for the nose or the solar plexus, and down they go."

He was midsentence when he stopped instantly. In the newfound silence, he pointed out a deer standing in a cornfield. The man noticed everything. He was aware. He had an attention to detail that I marveled at.

I loved the competitive environment of karate, but more than anything I was just trying to find something that I was really good at. Success in karate seemed simple to me—you trained, learned the required forms, and tested for belt advancement. It was clear at a glance who was better than you were because they were wearing the proof around their waist.

On sparring days the goal was even simpler, if a bit more brutal: beat your opponent. Victory provided instant gratification. I was fiercely competitive, accepting challenges from older kids, knowing that I would get my ass kicked, but knowing too that I would get in a few good blows.

I also knew that my dad was watching.

With the Achatz Depot thriving, my parents tried to buy the building, but the owner refused repeated requests to sell. Minor problems that could be easily fixed turned into bigger problems, and the irritation of having a landlord took a toll, even though the rent was cheap.

Once they realized that the purchase would never happen they began looking for a bigger space to capture the excess demand. A co-op–owned restaurant that was inside of a 95,000-square-foot farmers' supply store a few miles away presented an opportunity to expand.

My parents made the move.

When we took over the new space it was a complete disaster. The owner wanted to be gone in a bad way, so he literally walked out to the parking lot and handed my parents the keys, leaving garbage in trash cans and food in the refrigerators. A small team was hired to begin the cleanup while the current crew kept the Depot running until the new restaurant opened. I helped my parents clean the filthy kitchen and declared the walk-in refrigerator my personal project. I went in armed with rubber gloves, a bucket of soapy water, and a jug of bleach. The previous owner had only been gone one day, but what I found there made it seem like it had been months. Five-gallon pickle buckets sat one-quarter full of tomato sauce with a thick moldy crust on the surface. Iceberg lettuce heads were liquefying in the cardboard box they came in. Then I came upon a partially unwrapped hotel pan of what seemed to be a meatlike substance that smelled so bad I ran out of the cooler to keep from vomiting. I took a deep breath, ran in to retrieve the pan of rotting flesh, and ran out to the Dumpster as quickly as I could. It was the single most disturbing thing I have ever seen in any kitchen, and the smell haunts me to this day. Some people just don't have standards. I learned that at an early age, spending the better part of three days scrubbing down that walk-in until the smell lingered no more.

The Achatz Family Restaurant opened one month later in March 1983 to a flood of business. Revenue grew 30 percent that year and the next, and when, after two years, investors bought out the co-op, the opportunity to expand presented itself once again.

My parents borrowed $175,000 from a local bank at the stratospheric interest rate of 17.5 percent, signed a ten-year lease, and expanded to 4,000 square feet. The dining room was gutted and all-new booths, fixtures, carpet, and wall coverings were added. After a major six-week renovation, the place could now accomodate 165 people. Our little diner was not so little anymore.

When the restaurant reopened, the whole town showed up and pretty much never left. My parents had to hire nearly every one of our relatives to keep up with demand, and the Achatz Family Restaurant had its first $1 million gross revenue year.

Things were good in the Achatz household.

I arrived home from school one afternoon when I was eleven to see what looked like a spaceship parked in my driveway. The sleek silver object glistened in the afternoon sun. The doors, hatch, and hood were all open. I ran up to the car, stuck my head in the window, and was struck by the smell of new-car leather. As I was pulling my head out to run around back, I heard my dad say, "Pretty cool, huh? Nineteen eighty-five Corvette. Check out the gauges. They light up like *Knight Rider.*"

My dad closed down the doors and the hood, and I hopped in the passenger seat. The engine rumbled. I was in heaven. He slowly backed out of the driveway and I heard my mom yell from the house, "Put your seat belts on! Don't drive crazy!" We both laughed. My dad crept down the street away from our house and turned the corner—he was taking it easy while my mom could still see us.

And that moment, blasting down the road in a brand-new Corvette . . .

CHAPTER 2

My paternal grandfather died at forty, when my father was very young. I think my dad was determined to enjoy his success—after all, it was hard-won from hard work. Nothing was given to us, and we all contributed.

But my dad had a hard time with success.

My mother and father were married in August 1973, exactly eight months before I was born. It isn't hard to do the math. My family was stable as long as the work was hard and steady, but marital turbulence was frequent during my childhood. My dad's drinking was the source of many temporary separations between he and my mother, although I was largely unaware of the problems.

By 1986, three years after my parents' restaurant opened, the stresses of running a demanding business coupled with my father's increasingly heavy drinking led to a split that became a divorce. By this time I had graduated to working the line during the weekends, but once my parents separated, my mom stopped going to the restaurant, and so did I. The weekends that were normally filled with flipping pancakes, French toast, and hash browns were now consumed with riding dirt bikes and hunting with my cousin Tim at his house in the country. These were my first real idle weekends of just hanging out with friends in the neighborhood. But it didn't seem as satisfying.

Throughout my parents' separation and divorce, my mom shielded me from the issues surrounding my dad's drinking. I didn't know quite what was going on, I only knew that they still talked, that the restaurant still existed, and that my dad wasn't around the house. In fact, I never saw him during the times he wasn't living in the house. He visited rarely. He was either in or out, and when he was out he simply vanished.

Nearly a year later my father returned. Suddenly he was back, and we didn't talk about the time away from each other. And for my part, I was just happy he had come home. As quietly as my parents divorced, they reconciled and were quickly remarried.

Everything became remarkably normal again.

In the spring of 1988, when I was fourteen, my dad asked me what kind of car I wanted when I turned sixteen. He loved cars, and he wanted me to love them too.

"A fast one," I said.

My dad had the idea of buying an old muscle car and restoring it with me. I couldn't have been more excited. I read about cars often and had a fairly good knowledge of the different makes from building 1:24-scale plastic models with my dad. He would guide me through the building process, but I was in charge of figuring out the instructions and doing the assembly. A dozen of these projects were lined up on my dresser, and you could see the progression of build-quality from early childhood on. The first one was the "General Lee" from the TV show *The Dukes of Hazzard*. It had crooked decals and thick, drippy paint. The roll cage looked like it was melted because of the thick globs of glue that hung off of it.

Eager to find the first real car that I would build with my dad, I would ride my bike every week down to the Speedy Q gas station to pick up an *Auto Trader*. After searching for a few months we settled on a 1970 Pontiac GTO that was about a two-hour drive away in Flint, Michigan. My dad called the owner, who had a pole barn full of old muscle cars, and they haggled out a price of $1,400.

The GTO was not really a car at this point. It was disassembled and in about fifty boxes, but the guy promised my dad that all the parts were there. Sight unseen, we arranged for a flatbed wrecker to follow us to Flint to pick up the car, and Uncle Norm came along for the ride.

Just before we got there my dad looked at me and said, "Now don't be disappointed when you see it, Grant. Remember, this thing is not even going to look like a car. It's in a million pieces and the back fender is smashed in. I promise you, we are going to make this thing look like new, but it's going to take real time and effort."

As we hopped out of the pickup truck the owner of the pieces came out of his house and greeted us with a firm handshake. As we walked back to the barn he looked at me and said, "So, son. Is this going to be your car?"

"Yes," I said quietly.

"You know what kind of car it is?"

"Yes, sir, I do. It's a Goat. This one should have a 'YS' stamped 400, right?" That referred to the code on the engine block with a 400-cubic-inch, 350-horsepower automatic. Over the past week I had read everything I could find on Goats and was trying to act smart.

"Well, I guess you do know then! You're a lucky kid, but I hope you're good with a wrench, too."

"I think we'll be fine," my dad said as he shot me a wink.

We shoved the front fenders inside the empty chassis shell and the flatbed started to pull the car up the platform. We loaded the doors, boxes of parts, and bags of unknown stuff into the back of the pickup and headed home to St. Clair.

My dad knew that this would be a fantastic life lesson on organization, hard work, and persistence. You want a great car? Build one.

At first my motivation waned. The car didn't look like anything I wanted to drive, and it was difficult for me to visualize the end result. It was also really hard work to build it.

The first step was restoring the frame to its original condition and that meant the miserable task of sandblasting years of rust, grease, and tar from the skeleton. I would suit up in a thick ski-coat with gloves, put the hood up, and drop a shield in front of my face so the sand wouldn't get in my eyes or rip off my skin. As the sand whizzed out of the nozzle it would bounce off the frame and scatter everywhere—down my shirt, and in my pants and my hair. I would shower twice after finishing but still find sand behind my ears the next day in school.

My dad sensed when my motivation wavered and kept me interested by letting me choose cosmetic improvements: a chrome air filter, metal-braided plug wires, and eventually the wheels. He gave me books and encouraged me to learn about everything we were doing. Before work began we talked about what we hoped to accomplish that day, and he'd hand me the giant builder's manual to look up the procedures. We then carefully grouped, labeled, and boxed up all the loose parts in the order they would be needed.

It was a lot like organizing a kitchen.

The deeper we got into the project, the more it grew. I don't think my dad realized how involved it would become. We converted the garage into a miniature body shop and my dad took crash courses on painting, bodywork, and welding. Before long we had giant air compressors, a host of specialty tools, and were as adept at talking the lingo as mechanics.

For Christmas my parents got me a complete Alpine sound system for the half-built car: equalizer, six-disc CD changer, and radio. I opened the presents in rapid succession and the signature black and green boxes piled up. I was shocked that the biggest of the bunch read ROCKFORD FOSGATE.

"Wow! You guys got me Rockford Fosgate subwoofers? Unbelievable! But where is the box?" I asked, referring to the enclosure for speakers.

"You're going to build the box, Grant."

"Build it? Build the box?"

None of the prefabs would fit level in the trunk—they were all made for flat trunks. My dad thought that if we studied the way the boxes work, we could make one that was louder—and cooler—than anything we could buy.

At the two-year mark we were nearly done. We took the entire body off the frame and disassembled the main pieces, painted and cleaned each one, and put them back together. My dad painted the body bright red, the original color, and I helped him stretch and glue down the black vinyl top. We bought reproduction material for the seats, brand-new premolded carpet for the floor, and had the dashboard and rubber bumper sent out to be re-dipped so that they'd look like new. Then, at last, we bolted on the oversize centerline wheels.

On my sixteenth birthday we stood in front of the car and my dad dropped the keys into my hand. We looked at a show-quality 1970 GTO that my dad and I had built together.

"Let's go for a ride."

I was making dinner at home one evening in 1995, chatting with my mom and waiting for my dad to return from his weekly golf league outing when I heard the phone ring, watched my mom answer, and could tell immediately that something was wrong.

"That was the golf course. They want me to come get your dad."

"What? Why?"

"Apparently he's too drunk to drive."

I offered to go, but my mom refused. Instead, I rode with her. Anticipating his reaction, especially when he saw me, I suggested we make sure he was somehow unable to jump in his truck and drive off. When we reached the course, I popped the hood of his truck and pulled all of the wires from the spark plugs and the distributor. I knew from building the GTO that each plug wire aligns with a specific plug on the cap to ensure the engine fires in succession. Once the order is lost it would take him an hour to get the plugs synchronized—when he was sober, that is. I closed the hood, and we walked inside to retrieve my dad.

He insisted, of course, that he was fine as he stumbled out of the club toward the truck. Instead of fighting him, I motioned to my mom to let him get in and turn the key.

The truck sat there silently as he turned the ignition. He figured out what I'd done and shot me a look with a raised eyebrow and faint smile before he got angry. I suspect he appreciated the cleverness for a moment; he had no choice but to surrender to the backseat of my mom's car.

The fifteen-minute ride was painful.

"What the hell is wrong with you?" my mom lectured. "Is that want you want? To have your son see you like this?"

My father sat there in silence, his head bobbing up and down a bit with the bumps in the road, not saying a word or reacting in any way. It was as if she didn't exist.

I just shook my head, still trying to process what I was now bearing witness to.

When we arrived home, I went upstairs to my room and immediately put on my headphones. I knew that an argument would start when my dad sobered up enough to process everything, and I didn't want to hear it. A few minutes went by and suddenly my mom opened my bedroom door.

"He snuck out, Grant. I think he's on your mountain bike."

"What! Jesus . . ."

"I hid all the keys thinking he would try to take a car or a dirt bike. So I guess he took your bicycle."

I rolled out of the driveway and turned left down the pothole-riddled dirt road that was the route back to his truck. I figured he would go there and try to fix it. I had driven about three miles when I saw some movement in a ditch about 100 yards ahead of me. I slowed down and was pulling up when I realized it was him. There was Dad, crawling out of the ditch, covered in mud, carrying the bike in one hand.

I got out of the car and walked up to him. "What the hell are you doing, Dad? You stole my fucking bike? Really?"

"I think I hurt my shoulder," he said without expression. He dropped the bike, and his right hand reached across to his left shoulder. He started to lift his shirt up but couldn't move his left arm.

I walked him over in front of the car so we could use the headlights to look more closely.

When he lifted his hand away from the area I saw a protrusion lifting his shirt like a tent pole.

We wrestled his shirt halfway off to find his collarbone fighting to break through his skin. "We have to get you to the hospital."

"No, Grant. I'm fine."

"Fine? You have a goddamn bone sticking out of your shoulder!"

"I'll go tomorrow."

For all of my childhood right through my teen years, in part because of my mother's tenacious protection of me and her ability to shield and conceal my father's growing debauchery and drinking, I was able to pretend that everything was fine. He was my dad, and an amazing one much of the time.

Most kids get to go to work with their dad once a year. For them it's a cool experience to head to their dad's office and imagine themselves in his shoes, grown up and in a position of power and responsibility. I got to work alongside my dad my whole life. I understood early the sacrifices that were made for our success.

There was a wild irony that came with our relationship. We spent real quality time together hunting, fishing, building the GTO, playing T-ball, and going to karate. He showed me how to ride a motorcycle and throw a football. Then he would simply disappear for a day, a week, or even a year. The time would go by and we would not speak at all.

When he would return home, as he inevitably did, nothing was said. I chose to pretend everything was fine because I so desperately wanted it to be fine. I wanted him to come back to my hockey games, to go fishing by the river, and to cook together at the restaurant.

But he slipped in and out of our lives with increasing frequency. As I grew older I learned about the DWIs, the jail time, and the adultery.

That day in the ditch was my shot at confronting who my father had become. It was the reason I insisted on going to the golf course with my mother—I needed to see him in that state that I had only wondered about, that my mother dealt with her whole life while trying desperately to hide it from me. When I found him in the ditch with a broken collarbone he couldn't even feel, I thought it might embarrass him enough that he might quit drinking, quit leaving.

But more than that I just wanted so badly to know why. So I took the opportunity to ask him—why he couldn't take more responsibility, why he couldn't stop.

With surprising tenderness my dad admitted to his addiction and his inability to control it. He spoke of the hold it had on him and how he had worried that I would fall into the same destructive habits. But ultimately, he believed I'd be stronger than he was.

And so that night, on the hood of the car with a bone piercing through his shoulder, we had a real conversation. I asked him where his addiction came from, when it started, and whether he thought it was genetic—his father had had similar issues—or whether it was brought on by the social upheaval of the sixties. I asked him pointedly about the affairs I suspected him of having and his twenty-five-year relationship with my mother.

I asked him if he would ever quit drinking. I asked him if he even wanted to quit.

We talked for an hour, then we drove home, and he slept all night in the recliner in the living room.

My mother took him to the hospital the next morning.

CHAPTER 3

I was an average student at best. I got good grades in the classes that I found compelling and challenging, like architectural drafting, art, and mechanical drawing. But the core curriculum classes of English, math, and science were across-the-board C's and D's. I was more interested in the restaurant than I was in school.

My parents wanted me to learn every aspect of the business. Despite my experience throughout my childhood in my grandmother's restaurant and at the Depot, when I hit middle-school age my parents made me start over. Now I was a real worker and was relied upon. At twelve I was back to being a dishwasher, but this time as an actual employee. I was allowed to do some basic food prep, and when I was thirteen, I had moved up to making and buttering toast.

At fourteen I graduated to cooking on the line and was scheduled for three to five shifts a week, just like the other cooks. I was given unusual responsibility for my age—I had a key to the restaurant and the alarm code. I would head over after school around 4:00 P.M. and work straight through closing, which by the time cleanup was over was around ten.

The Achatz Restaurant was all about volume, and like all restaurants, profit margins were low. But here, in a small town where prices had to be kept as low as possible, the margins were razor thin. My parents knew well that in order to make money the place needed to keep people flowing through constantly. They also knew that the people of this tiny farming community didn't care if an orange slice or a sprig of parsley adorned the plate for decoration. They wanted a big mound of hot, tasty food for little money, and they wanted it fast.

My dad ensured that they got that, and that he kept a tight control on costs.

I learned quickly that in order to be a successful line cook in a high-volume operation you needed to keep your cool and be highly organized. It wasn't that different than building the GTO: sort things out, keep them straight and organized, and plug away deliberately.

In the summer of 1991 I was given my first opening shift. I had to get to the restaurant by 5:00 A.M. to open at 5:30. I was pretty terrified at first since the restaurant was now solely my responsibility. But I quickly got used to the pressure and grew to love the feeling of opening up and letting the staff in.

Sherry, the opening waitress, was the second to arrive in the morning. The early risers would then trickle in for the first few hours. These were the hard-core regulars, the guys you saw nearly every day at exactly the same time. They walked over to the same seat, nodded hello to Sherry and their neighbors, and simply waited for their food to come. They wouldn't even have to order because Sherry knew what they wanted. She would head to the window and say, "Rycer is here."

"Got it."

Rycer's extra-crispy bacon, which for him meant that it was basically burnt, was on the griddle at 5:12 A.M. every day.

The next guy in was usually the kitchen manager, Jim. Jim was a short, stocky guy of Scottish descent, complete with the reddened cheeks and neck. My dad hired him to take over some of the kitchen management responsibilities in order to loosen up his schedule. Jim would arrive early and spend the start of his day preparing the daily specials, then transition to service around late breakfast time to help the opening cook push through the busiest moments.

Jim and I connected right away. He was fourteen years older than me, but he still knew how to have fun. He told me stories about his days cruising Gratiot Avenue and tall tales of hunting misfortunes. I soaked up these stories like he was my long-lost older brother, and he responded by calling me "Junior."

It was my goal to have the place buttoned up by the time Jim came in each morning. All of the produce and meat deliveries that arrived early needed to be put away, the kitchen had to be cleaned, and the *mise en place* for the breakfast run was set. I had to focus and move quickly from the moment I opened the door until Jim showed up.

The menu at the restaurant was vast. Breakfast was served at any hour, and the rest of the menu was diverse. That required a long line, about thirty feet, that held two griddles, two deep fryers, a twelve-burner stove, a char broiler, steam table, and a couple of stand-up refrigerators. Cooks had to run from one end of the line to the other whenever they were working on several tables at once. I learned very quickly to prioritize my steps in order to reduce movement and to not waste time running around in circles.

I began playing a game, challenging myself to see how long I could run a service by myself while Jim worked in the prep kitchen. He would be back there prepping the specials—Cajun meatloaf, Salisbury steak, Stroganoff, and soups and gravies—but he kept one eye on me in case I started "going down."

"You okay over there, Junior?"

"Yep. Never better," I would shout back while juggling four sets of over-easy eggs, pancakes, hash browns, and a BLT while dropping an order of fries in the fryer.

I spent my free time with a close group of six friends who shared the same interests: girls, cars, four-wheel-drive trucks, motorcycles, and sports. We were a clean-cut group. I never drank alcohol, did any drug, or even tried a cigarette—it just wasn't part of our program. We found other ways to get in trouble.

We rode around on ATVs well before we got our driver's licenses and thought nothing of driving them straight down the middle of the road. The police frowned upon this behavior and would escort us home. But on the fifth or sixth offense they made us stop in our tracks and called our parents to come pick us up—regardless of where we were at the time. They figured if they made it highly inconvenient for our parents that maybe they'd have an incentive to stop us. It did not, however, seem worth a ticket, since it was such a common offense.

Right after my sixteenth birthday I took the GTO out on its official maiden voyage with my buddies. My parents watched from the door as I pulled out of the driveway to gather my friends, who fought to see who rode shotgun.

I didn't get pulled over once during that first day. Nope—I got pulled over *twice*.

I was driving toward the highway at a very reasonable speed when a police car swooped in behind us. I eased off the gas slowly so he wouldn't hear the popping noise coming from the cherry-bomb mufflers. I wasn't speeding and the radio wasn't even on—I had no idea what the problem was. The officer explained that the back bumper was too high off the ground. I told him that it needed to be that high to make sure that it didn't rub on the oversized wheels. "Get smaller tires," he suggested, without missing a beat. He then promptly wrote me a ticket before pointing out that he'd also be writing me up for my tinted windows. "You do realize that tinted windows are illegal in Michigan, son, right?" Well, no, I hadn't, and now I was twenty minutes into my solo driving career and had two tickets.

At the urging of my friends I decided to press on, taking a few laps in town with the subwoofer thumping out Sir Mix-A-Lot. I headed to the school parking lot, then pulled a U-turn and headed toward a long, straight road right in front of the school.

I slammed my foot down on the accelerator and instantly the car slowed down. The tires were just spinning in place, smoking like crazy. Huge plumes engulfed the car.

The tires heated up and gained traction, and we shot forward like a rocket. My foot did not come off the gas until I had to brake hard for a stop sign at the end of the road. We could see the cloud of blue smoke trailing behind us, and we were positively giddy for about three seconds until my friend Mike saw the police car directly in front of us.

"Uh-oh."

When the cop looked at my license he shook his head disapprovingly, "First day, huh?

My maternal grandfather was a retired fireman in St. Clair, and in his house you could always hear the blare of the police scanner. It didn't take long for my mom to find out what we were doing that day.

The cop, too, must have figured out who I was, because he let me go with only a stern warning. Either that or he figured two tickets and a near miss were enough to set me straight. We resumed driving around town—very slowly—and ended up in the Burger King parking lot, chatting with some schoolmates and trying to find some girls, when my mom came rolling up to us.

She lowered her window, looked at me in the eye, and said, "Grant, you take that car home, and I mean right now!"

I was deflated and embarrassed in front of my friends and schoolmates. It had the intended effect.

On the weekends my friends and I organized camping trips on land that my parents had bought on Puttygut Road. It was an easy way for us to break free from the supervision of protective parents and stay out all night. We'd stock up on supplies at the Achatz Restaurant on the way out of town, eating dinner first then grabbing coolers full of eggs, milk, cheese, butter, sausage, bacon, and bread. We did it so frequently that my friends just walked in the back door like they owned the place. It was as though they were coming by my house.

I was the obvious choice to be designated the campfire cook. We would sit around the fire and talk about life in St. Clair. Most of us wanted to get out of there. Within our group, guys were applying to colleges, considering the U.S. Air Force, or taking computer classes in AutoCAD. There was genuine angst about what we wanted to do with our lives, how we could see the world beyond Michigan. But whenever talk came around to my ambitions, no one understood why I wouldn't just take over my parents' restaurant. They saw that I had plenty of toys, and my parents seemed relatively well-off. And they knew I was capable of running the place.

I assured them that that was not the case, and that I wouldn't be staying in St. Clair. I had started thinking about culinary school and had read about the Culinary Institute of America in New York. I explained that I wanted to cook fancy food and one day own my own restaurant—a great restaurant. But my friends, who wrote me off as a deluded dreamer, laughed. Soon we were all wailing with laughter. But I thought, "If you can fly a fighter jet, great. But I'm going to own a great restaurant, a famous one."

I had one long-term girlfriend throughout my school years, Cindy Morgan.

Cindy grew up on the other side of the metaphoric tracks. Her family was upper-middle-class, well educated, and fiercely Catholic. Her father, John, was a successful civil engineer and former Air Force pilot. She had two older sisters and a younger brother, all smart and engaging. The Morgan home was "on the river," as was said in the town. The affluent families gathered along the St. Clair River in large homes situated close to boathouses, docks, and piers. Cindy and I started out as mutual friends of my first real crush, Stephanie Petrone. After Stephanie and I had a falling out, Cindy and I grew closer, transitioning as we grew older from friends, to best friends, to boyfriend and girlfriend.

I always felt slightly discomforted by Cindy's family. They had an overt awareness of religion, social class, and educational achievement that made me realize I had a very different upbringing. I was a cook, after all, and that wasn't—in my mind—a manly or lucrative career. Cindy always told me that it was my own insecurity that made me feel that way, and of course she was right. But I never liked going over to their home. I always felt like I didn't measure up.

Knowing that her family was incredibly important to her, though, I always made an effort to spend time with them. In an effort to prove my worth to her father, or perhaps to myself, I offered to cook dinner one night.

Earlier that week I had learned a new recipe from watching Jim cook a dish he was running as a special. He had worked at some of the nicer restaurants in the area and I always looked at him as a Chef— capital "C." One night he was preparing a simple chicken stir-fry when he leaned over to me and said, "Watch this. This here is the secret."

He grabbed a spoon and stuck it in a jar of apricot preserves, removed a dollop and snapped it into the sauté pan. He shook the pan and tossed the vegetables in the air with a bit of showmanship. Then he poured a splash of white wine in the pan and it burst into flames.

I thought that was pretty damn cool. And it tasted fantastic.

Armed with the amazing technique of adding sugar and booze to a pan of vegetables and some chicken I felt confident that I could impress the Morgan family. I set up shop in the kitchen while Cindy and her mom went to the living room to read. The rest of the family wasn't home yet. I was plowing through my prep when I heard Mr. Morgan come home and Cindy's mom mention that I was in the kitchen cooking them a fancy dinner. I tensed up.

I had all of the vegetables washed and the rice cooked when I pulled out the only chef knife they had from its wood block holder. I ran my thumb over the eight-inch knife's blade and winced. I couldn't tell the sharp end from the back of the knife. I walked into the living room to find most of the family reading and her brother, John Jr., watching ESPN.

"Uh, do you have a steel?" I asked.

"A steel?" Mrs. Morgan replied.

"Yeah, you know, a round metal tool used to sharpen knives."

"Oh. No. We don't have a knife sharpener. Never needed one."

"Great," I thought to myself.

I went back to the kitchen determined to make do and started slicing and julienning the vegetables. I worked my way through the red bell peppers and moved on to the carrots. As I neared the end of a large carrot I took a hard downward rock that the dull knife required and was all of a sudden struck by intense pain in my left hand. I immediately dropped the knife and clinched my hand into a fist and jammed it into my waist. My nausea intensified when I looked down to see a chunk of my index finger, nail still attached, lying there next to the carrots.

I tried to compose myself, but my forehead was beaded with sweat and my hand pulsed like my heart had relocated there. I knew I had to walk through the living room, past the entire Morgan family, to get to the bathroom. I scooted past everyone quickly and closed the door behind me. I flipped on the cold water with my good hand, opened my fist, and the sink turned red.

"I am so screwed."

I riffled through the medicine cabinet and under the sink. No Band-Aids.

I mummified my finger in toilet paper, sat down on the toilet, and raised my arm above my head. I had to get the bleeding to stop.

"Grant, are you okay?" It was Cindy checking on me. I must have been in there for a while.

"Um . . . yeah, yeah. Fine. I nicked myself with the knife, just running some water over it and getting the bleeding to stop. Um . . . yeah. Do you have any Band-Aids? And I think I'll need some gauze, too."

She brought me some supplies, and I wrapped my wound as best I could. I glanced at Mr. Morgan as I walked back toward the kitchen. He peered over the newspaper at me. When our eyes met he darted back behind the paper, but I could still see the top of his head— shaking back and forth.

"I'm thinking about going to culinary school. What do you guys think?"

I had officially decided to make good on my dream to go to the Culinary Institute of America and now needed to see how my parents would feel about it. My mom and dad looked at each other, unsettled, before my dad spoke. "Well, I don't know. Are you sure you don't want to study drafting or architecture? You enjoy that and you do it very well."

My mom interjected, "We will support you in whatever you decide. We've set aside some money for school, so you don't have to worry about that."

"But you see how hard your mom and I work," my dad countered. "It's not easy and you don't make a ton of money for the amount of time you spend on it. And it's hard to have a good family life, too." Clearly my dad was pushing for me to do something else.

"That's okay," I blurted out, "I don't want a family."

My mom, taken aback, reminded me that I was her only hope for grandchildren. My father laughed quietly, as if he knew something I didn't. Ultimately we decided that I should at least do some research about the school before committing to anything. But I had already made up my mind.

CHAPTER 4

The fall after graduation most of my friends went away to college. Cindy left for Michigan State to study pre-law; my longtime friend Jim Stier joined the Air Force after all. I didn't go anywhere. I was still working at my parents' restaurant, growing more restless each day while awaiting acceptance to the Culinary Institute of America.

The letter finally came, and in February 1993, I packed my things and moved to Hyde Park, New York, with my friend Don Golder. Don was four years older than me and had been cooking for a long time. When Don got wind that I was applying to the CIA we decided to try for the same entry date so we could move out there together.

I expected the CIA to feel like the other colleges I had visited. But it was very different. The entire student body was older than me. Many were in their late twenties and were career-changers, or people who had started at a traditional university before deciding to pursue a culinary education.

Even more surprising was that the general attitude of the students was poor. I went in there to do one thing and one thing only: cook. I wanted to soak up all of the knowledge I could in the shortest amount of time possible. I had been a cook for years already, but this was my ticket to becoming a chef. Most of the students looked at the classes as an inconvenient interruption of their leisure activities. While they were going out to bars and partying, I hit the gym every day and then spent each night reading cookbooks.

I started buying culinary magazines like *Food & Wine* and *Gourmet* while standing in the grocery store checkout line. They didn't carry those titles in St. Clair, and I had never been exposed to fine dining. Suddenly, these cookbooks and magazines vastly expanded my awareness of the scope of the gastronomic world. There was this huge world that I wanted to explore, but I was incredibly naive. I had no understanding of the difference between haute cuisine and the classical education that I was exposed to every day. I joined the ice-carving club thinking it was going to be an important skill for me as a chef. I had no idea what a Michelin star was.

I breezed through the first several classes without any problem— they were incredibly basic. We began by learning how to hold and sharpen a knife, and then over the course of a week or two we progressed to actually learning how to cut something properly. Don and I would roll our eyes at these tasks—the knife already felt like a natural extension of our hands at this point—but to most of the class this was new information.

"This is stupid and a complete waste of time and money," Don would say after we came home from class and settled into the tiny dorm room we shared. And really, I didn't disagree.

We already had basic knife skills, knew basic kitchen etiquette, and most important, understood how a commercial kitchen operated. We were quick to task and had a strong sense of urgency. And we knew how to season food.

But slowly I changed my opinion, and I began to understand why the CIA curriculum started every student at point zero regardless of his background. Just because I worked in a diner since I was five didn't mean that I knew the right way to do things. Sure, I could get by, but what they were teaching us was based on years and years of refinement, so much so that they were culinary traditions. I was willing to rethink the basics because it became clear that I had a lot to learn. And one of those things was simply patience.

Before I left home, my dad bet me that I couldn't stay on the dean's list the entire time I was there. I had nothing but my pride to wager, but my dad offered up his 1985 Corvette, along with a personal restoration and paint job—any color I wanted.

During my entire enrollment at the CIA I received only one mark below 85. Most of my scores were in the nineties, and I was confident I would finish my first six-month semester still above water on the car wager. The only class remaining before we went on our six-month externship was AM Pantry.

AM Pantry was basically cooking breakfast. It was going to be a lay-up. If there was one thing in the kitchen that I felt comfortable with, it was eggs and frying pans.

We had to wake at 4:20 every morning and make our way into a cafeteria-style kitchen, where we were lectured on the proper way to cook hash browns and flip eggs. I got a better course on that when I was seven years old. The instructor tried to humiliate the students one by one, and when she was done we would cook breakfast for the rest of the student body, manning the cafeteria line shoulder-to-shoulder to scoop the food out institution-style.

"Why don't you show the group how well you can do this," she snarled in my direction.

"Okay. How many orders do you want?" I asked as I reached across the stove for more pans and turned the gas on to fire up a few more burners. I really didn't like this instructor and had decided to show her how to cook eggs. "You want humiliation?" I thought to myself. "Game on."

I dipped the ladle into the clarified butter and splashed it into two pans. As I started for the third she physically stopped me and said, "Why don't you start with just one?"

I ignored her, grabbed two eggs in each hand and with a swift, smooth motion cracked them simultaneously on the edges of the pans. My fingers hinged the shells open one egg at a time, while keeping the other eggs at the ready. Five seconds later the eggs were in their respective pans—boom, boom, boom, boom. I dropped the emptied shells in the garbage and repeated. The eggs bubbled in the butter. She was pissed.

She leaned in close to the pans to find eggshells that had fallen in. Nothing.

I flipped both sets over, waited forty-five seconds, and flipped them back. Then I turned them onto the awaiting plates. They were absolutely perfect, the best I could do. I quietly stepped back to the group and Don gave me a big smirk.

I got a C minus in AM Pantry. But it was worth it.

The CIA required all students to leave the school and gain practical experience at an accredited food-service establishment for the six months directly in the middle of the eighteen-month associate-degree program. Even though I wasn't entirely convinced that I needed or wanted any more practical experience, I started doing research on my externship early. Don kept trying to convince me that this was an opportunity to head to a warm-weather climate for a season, so I applied to a series of large hotels and golf clubs around Florida: the Fontainebleau, The Breakers, and the Sawgrass Country Club, amongst a host of lesser names. None of them bothered to respond to my inquiries.

I sent fifteen letters out. I got exactly one response: the Amway Grand Plaza Hotel in Grand Rapids, Michigan. I wasn't thrilled. Grand Rapids is definitely not Florida, and certainly not warm. I had never heard of the Amway or heard any talk about its culinary reputation. But it was close to home, it was close to Cindy at Michigan State, and it was my only option.

I picked up the phone and called the executive chef of the hotel, Steve Stallard, to confirm the details of my externship. He seemed cold, distracted, and wholly uninterested when I reached him. "Another inexperienced CIA extern that we'll throw in the banquet kitchen," is all he could be thinking. Midway through the call he suggested I speak with the current CIA extern at Amway, Ray Cuzmak, who was halfway into his six months. Chef Stallard put me on hold to transfer the call.

"Hello, this is Ray."

"Hi, Ray, my name is Grant Achatz and I will be starting as an extern there in a few weeks. Chef Stallard suggested we chat for a minute so you could give me an idea of what to expect."

"Yeah, okay. Well, what do you know about this place?"

"Not much. I noticed there are two fine-dining restaurants there. That's why I applied."

Ray chuckled. "Well, Grant, you'll never see those. They'll shove you in banquets or down in veg prep. I spend most mornings peeling potatoes and carrots. Tomorrow there is a banquet for nine hundred that I'll work. I don't know, man, this place is not what I expected."

I hung up the phone deflated. I went to the CIA to become a chef, not peel spuds. This was going to suck.

In August 1993, my dad helped me move into a small one-bedroom apartment in Comstock Park, about a fifteen-minute drive north of Grand Rapids. I entered the massive hotel the next day and headed to the human resources department. They shuffled me over to an all-morning orientation program that was incredibly dull. It all seemed so foreign and corporate.

After they dismissed the batch of new employees I made my way to the main kitchen so I could find chef Stallard. It was like a maze. I wound my way through the labyrinth of hallways and finally found the giant set of super-wide double doors and entered the football field–sized kitchen. Cooks were everywhere. There were guys using what looked like shovels stirring food in giant tilt skillets. A conveyor belt ran down the back of the space, and ten chefs stood on each side of it adding one component of the plated dishes as they slowly crept by. Mountains of dirty pots and pans were stacked up next to enormous pot sinks.

I had definitely never seen anything like this before. As I was soaking it all in, I nearly bumped into a cook pushing a hot box through the kitchen, swerving like a drunk driver.

"Hi. Sorry. Where is the chef's office, please?"

"Over there, kid," he said pointing.

I approached the door, took a deep breath, and knocked.

Chef Stallard lifted his head and slowly stood up out of his chair. He reached to shake my hand and welcomed me to the Amway.

He was quiet and deliberate as he spoke, pausing slightly as if to take a breath before he started each sentence. He was intimidating, a giant version of Charlie Sheen with no smile. And he exuded professionalism—his chef coat was flawlessly white and pressed, his jet-black hair was combed back, and his face was perfectly smooth.

"I am afraid there has been a change of plans, Grant. Originally we were going to put you in banquets, but a cook in Cygnus quit yesterday and they need a hand. So we are going to send you up there instead."

"Yes, Chef."

Chef Stallard gave me directions to the tower elevator, told me to ask for Jeff when I arrived, and sent me on my way.

I caught a lucky break.

If it were up to chef Jeff Kerr he would have continued to follow the Grateful Dead from city to city, partying with the Deadheads and trading bootleg cassettes along the way. Instead he ended up as the chef de cuisine at Cygnus.

Cygnus was one of the two fine-dining restaurants in the hotel and was located on the twenty-seventh floor of an all-glass tower. It was definitely the best restaurant in Grand Rapids and was considered among the best in northern Michigan. But it is fair to say that there was not a whole lot of competition for that title.

The restaurant was aiming to be more modern than its counterpart in the hotel, The 1913 Room, which was heavily rooted in classic French fare.

When I entered the kitchen I immediately looked for the telltale sign of the chef in charge: the colored stripes on the collar of the chef coat. I spotted a small man moving quickly around the kitchen giving instructions to a handful of cooks. He had red and blue stripes on his collar, but with the odd addition of a tie-dyed T-shirt poking up from under his neckline. He turned, spotted me, and came directly over.

"Hey, man, I'm Jeff. You Grant?" It seemed like he was panting the words out. He didn't make much eye contact. He was distracted.

"I am. I just started my extern today from the CIA. Chef Stallard sent me up here."

"Wow, man. That sure was nice of him," he said sarcastically. "We had a guy walk out of here yesterday. We're totally in the shits, man. I'm going to have you work in the back doing some prep for us. Cool?"

"Yes, Chef."

"Whoa. Hold up there a second, Grant," Jeff said, rolling his eyes. "I know they play that 'call me chef' game at school and downstairs, but up here we call people by their names. I'm Jeff." Despite his lingo he spoke quickly and his eyes darted around the room. He was fidgety and it was common for him to stop a thought midsentence and just walk away. Then he would pop back five minutes later and say, "Okay, what was I saying?"

Turning around suddenly he scooped a piece of raw foie gras scrap from a cook's cutting board and popped it in his mouth. I don't think he meant to eat it, or didn't notice what it was. "Why would you eat raw foie?" I was thinking. But that is how Jeff was. His mind raced ahead of his body, or vice versa. He winced for a second, leaned forward to spit the liver in the garbage can, and turned to face me.

"I just don't get why people like that stuff," he deadpanned.

Despite his hyper behavior he took his time when explaining things to me. I was getting the one-on-one instruction critical to my growth as a cook. As we got to know each other and he learned how ambitious I was he said to me, "You need to get some experience burning your forearms on a stack of sauté pans, Grant. Real cooking, know what I mean? Deep down into the pain stuff. I like food that is from the soul. Rustic good food. Tastes good. Bold flavors. Stuff you have to chew. Good-looking, sure, but not pretentious. You need to learn all of that before you can act like a prima donna."

I worked the prep station, making soups, salad dressings, and some *mise en place* for about a month before Jeff moved me to the roast/grill station on the hot line. I was a nineteen-year-old culinary student—I was not supposed to be working the hot line burning my forearms. But I was right where I wanted to be. Every once in a while

I would bump into my counterpart Ray in the locker room. He ended up working for a couple of weeks in The 1913 Room but spent most of his time in banquets.

Three months into my externship Jeff pulled me aside and told me to go see chef Stallard in his office. This didn't sound good, but I left immediately without asking why. To my surprise, chef Stallard relayed that he and Jeff would like me to stay at Cygnus for the duration of my externship. That is, under the condition that I be available to help him with things from time to time. I enthusiastically consented.

Every couple of weeks chef Stallard would call up to Cygnus and tell me to arrive early the following day. He was an avid outdoorsman who loved to hunt game birds and fly-fish. Whenever he went on a hunt he brought back a few birds and gave me a demo on breaking them down, describing how they were traditionally hunted and hung in Europe.

One morning I arrived to find an entire pig on the counter. We took it apart piece by piece as he explained the cuts, what they were commonly used for, and some of the favorite dishes he had created with them. He spoke with great nostalgia and reverence for the restaurants of France, especially the Michelin three-starred Taillevent in Paris, where he'd spent time working. "You think I should go to Europe after I graduate?" I asked.

"It would probably do you some good, in a lot of ways. Between a good friend, chef Angus Campbell, and me, we should have enough connections to place you somewhere. But the deal is that you have to come back here and work for a year before we do so. I want to prepare you personally if I am recommending you."

This was awesome. I could see things moving in a new, right direction.

"Now go get that big white plastic container over there and fill it half-full with salt. We are going to make some prosciutto with these hams."

Amazing. Just amazing.

———

When I returned to the CIA the following April, I was anxious to get back to Cygnus and keep moving forward. The final six months at the CIA went by very quickly as the curriculum shifted from primarily classroom lessons to real restaurant situations. We spent most of our time working our way through the four operating restaurants on the campus. It suited me, and furthered my comfort in a busy kitchen. I was extremely fortunate to land with chef Stallard at the Amway, and once I compared my experience with other students' I could tell that it was unusual. Most didn't love their externships.

As graduation grew closer, I had phone conversations with chef Stallard about returning to the Amway and working once again at Cygnus. Everything was lined up for me to go back, and the deal to move on to Europe was in place.

On October 28, 1994, my mother, father, and Grandma Achatz arrived on campus to watch me graduate. I returned home to find the Corvette restored and painted a dark purple, my requested color. I had graduated with honors despite the C minus in AM Pantry.

I packed what little I owned—a few cookbooks and some knives— and moved to Grand Rapids. I felt like a different person walking back into the Amway than I did just a year earlier. This time I knew they wanted me there, and I knew I could contribute in a meaningful way. I stopped by chef Stallard's office on my way up to Cygnus to say hello and to make certain that he was taking the first steps to contacting his leads in Europe. Setting up a "stage"—or apprenticeship—with its work visas and such could take forever, so it wasn't too early to start planning. I wanted to get experience at the Amway, but I saw beyond it. I was on a mission.

"Hello, Chef," I said.

"Chef! Welcome back, how are you? I want you to meet chef Angus Campbell. He is the culinary instructor at the Grand Rapids Community College that I was telling you about. Angus wanted to meet you face-to-face before he started making any calls on your behalf." Apparently chef Stallard was as serious as I was.

After the formalities, I settled into a chair and the three of us started to talk about the range of opportunities abroad. Angus was set on sending me to a hotel in Edinburgh. He was born in Scotland and had worked there for many years before coming to the States. Heck, his name was Angus! He knew the chef of the hotel well and said it would not be a problem getting me an apprenticeship there. I couldn't help but wonder why they hadn't already started organizing my trip. The connection seemed like a lock and chef Stallard had to know that. Further, why Scotland? I had been dreaming about the Michelin-starred restaurants of France that Stallard had waxed poetic about.

"How long do you think it will take to get this together?" I asked, not wanting to sound unexcited.

"Likely six months or a bit more by the time you get all of your visa requirements in place," said chef Stallard. "If we secure the position and everything falls in place early, I will let you go when it does."

I couldn't argue with that, but I had never imagined Scotland. When I read about the great restaurants and cuisines of the world I couldn't recall Scotland being mentioned even once. Italy, sure. France, of course. Scotland, not so much.

Jeff and the Cygnus kitchen looked the same. We exchanged greetings and caught up quickly before we started talking shop. Jeff explained that Mike Martin, who was running the sauté station when I was there last, was the only guy left from the team from a year ago. Mike was a solid cook who really cared about the food he was putting out, had an even temper, and took the time to explain things to me. Through both his talent and the attrition he was now sous chef, though still running the sauté station.

Jeff wanted Mike to train me on sauté so he could become more of a floater, picking up some of the tasks that Jeff had been doing so he could spend more time with his young son and work in his massive vegetable garden. It sounded good to me—sauté was the hardest station in the kitchen and the one I had worked in the least during my externship.

Jeff seemed more relaxed than I remembered him, and the three of us had long conversations about food and cooking during prep and slow periods on the line. Mike was going through a divorce and was blaming it on the long hours, stress, and low pay of the kitchen life. He talked constantly about parlaying his culinary knowledge into other potentially more lucrative facets of food service, like creating an ice-cream brand or a host of other pipe dreams. They both knew I had very high aspirations and could sense my impatience. "Why do you need to go to Europe anyways?" Jeff asked. "There are plenty of great restaurants and chefs here in the U.S. now. I was in Borders the other day and saw this new cookbook I bet you would like. It was very modern. Trotter. Charlie Trotter from Chicago. Ever hear of him?"

"No."

"Right up your alley. All froufrou and composed with elements and ingredients from all over the place. Kinda fusion, kinda not. Multiple sauces, organ meats. I was going to buy it for you until I saw the price."

The next morning I woke up early and went to the cookbook section at the nearest bookstore. A group of burgundy books sat on the shelf like a red siren flashing at me—Trotter. I grabbed one, sat on a bench, and started paging through it. I didn't move for forty-five minutes. The book was amazing. Every recipe was incredibly detailed but yet somehow abstract. The food was at once complex and simple. Jeff was right. This was right up my alley. It was exactly what I suspected existed somewhere but couldn't find.

Over the next month Jeff let me create a different special or two each night, each of them influenced by Trotter's book. I would stay up late at night reading the introductions to each dish. Chef Trotter would explain how the dish came together a certain way or why a particular ingredient was selected. He wrote about achieving excellence at all costs. The book was like a drug for me. What started as a weekly check-in with chef Stallard to assess progress on the Scotland front turned sporadic. I lost interest in Europe and became infatuated with Trotter's philosophy. And Chicago wasn't that far from Grand Rapids.

One day I saw chef Stallard talking to his executive sous chef Larry Johnson. I walked up to them and said hello.

"What's up, Chef?"

"Well, Chef, I have been thinking. Do you remember that Charlie Trotter book I showed you a couple of months ago? I was thinking that maybe I should just go work there. You know, instead of going to Scotland."

A smile broke over his face. It wasn't the reaction I was expecting.

"It's supposed to be a great restaurant, that's for sure. But there is something about being trained in Europe. I tell you what—if you want to try to get a job there, go ahead and pursue that. We will continue to work on Scotland. I bet it will be really hard to get into Trotter's, and realistically it may never happen. So we'll work on both fronts and if one hits, you can decide what to do then. Sound good?" Chef Stallard couldn't have been more supportive.

"Yes, Chef. That sounds good."

wrote a cover letter to Charlie Trotter's and sent in my résumé. A few weeks went by, and I thought it was likely he had tossed it in the garbage. Most of my cooking experience had been flipping eggs and making mashed potatoes. Surely the best restaurant in the country screened applicants rigorously and only hired the best. Why would he possibly want me? I started to think that working in Scotland would be a good place to start. I could possibly go from there to a Michelin-starred restaurant in France, then come back and have a shot at working at Trotter's.

Every night I propped up some pillows in bed and studied the book—it would be my only chance to get to know the food and techniques. I knew the dishes and the techniques cold.

Three weeks after I sent my résumé I had almost given up hope when I came home around midnight and saw that the light was blinking on my answering machine. I hit play and started to pull some leftovers out of the fridge to eat. A voice I didn't recognize echoed faintly through my tiny apartment.

I started making an egg-white omelet when . . . holy shit . . . did he just say Charlie Trotter?! I ran to the machine, almost knocking it off the shelf. I hit rewind and listened to the message again. The soft, poised chef's voice now seemed deafening. He mentioned an open position at his restaurant and asked me to call him back. My heart pounded as I picked up the phone and began to dial. Then hung up. Then dialed again, then hung up. It was like calling a girl to ask her on a date when I was thirteen. What would I say? What would he ask me?

I composed myself and let it ring. The phone was answered by the familiar noise of a busy kitchen. The chef on the other end sounded annoyed. "Is chef Trotter available?" I asked.

"Of course he is here, but he is busy . . . we are . . . IN SERVICE."

"In service?" I thought, "But it's past midnight in Chicago." I had no idea that the service schedule at an elite restaurant could go until 2:00 or 3:00 A.M. At the Amway I was home by midnight, even on the weekends. I sheepishly left my name and phone number with the gruff chef, knowing it was unlikely that chef Trotter would ever receive my message.

Over the course of the next week I continued to call the restaurant. Chef Trotter proved to be an elusive guy. On the ninth day someone finally said, "Sure, wait a minute," and chef Trotter picked up the phone. I was incredibly nervous—I was talking to the best chef in the country.

The conversation went like this: He asked questions, I gave answers, and he crushed me. I didn't have a correct answer for anything, and by the end of the five-minute interview he could have asked me my own name and I would have believed him when he told me I was wrong. Chef Trotter was introducing me to his management style.

At the end of the phone call he asked why he should hire me.

"I am a highly motivated cook and will do whatever it takes to do things right."

Trotter chuckled. "I have an entire restaurant full of people like that. What makes you different?"

I was floundering. I had nothing to add. I thought, "Ask me something about your food! I know it cold. I can cite the awards, the press, and quote you to yourself. Ask me something I know, dammit!" But he knew that I knew all that, so he didn't ask.

I muttered something about "being prepared each and every day," and to my surprise he abruptly ended the call with an invitation to try out at the restaurant. Two days working in the kitchen would be followed by a mystery-box cook-off. The chef de cuisine would give me a box of ingredients and I had to produce four courses for four people—chef Trotter and the three sous chefs—in three hours. He asked if I had any questions.

"Is there anything special I need to bring?" I ventured.

"Your A game," he replied.

Over the next two weeks I studied his book maniacally. I located the hotel closest to Charlie Trotter's and booked my stay there, regardless of the cost. I reserved a table at the restaurant the night before my try-out so I could taste the food. I was doing my homework. Despite the fact that I couldn't afford the meal, I wanted a chance to see the plates I would have to work with, study the flavor and seasoning profiles he preferred, and even peek into the kitchen to see the layout and equipment. These were naive plans.

I arrived nervous and on edge. Everything about the neighborhood and the restaurant made me uncomfortable. I was a small-town kid and the drive into Chicago was enough to freak me out.

The dinner was revelatory. I had never eaten food like that before. I surprised the staff by ordering two bottles of wine that fit the menu and were reasonably good values, but that I clearly could not afford. I couldn't drink all of the wine so I had a glass or two of each and left the rest for the staff. I thought I was being clever by giving them a gift.

I looked ridiculous. I was twenty-one years old, in a cheap, frumpy suit, armed with too much knowledge about the food and not afraid to ask questions that were too pointed. I was being overly observant and was far from relaxed. I wondered the whole night whether Charlie knew who I was and whether he was throwing curveballs at me. Was he giving me food that wasn't on the regular menu? Presenting it abnormally? Noting what I was eating so that those ingredients would not be in the mystery box? I hadn't spent a moment in his kitchen, but Trotter was in my head already.

Despite the wine, I didn't sleep well that night.

After two walks around the block to get the timing just right, I arrived at the back door of Charlie Trotter's precisely at 9:30 A.M.

on a Friday morning in July. A chef named Reggie greeted me. Reg was both gregarious and standoffish at the same time. "So, you the tryout?" he asked.

I reached out my hand and said, "I'm Grant."

"Whatever. I don't remember names until you have been here three months. Too many people break and run, ya know?!" He laughed, clearly enjoying his chance to intimidate the new guy.

I walked in and surveyed the space. It was spotless. I didn't know kitchens could be this clean. I thought that they must have a dedicated cleaning crew that kept it like this.

Reg liked to talk and wasn't shy about imparting little bits of wisdom, but I wasn't listening. I was too busy studying the kitchen. He showed me the rack full of perfect tomatoes, tiny onions, and fresh squashes. "Wow, produce at room temperature the way they should be," I thought. They were all perfectly lined up on sheet pans instead of jammed on top of each other, still in cardboard boxes in a giant walk-in refrigerator.

"No. No walk-in here, G—the food comes in, the food goes out. Same day. No playing here."

The Bonnet stove with the brass fixtures and rails gleamed. The rows of copper pots hung in size order overhead, and glass cabinets held jars of spices and beautiful French porcelain. Reg opened one door and showed me the mushroom cooler.

"Uh . . . all you keep in there is mushrooms?"

"Yessir."

A fucking mushroom cooler . . . a cooler just for mushrooms. No shit.

"I am the guy. You need to know something about this place or Charlie, you come to me. I've been here since day one. Started out washing dishes." That meant Reg had been here seven years. This place can't be that tough, I thought.

"And by the way, I am the only one who calls the man Charlie. Me and his mom, Donna. You best call him 'Chef' and you best say a polite hello to him."

After the tour, Reggie walked me back into the kitchen, which began to fill up with cooks. He introduced me to a few of them, one of whom was the chef de cuisine, Bill Kim. At that point, Reggie passed me off to Bill. Chef Kim looked down at me expressionless, his height accentuated by his toque. He spoke quietly, almost in a whisper, trying to impart a sense of calm to an otherwise chaotic kitchen.

Chef Kim asked me if I was ready, and for the first time he let a little smile creep onto his face as I nodded. He introduced me to the pastry chef and said, "I think you can start here."

The pastry chef, a young woman of twenty-eight, looked me over quickly and said, "Here's a rondeau of water and some peaches. Just blanch and peel them for me."

Her tone was frigid and I could tell she was stressed.

After I took the first batch of peaches out of the hot water and placed them into the ice water, shocking them to make them easier to peel, I quickly started on the second round. As any cook knows, you have to have two things in order to blanch a fruit or vegetable correctly: boiling water and ice water. I had both on the first batch, but loading the pot too soon with peaches the second time killed the water temperature. The pastry chef came running over and slid to a screeching halt next to me, grabbing the spider out of my hand. She quickly removed the peaches from the warm water and got them into the now not-so-cold ice bath to cover the error. It was too late.

A familiar voice said quietly, "Sorry to interrupt, Chef."

[Long pause.]

"Is that how we blanch peaches?"

[Longer pause.]

"In warm water?"

I turned to see Charlie Trotter standing before me, head tilted to one side, peering over his John Lennon–style glasses. His hands were together in front of him like a praying mantis, and he leaned forward slightly to intimate that he was looking into the ice bath, even though his eyes were on the pastry chef.

I cringed at the thought that the first impression I made on the *best chef in the country* was that I didn't know how to do something as simple as peel a peach. But I didn't have much time to worry, as his fury was not going to be directed at me. It was about to be directed at the pastry chef, who had nothing to do with the error but whose responsibility it was to look after me.

His voice began to crescendo. "You are disrespecting these beautiful peaches! You have no idea how to cook. This is basic cooking and you have failed. Perhaps you should waste more money and go back to culinary school because you obviously didn't absorb the mediocre education you received the first time you were there."

Each sentence grew louder and each was a massive blow to her already fragile ego. I stood there and watched him yell at her, the poor pastry chef who drew the short straw and got me for the day. Trotter knew full well that she wasn't blanching the peaches. He spotted me supervising the failure from across the room. He knew exactly who I was and why I was there. But I was invisible to Charlie Trotter. I didn't exist yet.

He walked away from the pastry station and announced loudly to the whole kitchen in a grand gesture with arms flailing upward, "We will not be serving the dessert with poached peaches this evening because we don't know how to properly remove the skin from the fruit." He paced around the kitchen so that everyone could look him in the eye.

Then suddenly he stopped, frozen in the center of the kitchen with all eyes on him. He turned, walked back over to the pastry station, and stopped squarely in front of me.

He reached out his hand and introduced himself.

"I am Charlie Trotter. If you give a shit."

Cleanup every night in a four-star kitchen meant scrubbing every surface intensively. The whole kitchen staff participated. The stainless steel is washed and buffed and then the entire kitchen is literally wrapped in cellophane before a power washer is used to clean the floor.

The worst job of the day—after a sixteen-hour shift no less—was reserved for the FNG. The Fucking New Guy. The veterans called it "going up," which meant climbing on the Bonnet stove, the flattops still radiating heat, and cleaning the inside of the hoods right up to the point where they meet the black iron. With the heat climbing up your legs, getting trapped inside your pants right at your crotch, you sprayed the degreaser and were enveloped in a cloud of toxic gas. Even if you managed to hold your breath, it would make your eyes sting and water. It was exactly what you didn't need after a long day.

If there was one upside to the task, it was that it afforded a degree of privacy. Despite the shit-cloud of chemicals, the shelter of the hoods provided the only place of refuge in the kitchen where you could speak freely with another cook. Mike, the not-quite-so-fucking-new-guy, and I were bobbing in and out, alternating spraying the degreaser and dipping outside the stainless box to take gulps of fresh air.

"Mike, this is nuts, man. I have to go," I found myself saying.

"You leaving so soon, G? You just got here! Total pansy. I told Bill you couldn't hang. Too bad. I was pulling for you, fellow Michigander and all." Peer pressure, comfort in numbers, and typical kitchen machismo—but still, this is how you help a young cook through.

Mike had just crossed over the year mark at Trotter's and was singled out for the next sous chef opening. Although he acted like it was a burden, he secretly liked the fact that he was assigned to watch over and train me from day one. It gave him the opportunity to show the arrogance that top chefs are known for. Despite his exaggerated attempts to act overly tough, he managed to pull it off. In my eyes at least, he was a badass. He never flinched when Trotter was twisting him up, messing with his mind. He worked clean and tight and he had made it a year. The pressure of the service, the shit job of scrubbing the Dumpsters, and the sheer marathon of five days in a row of 10:00 A.M. to 4:00 A.M. never seemed to bother him. In fact, he somehow seemed energized by it all.

One hundred and eighty-nine covers was the record number served at Trotter's until a day shortly after I arrived. On this particular night, somehow, even more were booked. At the peak of the push, with the kitchen becoming completely overwhelmed, Trotter began yelling for food. Bill and Reggie reacted in a way that I had never seen. As Trotter directed his fury at a particular cook, Bill stepped between Trotter and the poor chef and absorbed the verbal lashings in a primal, almost parental fashion. He knew that if Trotter succeeded in mentally unhinging a cook in the midst of this service the kitchen would fall into a terminal avalanche. Bill and Reggie made sure that didn't happen.

At the craziest moment of the night, with the optimum opportunity for disaster, Mike and I ran out of space on the pass to plate our food. The queued plates had grown to a point where the pass was covered with partially finished platings. The cooks were spinning in circles, growing more frustrated and unable to think clearly enough to take a task to completion.

"What do we do, Mike?" I whisper-barked in his direction, knowing that even a pause would be a crushing break in rhythm.

"Make the shit happen, G!" he said with a grin. He was loving this.

Mike stretched upward and grabbed a stack of plates on the shelf above our station and with a single deft motion spun left while tucking them under his arm like a football. With his free hand he snagged a spoon out of the *bain* and removed eight nuggets of lobster that had been poaching in an orange-infused broth and placed them on a drain rack. Without breaking stride he slid over to the dish machine, and again using his free hand, squeegeed the water off the rack and started laying plates down.

I thought to myself, "Holy shit, this guy is going to plate food on the dish-machine drain board! No fucking way."

As Trotter began to call for lobster—gleefully anticipating another problem—Mike was saucing the seventh plate. He had a shit-eating grin on his face.

Trotter bellowed, "How long? How long? Will I get some food from you tonight? These poor people are hungry!"

"Now, Chef!" Mike called back. He turned immediately and placed the first two of the eight on the pass in front of chef Trotter.

Perfect.

Mike was the shit.

"Just don't break and run, man," Mike said to me. "You have to give notice. It has nothing to do with Charlie. It's about us cooks. Don't leave us dry, G. It will make our lives that much harder. Bill is going to be pissed . . . so tell him first, then Charlie. Poor Bill." Mike shook his head with genuine worry.

After we finished the hoods I approached Bill and told him I wanted to talk to him after we were finished with the scrub-up.

Bill knew. He put his head down and sighed, "You too?" It was barely audible.

"Bill, I just gotta go," I said with a shaky voice. "I am a better cook than I am performing now. Something about this place . . . it is making me worse, not better."

Clearly, this was not the first time Bill had heard this. He didn't say anything other than, "You have to talk to the man. He's in his office. I'll call over there and see if he'll talk to you now."

I got the nod from Bill while he was still on the phone. "Go over there, G, make sure you knock, and take off your shoes before you enter the office."

I was incredibly nervous and confused as I rapped on chef Trotter's office door. Part of me questioned what I was about to do. It was my goal to become a great chef and in order to do so I knew that I would have to work in some great restaurants. I knew I had to endure being the new guy, to eat a fair amount of shit in the process. I was fine with that. But this wasn't working. Trotter was rarely in the kitchen during the day, and when he was, he was giving a tour or simply walking through to discuss some aspect of the business with Bill.

I never saw Trotter cook.

Perhaps my ideal of learning from the man that created this amazing restaurant—and that amazing book—was unrealistic. I wanted to watch him work, learn how he cooked, hear his creative thoughts and processes. I wanted it to be like working with Jeff and chef Stallard. I wanted one-on-one time and mentoring. But the personality of this kitchen was the antithesis of that. The behavior of Trotter made such mentorship of cooks impossible. I wanted to grow, but instead I got ass-kickings.

I sat down across from chef Trotter. "Chef, I'm sorry, but I need to leave."

Instead of the response I expected—yelling—I received for the first time in my young tenure something amazing—encouragement. In a matter of minutes, chef Trotter convinced me to stay. It was some sort of Jedi mind trick that was almost magical—*this is not what you want to do, Grant. You want to stay.* Clearly he knew how bad I wanted to succeed, and he knew how intimidating he was to a twenty-one-year-old cook. He complimented me on my work in his kitchen. He reminded me how great this restaurant was and how it could help me become a leader. My experience at Charlie Trotter's would open doors. I walked out of his office in a daze, confused by what had just happened. When I returned to the kitchen to finish up the cleaning Mike walked over and bumped into me on purpose, spilling the soapy water I was holding. As we bent down together to clean it up he whispered, "Did you do it?"

"Well, yes and no," I said.

Mike popped up and began laughing loudly. He strode over to Bill with excitement and announced, "Charlie got another one, Bill. G caved!"

I left the kitchen at nearly 3:30 A.M., strapped on my Rollerblades in the back alley, and began skating to my minuscule apartment just north of the restaurant. The October air was crisp, and the smell of autumn in the Midwest made me intensely homesick. As I passed the late-night bars and blues clubs along Halsted, people were falling into the street after last call, and the encore music spilled out the door, mixing with the noise of the cabs and the wind.

I don't belong here. This just doesn't feel right, none of it.

I lasted a few more weeks at Trotter's. I pushed hard and actually did some good work. But the feeling only grew more intense—I needed to leave.

The atmosphere was genuinely eerie as I walked out the back door of Trotter's for the last time. The alley was dead quiet and an orange glow from the light affixed to a nearby telephone pole made chef Trotter's skin the color of a carrot. He was sitting on the hood of his maroon Jaguar, one foot up on the front, one foot on the ground. I knew I had to present myself confidently. But as my foot touched down on the last brick of the alley I realized I was looking at it, head down sheepishly.

"What can I do for you?" Trotter asked.

"Chef, I am really very sorry, but I have to go. If I leave now my landlord is willing to change my lease to a three-month, but that means I can only give you two weeks notice so that I can be out in time." This was not going as planned.

Trotter looked me in the eye. "Well, that is really quite unfortunate. Because if you do not stay at this restaurant for a full year, you will simply not exist to me. Period. That means don't ever call me. Don't ever use me as a reference. Don't put Charlie Trotter's on your résumé. As far as I am concerned, if you don't work here for a year, you haven't worked here for a day."

It took everything I had to pick my head up and look the best chef in the country in the eye. I wasn't afraid of Trotter, but I realized that I had failed.

"I understand, Chef," I mustered.

There was an odd pause and we stared at each other for a moment. Then Trotter slid off the fender of the car, walked to the driver's door, got in, and drove away.

CHAPTER 6

I returned to St. Clair and brooded.

When I got the job at Trotter's, I thought for sure it was the break I needed. The restaurant was amazing, the food exciting, and Trotter was certainly on an all-or-nothing mission to be the best. He was succeeding, but I was getting exactly the opposite of what I needed. Instead, in a very short time, the Trotter experience managed to drain all of the confidence and drive that I had built up over years of cooking and thinking about food.

Maybe I wasn't cut out for fine dining after all. Maybe I belonged in a diner.

My dad pulled me aside one afternoon. "You okay, kid?"

"That was my shot and I blew it. I have no idea what to do now."

"Ahh. That place wasn't right for you. Whenever you called home you didn't sound like yourself. Restaurants are like girlfriends; you just gotta find the right one. You didn't fail, you just haven't found the right partner yet and were smart enough to realize it. You'll figure it out."

His words rang hollow.

I decided to visit Cindy at Michigan State in an effort to connect with someone who knew me well. We talked for hours about my goals and desires and came to the conclusion that I needed to connect with food again. I had to find something that would get me excited about cooking. I needed to go see the Michelin three-stars for myself, to experience the perfection that Trotter was trying to emulate and that Stallard had spoken so passionately about.

Cindy and I planned a trip to Europe. It would be a culinary tour for me, museums and cathedrals for Cindy.

Jim Stier, one of my best friends from high school, was stationed at Mildenhall Air Force Base in London, so that was our first stop. It had been nearly four years since I had seen him, and it was great to catch up. He spent a few days playing tour guide in London, and we hit the usual tourist attractions: Big Ben, Parliament, and the pubs. In return I treated us all to dinner at Midsummer House in Cambridge. During the meal I tried to explain to him why it was important for me to take this trip and to experience some amazing restaurants. While he understood the logic, he couldn't understand the bill. "Holy shit, Grant! That's more than I spend in a month on food."

"It doesn't matter what it costs. I have to find that holy grail. I am visionless," I said. They looked at me like I was being melodramatic.

We said good-bye to Jim the next day and took the ferry from Dover to Calais, then headed by train directly for Paris. Cindy had a full schedule planned for us there. Like me, she was in her holy land, and we visited the Louvre, Notre Dame, and the Eiffel Tower before making our way by train to Reims for our first three-star meal.

The *Michelin Guide* was first published in 1900. It started in France, and it ranks restaurants from one to three stars. It is an honor to get mentioned in the guide with even a single star. Any starred rating means that it is a fine restaurant certainly worth the reservation. But the highest rating, three stars, denotes exceptional cuisine "worth the journey." It is the very essence of a restaurant worth traveling to find, and only a handful of chefs ever achieve the honor.

I was both nervous and excited as we walked into the door of Gérard Boyer's Les Crayères. This was it. I was in France and was ready to get my mind blown by my first three-star experience. I managed to save enough money from working throughout high school and from the Amway to make this a blowout trip. There aren't a whole lot of ways to spend money in St. Clair or Grand Rapids, and I was going to spend it all right here on my fine-dining education.

We must have looked ridiculous, especially to the French. We didn't speak the language well, and despite my knowledge of cooking, were totally in over our heads in terms of dining. Plus we were both twenty-one, and I looked fifteen.

I tried to compensate by ordering expensive wine and the largest of the tasting menus, plus an additional à la carte dish of *truffes en croute*, a 550 French franc supplement that was a signature dish.

But after all that, the meal was just okay. The service was unremarkable and condescending. They made it clear that we had no business eating there, and that inevitably colored the food.

I wasn't terribly disappointed, though. This was just the start. I had booked three three-star experiences during our trip. Les Crayères, Enoteca Pinchiorri in Florence, and Georges Blanc in Vonnas. I had it in my head that Blanc was going to be the meal of the trip, the one that jolted me back to life. He is a fourth-generation member of the Blanc family of restaurateurs and innkeepers, and, like me, worked side by side with his mother in the restaurant. He took over the business at twenty-five and slowly transformed it into one of the best in France. He was awarded a third Michelin star in 1981. Here was a guy that I felt I could relate to: humble beginnings, grand ambitions. And because of that I wanted to go big. I booked a room in the inn despite the extravagant cost of nearly $600 a night. I was putting all of my eggs into the Blanc basket.

We arrived at the Vonnas train station and asked the conductor for directions to Georges Blanc. With a raised eyebrow he looked us over but said nothing. We repeated the name again, making sure he heard us correctly. "It is about a fifteen-minute walk, not especially far." We decided to hoof it.

We grabbed our giant backpacks and set out through the town. It was an unusually hot day and we were wearing shorts and T-shirts. By the time we arrived in the Georges Blanc lobby we were panting and dripping with sweat. The receptionist looked puzzled at first, then genuinely concerned about having two American students wander in by accident. She figured we were lost and needed directions.

"Bonjour. We have a reservation," I said.

She looked horrified. "Here?"

"*Oui. Je m'appelle* Grant Achatz."

She frantically searched the reservation book, running her finger over my name at least half a dozen times before she regained enough composure to see it.

I gave her my credit card and she reluctantly handed over the key. "Do you, um, need help with your . . . luggage?"

"*Non, merci,*" I said as I hefted my North Face backpack over my shoulder, "we can manage."

We took showers, put on nice clothes, and went for a stroll through the garden at the back of the property. We walked past the windows of the kitchen and peeked in. What appeared to be thirty cooks were meticulously prepping *mise en place* for the night's dinner service.

"Wow. Look how calm it is in there," I said to Cindy. "This will be amazing."

We turned a corner and walked past the pool. A helicopter flew overhead, circled, and landed on an expanse of lawn nearby, dropping off what appeared to be two Swiss businessmen in bespoke suits.

"Look at that! A helicopter to dinner."

With that we went back upstairs and I grabbed my sports coat. I was ready for dinner.

The dining room was completely empty when the maître d' escorted us to our table. The room had an odd mixture of elegant Parisian elements—ornate mirrors and huge floor lamps—tucked into a farmhouse with large stone floors and exposed wooden-beam ceilings. Despite our youth and appearance we were seated side by side at a great corner table with a view of the entire room and the windows that encase the kitchen.

The captain greeted our table promptly and warmly, and I ordered two glasses of champagne. I didn't want a repeat of the treatment we received at Les Crayères, and while we looked out of place, I wanted him to think we knew what we were talking about. He left the menus and the wine list.

He returned quickly with the champagne and offered to help us "assess the menu." He wanted to make sure "you will eat such things as pigeon." He wasn't so much helping as he was trying to steer us clear of our certain ignorance.

The sommelier came over and I ordered half bottles of 1986 Drouhin Chassagne Montrachet and a 1989 Gevrey-Chambertin Clos St. Jacques from Rousseau. With him, at least, I scored some points. We were on our way.

I was literally on the edge of my seat with anticipation as my eyes swept the room trying to absorb the details.

"Grant, I'm over here," Cindy said with a wave of her hand in front of my face. She was on a different mission than mine. Romance.

"Sorry."

The food began to arrive. I ate. I wondered when it would happen, the moment of revelation.

About four courses through the seven-course degustation it dawned on me: It isn't going to happen. The food was all right. Some was even very good. None of it was revelatory. Cindy could see the disappointment washing over me. "Grant, I'm sorry this isn't what you thought it would be. Maybe Enoteca will be great?"

I was starting to think that maybe what I imagined to exist somewhere in the world simply didn't exist at all.

Then the squab arrived.

I picked up my knife and fork and cut the breast in half. I gently pushed one side of the supreme away from the other and glanced at the cut edge. It was gray. Hugely overcooked. I was staring at it in disbelief when Cindy whispered, "There's the chef!"

We had until this point quietly and dutifully worked our way through the food and wine without much interaction with the service team. Once we had ordered they did a fine job of keeping our glasses full and delivering the food, giving brief descriptions along the way and clearing the plates when we were finished. Now suddenly, at the low moment of the meal for me, here comes the man himself.

I looked up to see Georges Blanc striding through the dining room, greeting tables and shaking hands. I contemplated what to do, growing more nervous as he walked from table to table, slowly making his way toward us. Should I show him the overcooked meat? Should I cover it somehow so he doesn't see it? I knew I was not remotely qualified to question a chef of his caliber and standing, especially in his own dining room. But I was upset. I had come all the way to France, all the way to this restaurant in particular, to experience greatness. I was taught in school that France was the birthplace of all things great in gastronomy. The entire CIA curriculum was based on French technique. All the chefs I had worked with waxed poetic about the great French kitchens they visited or worked in. Even Trotter told the staff about his experiences eating at Girardet and Boyer, placing them on a pedestal. He told the staff how we should strive to be as great as they are.

I had come all this way to find something that I had lost.

Chef Blanc approached the table and I stood to shake his hand. His English was difficult to understand through his French, but I made out, "Where are you from?"

"Chicago," I said.

"Ahhh. Chicago. I know a chef there. Charlie Trotter," he replied.

"Yes, I worked for him," I said.

"Really. Very good then. How has your meal been?"

"Good, Chef," I replied. I took a long pause trying to decide what to do. "Chef. The squab breast. Is it supposed to be, uh, cooked through like this?"

I took the fork and impaled a section of the breast and tilted the cut side up so he could see the gray color in the dimly lit room. He looked at it closely but quickly, looked me in the eye, and said, "Yes. That is a pigeon."

Georges Blanc turned and walked away.

I sat there frozen, fork in hand, still holding the meat. I tossed it down.

"Look, man. I might not be a Michelin three-star chef, but I do know this meat is overcooked. Look at it, Cin!" I picked it back up and held it aloft in her direction.

"Grant, it's okay. I am sure he's making another one right now."

The captain arrived at our table.

"It there a problem, monsieur?"

"The squab is overcooked," I mumbled, not really paying much attention to him. I was saying it to the gods, to myself, not to him. I didn't care about the meat. The bubble had burst.

"Monsieur, this is why I asked you about the pigeon earlier. Most Americans are not used to eating this bird. Shall I remove it, monsieur?"

"Yes."

Cheese came quickly, followed by desserts. No further mention was made of the squab, no replacement course was offered, and no deduction was made on the bill. We went back to our room.

"I'm done here," I said to myself.

We made it to Florence after spending time in Venice and Rome to find the meal at Enoteca Pinchiorri good, better than the two meals in France, but certainly not at the level I had imagined. My culinary tour was over.

We only had two days left in Europe, and we planned to explore Florence by foot. We wandered through Piazza della Signoria on our way to the Ponte Vecchio and stopped in at a small café for an espresso. Pinned to the wall, in English, was a piece of paper that read:

BIKE TOURS OF THE TUSCAN HILLSIDES
Led by American college student.
Bikes included.
See: olive groves, winery, Italian countryside.

Cindy pointed to it and asked me if I was game. I had been so glum and self-absorbed that it was the least I could do. She grabbed one of the tear-off phone-number tabs at the bottom.

We wandered around Florence for the rest of the afternoon, taking in the sites and art. Cindy called the number that night and set up a tour for the next morning while I scanned the guidebook trying to figure out where to eat that night. We opted for a pizza.

We woke up the next morning and met a group of four other Americans at a coffee shop and waited for our guide. A van pulled up with seven bikes strapped to the top. We piled in, drove to the other side of town, and started unloading the bikes.

"The hard part of this trip is getting there," Tom the bike guide said. "It's all uphill. At the halfway point we'll stop at a winery where they make their own olive oil and wine. If you get tired before that, just stop and rest. There's only one road, so you can't get lost. Just look for a wooden sign for the winery." We huffed our way up the hillside, leaving two of the other four well behind us.

The winery was as magical as you might imagine. Storybook stuff. Two dogs rolled around the front lawn, light poked through a leafy canopy. The owner had leathery skin from years in the sun and spoke no English, but exuded warmth and calm. We walked the property, saw the old stone olive press still used to make the oil from the trees that lined both sides of the driveway, and tasted the unfiltered version on crusty pieces of bread. We had a few glasses of Chianti straight from the barrel to wash it down.

Mellowed by the wine and sun we climbed back on our bikes and continued our trek upward toward a towerlike ruin at the top of the hill. We arrived forty-five minutes later. "This is as far up as we're going," Tom said. "Take a few minutes to look around, take some pictures, and then we're going to head back down. We can stop for lunch on the way back if you're hungry."

On the road up all we saw were a few homes, the winery, and trees. I didn't remember any restaurant. We headed quickly down the hill, and fifteen minutes later we followed Tom into a small driveway just off the main road that led to what appeared to be an abandoned stone building. We hopped off the bikes and I could immediately smell grilled meats, herbs, and the strong scent of roasted garlic. Our group looked at each other skeptically as we ducked through the tiny wooden door.

"I found this place by chance," Tom said. "I was taking a group up here last year when my chain came off and got lodged between the

sprocket and the frame. So I walked up here to see if they had anything to help me fix it. I started talking to the owner and we worked
out a deal to make this part of the bike tour. There she is . . ."

He stood up and greeted her loudly in rapid-fire Italian, waving his arms and kissing her on both cheeks. She bear-hugged him
back. The woman appeared to be eighty years old, even though she
was probably sixty. She wore a blue dress with small white flowers
scattered across it and a white apron loosely tied around her rotund
midsection.

A man who I assumed was her husband walked over, plunked
down wineglasses and a plate of crostini with chicken liver, bean, and
tomato toppings. He filled our glasses with a hefty pour of red wine.

"She usually just cooks, well, whatever!" Tom said. "Today she's
made chicken under a brick, some gnocchi, wilted greens, and *fagioli
al fiasco*. You guys know what that is? Basically a very typical Tuscan
way of cooking white beans. She'll place them in a glass flask over a
dying fire until they're creamy. They're pretty awesome."

"Yes they are," I thought. "Yes they are."

I peeked around the corner and saw the woman bent over a makeshift grill with glowing embers beneath, pushing a plain old brick
on top of our chickens. Four glass flasks filled with beans were positioned around the edges.

We ate and drank for two hours. I didn't want to leave. Everything was more perfect, more delicious, and more inviting than any of
the three-star restaurants we'd been to. Even the service was better.

At the end of the meal the woman brought out a plate of almond
cookies and we dunked them in Vin Santo. *"Grazie,"* everyone said.

I left the restaurant in a daze, and not because of the wine.

I realized immediately that I had just had the best meal of my life.

CHAPTER 7

The meal in Tuscany was a wake-up call to what was most important in a kitchen—passion. Even though the Michelin three-stars in Europe fell short of my expectations, I felt that somewhere fine dining must meet with a genuinely passionate chef.

I dug out the March 1995 issue of the *Wine Spectator* that I purchased while I was at the Amway. That month, the magazine listed its picks for the ten best restaurants in the United States, and it had Trotter at the top. Now I wanted to examine the other nine. I read about each and jotted down the addresses and names of the chefs so I could send them my résumé.

A few pages past the feature was a small picture of a simple brown building and a short description of the restaurant it housed:

In Napa Valley wine country, Thomas Keller's The French Laundry seems to be one of those three-star country restaurants that so captivate us in France. The menu ($49 for five courses, $44 for three) has four to six selections in each category; consider starting with potato agnolotti enriched with mascarpone and dressed with black truffles and white truffle oil. Sea bass is pan roasted and served with a cassoulet of beans and preserved lemon, followed perhaps by a saddle of rabbit wrapped in bacon and accented with roasted fennel.

I read that and somehow knew I had to work there.

Perhaps it was the romantic lure of Napa or its similarity to Tuscany. Whatever it was, I never sent a résumé to any of the "top ten restaurants." Instead, I wrote a letter to Thomas Keller, explaining how much I wanted to work at The French Laundry.

Then the next day I wrote another. I changed it slightly, added a bit more about my experience, and sent it off. Then I did that again and again over the next twelve days—fourteen letters in all. Perhaps chef Keller would think I was nuts. Or perhaps he would recognize my persistence and think he could use that in his kitchen. But either way, he could not ignore me completely because he would realize that the letters would keep coming.

After two weeks I got a call from chef Keller himself inviting me to Napa for a two-day tryout. I didn't freak out this time like I did talking to Trotter. He was matter-of-fact and had a slight laugh in his voice. It must have been the letters I sent, though he didn't mention them.

I told my parents about the tryout and we decided that it would be nice for my mom to come with me. More than anything, it would be an opportunity for us to spend some time together, even if the job didn't work out. We flew to San Francisco, rented a car, and made the drive to Napa.

We checked into a hotel in the town of Napa and then set out to find Yountville, so we wouldn't have to search for it the next day. The drive up Highway 29 was stunning. Exiting the town and entering the valley reminded me of the hills of Florence. The light was soft and the smell of eucalyptus and vines was fresh. We turned off on Washington Street and drove slowly through the tiny town of Yountville.

I knew from the *Wine Spectator* mention that the building was probably unassuming, but we couldn't find it. I was expecting a sign of some sort, but we didn't see one. We came to the end of the town, turned around, and went back again. Nothing.

Finally my mom spotted a brown building with exhaust-hood covers on the roof. "That looks like it could be a restaurant," she said. We parked the car, stepped out, and saw the tiny sign on the wall: The French Laundry. "You want to move all the way to California to work here?" It looked barely more impressive, from the outside at least, than the Achatz Family Restaurant. I scurried away lest I be seen lurking around a day early.

Chef Keller told me to arrive at the restaurant at noon. I showed up at 11:30, making sure I was on time. I unlatched a small wooden gate and walked through the entryway, past a walk-in cooler, through another screen door, and onto what looked like the porch of someone's home. Baskets of vegetables were arranged on small shelves and the savory smell of veal stock filled the air. I approached the doorway to the kitchen and was nearly run over by a cook wheeling around the corner. "Hey, man. How are you?"

"I'm okay. I am here for a tryout. Is chef Keller here?"

"Yep. He's right inside."

I entered the French Laundry kitchen and saw a tall lanky man sweeping the floor. His back was toward me and he didn't hear me enter, so he kept doing his job for a few seconds. I peered past him looking for chef Keller, waited a few seconds for the sweeper to notice me, and when he didn't, approached him. "I'm Grant Achatz, here for a tryout. Is chef Keller in?"

"Yeah. That's me," he said, letting out a laugh. "You're early, Grant."

He stuck out his hand and shook mine vigorously with an exaggerated up and down motion.

I thought to myself, "Holy shit. He's the first one here, and he's sweeping the floor. What kind of restaurant is this?"

"I'm going to set you up with Kevin. He's in the back putting away produce, but he can show you around and get you started."

"Yes, Chef." My tryout had begun.

Kevin Kathman was a wiry guy with jet-black hair that he wore slicked back into a long ponytail. He looked like a young Steven Seagal, complete with muttonchops and pronounced, angular features. Along with a cook named John Gerber, inexplicably called "DJ" by everyone, the two made up the morning commis—or prep cook—team.

Kevin, who had almost run me over when I first walked in, came racing back into the kitchen before I could get out the door. "I'm with you," I said.

"Okay. Come and help me and DJ put away this order."

DJ was outside removing the papery skin from yellow onions and placing them carefully in a large woven basket. "Hey," he said, not bothering to look up from his task.

"I'm Grant. Here for a tryout today and tomorrow."

"Another one," he mumbled toward Kevin with a slight smile.

I helped organize the produce while cooks started to arrive and walk by us. A few would make sarcastic remarks at Kevin or DJ and the guys would fire back. It was in good fun, but there was an underlying tension to the place. It felt competitive. After the produce was put away I moved inside.

The kitchen had eight cooks in it now, each quietly producing the *mise en place* for their station. I helped Kevin roll and shape a batch of russet potato gnocchi while we quietly chatted. "So, where are you coming from, Grant?"

I hesitated. I remembered chef Trotter's admonishment, "If you don't work here a year, you never existed." But I could tell that Kevin was sizing me up. "Trotter's," I said.

"Oh. Trotter's. How was that? How long were you there?"

"Not very long," I said. "It wasn't what I expected." Thankfully, that ended the conversation.

We finished up the gnocchi and he put a cutting board down for me right next to his. "We're going to cut some brunoise. You okay with a knife?"

Kevin demonstrated the tiny dice, pushed the pieces over to the far corner of my board and said, "Leave those there for a reference."

I began cutting the turnip, carrot, and green leek tops into the miniature cubes at a good clip. Another cook approached my cutting board, looked at my work, then back at me. He spoke very slowly, making sure the others around us heard him. "Hi. I'm Josh."

"Grant is from Trotter's," Kevin spoke up on my behalf.

Josh immediately looked down at my board, poked his finger into a pile of my carrot brunoise and pulled out a single piece from the hundred that was cut on a slight angle to form an inconsequentially uneven cube.

"Kevin, you had better watch this guy. His knife skills aren't so good." Josh looked me in the eye and said, "You might want to start over." He slowly walked away.

I looked at the pile of carrots, dumbfounded. Kevin could see me thinking "What the hell?" and decided to encourage me. "They're fine. They look good. He's just trying to intimidate you. Josh is a friend of mine, but he can be a prick sometimes. He worked fish for Bouley and now he thinks he's a god."

"Where is everyone else from?" I asked.

"Well, all over the place, really. The poissonnier over there, Phil Baker, is a Jean Georges alum. The saucier, Jeffrey Cerciello, worked in Spain at some place called elBulli. Ron Siegel, today is his last day, but he's from Daniel."

The kitchen was loaded with talent.

As we finished up the brunoise, Kevin headed over to chef Keller, who was busy cleaning foie gras for torchon, and inquired what he should have me do next. "Have him peel and slice tomatoes for Eric," he said.

Eric Ziebold was manning the garde manger station, working on the components for a sliced tomato salad. We exchanged introductions and he instructed me to blanch, peel, and slice the Early Girl tomatoes using a deli meat slicer.

I made quick work of peeling them and headed to the slicer.

With every stroke across the slicer the tomato juice would run down toward the bottom of the blade then violently spray at me. I sliced thirty tomatoes, seasoned each layer with minced shallots, olive oil, *sel gris*, and black pepper, then meticulously stacked them back together so that they would appear to be a whole tomato. In the process, I looked like an ax murderer, my chef coat covered with tomato-juice splatter.

Chef Keller walked by, looked me up and down, and deadpanned with a wry smile, "Hey. Next time why don't you try to get a little more tomato all over yourself?" He paused a few beats for effect and smiled again. "Go change your coat."

I couldn't help but smile, even though I was embarrassed.

This place felt different. It felt good.

The day progressed into service, and I ended up camping out next to chef Keller, mainly observing. He was expediting and working the canapé station at the same time. It wasn't a particularly busy night, at least compared to the pace I had experienced at Trotter's. Plus, everything here felt calmer and more methodical. Chef Keller would move slowly and gracefully as he placed giant slabs of foie gras in a hot pan, turn back to expediting, and then turn back to the stove only at the very moment when the liver was ready to be flipped. He was able to carry on a conversation with me while working multiple pans on the flattop and serving as air-traffic control to the rest of the cooks in the kitchen.

"Why did you write me a letter every day?" he asked.

"I wanted a job, Chef," I replied.

He smiled. "So you thought that would do it?"

"I thought that might get me here, and I knew if I could get that far, then the chance of landing a job was good."

"So why did you leave Trotter's?"

I let out a sigh and tried to think of how to put things politely. "It just wasn't for me. It's a different place."

"Different than here?"

"Way different, Chef. Way different."

I sensed that he knew that before asking and wanted to see if I recognized the differences between the two kitchens. It was fine that I didn't articulate what exactly was different.

No chef should bad-mouth any other.

He finished sautéing a spoonful of julienned abalone, drained them on a towel, and seasoned them with salt and parsley. A brioche crouton was sautéed in the fat that had rendered off the foie, and after it was golden brown and crunchy he placed it in the dead middle of the oversized plate, gently laid the foie gras on top along with a few pieces of Meyer lemon supremes and fried abalone. A cordon of sauce was poured around and a pluche of chervil crowned the top. He moved back a half step to view the plate in its entirety, as he did with every plate before it left the kitchen.

Just as he finished, a front-of-house member ducked in the kitchen and said, "Chef, up on ten." That meant that someone at table number ten had gotten up from the table for whatever reason, probably to use the restroom. Chef Keller glanced at the tickets and, realizing that it was the table where the foie gras was headed, calmly picked up the plate and handed it to me. "You like foie?" he asked.

"Yes, Chef."

"Abalone and foie gras, with a Meyer lemon and lemon gastric. Surf and turf, get it?"

If a diner gets up from the table, the food at The French Laundry doesn't go under a heat lamp somewhere. It gets thrown out and the process starts again when the diner returns to his seat. This time, however, chef Keller gave me the plate.

A few of the cooks shot me wicked looks as I ate the dish standing next to chef Keller. Apparently, I figured, this doesn't happen very often.

Chef Keller approached me after the service was over and cleanup started. "You can go home; you don't have to stay and clean."

"No, Chef. I want to help. I'll stay until the end." He smirked and walked away. Clearly that was a test.

The next day was largely the same. I felt a bit more comfortable and less self-conscious. I was able to observe the cooks in action. They were good—really good. They didn't talk amongst themselves. They all just manned their stations with their heads down, meticulously working through the prep. There was no chaos in the kitchen, no yelling, and no fear on the faces of the staff. Everything was calm, quiet, and deliberate. At the end of service, before cleanup, chef Keller pulled me aside and asked to speak with me. I followed him to the patio-like space in the back. "So, Grant, you want a job?"

"Yes, Chef."

"When can you start?"

"Well, I have to find a place to live and move out here, but that shouldn't take too long."

"How about mid-October? We have a few cooks leaving around then. That should give you plenty of time to find a place and get situated."

"That sounds great. Thank you, Chef!"

We shook hands and walked back into the kitchen to finish cleaning. And that was it. I was hired. I had no idea what I would be doing; I didn't ask what the position was; and I had no idea what my salary would be. I never asked.

I didn't care.

CHAPTER 8

My dad and I loaded up the car with my few belongings and a cooler stocked full of snacks and caffeine. Then we set out to drive the thirty-six hours from St. Clair, Michigan, to California non-stop. I made arrangements to rent a one-bedroom apartment on the north end of Napa. It was furnished, so all I had to pack were clothes, cookbooks, and my knives.

My dad was curious why I was moving all the way across the country to work at a place that I knew little about, that had no national reputation, and that was in such a small town. I could tell he was worried that if this turned out like Trotter's I would be home again in eight weeks.

"I think this will be different, Dad. The food was perfect. And it was funny; it had a sense of humor. Chef Keller was the first one in every morning and the last one to go home. And he cooked!" I explained how rare this seemed, not just at Trotter's but also at the three-star restaurants in France.

We made it to Napa in record time, taking turns driving the whole way. My apartment was in decent shape, so we stocked it with groceries, took about ten minutes to put away all of my clothes, and sat down on the couch.

"Now what?" I asked. "Maybe we go to a few wineries? Explore the valley a bit?" I figured this would be my last chance to do that for a while, and my dad had never been out here.

"Sure. But you know, I was thinking. After hearing you talk about the Laundry the way you have, I would love to see it. To eat that food. It sounds magical."

"Man, Dad. I don't know. I think they're pretty busy. I wouldn't really feel comfortable asking for a reservation and actually eating there before I even started working."

"I understand," he said. "Let's head up the valley and see what we see."

I felt bad. I certainly had rocky moments with my dad, but both of my parents had been unbelievably supportive of my career. They put me through culinary school, moved me to New York, Grand Rapids, Chicago, and now Napa, and helped me pay my travel and living expenses in each city, allowing me to focus on the work.

And now, for the first time, my dad expressed an interest in learning more about fine dining and where I would be working. The last thing chef Keller said to me before I left was, "If there's anything you need at all, just give us a call. We're here to help." Chef Keller had known me for a mere two days, but his generosity seemed genuine.

I contemplated all of this for a few moments and then called the kitchen phone. Chef Keller answered. I explained that my dad had moved me out here, that he spent his life owning and working in a small restaurant in St. Clair, and that he really wanted to see where I was going to work. I sheepishly told him that I felt terrible calling and asking for a favor before I even started, and that while I didn't expect to get a table, out of respect for my father I had to at least try.

"I'll call you back in thirty minutes," chef Keller said. "What's your number?"

"I don't have a phone yet, Chef. I'll have to call you."

"Sure. Understood. Make it an hour then."

We sat around for an hour, dozing off a bit from the long drive, then I picked up the phone and called the kitchen again. I felt terribly uncomfortable as I was put on hold for a few minutes before chef Keller picked up. "Grant? You're all set for seven P.M. See you then."

We arrived at the restaurant and found a parking spot on the street right out front. Just like my mom, my dad saw the place and was surprised by how humble it looked. He seemed downright disappointed.

"Wait until we get inside the courtyard," I countered. "The ivy growing on the building is just turning red and the herb gardens are awesome."

We walked down the gravel-lined path that led to a lush garden courtyard. The flourishing honeysuckle and rosebushes created a wall around the property, almost hiding the charming stone facade of the building and the view into the serene kitchen. In the center of the courtyard was a baby Meyer lemon tree surrounded by a circular herb garden. The sun cast a golden glow from just over the mountains on the west side of the valley. A few people sat in the far corner of the garden, sipping glasses of champagne.

"Wow," my dad said while looking around. "This is beautiful. Just beautiful."

We walked in.

A statuesque woman with dark hair and large green eyes was standing behind a podium and greeted us in a soft voice. "Welcome to The French Laundry."

She simply nodded when I told her the name of the reservation and without so much as a glance toward a reservation book said, "Right this way." We were led to a downstairs table and seated.

I had observed service twice and even tasted the food, so I had a pretty good idea of what to expect. My dad, however, had never eaten like this before.

A food runner came over immediately, holding a clear triangle tray with what appeared to be miniature ice-cream cones. These, however, were filled with salmon tartar.

Next, a tapioca pudding with a heaping spoonful of caviar and two tiny rouget fillets stacked neatly on top of each other. They were cooked perfectly and without a single pin bone or scale.

"I thought for sure there would be bones in those fish," my dad whispered at me, although he was really talking out loud to himself.

I leaned toward him. "I watched them take the bones out with tweezers when I was here."

The meal stretched on—a chop of Atlantic salmon arrived on a ragout of lentils with truffles and lardoons; lobster came on a bed of creamy lobster-scented orzo.

Then the foie gras course came. A rosy-colored, puck-shaped torchon with pear relish and toasted brioche was placed in front of me, while my father received the sautéed version with abalone and Meyer lemon that I had eaten during my tryout. The captain, Kevin, approached our table, looked at me with a smile, and said, "Chef thought you might want to try a different preparation."

I thought to myself, "He remembered! He freaking remembered that I tried that. This is crazy."

I was in a stupor. To say that the food was delicious would be stating the obvious, but it would also be understating so much more. If it wasn't perfect, it was damn well close. But it was also so *smart*. It was clever without being cloying. And the service hit just the right mark. This flat-out blew away the meals I had at the restaurants in Europe. It wasn't even close.

"Grant," my dad said, snapping me back to reality, "if the chef comes out you should stand up and shake his hand. Don't stay sitting."

"Oh, I will, Dad. But I doubt he'll come out. I think he stays in the kitchen."

As we made our way into desserts Kevin came back around and asked if we would like coffee or an after-dinner drink. My dad showed interest in a glass of port; I ordered an espresso. As Kevin moved away I saw my dad start to rise out of his chair. I looked up slack-jawed to see chef Keller towering over our table. I pushed back my chair quickly and stood.

Chef Keller greeted my dad first, giving him a firm handshake and a warm smile. Then he turned to me and did the same. He had a modest way about him, and he seemed a bit uncomfortable in the dining room, as if he didn't belong. We heaped praise and thanks on him for a few minutes before he disappeared back into the kitchen.

I was in awe. I felt like a little kid again—like I knew nothing about cuisine, cooking, or food and was starting from scratch. It was a truly exciting night.

Kevin came back with the port, espresso, and some *mignardise*. "Well," he said, "I have never seen Chef in the dining room before. I guess he likes you guys."

We nibbled on the chocolates and cookies, recounting the meal play by play. To both of us, it was obvious why I should work here. And it was one of the best nights I ever spent with my dad.

"Can I get anything else for you gentlemen?" Kevin asked.

"No, thank you. Just the check," my dad said.

"Ah. There is no check. Thomas took care of it."

CHAPTER 9

f you ask a French Laundry cook the date he started at the restaurant, he'll be able to tell you without hesitation. The date is burned
into his mind like an anniversary or his mother's birthday. October
16, 1996, was my first day.

Also starting that day was Mark Hopper. But on our first day we
didn't work in the restaurant at all. Instead, chef Keller took us to a
charity event at the Culinary Institute of America at Greystone.

Mark and I served hundreds of salmon cornets that evening while
listening to chef Jean-Louis Palladin—who was in town promoting
the opening of his Las Vegas restaurant Napa—tell chef Keller stories
of the food he cooked at Jean-Louis at the Watergate Hotel. Thomas
mentioned to Mark and me that the meals he had there were among
the best of his life.

Being a commis, or prep cook, at the Laundry was not unlike the
work at any other restaurant, even a diner. The commis' responsibilities ranged from rudimentary to advanced, depending on their level
of experience. Starting out, I was slow on the uptake. There is a period of acclimation that every cook must go through in a new kitchen,
and I was no different.

"This is shit!" Jeffrey yelled as he took the strainer full of poorly
cooked green beans and threw them into the sink, beans flying everywhere. "If Thomas saw that, he would fire you right now."

He was right. Not about Chef firing me on the spot, but that the
beans were indeed overcooked. I knew it and wasn't planning on
using them, but I got caught before I could start again. I had lost
track of time while kneading pasta dough, and the beans started to

discolor. It was my second day there and I had yet to find my legs. A few of the cooks were not afraid to point that out. "They might do it that way in Chicago, but here we do things right. Do it nice, or do it twice."

Embarrassed, I gathered the beans from the sink, counter, and floor and threw them away. Mark swung around and whispered, "Don't let 'em get inside your head. Everyone is gunning for everyone right now. They all want that sous title."

It struck me for the first time that I had never been introduced to the sous chef. It was clear that a few of the guys had seniority and seemed to carry themselves like they were in charge. Chefs like Josh, Jeff, and pastry chef Stephen Durfee had authority but lacked the official title. Unlike most kitchens that had several layers of management to make sure standards are upheld, The French Laundry had chef Keller, and that was it.

The first few weeks were brutally tough. The cooks weren't interested in helping me out or making friends. They weren't vicious, they just lived by the standard set by chef Keller and everything else was meaningless and superfluous.

I continued to be trained by Kevin and DJ while most of the other cooks prowled, waiting for me to make a mistake.

DJ and I grew on each other slowly but surely.

We spent weeks of dragging ourselves out of bed at 5:00 A.M. to bang out a long list of menial and petty prep tasks that were passed down to us from the *chefs de partie*. It felt cruel and a result of their own laziness, but that is the kind of thing you can bond over: common misery.

DJ called me "Spanky," after the character from *The Little Rascals,* knowing that I hated it. I teased him constantly about being slow to the point of moving in reverse. He would counter that I was so aggressive that I would crash and burn, turning into an ember by the time I was thirty.

DJ was a purist and a dreamer. He would go mushroom foraging on his days off, have a batch of homebrew beer working in his apartment, and help his local farmer friends harvest or till their fields in exchange for some vegetables. He drove a beat-up VW bus, which summed up his personality pretty well.

One very busy morning we both entered panic mode. The lists left for us were enormous. On top of that it was a Saturday, which meant that we had lunch service to deal with and everything that came with it: extra *mise en place* to cover the extra service and a whole host of extra cooks in the kitchen taking up space earlier in the day. Every day, once the PM cooks came in, we would end up balancing our cutting boards on stacked-up milk crates. After all, we were just commis, and the *chefs de partie* needed the prime real estate in the kitchen.

DJ was watching me bounce off the counters and I heard him chuckle from the other side of the kitchen. "Spanky, you're going to kill yourself. When you move that fast, quality suffers."

In the French Laundry kitchen those were fighting words. To insinuate that another cook was compromising the quality of the food was the ultimate insult. As busy as I was, I took the time to stop and walk up to DJ and look him in the eye. "No chance, Gerber. I am on fire today. Untouchable!"

I dumped a batch of olives that I'd recently pitted into the Robot Coupe and just as I was about to fire it DJ put his hand on the lid and said, "I will bet you, Spanky. I'll bet you that there's a pit in there."

"No chance," I replied with supreme confidence. "I'll bet you anything you want."

"Okay. Here's the deal. When you turn that on I guarantee we will hear a pit hitting the blade. When we do, you have to fish it out and put it in your wallet. That pit has to stay there until I ask to see it. If at any time you cannot produce the pit when I ask, you owe me ten dollars. And it keeps going on and on."

"And if there is no pit?" I asked.

"I'll give you ten dollars right now."

"Deal!"

I cranked the lid closed and hit the green button. We both froze, listening carefully. The blades whipped around for about thirty seconds, breaking down the olives into a black paste. All seemed fine. But then it freed a single pit from its jacket of flesh.

Ting. Ting. Ting.

DJ reached over and pushed the red stop button with a huge smile on his face.

I emptied the contents of the bowl onto a sheet of parchment and searched for the culprit. I found it, washed it off, and pulled out my wallet. I held the pit up in the air between two fingers and held my wallet up in the other hand. In slow motion I lowered the pit into the wallet like a mom pretending a spoonful of food is an airplane while feeding her baby.

We both laughed. I knew I had been beat.

DJ has never asked to see the pit. It sits, waiting for him, in my wallet.

I worked as a prep cook for months. I was patient. But I was anxious to move up, or to at least know that I would move up eventually.

I approached chef Keller and expressed my concerns of being passed over or left behind as an eternal prep cook. A soft smile spread over his face and I imagined that he must have been thinking how I was very young, presumptuous, and naive. I was only twenty-two years old, and he basically told me as much. "Be patient," he said. "You don't realize it yet, but you are learning so much right now."

I nodded my head in agreement, but I didn't agree.

I wanted a life on the line.

I wanted to burn my forearms on the oven door and dig myself out of a giant black hole of tickets every night at seven. I wanted to feel the adrenaline. I wanted to be great.

"Eventually, Grant, we'll move you into a *chef de partie* position."

I was a commis at The French Laundry for eleven months. It was the most important period of my culinary development. I was surrounded by products that I had never seen before, let alone worked with on a daily basis. I learned how to cook pig ears and trotters, duck tongues, cockscombs, sea urchin, and veal brains. I was exposed to traditional techniques as basic as making veal stock and kneading the perfect pasta dough to more advanced preparations like cleaning foie gras for torchons or properly macerating short ribs in red wine, clarifying the marinade, and flaming it before the cooking process. I spent months making the innovative, savory oyster-flavored tapioca sabayon for the "Oysters and Pearls" caviar dish.

Chef Keller would take time out of his day to personally demonstrate techniques required to complete preparations. Many of these would be the more traditional or obscure techniques for preparing offal. Ingredients such as hearts, brains, sweetbreads, liver, trotters, cheeks, gizzards, tripe, and tongue typically require numerous preparatory steps and long cooking times over several days. These are projects, not simply cooking, and it was necessary to start early in the morning before the *chefs de partie* would fill the stoves with other elements of the daily *mise en place*.

Chef Keller was passionate about these preparations and loved teaching us how to cook them.

One December morning Chef came into the French Laundry kitchen carrying a beautiful antique copper *brassier*. He hefted it onto the counter, glanced at me with squinted eyes that had seen only three hours of sleep, and said, "Morning, Chef. Do you have the *mise* for the tripe ready?"

Three days earlier we had received a delivery of tripe. Chef Keller told me he would show me how to process it in the coming days, and he started me that day by giving me specific instructions, which I wrote in a notebook, on soaking and rinsing the tripe. This series of purging required pounds of salt, gallons of fresh water, several large containers, and about three days. When he brought in the *brassier* I thought we were ready to go with the final step. Little did I know that we were only halfway to the finish.

The task is not enchanting—the goal is to clean the lining of a bovine stomach. Despite the unglamorous work, or perhaps because of it, I could see the care and determination of his effort. Chef Keller understood something about the end result that I could not at this point in my career. Maybe he really liked tripe. But I think the point of all of this tedious work was to transform something that by definition is poor, worthless, or offensive.

And so we kept at it: repeatedly soaking the tripe and changing the water, scrubbing it with salt, scraping the lining, blanching repeatedly, and trimming after each step. Finally, after days of work, we had something that looked appealing. The pure-white honeycombed texture that was revealed was a satisfying conclusion to the effort. It was like waxing a car by hand. And we hadn't even cooked it yet.

The cleaned and polished tripe was packed carefully into the *brassier* between layers of carrot, onion, and celery—or mirepoix— that were added in an alternating, specific order. White wine, vermouth, and aromatics were added and the pot was placed in the oven for hours, only to be removed, repacked with fresh mirepoix and wine, and cooked again. We repeated this process three times.

Five days after the tripe arrived it was finished.

Every step along the way chef Keller was there demonstrating, watching, correcting, and guiding. He literally stood over my shoulder. It felt like I had been taken under his wing, like I was building the GTO all over again.

But this was different. Chef Keller was not just teaching me, he was protecting the tripe. He wanted that worthless piece of a cow to complete its transformation perfectly. And he was willing to get up early every morning to see that it did.

Chef Keller always talked about thinking "big picture." He drilled that into all of the cooks at The French Laundry. With the tripe, he knew that if he showed us the right way to prepare it, he would be passing down not just a recipe but also a philosophy of cooking.

And chef Keller knew that someday, later in my career, I would pass along that same ethos.

I became good friends with Eric and would tell him regularly that if I didn't get moved to the line soon I would have to leave. Eric was on the meat station at the time and had worked nearly every station in the restaurant. He had a great rapport with chef Keller and was marked for sous chef. I figured whatever I told Eric would eventually filter its way up to Chef.

One morning Eric walked into the kitchen to find me rolling sweet potato agnolotti for the garde manger station. He said good morning as he passed, began setting up his station, and then slid next to me. "Ever been to Hawaii?"

"No, you? I hear it's amazing."

Eric looked at me and smiled. "I'm sure it is."

Thirty minutes later I passed chef Keller as he was on his way into the kitchen. We shook hands and he pulled me aside. "We have an opportunity to do an event in Maui in a few weeks. I was talking it over with the cooks last night after service and Eric suggested I bring you. He knows it'll be a busy trip, and he's been happy with the work you're doing. So what do you think? Want to come to Hawaii?"

Chef and I discussed the trip in detail and he filled me in on the events for the week. It was, in fact, going to be a lot of work. I could tell he was very concerned about leaving the restaurant. I had never seen him miss a service. Chef had already decided to bring the pastry chef Stephen Durfee along, and he asked me who else we should bring.

I was working closely with a new extern at the time named Richard Blais. He fit right in with the personality of the restaurant, taking the all-or-nothing approach and showing a good amount of natural talent despite still being a CIA student. I suggested we bring him along. He worked mornings, so it wouldn't impact the service team, and I knew he would kill himself to get the job done while we were there. Plus, I liked him and we got along well.

The suggestion was unorthodox to be sure. The trip was a golden ticket among the cooks. A weeklong trip anywhere with chef Keller was the stuff of envy, but throw Hawaii in the mix and people would be fighting over it. Typically, such perks were reserved for chefs with the most seniority. Bringing an extern would ruffle some feathers, but it was the way to least upset the flow of the restaurant. Chef Keller agreed with my suggestion.

Rich and I spent the next week organizing, prepping, and packing the *mise en place* for the event. Stephen and Rich left a day ahead to unpack the boxes and set up so that Chef and I could spend one more day at the Laundry making sure everything was set there.

Chef Keller and I got off the plane, recovered our bags, and hopped into the awaiting convertible for our ride to the resort. I felt uncomfortable being around him outside the kitchen. Here we were, sunglasses on and cruising in a convertible in one of the most beautiful places in the world—and I didn't know what to talk about. I wanted to ask him about his career, The French Laundry, the risks he took to make it happen, and the secrets he held about cooking, but I censored myself, knowing he must get asked those things a million times. We enjoyed the thirty-minute drive in silence.

We pulled up to the Kea Lani resort and were met by two women in hula skirts and white tops. They handed us cold towels to cool our foreheads and offered us fresh-squeezed guava juice.

This was unreal. Thomas Keller was being treated like a rock star.

I was rooming with Rich, and after getting a key of my own, Chef and I made plans to take an hour to relax before heading into the kitchen to check on the food that had been shipped ahead.

As I was about to put the key in the door it swung open quickly. "Dude. Man. This is off the hook. You have to see this."

Blais was bouncing up and down and pulled me into the room and led me to the back door. It was March 1998, and El Niño had interrupted the migration pattern of the humpback whales, forcing them closer to shore. "The whales are coming right out of the water. Check that shit out!"

I stepped out onto the patio and watched one whale after another breach the water. We stood for a few minutes surrounded by palm trees, warm air, and the whales and I couldn't help but think I was the luckiest cook in the world. Except maybe Richard, who was here on his externship.

The weeklong event required us to prepare a demonstration, a lunch, and a dinner. Each event had nearly two hundred guests in attendance. We flew 2,500 miles and were cooking in an unfamiliar kitchen with makeshift equipment and a skeleton crew. Most chefs would create a menu that was low-maintenance in that situation, one that would allow them to spend more time on the beach sipping mai tais. Chef Keller did the opposite. His pursuit of perfection extended beyond his restaurant. The menu he created was the polar opposite of safe—it was highly ambitious. The lunch menu included a rabbit course that required the tiny racks to be meticulously frenched, a morel and asparagus course garnished with thumbnail-size gnocchi, and the first course on the dinner menu was a foie gras torchon.

The four of us arrived in the kitchen to find the resort kitchen team sitting on stools while prepping. We exchanged glances, confirming our mutual derision for such heresy and isolated an area of the kitchen where we could work by ourselves. Chef Keller immediately grabbed a bucket, filled it with soapy water, and began to scrub the area where we were working. A couple of members of the resort kitchen offered to help, no doubt as the management sensed that the famous chef should not be cleaning, but chef Keller politely declined. "I think we're in good shape, thank you."

The task of deveining foie gras for the torchon preparation was extremely time consuming. The foie gras had to be cleaned, cured overnight, rolled, poached, and rerolled. The restaurant processed between eight and ten lobes a week, but Rich and Stephen returned from the walk-in carrying a giant plastic tub filled with milk and twenty-four lobes of foie gras bobbing about. Chef suggested we let the liver temper while we butchered the rabbits. As Rich broke off and started making the thousands of gnocchi for the morel course, and Stephen began to prepare the coffee semifreddo for the signature dish "Coffee and Doughnuts," Chef and I started to break down and french the rabbit loins.

When it finally came time to put out the 205 plates, the resort's kitchen staff lined up to help. There were nearly twenty guys.

"Great," I thought, "we will rock this out quickly." Then chef Keller told everyone except the four of us to go away. He did this for each of the three events, and though it made for a crazy stretch of breakneck plating, we knew that each and every one of the dishes went out perfectly.

Chef Keller, it seems, never let the bar drop no matter the situation. In the restaurant, or out.

After the final event Rich and I returned to our room to decompress and clean up before heading out for dinner. We sat giddy with excitement on the balcony of our suite overlooking the ocean. The events had gone smoothly and we were about to board a plane, fly to the big island, and eat dinner at Alan Wong's.

"We are taking an airplane to dinner. With TK. How cool is that?"

We had grown pretty comfortable with each other and sat there talking for a while. We couldn't believe the way the guests and the staff treated chef Keller like a star. We had never seen a chef as a celebrity, and clearly Thomas Keller had become one.

Blais asked me if I thought I would stay at the Laundry for the long haul.

"Yeah, I'll be there for a while. But it's a stepping-stone for me, not the end point."

"Really? What do you mean?"

Having been in his shoes not too long ago, I could understand how hard it was to wrap your head around life beyond the Laundry. It was the pinnacle of gastronomic excellence, not only in America but also—as I learned the hard way—in the world. But I knew that I wanted something more. I wanted a place that was mine. That was what I grew up with, and that is what I knew.

"I have a lot more to learn from TK. But even as I'm frenching rabbit for what I know will be an amazing dish, I can't help but think about how I'll do it differently. I'm over buttered-out reductions, not because they aren't great but because there is something beyond them. I want to use it all but leave it behind, if you know what I mean. I want to do my own thing."

Blais looked at me like I was posing and being a cocky bastard, but he didn't say anything. He was ambitious, too, and had landed here well. And we were about to hop on a plane to go to dinner. Anything seemed possible.

I wasn't just running my mouth, though. Even in the thrall of The French Laundry I tried to do as Thomas instructed—to see the big picture.

And while I couldn't see the details, I could see how things might fall in place.

Mark was the *chef de partie* on the garde manger station and would soon be moving to fish to replace Phil, who was leaving to join chef Daniel Patterson's restaurant Babette's in Sonoma. Mark emerged as one of the strongest cooks on the team, and I was happy that he would be the one training me for my shot on the line. He was like a drill sergeant, incredibly focused and serious. There was only one way to do something—his way. The *bain-marie* was in the same spot every time, and the spoon and palette knife handles always faced the same way. The *mise en place* rail was set up in the same order every day at the exact same time. The section ran like a machine because it was consistent and almost mechanical. "This is the way Chef likes it. Do it this way," was the only explanation ever given.

I wouldn't argue with him. He obviously knew what he was doing, made clear by the way he interacted with chef Keller. Mark spent a week training me on the station and then moved on to work fish.

Finally, I was on the line.

Traditionally garde manger stations are removed from the hot line, but at The French Laundry it was one of the four stations surrounding the stove and directly behind the expediting station where chef Keller stood every service.

The Laundry had two menu options: the nine-course chef's tasting or the five-course prix fixe, in which the diner chose among several options in each category. I was responsible for between six to ten dishes, all of which I had some familiarity with from producing the mise en place for them. Other ingredients I had cooked before with chef Keller, such as the veal tongue and beef cheeks that made up the dish "Tongue 'n' Cheek." I locked into the work quickly and with the support of Eric, who was on the meat station to my immediate right, and Mark, who was coaching me from across the stove, the transition from prep cook to line cook went smoothly.

At the end of service each night the cooks would huddle around the chef's pass and go over the orders and menu changes for the following day. One night, a few months into my time on the line, chef Keller let us know that a very important group of journalists would be in town for a food journalism symposium at CIA Greystone that weekend, and that a group of them would be dining at the restaurant the next evening. Among them were some of the most influential writers in the country: Ruth Reichl, head critic for the *New York Times*, Phyllis Richman, and Corby Kummer.

Not only did we have the most important critics in the country coming in, but they were all sitting at the same table. Chef Keller led the discussion about the menu we would prepare for them by asking the group what they would suggest. We spent an hour writing a menu that would showcase a broad variety of the best dishes we could prepare.

The next day we all arrived early knowing how busy the night would be and how critical it would be that everybody was ready to go when service started. We also knew that chef Keller would be tense and a bit edgy, especially if he sensed that the kitchen was unprepared.

I was rolling out pasta when he arrived. He walked briskly past me, reached out his hand and squeezed my elbow as a hello gesture that did not interrupt my work. Two steps past, however, he stopped abruptly and turned toward me. "We should do a different pasta course for them tonight. What do you want to do?"

"Are you kidding me?" I thought. Why the hell was he asking me, a twenty-three-year-old cook who had been on the station for a few months, to come up with a course?

I said nothing but immediately ran to the walk-in to see what ingredients we had available that were not already on the critic's table menu. I settled on foie gras, chanterelles, sage, and Swiss chard. I went back to chef Keller and proposed the dish. "Chef, how about a single foie gras tortellini garnished with chanterelles, Swiss chard, and sage? Maybe an acidic brown butter emulsion, spiked with sherry or banyuls vinegar."

"Sounds good. Don't make them too big; they're getting a lot of food."

"Yes, Chef."

I rolled the pasta and worked on the emulsion and garnishes first so we could taste the finished product in plenty of time to make adjustments.

When service started the kitchen was buzzing with energy. Mark looked across the stove at me and gave me a serious nod while his eyes stayed focused on mine. It was his way of saying, "Don't be the guy to fuck it up tonight."

Chef Keller was typically unflappable. But this table had him keyed up. And nobody wanted to let him down.

The service sped up and the team locked into a rhythm. Chef Keller would call out an order, "Order in, four tasting."

The cooks fired back the order in unison like an adrenaline-fueled football team on Super Bowl Sunday: "Four tasting!"

We were all on top of our game, and Chef knew it. About halfway through the critic's menu he gave his classic "tell." Whenever chef Keller was happy and things were cruising along, he would click the heels of his wooden clogs together. The sound must have brought him pleasure, like the clink of two wineglasses during a toast. He would only pull that out when the kitchen was rocking.

I was dipping into the oven to grab a stack of warmed plates when I heard it. I stayed low but picked my head up to see if I could catch Mark's eye across the stove. He was looking at me, giving me the nod again, but this time with a big grin on his face.

After the last course went out, Chef went to the dining room to say hello to the table. Eric, Mark, and I cleaned the kitchen and anxiously awaited word from the dining room. "What did they say, Chef?" we asked in unison.

He smiled. "They liked it. I think they really liked it. That was a big one, guys," he said as his heels clicked together once more. "Thanks, guys. Go get some rest. That was a long day."

It is hard to overstate how exciting that day was and how good it felt that we pulled it off so well.

A week later the cover page of the *New York Times* dining section featured a review, by Ruth Reichl, of the meal: IN NAPA VALLEY, A RESTAURANT SCALES THE PEAK.

The article heaped praise on the restaurant and chef Keller, but one line gave The French Laundry the mythic aura that it carries to this day:

> Today his restaurant in Yountville, still called The French Laundry, is the most exciting place to eat in the United States.

CHAPTER 10

The praise from Ruth and the Outstanding Chef Award from the James Beard Foundation that followed in May catapulted chef Keller and The French Laundry to legendary, destination-dining status. The phone rang and did not stop. Reservations became impossible to get for lunch and dinner, a total of ten services per week. It became common to have a hundred patrons for dinner and eighty for lunch.

Chef Keller arrived around 10:00 A.M. on the weekends, expedited lunch service, then rolled right into butchering fish or cleaning foie gras as soon as lunch was broken down. The team prepped frantically until service, and most of the staff meals were eaten from deli containers while monitoring sauces as they reduced or garnishes as they cooked.

In addition to the immense pressure brought on by the onslaught of popularity, chef Keller was in the process of opening his second restaurant, Bouchon, and had begun work on *The French Laundry Cookbook*. The man did not stop moving for a second. One day he overheard a cook complaining about being tired and sent him home. "You're tired? Why don't you go home and sleep, then." That became the running insult that cooks would jab at a yawning coworker or when they sensed a lull in productivity.

While all of the cooks were talented, a core group emerged. Mark, Eric, Greg, and I were the guys who chef Keller would rely on to anchor the busy services, train incoming cooks, or lay on a few extra courses for a special table of guests. There were a few unspoken rules: chef Keller was God; try to be like chef Keller, exactly; the food was perfect or it was wrong; failure was never an option; and "yes, Chef" was the only proper response to any request.

When chef Keller asked us to help in the recipe documentation and plating of the dishes for the cookbook, we jumped at the opportunity. Mark and I arrived at chef Keller's house every Monday afternoon during the month of June to join recipe writer Susie Heller and photographer Deborah Jones. We prepared the recipes while Susie documented every pinch of salt. Then Mark and I would plate the dishes for Deborah to photograph. It was an amazing experience that made us feel connected to the chef and the restaurant. It also gave us a false sense of superiority over the other cooks, and rifts began forming in our kitchen relationships.

After service each night the cooks gathered around chef Keller's workstation. We would go through menu changes and orders for the following day, or discuss VIP courses that had to be created. At one point Mark and I suggested that we would be happy to come in and work the service on our stations in the morning as well, replacing the AM cooks.

"You really think you guys are better?" chef Keller asked.

"Well, Chef," I said. "I think we could do a better job, yes. I think the night would go smoother given all of the special dishes going out tomorrow."

"I agree, Chef," Mark said.

Chef Keller expected this level of arrogance from Mark, but was both surprised and disappointed that it had seeped into me. He turned directly to me and said, "What happened to you?" It was the first time he'd ever raised his voice to me, and the question cut deeply.

Mark and I pulled into our parking spot on the street and got out of the car with a protein shake in one hand and our blue aprons in the other. "I feel a bit off today," he said. "Might be a shit day."

We changed into our coats and headed for the kitchen. It was Saturday and the AM team was about to start a busy lunch service. Mark headed toward chef Keller to check on the status of his PM station with AM *chef de partie* Kirk. He seemed to be gone for a while, and I glanced at the empty cutting board next to mine wondering what was taking so long. A few minutes later Mark came storming back over, grabbed his knives, and turned to me: "Um. I'm leaving."

"What? What are you talking about?"

"I just got fired." He walked toward the back door.

"Dude. What the hell? How are you getting home?"

"I'll walk. It's nice out."

"It's ten miles, man. Let me give you a ride."

"No. Only one of us needs to get fired today. I'll be fine. Happy Fourth of July. I guess the fireworks came early."

Mark had trained me on the garde manger and fish stations before moving on to cook meat. Not only did he take the time to train me well, but he watched over me closely, supporting me when I was slipping. He was the reason I moved from the commis position to the line. He had tenacity, confidence, and the respect of everyone in the kitchen. Nobody fucked with him. He backed up his arrogance with extreme discipline and pure talent. We had become close friends and roommates, and I looked up to him like a big brother. When Mark walked out the back door I felt vulnerable. Together we felt like an unstoppable team. We pushed each other to do better—faster *mise en place*, more VIP options for Chef to choose from, who could be the guy who is so together and ahead that he can walk to Ranch Market at staff meal and buy the other guy a sandwich and a Gatorade?

It turned out that Mark was wearing black jeans that day. No jeans were allowed, and when chef Keller noticed Mark's clothing choice, his mention of the jeans sparked a comment about acting privileged and above the law. Neither of the chefs felt like backing down that day. When chef Keller asked Mark if he had an attitude and Mark replied yes, Thomas told him to take his attitude home and not bring it back.

My parent's marriage hit ground again.

I called home one afternoon to speak with my mom and see how she was handling a new separation when my uncle Jim answered instead. I heard the voices of my mom's sisters in the background and figured they were over at the house for dinner.

"Hey, it's Grant. Can I talk to my mom?"

"Grant, I think it's best if she gives you a call tomorrow. She isn't feeling well right now. Everything is fine; a bunch of people are with her. But she'll have to call you tomorrow."

I found out the next day that the separation from my dad had taken a more insidious turn— my mom had swallowed a handful of painkillers. I wrote my dad a letter explaining that if he didn't treat her with respect, then we no longer had a relationship. I never heard back from him.

My relationship with my father was crippled, my mother's life was a mess, and I was halfway across the country and couldn't help in any meaningful way. My parents were heading for divorce and my fantasy of one day opening a restaurant as a family had vanished. My relationships at the Laundry, after Mark was fired, fueled a new sense of displacement.

Cindy had moved to Sacramento for the summer of 1998 to fulfill an internship obligation for the law degree she was completing at Notre Dame. Our relationship had been a long-distance, on-again, off-again affair since we graduated from high school. In theory this was going to be an "on-again" time. The reality of my working in the restaurant industry did not mesh well with the home life she wanted in the long run, but she was willing to give it a try. We settled into a routine of making a day-a-week commute between Napa and Sacramento. That worked for a few months before my work demands got in the way. I was more aware of the sacrifices I was making, though, and I started to entertain thoughts of living a more ordinary life on a schedule that would permit me personal time.

"I think it's time for me to leave, Chef. I just don't feel like I'm mentally in it right now."

"I agree," he said.

"What do you think? Should I move on?"

"I can't make that decision for you, but it seems like it might be the best thing."

"I want to leave on good terms. I don't want to jeopardize the time I have spent here or put my relationship with you in danger. I'll give you as much notice as you need."

"How about two months?" His words rang in my ears—it sounded like I had quit.

"Two days left, old man; you're going to miss me," I mumbled quietly to DJ as we stood shoulder to shoulder prepping.

"You know, I didn't think you had it in you to leave. I thought you might follow your bro Mark out the door, but figured they would pull you back in. What are you going to do, Spanky?"

"I'm not sure. Maybe wait some tables and try to make some real money. Have some free time. I'm just not sure yet."

"I told you—crash and burn. I knew you would fry out." DJ was making fun of me, but I knew he was sad to see me leaving. "Hey. A friend of mine told me about a winery job that's open if you want to give that a shot. Seems like a good gig, too. It's a small place run by an older guy. He basically wants help so he doesn't have to do everything by himself. I was considering it myself. You know it's just a matter of time before TK fires me or I implode."

When I accepted the job at the Laundry I had the unrealistic notion that I would be able to find the free time outside the restaurant to learn the wine trade. Surrounded by vineyards and the core of the American wine industry, there was no escaping that Napa meant wine and that my culinary education should include an immersive experience in the vineyards. Once I began working fourteen-hour days, however, it became obvious that that was never going to happen. Outside of work I barely had time to lift weights, wash my clothes, and try to catch up on sleep.

The job sounded perfect.

The next day DJ slid a c-fold towel across my cutting board. In blue Sharpie it had written on it: LA JOTA. BILL SMITH. 965-4327.

I called Bill the following day to learn about the position.

"I understand that you've been at the Laundry for two years, so I know you're not afraid of work. Still, I need to see if I like you before I bring you on—we'll be spending a good amount of time together. Can you come up and visit the winery for an interview tomorrow?"

The thirty-minute drive up the valley to La Jota was stunning. After turning off Highway 29 onto Howell Mountain Road the foliage became dense with manzanita and redwood trees. It was a peaceful, quiet world that was so close, yet I didn't know it existed.

I pulled into a narrow blacktop driveway with the address hand-painted on a white board. As I slowly drove up the road to the winery, an oncoming truck approached and a hand appeared out the window, waving me over to the side of the drive. The truck pulled up next to me and the driver rolled down the window. A small man with big, saggy cheeks and white hair that stood out against his tan complexion flashed me a huge smile. "Howdy. You Grant?"

"I am."

"I'm Bill. I thought I'd be able to sneak out to the store for some coffee before you got here."

"Sorry, I'm early. I wasn't sure how long it would take to get up here."

"No worries. Let's go back to the winery and drop your car off and then we can go together. We'll head to St. Helena and get one of those good lattes. They don't serve any caffeine in Angwin."

I wasn't sure what that meant, so I just smiled and nodded. Bill turned the truck around and I followed him back to the winery. I knew from DJ that Bill was an older man, but I was surprised to find that he appeared old enough to be my grandfather. I wondered why he was still working so hard.

We made our way back down the valley to grab a coffee while we chatted. Bill went over his story: He was in the oil business in Bakersfield and did well for himself but disliked the location and the work. He loved food and wine, so in the midseventies he decided to buy some land in Napa and try to make his own wine. He bought La Jota, a small winery that had fallen into disrepair and had not produced any wine since Prohibition. Bill planted most of the twenty-five acres with the Bordeaux varietals of Cabernet Sauvignon and Cabernet Franc, but his affinity for Condrieu led him to plant a small amount of Viognier as well. In 1982 La Jota made its first commercial vintage.

As Bill wrapped up his life story I asked him about the job.

"Basically the person has to wear many hats. Up until now I have done all of the winery work myself—pressing, pumping over, racking, and maintaining the wines once they're in barrel. But I'm not getting younger, and my wife, Joan, and I are building a new house on the back of the property. So I need someone to lend me a hand. You'll do all of those things, plus help the vineyard team prune and plant. You'll probably help out around the new house, too. Joanie likes tulips, so we'll give her some tulips around there," he said with a shrug and a smile.

I had toured a few of the big wineries in the valley and they were anything but romantic. Dozens of workers wore hard hats and lifted zip palettes of wine on forklifts while giant fire hoses moved enough wine to fill a small pond. La Jota was the opposite of that—it had character. The stone structure was built in 1867 and was largely unchanged. The surroundings were magical, and Bill seemed to be the gentle grandfather of every kid's fishing dreams.

Bill showed me around the cellar and grounds and then we settled into his office. "Well, Grant, you sure are quiet. I like that. Do you want a job?"

"I do. Thanks."

Despite everything Bill had told me, I was expecting to find some technology at the vineyard once I started. At the very least I assumed there'd be automated machines for the pressing, pumping, and bottling of the wine. Once I got there I found that the reality was as far from my expectations as possible—in a good way. Absolutely everything was done by hand.

I spent the first few weeks preparing for the onslaught of the harvest. I cleaned the large stainless-steel fermenters using buckets of bleach and citric acid, climbing inside with a scrub brush attached to a long pole. I spent days organizing the cellar and moving in the new oak barrels.

Bill and I measured the grapes' Brix—or sugar content—religiously as they hung in the vineyard nearly ready to pick. While we were collecting samples one day Bill mentioned that the fruit at the Sonoma vineyard where he purchased his pinot noir grapes was ready. "Jim says they look good and we should plan to pick tomorrow or the next day."

"Cool," I thought, "I finally get to make some wine."

The following day we drove to the Sonoma coast with our vineyard team and harvested the grapes into three large bins and trucked them back to the winery.

"Bill, why aren't we unloading these up top by the press?" I asked.

He explained that with the pinot grapes he liked to do things differently. He put them through what's called "whole berry fermentation." The fruit is encouraged to begin fermenting inside its own skin, which helps develop flavors like banana, cherry, and even bubble gum. It also helps reduce the malic acid and increase the chances of higher alcohol content—Bill liked strong wines.

It was cold enough that we could cover the grapes for the night and start processing them in the morning.

The next day I walked into the office to find Bill sitting at his desk doing some accounting. He welcomed me as I pulled up a chair to hear what the plan was for the day. Bill paused, looked at me, and a big grin came over his face. "Grant, today you're going to crush the pinot grapes in the fermenters outside."

I clapped my hands together, excited to be really making wine and said, "Okay . . . show me what I have to do."

Bill's grin widened further as he reached into a desk drawer and pulled out a pair of purple swim trunks. He tossed them in my direction. "You'll need these." I figured that it would be a messy process and he was trying to spare my jeans from stains.

He led me outside and down the hill to the front of the winery where the fermenters were located. They were three white plastic tubs, each chest-high and six feet square. He glanced at the shorts and told me to put them on as he lifted the lids off the fermenters.

I was starting to figure out what he had in mind but wouldn't let myself believe that he was going to ask me to take my clothes off and wade around in the warm grape bog. As I was getting undressed he said, "There are a few bees on the surface and the cap will likely hit you about waist high, so, well, you aren't allergic to bee stings, are you?" He was now laughing out loud in a good-natured way. I glanced into one of the fermenters and shook my head at the swarm of bees gathered on top. Every second a few more would dive-bomb into the vat of sugar. It vanquished my romantic notions of crushing grapes underfoot in the middle of wine country.

"Uh, Bill. Why are we doing this? I mean, don't they have machines for this kind of thing?"

"They do, but we want to be very, very gentle on the grapes. Your feet are nice and soft."

I managed to wade carefully through the grape baths without a sting while I gently crushed the grapes. It even became enjoyable. But while hosing down after finishing, I stepped on a bee. Seems I needed one sting to prove I did it.

A few months later, after the wine was well into the barrel and the vineyard was cleaned up for the following spring, Bill asked if I could cook a dinner party for a small group at the new house. "Of course," I said, happy to show him what I could do in a kitchen.

"Good then. By the way, it's for *Food and Wine* magazine. They want to do a profile on our Cab Franc." Whoa.

Once *Food & Wine* found out that Bill had hired an ex–French Laundry cook as an assistant winemaker, they decided to turn the article into a dinner-party theme, with me cooking dishes that paired well with the luscious Cab Franc. It was my first press of any kind and a fairly substantial piece.

I thought it was pretty cool that my photo and food were in a major magazine, and when the article came out I got plenty of phone calls from people I hadn't spoken with in quite some time. One of them was Angela from The French Laundry. She had seen the piece—someone had pinned it to the wall in the coffee station in the restaurant.

Angela and I met at the restaurant in 1996. She was by then already considered a longtime employee, one of the few people around that knew the "old" French Laundry. That basically meant the period between 1994, when the Laundry opened, until the first of many major renovations in 1996, just before I arrived. Angela and a few other veterans would tell stories about taking reservations while sitting on milk crates, since there was no real furniture around. Thomas would create four-star meals from a residential stove and refrigerator in a kitchen the size of a small bathroom. Angela had worked during that heady time as a reservationist, hostess, and, as the restaurant grew, the director of group sales and private events.

When I left, everyone there thought I had committed career suicide. So to make a splash with the *Food & Wine* article somehow legitimized my departure, at least in my mind, and this phone call from someone at the Laundry let me know that they had indeed seen it. It felt great.

After working at the winery for ten months I realized I wanted to be more entrepreneurial and to start making some money.

I talked to Bill about starting my own wine label, and he agreed to help me get going by giving me some space in the La Jota cellar and loaning me a few old barrels. He put me in touch with key people to help buy quality grapes. I started taking viticulture and winemaking classes at Napa Valley College three nights per week and making industry connections to give me insight into how to plan for my own bottling.

The idea was to start small—by necessity but also by choice. If I could find a vineyard owner willing to sell me a ton of grapes, I could produce two barrels, or about seven hundred bottles of wine. It was a modest plan, but doable.

As time went on, the work at the winery slowed significantly compared to the high season when we crushed the grapes. Most of my days were spent doing vineyard work such as installing irrigation lines and planting rootstock, pruning the vines, repairing trellises, and weeding. I was farming. It was a side of the wine industry I hadn't considered. The pace slowed, and as it did my desire to make my own wine waned. I became anxious about what I was doing with my life.

I talked about these uncertainties with my mom and Mark, and both of them suggested I return to The French Laundry. I had no idea how I could possibly do that. It had crossed my mind, but I couldn't see myself joining the team having missed nearly a year. I would be pushed back down through the ranks in terms of seniority, and more significantly there would be the awkwardness of my relationship with chef Keller. I went from being one of his most dedicated cooks to—in my mind—letting him down.

One morning I popped in to see Bill and get my tasks for the day. He wasn't in yet but his daughter, who handled some office work for him, was behind the desk. She said hello and handed me a piece of paper. "There was a message on the machine for you this morning."

I looked down at the Post-it note and saw the name "Thomas," followed by the familiar number of the French Laundry kitchen. I walked outside in a confused panic. Why would he be calling?

Chef Keller and I played phone tag for a couple of days before we were able to connect. When we finally talked I was surprised to find his manner warm and friendly. He asked about the winery, how I was doing in general, and what was new. This was the first time I had ever heard him make small talk. Finally, he got to the point of the call. "So, I have a sous chef position opening up. Are you interested?"

I was flabbergasted. "I am hugely interested, Chef. But give me a few days to think about it, if you could."

The decision was not completely cut and dry. Despite thinking that perhaps winemaking was not for me, I greatly appreciated Bill, La Jota, and everything I had learned there. I found the free time wonderful as well. I had never had a seven-hour workday in my life, and I now had time to devote to other interests. But with all the stress of a long-distance relationship and different long-term goals, Cindy and I had broken up. And without her around, I really had no other interests. I returned to The French Laundry as a sous chef in June 1999.

CHAPTER 11

was only at the winery for ten months but the Laundry had gone through significant changes in my absence. Chef Keller was spending more time away from the restaurant, and many of the faces in the kitchen were new. Eric was promoted to chef de cuisine and Greg to sous chef. The restaurant had become more corporate in its organization—the cooks had a posted schedule to follow instead of arriving whenever they felt they had to in order to accomplish the work, a series of clipboards outlining tasks hung on the kitchen wall, and the kitchen management was asked to post entries in a journal after each shift. Instead of having one expediting station there were now two. Chef Keller would still call in the tickets but focused primarily on the canapé and fish stations. Because the majority of my time on the line was at the fish station, chef Keller typically had me take over for him when he was away. I was twenty-five years old and standing in the shoes of one of the most respected chefs in the world.

In a conversation with Angela at work one morning, I mentioned that I was running out of time to find a new place to live. Conveniently, she was looking for a roommate. The fact that I had no furniture or even a security deposit made it as easy as moving my clothes, books, and knives once again. I moved in with Angela—and *then* we started dating. Pretty much the opposite of what most people do.

Chef Keller treated each of us like specialists, delegating the responsibilities of the kitchen to us based on our strengths and personalities. Greg led the morning team and did most of the ordering, Eric would oversee the entire operation but concentrate on the meat and butchering stations, and I spent most of my time looking over the fish and canapé sections. The creative process was always collaborative, but it became clear that Chef appreciated my imaginative spirit. He knew that while I respected the idea of flawless repetition required in the pursuit of perfection, I grew bored easily. I found making the same thing the same way monotonous, and I commonly pestered him to change my dishes.

In a menu meeting, Chef threw out a challenge to the group: to come up with a new summer-focused caviar dish. We'd run the same two—"Oysters and Pearls" and "Cauliflower Panna Cotta"—for a long time, and even though the former dish is amazingly delicious, it is very heavy for the summer months. I went home that night and sat down with a few books and a pad of paper to figure out a new dish.

I wanted a cold preparation, something that was light and refreshing—the complete opposite of the rich, hot sabayon in "O & P." As I started to think about caviar my mind naturally drifted to champagne. It is a classic match, and the cold effervescence of the wine is energizing. I next thought of things that paired well with champagne. I imagined a cocktail reception with people wearing fine clothes, sipping champagne, and eating . . . prosciutto-wrapped melon on a toothpick.

Cantaloupe, champagne, and caviar. It makes sense.

I called the produce purveyor at 3:00 A.M. and added a few cantaloupes so I could play around the next day.

I arrived early with a condensed page of notes and an annotated sketch I drew up showing each of the components and their composition in the finished dish. After giving it more thought, I wanted to create a dish that highlighted the texture of the caviar itself. I decided to turn the melon into a *bavarois*, or mousse, so it would gently dissolve in the mouth and give a textural priority to the eggs. A thin layer of champagne gelée would form the barrier between the caviar and the mousse, and a paper-thin slice of ripe melon would act as a foot to prevent the *bavarois* from melting if the plate was not super cold.

I began to prepare the dish as John Frasier, the canapé *chef de partie*, walked past. "Oh, God. Now what are you up to?"

"The new caviar course you're going to be picking up tomorrow. You might want to watch how I do this so you don't go down in a couple of days." John and I ego-jabbed each other all the time.

"Is that melon? You're making a caviar dish with melon? Yeah. That ought to be good. Can't wait to hear what Chef has to say about this one."

I finished plating the prototype, placed the dish on chef Keller's desk, and handed him a spoon.

"Cantaloupe Melon Bavarois with Champagne Gelée and Osetra Caviar."

He looked down at the dish and slowly lifted his head up to meet my eye. With a raised eyebrow he smiled. "Uh, you put caviar on dessert?"

I laughed. "No, Chef. It's not desserty sweet. It's just as sweet as the melon is naturally, about twenty Brix. But it balances really well with the acid from the champagne and the salinity of the caviar. Try it."

He skeptically dug his spoon in and took a bite.

"Wow. It's really good. *Really* good. I never would have thought . . . Is it producible?"

"Yes, Chef. I can train John in a day or so, no problem. Can we put it on tomorrow?"

"Yes." He paused for a moment and continued, "But you know the minute we put this dish on the menu it's no longer a Grant Achatz dish. It will be a Thomas Keller dish. You won't be able to use this when you eventually become a chef. People will think you are stealing from me."

I thought about it for a moment and decided to say what came to mind. "That's okay, Chef. Plenty more ideas where that came from."

I arrived at The French Laundry early one night so I could get some prep done for a table of regulars—we called them VIPs—when I saw chef Keller gliding through the kitchen directly toward me. Every morning he would greet each cook with a handshake and usually, depending on the day, a smile. On that day, I noticed something in his hand. He placed the October 1999 issue of *Gourmet* magazine on the stainless pass and asked me to open to the page marked with a yellow sticky note.

I thumbed to the page, finding an unfamiliar, gruff-looking chef surrounded by floating oranges. "Who is this guy?" I wondered. "And why is he juggling citrus fruits?"

That guy was Ferran Adrià, the chef at a restaurant in Spain called elBulli. "Bulldog?" I thought. "A restaurant named Bulldog?"

Chef Keller looked down at the magazine and almost whispered at me, "Grant, read this tonight when you go home. His food sounds really interesting and right up your alley. I think you should go there and stage this summer. I'll arrange it for you."

Seven months later I landed at the Barcelona airport. I hadn't planned very well and had neglected to make arrangements for traveling to elBulli, two hours north of Barcelona by car.

While walking through the airport I ran into a group of American chefs. Wylie Dufresne, Paul Kahan, Suzanne Goin, Michael Schlow, and a couple of journalists had been flown to Spain by the local tourism board to promote Spanish gastronomy. I recognized them and we chatted for a while before I asked where they were headed. "A restaurant called elBulli," Wylie said. "Have you heard of it?"

I hitched a ride with them on their posh tour bus.

When I arrived at elBulli with the American chefs I felt like a leech. After all, I was an unknown, uninvited sous chef there to work, not to be wined and dined. None of them had ever heard of me. The elBulli co-owner and maître d'hôtel, Juli Soler, welcomed the group at the door, along with the Spanish government official who was leading the tour. I pulled him aside and explained my story. He told Juli who I was and walked off to the kitchen to tell chef Adrià that I had arrived with the group.

"Ferran wants you to eat with them," he said. Well, now I really felt like a parasite, but thought to myself, "If you insist."

I sheepishly joined the group for dinner. Despite being uncomfortable with the chefs, I wasn't going to pass up this opportunity. I would just lay low, stay quiet, and pay attention.

I had, at this point, been cooking for twenty of my twenty-five years. I had literally grown up in restaurants. I had graduated from a top cooking school and worked as a sous chef in one of the best restaurants in the world. I thought I knew food and cooking.

I had no idea what we were in for. None of us did.

The dishes started to come out, and I was disoriented, surprised, and amazed. Completely blown away.

Trout roe arrived, encased in a thin, perfect tempura batter. I shot Wylie a skeptical glance and he immediately returned it. You simply don't deep-fry roe. You can't. It isn't possible.

We popped the gumball-sized bite into our mouths. There was no obvious binder holding the eggs together, and they were still cold and uncooked! How did they hold the eggs together and then dip them into a batter without dispersing them into hundreds of pieces? And how are they uncooked? Whoa.

A small bowl arrived. "Ah, polenta with olive oil," I thought. "This isn't so out there. This I can understand." But as soon as the spoon entered my mouth an explosion of yellow corn flavor burst, and then all the texture associated with polenta vanished. I laid my spoon down and stared at it with mock calm. I was astonished.

What the hell was going on back there? This is the stuff of magic.

On it went. Pea soup changed temperature as I ate it. Ravioli made from cuttlefish instead of pasta burst with a liquid coconut filling as soon as I closed my mouth. Tea showed up looking like a mound of bubbles but immediately dissolved on my palate. Braised rabbit arrived with a *hot* apple gelatin. How is that possible? Gelatin can't be hot! That much I knew for sure. Hell, my mom taught me that.

The meal went on for forty courses—over five and a half hours. It was, quite simply, mind-altering.

Still, I walked into the elBulli kitchen the next day expecting some familiarity. A kitchen is a kitchen, right? Chefs were coming from all over the world to learn this new style of cooking, yet it didn't feel like cooking at all. "Concepts" better described the dishes. There were no flaming burners in this kitchen, no proteins sizzling in oil, no veal stock simmering on the flattop. This was like landing on Mars.

I saw cooks using tools as though they were jewelers. Chefs huddled over a project such as wrapping young pine nuts in thin sheets of sliced beet or using syringes to precisely fill miniature hollowed-out recesses in strawberries with Campari. Everything was new and strange to me: the way the team was organized, the techniques being used, the sights, even the smells. Here was a new cuisine where nothing was routine.

René Redzepi from Copenhagen, who spoke French and English, was given the task of being my ears and voice during the stay. I didn't speak any Spanish. So an elBulli chef de cuisine would speak in Spanish to an Italian chef, who would translate to a French guy who would pass on the instructions to René. René would then pass along what was left of the initial conversation to me in English.

I spent just three days in the kitchen of elBulli, but it sent me home reeling.

I knew that quickly that I still had much to learn.

I arrived back at The French Laundry to find myself working the canapé station, filling a spot vacated by a cook who was fired while I was gone.

I couldn't stop thinking about the elBulli trip. The idea of letting my imagination be the guiding source of inspiration had resonated with me for a long time, but now the urge to create outside of The French Laundry became irresistible.

A few days later, chef Hiro Sone from Terra restaurant in St. Helena was coming in to dine. We always tried to come up with a few twists for visiting chefs, especially ones we knew well and appreciated. I looked over at chef Keller and said, "How about a foamed lobster broth in between the canapé progression?"

Thomas looked at me oddly, as if he dreaded the day I would want to implement some of the techniques I saw at elBulli, but knew it was coming. Suggesting such a thing at The French Laundry bordered on heresy. It was not under the Laundry umbrella, and I certainly did not want to insult chef Keller or compromise his style. But I was so incredibly inspired and excited by what I saw at elBulli that I wanted the other chefs to learn about it and feel the same way.

Chef Keller heard me out. "The flavors will be classic French Laundry, Chef," I said. "It will be delicious. We will simply take our exact lobster base, put it in an ISI canister, and aerate it over some classic garnishes in a glass. It should come out part soufflé, part soup, and part parfait. We will only be playing with the texture. The rest is TFL all the way."

Chef Keller paused, then nodded his head and said simply, "Okay."

That was the moment I knew I had to leave The French Laundry.

I was so excited to explore and push new boundaries with food that I was in danger of compromising the vision that chef Keller had crafted over many years in his kitchen. I wanted to experiment and take risks, and I would need to risk failure and imperfection to move forward. Chef Keller had taken those same risks over and over early in his career, but now he and The French Laundry were at a different stage of maturity. Every day in that kitchen was about striving for perfection through refining years of ideas that were known and comfortable. The team continued to finesse dishes and increase the level of sophistication, but it was done in a set style.

I mentioned all of this to chef Keller, and while he was too generous to say so, I knew he could feel the conflict as well. Maybe he recognized the new instability I was feeling, the renewed creative energy, and realized it was time for me to go. He probably saw that I was no longer a soldier fighting his fight.

Two months of uncertainty went by and I contained my urges to mess with his dishes. I spent my free time trying to figure out what to do. I wasn't the chef de cuisine, but I was certainly in a position of leadership, and I felt confident that if and when Eric left I would be the heir to that coveted throne, right under chef Keller. I loved everything about The French Laundry: the people, the place, the food, and the memories. I learned more there than I had ever hoped to in one restaurant or from one chef. But I had to forge ahead on my own. I had, after all, seen my mom and dad do the very same thing. They took that leap and it paid off.

Thomas, armed with an espresso in one hand, put his other on my shoulder as we walked into the dining room on a sunny October morning. We tucked into the downstairs alcove for some added privacy, and I began to talk right away so I didn't waste his valuable time.

"Chef. I have been thinking about leaving, about trying to find my own kitchen to run. I wanted to hear your thoughts about that."

Thomas smiled at me and nodded his head. This was not a surprise. "If you think you're really ready, I mean really ready, then you should go. But you need to understand that it is going to be incredibly difficult.

"What we have here is an amazing restaurant, built over many years. The infrastructure is in place and we are fortunate to have everything we need. If we need a Pacojet, we buy it. If we want new china, we buy it. And the staff, the staff is amazing both in the front of the house and the back. All of the things you take for granted here, well, they don't exist in many other places. Those are the things that allow The French Laundry to be among the best in the world.

"I know how frustrated you get when things are less than perfect, and I am telling you that it happens here far less frequently than almost anywhere else. You have to ask yourself if you really want to leave all of that behind so soon."

He paused for a moment, but I didn't say anything, so he continued. "I assume you're talking about being a chef de cuisine, right? I mean, you are not opening your own place. So you are going to have to find an owner who is willing to let you have carte blanche. And knowing what I think you want to do . . . well, it will be extremely difficult to find that person. Especially for a chef who has no experience and no reputation."

"I know, Chef, thank you," I replied. "I want you to know that I really appreciate that you understand all of this. The Laundry means a tremendous amount to me. I just think it's time for me to try my own thing."

He encouraged me to keep him in the loop on any developments as they happened and asked me to give him ample notice if I did find anything solid. I could tell that he figured this could take a while.

Indeed, I had no idea where to even start looking. Where do you find a fully operational restaurant that has all of the materials necessary to run at a four-star level, minus a chef? Most of the genuinely great restaurants in the United States were chef owned. While there might be an outside chance that one of them would consider hiring a chef de cuisine from the outside, that person would still have to cook in the style of the chef owner. I knew that a situation like that wouldn't work for me.

I was using the best restaurant in the country as a model for my ambitions. I knew exactly what I desired in terms of standards of operation, protocols, purveyors, and even cooks. What I lacked was a building suited for a great restaurant and an owner willing to let me complete my vision. And as Thomas said, who the hell would bet all of that on an unknown young chef with no reputation who never really ran a kitchen on his own?

For a couple of months I scanned the Internet, visiting hospitality headhunter and job-posting sites. I sent out a few e-mails and put out a few feelers to people I knew in the industry. Nothing.

The typical postings were for executive chef jobs in hotels and resorts located in far-flung places like the Caribbean, Mexico, or, if you were lucky, Florida. There were a few private chef positions. Not a single posting was remotely close to what I was looking for. I plugged along at the Laundry thinking I would have to change my expectations and my path. But I kept looking, almost out of habit.

One night, while scanning the fine-dining category on a job site, I stumbled across an ad for a tiny restaurant in Evanston, Illinois, called Trio. I had never heard of the place. According to the ad, Trio was a nationally acclaimed restaurant formerly run by Rick Tramanto and Gale Gand. It went on to describe the food as eclectic-fusion, offering some of the most innovative and visually dazzling presentations in Chicago. I copied all of the info down and wrote a cover letter to the owner, Henry Adaniya. But before I sent it off I figured I should ask some people about the restaurant.

I contacted Dan Swartz, who owned a company that specialized in smoked salmon and was based just outside Chicago. I had met him on one of my winter breaks from the Laundry while working with chef Stallard at a dinner at Midland Country Club. I figured if Trio was "nationally acclaimed" then a purveyor from Chicago ought to know about the restaurant and its owner.

Dan heaped praise on Henry's character but noted that the restaurant was experiencing some recent growing pains. He told me that its current chef, Shawn McClain, was moving on to open his own place in Chicago called Spring and that information had leaked out, causing Trio to slow down. Still, on the whole it was a positive review. I thanked Dan and hung up with enthusiasm.

It sounded perfect. Henry wasn't a chef, and from what Dan said, Trio had a history of embracing each chef's vision for the restaurant. Certainly, the transition from Rick and Gale to Shawn produced radically different cuisines. And the restaurant did indeed garner four stars from both the *Chicago Tribune* and *Chicago* magazine.

I e-mailed my cover letter and résumé to Henry. Ten days passed with no response.

I wasn't devastated, but I was certainly annoyed—and surprised. I had by this time developed quite an ego. I was a sous chef at The French Laundry, dammit! "This guy doesn't know what he's missing," I kept telling myself. But really I was worried that perhaps my résumé was not as solid gold as I had thought.

A few more days went by when I received an e-mail from Dan telling me that he saw Henry and took the liberty of recommending that he consider me. It worked. The next day I got an e-mail from Henry introducing himself and opening a line of communication. Clearly, he was far from sold on me, as he suggested that we take the first steps via e-mail.

Our exchanges started simply with quirky questions from Henry: "What is your favorite junk food?" I didn't really have a sense of humor about that. My response was, "None. I'm a workout fanatic and eat very healthy." He followed that with, "You're only twenty-five years old and have never run a kitchen by yourself. What makes you think you can possibly be ready?" And: "What is your vision for the restaurant you want to create?" I followed with lengthy replies and our dialogue continued for a month. I liked Henry's frank and playful questions, and he must have appreciated my earnestness. At the end of the month he admitted that he had virtually no other serious candidates and he agreed to fly me to Chicago for an interview and tryout.

Because the dining experience I described in my e-mails sounded much different than what Trio was known for, Henry said it was imperative that I try to create for him a three- or four-course menu that was indicative of the style I wanted to serve. I would be cooking for a committee of one: Henry Adaniya.

It was unlikely that another opportunity like this existed anywhere in America. I knew I had to nail it.

I spent the next two weeks coming up with a seven-course menu. I was very calculated in my process. The menu would be composed of dishes that were based on flawless execution—things I could do perfectly. I would do a saddle of lamb roasted on the bone that I could present tableside and then carve. That would show that I knew the classic technique cold. But then I also wanted to show him flashes of new concepts that he had never seen before. The menu would start with the known and end with the future.

I e-mailed all of the ingredients I wanted Trio to have on hand before I arrived, followed by a precise equipment list to confirm what would be available to me in the kitchen. I wrote prep lists to prepare prep lists for the prep lists and arranged them in chronological order from the moment I stepped into the kitchen. I was thinking of every contingency I could possibly conceive of happening. Because I knew one thing for sure: when Henry saw me, he was going to think that

I was sixteen years old. I looked really young and was constantly reminded of that in the Laundry kitchen.

I told myself that even if I walked into Trio and knew that it wasn't the right place for me I would still try to blow him away. I wanted that job offer even if I didn't want the job. That way, the choice would be mine.

I was ready.

"And by the way, Grant. I think I'm pregnant."

My hand fell off the doorknob as I froze. My mind flashed back to a moment when a girlfriend's mom once asked me when she would get grandchildren. I looked her square in the eye and said, "Never."

Still facing the door I said to Angela, "That's unlikely."

A quick drive to Target in Napa, an hour, and a little red line would confirm it.

There is no doubt in my mind now that if I had walked out that door that day without hearing "I'm pregnant," I would have only walked back in to gather my belongings. The relationship we had was over. I was ready to move on, to take on my future and my career.

She knew I was leaving.

Now, I knew, I was staying. I said nothing about breaking up. How could I?

The week before my tryout at Trio I woke up one morning feeling like a truck hit me. A deep throbbing ache coursed through my body and I was shaking uncontrollably while sweating profusely.

I had felt increasingly ill over the past few days, but of course I had gone to work as usual. This, however, was a new level of sick. Something was really wrong.

I forced myself to the bathroom and got the shower as hot as it would go in an effort to stop the chills. I stood there shaking like I had hypothermia. I got dressed and walked into the living room, ready to go to work, when Angela felt my forehead. Despite my chattering teeth and uncontrollable chills, I was burning up.

Angela put the thermometer under my tongue. When it beeped I pulled it out and squinted to read the number. Angela peeked over my shoulder. "Grant, holy shit, 104.3! You have to go to the hospital. This is ridiculous. I'm taking you right now."

Calling in sick to work was not an option in my book. I had never once done that in my life. Never. Then again, I was incapable of arguing with her. My body felt completely out of my control. We drove to the emergency room at Queen of the Valley Hospital.

When I walked up to the registration desk the nurse looked at me oddly. "What's the problem?"

"Well, I c-c-can't stop shaking. I'm freezing, but I'm sweating. I have a fever."

"What's your fever, sweetie?"

"It was 104.3 a few minutes ago, but I feel worse now."

She looked worried. Never a good sign in a hospital, I thought.

I was led to a small room, and a minute later a nurse came in to do a series of diagnostic tests. She started by taking my temperature.

"It's 104.7. Hmmm. You have a nice one going there, huh!"

"It's climbing," I mumbled. "It was 104.3 a while ago."

She flashed a look of concern but continued taking my vital stats. The doctor entered shortly, looked at the chart, and led me immediately to a different room. He poked and prodded me, then ran me through a series of odd exercises, like lying on my back and instructing me to lift my head and legs at the same time. "I'm not really into yoga, doctor." He chuckled.

"We won't be doing yoga today. We are going to draw some blood and run some tests. It will take time for the lab to process the results, so you just rest here for a while and we'll keep an eye on your fever."

"How long will that take?" I asked. "I have to be at work in three hours."

"You won't be going in to work today, that much I can assure you."

The nurse returned with some medicine to reduce the fever. "Does that phone work?"

"Sure. Do you need to call some relatives?"

"No. I need to call work and let them know I'll be late."

The nurse looked at me like I was nuts and said, "Just dial seven first. I'll get the blood while you call."

I held off calling, giving her my arm instead. I knew I had to tell chef Keller I would be late, but decided to hold out in case my fever went down or my blood tests came back quickly.

They led Angela in and we sat in silence, waiting. The nurses came back every thirty minutes to check my fever. It wasn't going anywhere. Two hours in, the doctor came back. "Well, we don't know what you have yet, but you certainly have something. Your white blood cell count is through the roof, and that means your body is fighting some type of infection. Because you have such a high fever and chills, we want to test you for meningitis."

I had no idea what meningitis was, but it sounded serious. The tone the doctor was taking was equally serious. I was still more worried about work, however. "How long will that take, doctor?"

"You ever heard of a spinal tap?" he asked.

Holy shit, did he just say spinal tap? The doctor explained that they would have to put me on an IV drip and stick a long needle into my back to collect some spinal fluid. "It won't hurt, but most people find it a tad scary."

"Then what?"

"We take the fluid to the lab and have it analyzed."

"So I can leave after the tap and have you call me with the results?"

Clearly the doctor thought I was stupid. No one leaves the hospital with possible meningitis. "Ha. No. You'll spend the night here."

I looked at Angela, and she could read my mind. "I can call him if you want," she said.

I used Angela's cell phone to call the French Laundry kitchen only twenty minutes before people would begin to wonder where I was. Eric answered, "Hey, where are you?"

"Queen of the Valley. They are running some tests on me. I have a high fever. Is Chef around?"

Thomas came to the phone, "Grant? Everything okay? Where are you?"

"Yeah, I'm at Queen of the Valley. They are running tests."

"You didn't look good last night. What are they saying?"

"They are worried about meningitis and are giving me a spinal tap. But I might be in later tonight if they let me go."

"Grant! You're in the ER. You can't come in here if you might have meningitis! We'll manage. Have Angela call us when they figure out what's wrong. Feel better."

Moments later a couple of doctors and a nurse came into the room with what looked like veterinary needles. They were huge. And just like the doctor said, I got scared.

They instructed me to lie on my side, facing away from them, and to pull my knees to my chest in the fetal position. The doctor explained that the first poke would be the painful one. It was the local anesthetic to numb the area. It wasn't bad. I glanced over at the needle he picked up next to extract the cerebrospinal fluid.

"Relax," he said. Which was pretty funny given the size of the needle.

"Do not move. Don't even flinch while I'm doing this. And try not to tense up or hold your breath."

Yeah. Right.

The doctor worked quickly, and I tried to remain calm. "That wasn't so bad," he said. "The fluid looks clear, which is a good sign. But it will take a few hours to get the results. Take a rest."

I reluctantly spent the night in the hospital, and even though my test came back negative the next morning the doctor strongly recommended that I stay away from work for an entire week in case the virus I was carrying was contagious.

I was totally depleted and really couldn't argue. I let chef Keller know that I was fine, but that I couldn't come in. I hadn't eaten in days and had lost nearly ten pounds. My energy level was zero. But my most pressing concern was that four days from now I was supposed to travel to Chicago for my tryout with Henry at Trio.

Henry had already paid for my plane ticket, and the thought of canceling or postponing made me feel even worse. I was also freaking out at the thought of missing a week at The French Laundry, then following that up with three days off so I could find a new job. I called Henry the next morning and told him I wasn't sure I would be able to make the tryout. He immediately thought that I had changed my mind or that chef Keller had persuaded me to stay at the Laundry. I explained my stay at the hospital and my illness, but it sounded phony. After all, I wasn't diagnosed with anything in particular. Henry kindly told me to rest up and feel better. I promised to call him within two days to let him know for sure.

I tried to go back to the Laundry early, but Thomas wouldn't have it.

When I finally returned, I pulled chef Keller aside and explained my precarious position. Chef knew about the tryout and had agreed to provide me with all of the ingredients I needed to prep ahead. In fact, he wouldn't even let me pay for them. The Elysian Fields Farm saddle of lamb, black truffles, truffle stock, lobster, and foie gras would all need to be partially prepared and brought along. Of course, all of these arrangements had been made before I got sick and missed work.

"Bad timing, Grant, but you should still go. It isn't your fault you got sick. Don't worry about missing the extra days here. But the real question is whether or not you feel well enough to pull it off."

Having chef Keller's blessing was all I needed. I felt guilty but relieved and called Henry to tell him that I was well enough to make it to Chicago.

I headed into the Laundry kitchen to prepare the *mise en place*, not for dinner that night, but for my future.

I landed at O'Hare and headed to the baggage claim to retrieve the box of food that I'd brought along. I headed outside to meet Henry, who had come to pick me up. We exchanged pleasantries and drove toward Evanston.

"I couldn't help but think that you were some punk kid who got cold feet. But man, you genuinely look sick. You're white as a ghost."

I assured Henry that I felt fine and we began to chat about other Chicago restaurants. The month of e-mails gave us a certain comfort with each other. He mentioned that he wanted to set up a dinner somewhere on the last night I was in town and asked where I wanted to go.

"Blackbird," I said. "I met Paul Kahan when I was in Spain and he seems like a great guy. I hear good things about his food."

"Blackbird it is," he said. "But tonight I want you to eat at Trio with me."

We exited the expressway and started east down Dempster Avenue toward Evanston. The road pierced a series of strip malls and some low-rise office building sprawl, with the not so occasional fast-food chain in the mix. Compared to the vineyard-covered mountains flanking Napa Valley, the view was depressing. I was worried that Trio would be in the third strip mall to the left.

Finally, though, the suburban grunge gave way to grass, trees, and beautiful homes. This was encouraging. We turned on Hinman Avenue and I recognized the name from the Trio website. It was a beautiful tree-lined street within the community of Northwestern University. Even in March, the Midwest had some beauty and charm.

We walked up to the inn that housed Trio, which looked like it could easily fit in rural New Hampshire. A sign hung in front of a white pillar: THE HOMESTEAD. "Nice," I thought.

As soon as we walked in, however, things felt a little dated. In the lobby area was an old green event sign—the kind where you pop in the plastic characters to announce private dining events in the restaurant. The gray carpet on the floor was dirty and worn. Henry had made arrangements for me to stay there for the three nights, so I checked in and went up to my room to catch my breath and get cleaned up. We agreed to meet in an hour.

The room was less like a hotel room and more like a studio apartment, complete with small kitchen. It was clean, but I couldn't help thinking that it was incongruous with a four-star restaurant.

An hour later I met Henry in the lobby and he led me through the front door of Trio. I got a glimpse of the small dining room as we walked toward a screen door that led to the kitchen. My eyes were drawn downward immediately. The kitchen floor was painted purple. I looked around and thought, "Thomas was right." Despite feeling normal to me, The French Laundry was far from a typical place.

Henry gave me the tour of the restaurant and we settled into the smaller of the two dining rooms for my first formal interview.

Henry asked me directly what my vision for the restaurant would be. I knew he was losing momentum at this point. Shawn had already left to build Spring, and the popularity of Trio in the Chicago media had waned. Customers were starting to figure out that Trio was not really Trio anymore.

"Someday, I want to run the best restaurant in the country. Every step along the way I will pursue that goal like it could happen the next day." Henry looked a little slack-jawed at me. He could tell I was serious, but he looked like my high school buddies that day around the campfire.

I went on to talk about the style of food with one word, "different." I spoke about crafting tasting menus of various lengths to evoke emotions and engage all the senses.

He began to go into detail: how many cooks, the expediting system, the role wine would play in the menus, the role I would play in service. The questions went on and on, but the answers came easily for me. I spent virtually every waking moment dreaming of running my own kitchen, and whenever I didn't know an answer I defaulted to what I thought the best restaurant in the country would do.

We spoke for hours, and then I headed up to my room to comb over my prep lists for the next day. I adjusted them based on what I saw in the kitchen—the equipment, the layout, and the fact that Henry said he would be sitting at Trio's kitchen table watching me prepare the courses and that I would serve it and describe it to him personally. Somehow I didn't account for that. When I mentioned to him that I was planning to give him seven courses, he made a face. "You don't have to give me that many. I don't want it to take too long."

I went through my notes and realized that the timing had to be tight. I rewrote my list to the minute.

Later that evening I joined Henry and his girlfriend, Mary, for dinner at Trio. This gave Henry a chance to continue interviewing me in a more informal setting as we ate the heavily Asian-influenced tasting menu.

The meal gave me an opportunity to size Trio up as well. The champagne was served in tall hollow-stem flutes, one of the plates early in the meal was chipped, and the bread was served on neon blue and orange glass plates. Our waiter, Peter, a bald man with a thick Bulgarian accent, was wearing a tuxedo and black bow tie, lending the service a formal if somewhat out-of-place feeling.

I watched the room closely, studying the front-of-house team and trying to understand the system that Henry used to facilitate service. It, too, was different than what I was used to. The food came out on rolling gueridons instead of being carried, the tablecloths were wrinkled, and a few of the staff didn't speak English very well. I knew immediately that I would have to make drastic changes to service if I landed the job.

After the meal I headed back to my room and went over my list again, assigning plates to each course based on what I saw during dinner. I went to bed early that night.

I woke up early and decided to take a walk before getting started. I grabbed a coffee in downtown Evanston, listened to some music, and cleared my head. I was ready.

I walked in the kitchen door at 10:00 A.M. and was greeted by Henry. "Hello, Mr. Grant. You ready?" He was as curious as I was anxious.

"I am," I said. We set a 2:00 P.M. start time for his tasting.

I had done some advance prep at the Laundry prior to heading to Chicago—time-consuming tasks like curing foie gras, breaking down lobsters, and cleaning and tying the lamb. But I still had plenty of work to do.

I fired up the stove, set my cutting board in place, and composed a couple of *bains-marie* with essential tools. I soaked towels in a vinegar solution for wiping the plates, and ran the serviceware through the dish machine to make sure it was spotless. I treated the setup like a busy service on the fish station at the Laundry. I knew that if I wanted to knock this out I had to be incredibly organized and it also had to feel familiar.

About an hour in Henry walked through the kitchen, acting like he needed something for the dining room, but he was really just evaluating how I was working. "How's your timing?" he asked.

"I can start early if you like. Shall we make it one?"

"Sounds good."

At 12:55 Henry seated himself at the Trio kitchen table armed with a camera, a legal pad, and a glass of water. "Whenever you're ready."

I promptly brought the first course of asparagus soup to Henry, described the dish, and bolted back to the line to tend to the black bass that was sautéing on the flattop. I flipped the fish and got the lamb saddle in a hot pan, then delivered the next course. Everything was flowing and the food was coming out great. Henry studiously took notes with each course and lobbed questions at me about techniques, portion size, or plating. He was a good poker player, showing no emotion as he slowly dissected the food. He deconstructed each component, tasted it individually, then combined them as intended.

Course five was the butter-poached lobster, followed by the roasted lamb with favas and truffles. I pulled the lamb out of the oven just as he was taking his first bite of lobster and squeezed the ends. It was there . . . done.

I placed it in a polished copper pot with the browned butter that I had basted it in and the bouquet of herbs. As Henry finished up his lobster I walked the saddle up to the table and presented the meat. "Roasted Saddle of Elysian Fields Farm Lamb with fava beans, black truffle, and spring garlic."

It looked beautiful and smelled even better. For the first time Henry cracked and a smile swept over his face. "You roasted that on the bone?" he asked.

"Yes, of course. Better flavor that way."

"Yeah, but how do you know when it's done?"

"You just know . . ."

I walked back to the line to slice the lamb. I pulled a large bowl from the oven where it was warming briefly and added the garnishes and the sauce. Out of the corner of my eye I could see Henry craning his neck to see my cutting board as I began to take the loin off the bone. I stroked the knife down and curved it out while hoping the meat was perfectly cooked.

The medium-rare loin slowly rocked on the cutting board as I sliced it thinly, seasoned it with salt and pepper, fanned it out on the garnishes in the bowl, and sprinkled it with thyme leaves.

When I placed the bowl in front of Henry he looked at it and said simply, "Wow." It was perfect.

He relished that dish, and when he was nearly finished he said, "I'm getting full. I normally don't finish all of the tryout's dishes. And we have Blackbird tonight! Oh, man."

"I have one more small bite and we're done."

Trio had a pastry chef, so I was not required to show Henry any desserts, but I had prepared a single bite of dessert anyway. In reality, the bite was more an *amuse-bouche* than dessert, but because it featured chocolate I placed it at the end as a logical conclusion to the tasting. It was meant to be a showstopper, something completely different than the traditional roast lamb. If I could pull it off, it would definitely be something he had never seen before.

This last bite was a risk. I wanted to show Henry where I wanted to take the food, how I saw my style evolving at Trio.

During our dinner the night before, the *mignardise* were served on a long granite slab not much wider than a ruler. While the captain was placing it down, Henry playfully grabbed a chocolate truffle before it came to rest on the table. When I saw this it struck me that I liked the idea of offering a bite-size composition to the guest directly. It produced an interesting, fun interaction and was more dynamic than placing it on the table.

I found one of the granite slabs and wrapped a white napkin around it. This would be my makeshift service piece for the final bite.

While at elBulli I watched the team make very thin sheets from invert sugars. I thought that you could perhaps flavor the sugar by incorporating a flavored powder into the base. I aimed to create a foie gras lozenge wrapped in a crispy chocolate. The bottle cap–size bite was designed to crack open when Henry bit down on it, revealing the creamy foie gras inside.

As Henry finished the lamb and stood up to walk his plate over to the dish machine I piped the cured foie onto a half dollar–size, chocolate-flavored sugar film and set another directly on top of it. I waved the tray briefly under the salamander and watched the top film conform around the foie gras like shrink-wrap. I flipped the candy and repeated it. The chocolate became perfectly enveloped. I placed the delicate bite on the linen-wrapped stick and walked up to Henry, who was now back in the booth thinking things were over. I extended the granite in his direction and held it out. He looked puzzled, unsure if I was trying to set it down or if he should grab it.

"Be careful," I said, giving him a hint on how to proceed, "it is very fragile. Bittersweet chocolate–wrapped foie gras. Eat it in one bite, because the inside might be a tad liquidy."

He picked up the lozenge and examined it closely, trying to figure out how it was made.

"This is where I see my food moving in the future," I said as he popped it into his mouth.

His reaction was immediate.

"Holy shit, man!" he exclaimed. "Wow, is that good. Holy shit, that is cool. How did you do that? That is from Mars, man. Incredible."

I nailed it.

That night Henry took me to Blackbird as planned. It was great to finally see Chicago proper and eat the food that Paul had talked about when I ran into him in Spain. Plus, the pressure of the tryout was off and Henry and I were getting to know and trust each other. He raved about the tasting, but told me he had a few more interviews lined up.

The next morning I boarded a plane back to San Francisco, confident that I would be offered the job.

When I returned to the Laundry I asked chef Keller for a moment of his time. I wanted to reflect on the experience and to get his thoughts. He quietly listened as I explained what I served and how well the tryout had gone. But I also mentioned the worn-out kitchen with purple floors, the dated decor, the tuxedos, and the chipped plates.

"I told you, Grant, there just aren't too many places out there like this one. And that's okay. Maybe it's better for you to start out in an environment like that—that's exactly what we did here. By working hard you appreciate it more when you finally get there, when you make it all happen. How was the owner? You trust him?"

"I do," I said. "He's a really nice guy. But I'm not sure he wants the same thing I do, Chef."

"What do you want?" Thomas asked.

"I want this," I said, laughing, gesturing to the whole of The French Laundry.

"Then why leave?" We laughed some more. "You think he'll offer you the job?"

"Chef, it was perfect. The food was perfect. And the place was cleaner when I left than it was when I arrived. The question is whether or not he offers the job to a guy who has never really run his own kitchen. He asked me that, actually. I told him that I had more responsibility being a sous chef here than most chefs have anywhere, but I doubt he believed me. Who would believe all of this?"

A week went by and I heard nothing from Henry. I became anxious. I continued to search for job openings online, and like before, there was nothing. Then I got an e-mail from Henry. He complimented my drive and passion and said the food was fantastic, but that it was simply too risky to transform the restaurant as I envisioned. Changing the food, service, and decor all at once was difficult conceptually and daunting financially. "I wish you all the best."

My ambition had cost me the job.

I told myself that I didn't want the position unless I could do it my way, so it wasn't really a lost opportunity. But I hadn't been offered the job, and I couldn't be certain why that was, despite what Henry said.

I told chef Keller about Henry's e-mail. "It doesn't look like I'm going anywhere, Chef."

"Well, you have to respect his honesty and the fact that he realized he didn't want to take that risk with his business."

"I guess."

I spent the next two weeks looking for another opportunity, but came quickly to the conclusion that I would be staying in Napa for a long time. Time was running out. If I was going to move I had to do it soon so Angela could have some stability during the late stages of her pregnancy. It had to happen quickly, or it would likely not happen at all. As much as I loved the Laundry, I was feeling that everything was conspiring to keep me there against my will.

Then it came.

Four and a half weeks after my interview with Henry he e-mailed to see if I was still available. I didn't even finish reading the e-mail before I picked up the phone and called him. "Hi, Henry. It's Grant. I got your e-mail."

"Here's the deal. I have gone through all of the applicants that I had scheduled and your food blew them all away. It wasn't close. The food has been haunting me. I can't get it out of my head. You are a talent and you're driven by a vision. So much so that I'm willing to entertain the changes you want for Trio. That is, if you're still looking for a job."

I was elated.

Henry and I exchanged dozens of e-mails working out the details. He decided to go all in, do or die. He would market this not as a gradual transition but as a reinvention of Trio. He commissioned his brother-in-law, Pavel Kraus, to design and install Mylar screens in the dining spaces to update the decor. We changed the logo, purchased new china and wineglasses, updated the website, ordered new uniforms for the service staff, and hammered out a labor budget so that I could hire a new team in the kitchen. Operationally, everything would change in a manner that would enable the best presentation of the cuisine.

Trio would become a new restaurant.

Chef Keller asked for a minimum of two months to work out the changes necessary in the French Laundry kitchen. Henry wanted me there sooner, but I told him that I would give chef Keller whatever he asked for. I would leave The French Laundry in June 2001 and start at Trio on July 1. Everything was set. I was about to run my own kitchen.

Chef Keller looked at me with a smile as he headed back toward the kitchen. "Chicago, huh? Trotter's going to crush you."

PART 2

A NEW TRAIN OF THOUGHT

CHAPTER 12

As my time at the Laundry wound down, I needed to make a plan for the kitchen at Trio.

Shawn McClain had already departed from his position to open Spring, and Henry had put in place a temporary kitchen team to fill the void until he hired the next chef. As soon as I committed to the job we began to talk about how I'd want to hire my own crew. Trio was never a terribly busy restaurant, and with the loss of customers after Shawn's departure and the expenses from the upcoming renovation weighing on him, Henry suggested I use a very conservative estimate for the number of cooks needed to operate the kitchen. He was equally adamant about offering a very low starting salary to all of the chefs, so much so that I was embarrassed to mention it to potential hires. I knew that I was going to drive the chefs hard, working them fourteen hours a day. To accept a job making barely over $20,000 with an unknown chef running his first kitchen at the age of twenty-six would require a huge leap of faith on their part. We settled on a crew of five cooks and I began building my team.

The French Laundry had a giant brigade of twenty-plus cooks. Having such a small team would be a significant departure, and I knew I needed someone who spoke the same language, knew the standards, and knew how to execute. I needed to bring someone with me from the Laundry.

While Henry placed ads in local papers and sorted through applicants for me, I approached chef Keller and asked him if I could bring David Carrier with me to Trio.

David was a commis at the Laundry, and I had gained a lot of respect for his drive and determination. He was a huge guy, the size of a middle linebacker, with a Queens accent and a fast pace. He didn't so much prep his *mise en place* as he plowed through it, sweat beading up on his forehead. Despite his effort and competence he never graduated past that prep-cook ceiling, and I wasn't sure why. I knew he would agree that it was time for him to move on in order to grow as a cook.

After Thomas said that it was okay for me to ask David along I decided to approach him by writing a letter. It read:

David,

Let me start by giving you an overview of what the restaurant is and where I plan to take it.

As you probably saw in the packet, I included the Zagat ratings, some reviews, and other items to give you some background about the place. It started out a huge success in '94 with Rick and Gale Tramanto. They left in '96 to open Tru, which has been a great success. When they left, their sous chef at the time took over and has been behind the stoves ever since. He is a young guy, thirty now, who will open his own place in the city in May. Seemingly good (I had a good meal there) but not the person to make the place recognizable on a national level. He maintained the four-star status, received some James Beard awards, but never made it big.

Enter me. I have been looking for about six months for a spot that would let me produce my own food. I was searching for the unique situation that an owner would hire me as a chef and let me have total "carte blanche." I found it in Trio. Henry, the owner, is a good guy who is a little goofy at times, but I can tell he is good people. He has agreed to "let me go," so to speak, to develop my own cuisine. It works out for me for a couple of reasons: 1. It is an existing four-star restaurant, so the media attention will be there. 2. That creates an opportunity for me to achieve the goals I have set for myself. 3. But more than any-thing it is a logical step for me, and this of course will be my first go at "chef." This allows me to take the reins of a restaurant that has the potential to become great under my direction, thus increasing my market value and putting me in a position for the next step. Ownership.

The food will be modern. Let me explain. My food will be true to itself. Integrity of the food and the way it is presented is my #1 priority. The style will be that of (are you ready for this?) FL + Atlas + elBulli. I want my technique rooted in French. We will clean foie and cook meat and fish the way I learned from Thomas. But I also want to be part of the revolution that is sweeping Europe. The new techniques and bold combinations of flavors. I want to help bring those to the States and develop my own along the way.

The menu format will be similar to that of the FL— a four-course prix fixe, an eight-course tasting, and a veg menu. The four-course will be a bit more conservative in comparison to the tasting, which will be the most avant-garde. But even the four-course will be modern and daring compared to the FL. I stress this, though—the technique will be exacting to the FL. . . . Flawless. I didn't spend four years here for nothing.

The kitchen will be broken down into five stations: Meat, Fish, GM, Canapé, Pastry. The savory side will have four chefs de partie *and 1–2 externs. That's it. Everyone is re-sponsible for his or her M.E.P. as well as working the station at night. I visualize it will be like the old FL, not the brigade of twenty-eight we have now. I will work the meat station first. I will not have a sous chef starting out. To me a sous is someone who understands the food and the way the chef thinks enough to replace the chef in his absence. Until I feel someone has that knowledge I will not name a sous. Training will be intensive in the beginning; I will need to teach everyone how I want things done.*

The restaurant will be slow during the beginning of my take-over. Average covers run 25–40 Tues, Wed., 40–65 Thursday, 80–90 Fri and Sat. This will give me a much-needed opportunity to train and perfect the food. August will be a big month—that is when we will push the media. The Trib *and* Chicago *mag will likely do dining reviews in August.*

The kitchen is not like the FL—not many are. It is solid, the equipment is sound and clean and the line is functional. It isn't the prettiest kitchen in the world but by far not the worst. It does have a kitchen table, so that tells you it can't be too bad.

You are leaving the best restaurant in the country. Be sure of your next move, Dave. I want you to join the team, but I am no Thomas Keller or Charlie Trotter. I am just a kid who thinks he has a shot. I am going in there confident with my ideas and I will execute the food to the best of my ability, using what I learned from Thomas as a base.

That's my story. Think it over.

When I next saw Dave the answer was swift: "You bet."

I had very little money saved up and he had even less, so we had no choice but to jointly rent a large U-Haul truck. Packing into the cab of a moving truck were Angela, nearly six months pregnant; her 140-pound Rottweiler; Dave; and me. Two thousand six hundred miles, a few arguments, a flat tire, and dozens of bathroom breaks and sleepless nights later, we arrived in Evanston, Illinois—twenty-eight hours before our scheduled first day at Trio.

David and I stood in the middle of the space, surveying the kitchen. It was his first time seeing it.

"Man, you were right," he said. "This definitely ain't The French Laundry!" He slapped me on the back hard and it was tough to tell if it was dismay or optimism that he was trying to convey.

Before we left Napa I warned him over and over that Trio was not what we were accustomed to. It was pretty much the same talk that Thomas gave me a few months before. The kitchen was rough, to say the least. Stacks of carbon- and grease-crusted pots were piled in the corner, and thick rubber mats lined the floor. The floor itself was painted purple and was slippery as hell. It pitched four inches into what we eventually called "ditches" on the hot line. All of the equipment was modular, raised on casters with broken brakes that not only moved around any time someone bumped into them but also created gaps where debris would collect, making it difficult to keep things clean.

As we walked down the line, David leaned in to inspect the condition of the stove and smacked his head on the exhaust hood. The ceilings were low and the hood extended down enough to make it an obstacle to any cook over six feet tall. On a far wall were framed magazine covers and old *Art Culinare* pages—reminders of the Rick Tramanto and Shawn McClain eras.

"Um, can we take those down?" he said to me with a grin.

We began the work of reconfiguring the kitchen ourselves. The shelving that towered above the hot line for holding the finished plates was disassembled, the low-boy refrigerators were rearranged, and a space in the center of the line was left vacant. We found a four-foot-square piece of granite in the basement and placed it on top of some metro shelving that we bought at Home Depot. That became our pass. The heat lamps were pulled out—we wouldn't need those for sure—and the steam table was converted into a workstation with the addition of another piece of found granite secured in place with duct tape. The line felt more spacious and clean and was an efficient use of an otherwise small kitchen.

Once the rest of our small crew came in, we gave the kitchen a scrubbing that it clearly hadn't had in years. Then Dave smiled and grabbed recently hired Nathan Klingbail, and a few moments later the two returned carrying rolls of black carpet mats, the same kind that lined the floor at The French Laundry. They rolled out the carpets and all of a sudden the purple floor disappeared.

It was not a high-end, well-designed four-star kitchen, but at the end of four days of cleaning and moving things around, the space worked. More important, the team felt united in the pride of what we had accomplished together—and we hadn't even fired up the stoves yet.

In the dining rooms, Henry was making the same effort to give Trio a new face. The walls were repainted, the table settings revamped, and new art was hung by his brother-in-law. Within three days it was transformed. The physical changes weren't dramatic, but to everyone working there the feeling was that we had just created a new restaurant.

As I got to know the team from our time cleaning I started to wrap my head around their placement in the kitchen. I knew I was going to put Carrier on the fish station, both because he was familiar with the *mise en place* from working as the fish commis at the Laundry and because its central location on the line would give him a good vantage point to help me supervise. Still, I needed to find a great meat cook to anchor the line, because I knew my own time would be stretched over multiple stations.

The group was downstairs attacking the basement and walk-in with bleach and deck brushes when I headed down and asked everyone to come up to the pastry kitchen to clear our heads of the noxious gases. "Who thinks they can cook the meat?"

John Peters took a small step forward while the others glanced at the ground. "I can do it," he said, his eyes making clear contact with mine.

John was my other linebacker, or perhaps more accurately, my lineman. He was a soft-spoken native Texan with a stature that rivaled Dave's. Speaking quietly but confidently, he told the group about his time working in steakhouses in Texas before moving on to culinary school at the CIA, and eventually landing in Chicago to work at Jean-Georges Vongerichten's Thai-influenced restaurant, Vong. Since I had nothing else to go on at this point, I thought to myself that putting a giant guy from Texas on meat made sense.

I placed the others in their respective stations based largely on the same process. It was more about their personalities than their cooking experience. With the help of a local culinary school extern named Jesse, Nathan would hold down the cold garde manger and Chris Sy would man hot garde manger.

I needed to articulate my goals to this small group of strangers. I wanted to turn a tiny restaurant on a sleepy street forty minutes outside of Chicago into a world-class establishment.

I needed them to start believing.

I tried the same method I used on myself to build up my confidence after I accepted the job at Trio. At the end of our first day of fourteen hours spent scrubbing and rearranging the kitchen, we retired to the dining room for a meeting. I grabbed an easel, a few Sharpies, and a giant pad of paper and had the group sit in a small circle. Then I started asking the same questions I had asked and answered in my own head a thousand times.

"What are the five best restaurant cities in America?"

The group shouted out the first two in unison, with Carrier's voice booming above the others. "New York. San Francisco."

Then there was a pause.

"Come on, now. I need three more," I pushed as I wrote headers with the city names side by side to create columns. I then wrote the numbers one through five below each city.

"Los Angeles . . . and maybe Boston," Nathan said with an inflection that suggested uncertainty.

"Okay," I said, "does everyone agree?" The group stared blankly at me, afraid to give the wrong answer on their first day.

John Peters spoke up, "Well, Chicago, right?"

I smiled a bit as I wrote down "Chicago" in the fifth spot and nodded my head. "Let's find out. Now I want you to list the very best restaurants in each of these cities. Let's start in New York since that will be the easiest."

The cooks started naming restaurants, and whenever I heard one that was generally agreed upon I wrote it down. The list looked like this:

New York

1. Daniel
2. Bouley? Ducasse? Lespinasse?
3. Le Cirque
4. Jean Georges
5. Le Bernadin

It didn't take long for me to realize that this exercise was going to do much more than I anticipated. My original hope was that by the end of the discussion I would be able to inspire the team and help them believe we could accomplish great things on par with these great restaurants. But the discussion also allowed me to understand the personalities and overall gastronomic knowledge of each cook. This was a young group overall, and with the exception of Chris Sy, who clearly spent much of his free time reading cookbooks and scanning food posts on the Internet, none of them had heard of many of these restaurants on the list. If they did know them by name, they had certainly never eaten at them.

San Francisco

1. French Laundry
2. Masa's
3. Fleur de Lys
4. Chez Panisse
5. ?

Boston

1. Clio
2. Radius
3. ?
4. ?
5. ?

L.A.

1. Spago
2. Melisse
3. Valentino
4. Ginza Sushiko
5. ?

We struggled to fill five slots in each city with what the group felt confident were "great" restaurants. Occasionally arguments would break out about what made a restaurant truly "great" or "world class." Of course, there were many restaurants in each city that were serving delicious food, but I made it clear that I wanted to list only the ones at the very highest level. My exact phrase was "fine dining, truly four stars"—exactly what we aspired to be.

After agreeing to leave a few cities with blank spots we came to Chicago. I shot Dave a glance and he smirked at me because he knew me well enough to know where I was heading.

"I am going to name some restaurants and let you guys vote them on or off the list. Certainly Trotter's is number one, right?" Everyone nodded their heads in agreement. "Tru? Arun's? What about Topolobampo and Blackbird?" We whittled a list of eight down to the four that everyone could agree upon. I left the fifth slot open on purpose, put down my Sharpie, and walked away from the board. I sat down in the circle with them.

"Take a look, guys. I think Chicago stacks up pretty well. David, why don't you take the board now."

Carrier unfolded himself out of the chair and stood up, "Yes, Chef."

"Okay, here's what we have to do now. Simply cross off the best restaurant in each city." Without waiting for input David slashed the Sharpie through The French Laundry immediately. "Wait, why did you start there, David?"

"It's the best on the board, Chef. The big dog!" Everyone started chuckling.

"Yes, it is," I replied, "but who's next best?" The room fell quiet and everyone looked at me. We crossed off Trotter and Lespinesse next. I prompted the group again, second best on the board? JG or Daniel? And so it went—we canceled out restaurants that were equivalents in each city until we had some cities with none left. New York was the clear winner with the most restaurants remaining, but we all knew that before we started. What the group was genuinely surprised by was where Chicago stood—a solid second.

I stood up and relieved David of his duties. "See guys, Chicago is a great restaurant city. New York is tough to beat, but we can take everyone else."

The Chicago list read:

1. Trotter
2. Tru
3. Everest
4. Le Français
5. ?

Nathan spoke up, "But Chef, you didn't put us on there."

"Exactly, Nate—but that's only because we're not open yet."

These chefs knew very little about me except that I was the sous chef to Thomas Keller and worked at The French Laundry for four years, despite looking like I was an eighteen-year-old dwarf standing between Carrier and Peters. They had never seen me cook, although a few of them had read a mention of me in Michael Ruhlman's book *The Soul of a Chef*. Their assumption was that I wanted to create food that was derivative of Thomas Keller's, even though I'd told them during the hiring process that Trio would be very different. But I didn't have notebooks filled with new techniques or recipes, nor did I have complete menus ready to implement. I had a vague notion that I wanted to explore new areas, and I had a very clear idea of how I wanted a meal to feel to the diner. That was the driving force, and everything else simply had to support that.

I was very much of the belief that if I built it, they would come.

I watched firsthand as The French Laundry exploded from a little-known restaurant tucked away in the sleepy town of Yountville to a globally known temple of gastronomy. I was optimistic that we could accomplish the same thing. I was very aware of all the things that we didn't have at Trio, but I was naive enough to tell myself that it didn't matter. The fact that Trio had been considered one of the best restaurants in the Chicago area for the previous seven years yet still struggled to draw people from the city simply wouldn't apply to us. The glassware, china, and silverware were dated, mismatched, and lacking in numbers. The best cooks would not want to work all the way out in Evanston. We had no budget. Servers would want to work where they could make more money on more covers.

I wanted to change all of that.

Three days after arriving in Evanston, two of which were spent cleaning, the team touched food for the first time. I had stayed up until 4:00 A.M. finalizing the opening menu and made packets for each cook containing recipes and *mise en place* lists. I ordered everything the previous night. For the first time in years I was nervous in a kitchen. I realized that I had to demonstrate every procedure to every cook except David. It wasn't just how to make a foie gras torchon, or how we were going to make avocado soup, it was every minor detail: how to check in the produce order, how we label every container, where to store all of the ingredients, how often to vacuum the floor, which equipment is hand-washed, and how we coil the cord around the blenders after they're used. The list was endless. The first time we did anything, even the most menial task, was critically important to setting a standard, and the bar had to be set high. "The only way to do it is the right way" was taken directly from the Laundry kitchen, and we made it our credo on the very first day.

Henry and I planned to hold a series of front-of-house training sessions and tastings in the days leading up to the reopening. The cuisine was a major departure from what they had been serving, and we knew that in order to be successful the staff had to be able to present it with confidence.

The menu format was different. The à la carte menu was abandoned, and two tasting menus took its place. The first was a five- to six-course menu with four or five choices in each category, and the other was a nine-course degustation. All of this made the service team quite nervous. Henry had warned them as well that the food we intended to serve would be radically different in appearance and in flavor combinations. Their job would be complicated by the fact that some courses would require special instructions to the guests to get the full, intended effect.

Just after 2:00 P.M. on day three, after the kitchen team spent six hours preparing the *mise en place* for the dishes, the front-of-house team arrived for their first training session. I had not met any of them formally, and had only seen them when I ate dinner during my try-out. Henry and the office manager, Peter Shire, printed the opening menus and recipe packets for the staff in preparation for the meetings. Henry came into the kitchen to let me know that the team was fully assembled. I lifted my head up as I heard his voice, tied my blue apron snugly around my waist, and nodded to Dave. "I'll be back in a bit. Keep it tight." I grabbed my clipboard and walked into the dining room.

It was a joy to listen to Henry speak. He had a thoughtful, poetic eloquence and a Zen-like demeanor that instantly put everyone at ease. As I walked into the room he turned his charm on full blast in an effort to "sell me" to the service team. After a gushing introduction, I thanked everyone for attending and began explaining what it was that we were about to embark upon.

The group I stood before was on average fifteen years older than me and had been in the restaurant business longer than it looked like I was alive. I tried to explain to them how and why we were going to create a dining experience that they had never seen before. The whole thing must have sounded absurd to them, coming as it did from a clean-cut guy who could be one of their kids. I spoke about my upbringing in the diner, culinary school, the brief stint at Trotter's, and my time with Thomas before I began to explain the philosophy behind the food.

"I want to create an experience that is based on emotions. I want people to be excited, happy, curious, surprised, intrigued, and even bewildered during the meal." That was my litmus test to see who was in and who was just there for the paycheck. A couple of the staff stared at me intently, a few drifted off, and one guy slyly nudged his friend with his elbow and raised an eyebrow as if to say, "Who is this clown?"

Henry and I took turns explaining how the restaurant would have to evolve and what our collective vision and goals were for this incarnation of Trio. I headed back to the kitchen while Henry went through service-related protocols and got the staff ready for the tasting we had coming up later in the evening.

The plan for the remaining portion of the afternoon was to serve half of the courses on the menu one by one. I would explain the ingredients and concepts behind each dish, we would settle on a wine pairing, the appropriate silverware, and practice descriptions for each. In the kitchen I plated the dishes for the first time and explained the critical elements of the presentations to the chefs while answering any questions they might have about technique or components. The team would then assemble the remaining dishes under my supervision.

We wanted the tasting to follow the progression of the menu as closely as possible, so we started with a small series of one-bite courses slated to be the *amuse-bouche* for each menu. First up was a course modeled after the one that won me the job. Called "Cumin Candied Corn," it was essentially a savory corn panna cotta wrapped in a cumin-flavored sugar film. The quarter-sized lozenge was salty and sweet, creamy and crunchy at the same time. David and I made ten of them and walked into the dining room. We didn't say much except to present it as we wished it to be presented to guests.

"Cumin Candied Corn. Please eat the lozenge in a single bite."

Nobody moved. Nobody lifted their spoons. Everyone simply stared first at the lozenge, then looked up at me blankly. Finally, Henry blurted out, "Eat it, folks!"

It was a delicious bite—that much I knew—but I could tell that this ambiguous-looking morsel did nothing to alleviate the staff's concerns about me. The tasting went on: strawberries laced with wasabi, shot glasses filled with bright orange carrot juice floating atop translucent green celery-flavored liquid, crab with clear raviolis made from lemon tea, and tomato salad with olive oil ice cream. A few in the group began to drink the proverbial Kool-Aid, but the majority showed signs of nothing so much as fear. By the time I got to the last course of the tasting, Rib Eye of Beef with Prunes and Wild Mushroom Perfumed with Tobacco, someone finally had the guts to voice the group's thoughts.

Barry Holton, the guy I quickly came to know as Earl/Driver 2—the name of the character he briefly portrayed in an episode of *Walker, Texas Ranger*—cleared his throat. "Um, with all due respect, this all tastes pretty good, but how are we going to sell mushrooms cooked with cigar ash to people? This stuff is pretty out there."

Henry quickly spoke up and tried to defuse the skepticism by reassuring the team that people would react positively to creative cuisine. As he launched into his belief in me and Trio's history of embracing food as art I quietly slipped back into the kitchen. I didn't like how this was all going down so far.

"Did the pasta dough get made?" I barked as I walked down the middle of the line. Dave could read my frustration and fired back with a respectful but aggressive tone.

"Yes, Chef!"

"Great, get a pot of water on. We're adding the Black Truffle Explosion to the tasting right now." As irritated as I was, I knew I had to get them back on my side.

And I knew that the BTE would do just that.

Henry did his best to get the local media fired up about my arrival, but the only thing that they had to go on was my connection to the Laundry. There wasn't much of a story at this point—just another young cook running his first kitchen. There were a few tiny write-ups in the local press, but that was about it.

Trio was not a large restaurant. The two dining rooms sat a total of sixty-two people. I thought it was reasonable to expect fifty diners per night, at least to start, and then once the word got out maybe we could fill the place and turn a few tables. Henry cautiously held such hopes as well, but he warned me not to get discouraged if the guests didn't knock down the door right away.

Joe Catterson, who had worked at Trio the first three years it was open, was brought back part-time to help run the wine program. He was far more realistic and told me that even during the heyday of Trio they could barely get fifty people in there on a weeknight.

Trio reopened for business on July 7, 2001, with fifty-one covers. It was a typical first night of service for a restaurant. We got totally crushed trying to figure out what we were doing on the fly. The wait times between courses were too long and when the food finally did leave the kitchen it often headed to the wrong tables. Well into the night I took a bite of the crab mixture that was the filling for the clear lemon raviolis garnishing the snapper dish and had to spit it out. It was full of shells. The intern, Jesse, simply decided not to pick them out, and Nathan and I were so busy that we failed to check it during the day.

Worst of all, perhaps, was the prep for the one dish I was certain everyone would love. Chris Sy's Black Truffle Explosions exploded all right, but not in the diners' mouths. Instead, as soon as they hit the simmering water that they were being cooked in, they popped and turned the water an inky black from the truffle juice.

After the kitchen was cleaned and our postmortem meeting was complete, I sat in the office with Henry to go over the night. It was, by my account, a disaster, but Henry was a veteran of restaurant openings and was unfazed. I mentioned that we might want to consider capping the reservations at forty covers or so for the first week until we worked out the kinks. Henry agreed and reached for the reservation book. As he flipped through the pages a look of despair crossed his face.

"I don't think that'll be necessary," he said grimly. We had twelve booked for the next night and only seven for the following Wednesday.

Weeks passed and the refinements continued. The kitchen began to learn the prep, the front-of-house staff learned the descriptions and service techniques. But the customers did not show up. Days with single-digit cover counts were common. I couldn't understand why Phil Vettel and Dennis Ray Wheaton, the two most prominent local food critics, hadn't shown up yet and penned their reviews. We desperately needed people to know that Trio had changed and that the food was new, exciting, and delicious.

And then when things seemed that they couldn't get worse for us, they did. And not just for us, but for the country and the world as a whole. Nearly two months to the date of our opening the terrorist attacks on the World Trade Center and Pentagon took place and the restaurant industry, like the rest of the country, folded up. Trio was limping along financially, and the understandable reaction to 9/11 made a bad situation far worse. The phones went from barely ringing to not ringing at all. Days went by without a single customer.

The staff went from generally nervous to almost panicked at the growing uncertainty, and the anxiety at home was intense as well. Angela was ready to pop. At any moment I was expecting a call letting me know that she had gone into labor. The situation evoked emotionally charged conversations. Here we were, living together in a nascent relationship, spending virtually no time with one another, and about to have a child. The country had just been attacked and the economy was in the tank. Angela was rightfully concerned that Trio would close and I would lose the job for which we had just spent everything we had to move across the country. Our relationship, such as it was, was more strained than ever.

But while the rest of the industry backpedaled to accommodate the financial and emotional downturn and the prevailing notion was a return to comfort food, Henry and I decided to do the opposite. We decided not to change Trio at all. We didn't change the cuisine, lower prices, create lunch specials, or change the hours of operation. We thought instead that people might actually enjoy being pulled into an experience allowing them to forget about the outside world, even just for a few hours. A Black Truffle Explosion would reinvigorate their lives more than wallowing in their sorrow with a plate of mashed potatoes.

Trio barely survived, but Henry's dedication to the staff and the vision for the restaurant became a source of inspiration. There were days the team would come in and prep the entire menu for a single table of three diners. I explained to the kitchen staff that we were in this for the long haul and that we were not going to panic. Instead, I reassured them, this was a time to work harder and to take advantage of the slow days by cleaning and painting the kitchen, and more important, by developing new dishes and concepts.

Things didn't recover all at once, but slowly the days with only a table or two booked gave way to a slow but steady business. The team worked six days a week from ten in the morning until midnight. I was the first one in and the last one to leave every day.

On Monday, September 24—the only day of the week that Trio was closed—and with impeccable kitchen timing, Kaden William Achatz was born.

I returned to work, on time, the next morning.

Trio's business returned to what Henry and Joe deemed "normal." To me it felt like we were barely keeping our heads above water. The lack of consistent covers made operations difficult. Weekdays we would bounce between twenty and thirty covers, and Saturday would always spike up to nearly eighty. With only six cooks and an ambitious menu, anything above a fifty-person night was pushing the redline. Saturdays were a battle we would sometimes lose, but we could not afford to turn people away. Trio was barely breaking even.

A few small reviews began to trickle out and were favorable: the *Chicago Reader,* the *Pioneer Press,* and a luxury, ad-laden magazine called *Chicago Social.* But still, there were no reviews from *Chicago* magazine or the *Chicago Tribune*. Finally, a call came in from Phil Vettel to do a fact check and an interview with Henry and me. I was relieved and nervous at the same time—the importance of this review was undeniable. Trio had managed to stay afloat during a chef transition, a reconception, the biggest attack on America since Pearl Harbor, and a recession, but anything less than a gushing four-star review from the venerable *Trib* would surely be the final nail in our coffin.

When the review was due to come out, Henry and I huddled around the office computer knowing it would get posted online some time after midnight. We did eleven covers that Thursday night during the first week in January. Henry took a deep breath and looked at me before striking the "Enter" key and accessing the website.

"Are you ready?" he asked.

A flood of emotions swept over me: excitement, fear, helplessness, responsibility, and a few I didn't even recognize. "Wait," I said, stopping him at the last second. "I want to thank . . ."

Henry interrupted me. He knew what I was going to say, and like a father he made it easier on my by letting me off the emotional hook. "Whatever this says, nothing can take away what we have accomplished here already," he said. "We have all worked hard to realize a vision. There aren't too many people who, one, have that creativity, and two, are willing to take a chance to make that happen."

I looked at him and nodded slowly, and we both turned to the screen to see our fate.

It didn't take long to figure it out. The headline said everything we needed to know:

"Dining at this four-star restaurant is akin to enjoying participatory theater."

Henry leaped out of the office chair, sending it flying across the room, and yelled, "Yeah, baby!" As I stood up he grabbed me in a bear hug and shook me back and forth. "We fucking did it, man—we did it! Congratulations."

The review was a grand slam. The fourth paragraph read:

"With the installation of its third-ever chef, Trio has definitely re-embraced its wild side. Grant Achatz (pronounced, and it's worth remembering, 'AK-etz') is the most dynamic, boundary-stretching chef to hit town in a long, long time. If you've been putting off luxury-dining lately, let me suggest that now is the time to jump back in the game."

And that is exactly what people did.

When I arrived at ten the same morning, I found Peter Shire intently listening to the voice mail while scribbling notes. He was giddy with excitement—the mailbox was completely full. The phone rang constantly in the background.

As the cooks arrived, each one would walk in the door with a copy of the paper in one hand and a coffee in the other. Ceremoniously they slammed the paper down on the wood counter close to the door of the kitchen, forming a pile, then shook my hand and offered some verbal encouragement that included some insanely profound and creative profanity.

The review was something. Once I saw it in the paper, I couldn't believe how much space they had devoted to it. The entire front page of the Friday section was a picture of the black truffle ravioli dish and huge block letters spelling out TRIO with four stars embedded in the "O." The review also dominated the front page of the dining section. If that weren't enough, William Rice wrote a feature on me in the Tempo section. It seems that the *Trib* was impressed.

The energy in the restaurant was palpable.

I gathered the cooks in the dining room once everyone had arrived and we took a second to bask in the reward for our hard work. Then I warned them of the consequences of the review. It was obvious that we were going to get a lot busier—we could all hear the phone ringing nonstop in the next room—and I reminded them that now we would be working harder to keep up. And yet just keeping up was not good enough, because there were real expectations. I thanked them all and then said, "Let's get to work."

I grabbed a roll of green tape that we used to label containers, ripped off an eight-inch-long strip, and wrote: "What Does Four Stars Mean To You?"

Hanging from the ceiling in the middle of the hotline was an antique pot rack that we used to display small copper pots. It was one of the few things that went unchanged during our kitchen makeover—we kind of liked it and left it there. I walked behind the line and placed the strip of tape on the vertical crossbar—so it was out of view of the rest of the kitchen but readily apparent to everyone standing on the line—as a reminder of who we were and what we were trying to achieve.

A few days later a large box arrived from Yountville, California. I opened the box to find a card from Thomas and a Methuselah of champagne.

I guess Trotter had not yet kicked my ass.

CHAPTER 13

Widely known as the tougher of the two major Chicago critics, Penny Pollack at *Chicago* magazine followed suit and awarded us four stars, which legitimized our status in the industry.

The positive press relieved the financial strain on the restaurant and allowed more creative freedom. Both reviews praised the innovative cuisine, calling it revolutionary, and this helped us to set people's expectations for the boundary-pushing food and meant that we could take more risks. We created dishes that showcased manipulations of ingredients like Atlantic squid "In Textures," where the seafood was fried, dried, pureed, braised, candied, and served raw. This highlighted the different mouthfeels that could be achieved with a single protein. We would also feature unusual flavor combinations that pushed expectations, such as a chocolate dessert that used strawberries and niçoise olives as supporting components.

This was the moment I began to define my own cuisine, the first major shift in my style of food. When I arrived at Trio, the food was certainly unique among contemporary restaurants in the United States, but it was still recognizably derivative of The French Laundry. Now we were clearly forging our own path.

The imagination of our kitchen exploded. Instead of a vague goal of making innovative food with new techniques, it shifted to an all-out mission to take food and dining further and further. I began thinking about food constantly. I would wake up at eight and play with Kaden for an hour before heading to Trio, usually arriving between 9:30 and 10:00. While I spent plenty of time on *mise en place* for the night, I also spent at least a few hours each day testing new ideas.

For me, the ultimate dining experience involved long menus composed of many small, sometimes one-bite, courses. Over the years I had helped to craft menus of twenty-five courses or more by adding small canapés for the beginning of the VIP menus at the Laundry. But the basic offering was only nine courses. In order to receive the ultimate experience you had to either be in the industry, know the chef, be famous in some manner, or best of all, arrive as a single diner. I wanted to be able to offer every guest the most expressive menu the kitchen could produce—to democratize the VIP menu.

We introduced the first Tour de Force menu shortly after the reviews. It was eighteen courses long and composed mostly of the five-course menu and the nine-course menu smashed together. We priced it at $175 and billed it as the complete current repertoire of the kitchen. Now anyone could be a VIP.

Each of our staff was encouraged to dine at the restaurant once a year, free of charge. We thought it was both a nice bonus as well as a way for them to experience the restaurant from the diner's perspective. Bryan Black, a recent addition from Trotter's To Go, requested the evening off to dine with his father. It was customary to surprise an employee by creating a special course that they had not seen before, since it added the element of surprise that a typical diner would have.

That morning during prep I started to daydream about my meal at elBulli a year earlier and was reminded of a course where Ferran suggested that the guest lift a vanilla bean to their nose before each bite of a vanilla-scented potato puree. I enjoyed the course but didn't like the repetition of lifting the bean up to my nose. It felt somehow inelegant to present it that way. I really wanted to find a way to present an aroma constantly throughout the consumption of a course without asking the guest to do anything except eat.

I ordered lobster the night before, thinking it would fit nicely into Bryan's menu, and that we would figure out something to do with it. I ducked into the walk-in to see what we had. When I opened the door to the walk-in a waft of rosemary floated out and hit my nose. At the time we were buying herbs that were still growing in dirt. This rosemary was particularly fragrant, and Nate had just unpacked the shipment and put it away. I grabbed the rosemary and headed back upstairs.

I asked the cooks if they had any extra *mise en place* that I could work with and Chris offered up some roasted bell peppers. Bell peppers, lobster, and rosemary made sense, but felt safe and boring. I threw a pot of vinegared water on the stove to cook the lobster, covered it with a sheet pan, and started looking through the freezer for lobster stock. I went back and lifted up the sheet pan and a cloud of steam bellowed up and surrounded me, the vinegar stinging my eyes. I threw the lobster in, turned to my cutting board, and caught another whiff of the rosemary on the counter.

That was it.

Instead of vinegar steam we can do rosemary steam. Rosemary vapor surrounding the lobster.

I grabbed a handful of rosemary, threw it in the pot with the lobster, and breathed in while leaning over the pot. Out of the corner of my eye I noticed John looking at me. He cocked his head and smirked. I dipped into the cabinet that held our plateware and grabbed a large, flat-bottomed soup bowl and a smaller bowl that we used for canapés. After covering the bottom of the large bowl with rosemary branches I placed the small bowl on top of them, in the center of the larger bowl. By now the rest of the cooks noticed something was going on and gathered around. I explained that we could fill the little bowl with food that was going to be eaten by the guest and place it within any aromatic we wanted. The table service team would then pour hot water into the large bowl, activating the aromas and producing a vapor that would "flavor" the dish solely through smell.

I knew instantly that this would be fantastic.

Later that evening we served the course to Bryan and his father. After the meal he walked back to the kitchen to show his father around and introduce him to the staff. He walked up to me to say thanks, and a giant smile came over his face. "That lobster course is off the hook, Chef. It's badass. Everything was great, but that's another level."

The increased business translated into the ability to hire a few more cooks, buy more kitchenware that was much needed, and trade our overworked Costco-bought FoodSaver vacuum sealer for a real commercial-grade Cryovac machine. But I was growing restless.

On a cold Saturday morning in February, while the team was in full swing prepping for the night's service, the phone in the kitchen started to beep. Everyone knew this noise, and it was usually an unwelcome interruption of the kitchen pace. Peter was, once again, paging us. "Is Chef there?"

"Yes, Peter, I'm here." The annoyance in my voice was hardly disguised.

He asked me if I wanted to take a call. Peter knew that I rarely took calls during the day. Basically, I only stopped work when Angela would help Kaden call so he could hear my voice. So this must have been important. "Who is it?"

"Some woman named Dana Cowin. She claims she is from *Food and Wine* magazine. Might be an advertising call."

I set my knife down slowly and wiped my hands. "Yeah, I think I'll take that one, Peter."

Rumors had been floating around for a while that the editors from the magazine were in town scouting for the annual Top Ten Best New Chefs issue, and we knew that a few had been in to dinner.

"Hello, Grant, I have some exciting news that I wanted to call and tell you myself. You've been chosen as one of this year's *Food and Wine* best new chefs. Congratulations!"

The top ten had been a goal of mine, but I was still surprised to hear the news. I thanked Dana profusely, hung up, and went to tell Henry.

As part of winning the Top Ten I flew to New York City for the announcement party and in July traveled to Aspen for the *Food & Wine* Classic. There I was responsible for producing a tasting-size portion representative of my food for six hundred people. Six hundred portions of anything requires a giant effort from any chef, but the fragile,

• Me at three years old
making Jell-O

• Karate with dad

• Me at age fourteen,
hunting. (From left to
right) my dad, me, Jim
Achatz Sr., Jim Achatz
Jr., and Norm Achatz.

Carcass of the GTO being stripped for restoration

Maiden voyage of the GTO on my sixteenth birthday

CIA graduation day. (From left to right) dad, grandma Achatz, me, and mom, October 1994

1995 trip to Europe, meeting James Stier at the ferry

• Me (second, front row) with chefs Steve Stallard (front row, third from left) and Angus Campbell (front row, far right) at an event at Midland Country Club

• In the kitchen at The French Laundry, 1997

• (From left to right) Richard Blais, me, Thomas Keller, and Stephen Durfee in Hawaii, 1998

• Working on The French Laundry cookbook in Thomas Keller's home kitchen with Mark Hopper

franc TALK

CABERNET FRANC HAS LONG BEEN AN INVALUABLE BLENDING GRAPE. NOW NAPA'S
LA JOTA WINERY IS GIVING IT STAR TREATMENT—AND THROWING A PARTY TO CELEBRATE.

• *Food & Wine*
magazine
feature on a
dinner party
I prepared at
La Jota

• Ferran Adrià signing his cookbook after
my four-day stage at elBulli in 2000

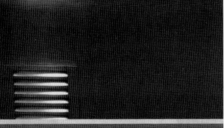

Tour de Force Tasting Menu
Wednesday February 20, 2002

Spice Water
Savory Mignardises
Grapefruit Cells - Black Truffle
Ice Cream and Ice
Salmon Roe...Three Ways
Hot Coconut - Cold Coconut
"Tuscan Jelly Beans"
Liquid Black Truffle Ravioli
Poached Maine Lobster
Everglades Frog Legs
Virginia Striped Bass-Redeye Gravy
"Hasenpfeffer" Rabbit
Elysian Fields Farm Lamb, Salt and Pepper
Juniper Ice
Roasted Banana Black Truffle Shake
Lemon Soufflé Parcels
Smokey Chocolate Tart
Mignardises

$175

Accompanying wine tasting
$85

Complete table participation required

- A Chefwear ad featuring the kitchen of Trio, including (starting second from left, then left to right) Nathan Klingbail, John Peters, me, and David Carrier; and Michael Carlson (third from right)

- First Tour de Force menu at Trio

Courtesy of Chefwear

• With Henry Adaniya at the James Beard Awards, shortly before
winning the Rising Star Chef award

• Kaden and Keller with me
at The Chef's Garden, Huron, Ohio, 2004

detail-oriented cuisine we were producing at Trio made the task seem impossible.

After Henry and I returned from New York, I sat with the team to figure out what we would produce for Aspen. I knew that Henry would want to attend, which would mean that I wouldn't be able to bring a cook along on the trip. I wanted to serve a course that represented our philosophy, but we had to take into account the limitations of traveling with prepared ingredients, the limited space we would have to work in, and the manpower—just me—to pull it off.

One of our recent additions to the team, Michael Carlson, suggested we do the Parmesan and olive oil ice-cream sandwich that we were currently offering as an *amuse*. If we could prep the six hundred–plus orders at Trio and somehow transport them frozen, already cut into small pucks, I could bake the cookies on-site, assemble the sandwiches, and wrap each in a small foil wrapper.

This seemed insane. We had limited kitchen resources, and producing six hundred of these would be nearly impossible. John reminded us that we would have to make the ice cream as close to the ship date as possible, otherwise ice crystals would form as the ice cream sat. And, of course, the ice cream had to be made, spun, laid out in trays, frozen, and then punched out with a ring cutter and immediately refrozen. Then, after all of that, it would be packaged and shipped halfway across the country.

"There is no way to pull that off," John said. "We can barely serve forty of them per night here. Our freezers are more like refrigerators. How are we possibly going to keep seven hundred of them frozen? We would have to buy another freezer here just to keep them ready. And what happens when FedEx loses the box or the ice cream melts en route?"

Carlson chimed in, "Chef-man, you get me a two-hundred-dollar chest freezer and I will bang this shit out. That *amuse* is killer. We have to show well in Aspen, Chef, we have to. You cats focus on service, I'll do the rest."

I thanked Michael for his dedication, but voiced the same concerns as John. "It will take you days to do this by yourself."

"I got it, Chef. I got it. This is Trio, guys. Come on. Quit being a bunch of pussies."

Mike was right. He was on fire, smiling, and he was right. Everything we had accomplished to this point happened because we took risks. I knew Mike would kill himself to get it done on time if he said he would, and for that I had to back him up. I told him, "Let's do it."

Carlson showed up early, stayed late, and came in on his days off to get all the *mise en place* for ice-cream sandwiches done, packaged, and boxed up with dry ice, all the while holding down his station during our normal service. The FedEx driver loaded up the boxes on a hand truck and our 725 ice cream sandwiches left for Aspen. The extras were just in case.

I headed to Aspen with Henry. The boxes arrived shortly after we did in perfect condition, and Henry and I stood in a giant walk-in freezer colder than Antarctica wearing layers of clothing and assembling and wrapping the sandwiches.

"Man, if the guys could see us now," I said to Henry, chuckling as my breath formed clouds.

In the matter of a year I had gone from an unknown young chef in his first kitchen to the cover of *Food & Wine*. Then I got nominated from a national pool of chefs under thirty years old for the James Beard Rising Star Chef of the Year Award. All of the good press begat new good press, and more articles began hailing the food as avant-garde, or even "molecular gastronomy"—a term that I had never heard.

When I was in Aspen I met chef Michael Anthony. He and co-chef Dan Barber had made the list from their work at Blue Hill restaurant in New York City. Michael asked me if I read any of the food forum websites that had begun to come out recently, and if so, how I was reacting to the public reviews online. This piqued my curiosity. I did a Web search one night after service and found the site eGullet, where I was surprised to find that there were more than a few comments about

Trio. Most were great, but a few were wildly misinformed. Posters to the site would be arguing over dishes that neither had ever eaten. Their speculations prompted me to join under the name "Chefg." I started a new Trio thread with the subject line:

IF ANYONE HAS ANY QUESTIONS REGARDING THE FOOD AT TRIO, ASK ME.

The statement was as absurd as the fact that I wrote it in all capitals. I was a computer idiot and a Web neophyte who didn't know any of the etiquette and had no real idea of the wealth of information and the power of the online crowds. But I saw in the posts that people were passionate about food and more than a little curious about Trio. Plus I figured I could entice a few to drive up to Evanston and check it out in person.

Every day during staff meal and after service was complete I diligently logged onto eGullet and answered the questions that had been posted that day. I enjoyed the unfiltered and immediate interaction, and many of the questions were thoughtful and thought-provoking. Typically, if a chef were to talk to a guest it would be briefly after their meal in the kitchen. These interactions online were very different, far more academic, and forced me to really think about what we were doing at Trio. The exchange of ideas began to inform our creative process. I learned about other chefs throughout the world who I hadn't previously heard about who were also pushing the envelope. Guys like Andoni Aduriz at Mugaritz, Quique Dacosta at El Poblet, and the Roca brothers in Spain. eGullet was at the time the ultimate research guide to all of the best restaurants in the world, and it was full of authentic reactions to the food.

After four weeks of steady posts with tons of detail the site administrators took note and invited me to participate in a formal Q&A session where the subjects would be sorted, grouped, and focused. They offered to help with the legwork and promotion, and in return I promised to spend a good deal of time answering the questions.

The eGullet sessions were a turning point of sorts. I realized quite suddenly that despite my successes at Trio and the recognition I was receiving, I was barely scratching the surface of the interested audience. And the level of knowledge and passion exhibited by these people posting from all over the world was inspiring.

I felt a sense of freedom that I had not felt previously. eGullet allowed me, by writing down my thoughts, to focus my attentions and create a written philosophy of my ideas. This was something I would never have done on my own, and the process was incredibly instructive.

It made me want to push the boundaries much further outside the norm. And suddenly I had a small but vocal crowd letting me know that that was not just okay, but hugely exciting.

I was already deep into butchering a pile of Elysian Fields Farm lamb saddles when Curtis Duffy, the young, fit Tom Cruise–esque cook who we recently lured from Trotter's, walked in the back door of the kitchen holding a ziplock bag full of what looked like paper.

"I picked this up in Chinatown yesterday," he said. "I thought it was pretty cool."

Curtis ripped off a corner of the paper and popped it in his mouth. He motioned for me to do the same. I picked up what looked like paper and placed it gingerly on my tongue. Within a second it was gone, completely dissolved. I did it again.

We quickly started chatting about what to do with this potato-starch paper. The rest of the cooks stopped at my cutting board, and Curtis kept ripping off samples for them to try. We decided that whatever it was had to be small. Even though the paper dissolved efficiently it did leave an unpleasant starchy film if you took too big a piece.

I immediately told them that if we were going to serve a tiny bite, it had to have intense flavors. The paper would also dissolve in the presence of any moisture. So the ingredients had to be dry. What about with fat? Chef Carrier grabbed a bottle of olive oil and dripped a bit on the paper. It held together. After nothing happened we knew we had our culinary glue. We began rattling off foods that would be imbedded in everyone's memories and that had intense flavors. We quickly got to pizza.

Almost everyone has had pepperoni pizza and can remember exactly what it tastes like. While there may be variables that come with pizza's numerous toppings, the core flavors of tomato, cheese, and garlic are nearly universal. The pepperoni merely adds a paprika and fennel seed element to the mix. We all became very excited by the prospect of turning this edible paper into a culinary joke, and Carrier sent one of the externs to the grocery store to buy some mozzarella. I began mixing powders of garlic, tomato, smoked paprika, and fennel pollen together in a ratio that tasted about right. When the extern came with the cheese I grated it into a large sauté pan and fired it in a hot oven. I wanted the cheese to caramelize the way it does on the edges of the crust of a pizza that has been overladen with cheese. Once it was browned we hung the pan and collected the rendered cheese fat in a small cup. The fat was then placed in the fridge, where it set up into a butterlike consistency.

We cut the potato-starch paper into half-inch squares, spread the congealed cheese fat on it, and sprinkled the powder mixture over the whole thing. It tasted exactly like the essence of pizza.

The experience of eating this pizza-flavored stamp was of course nothing like eating a slice of molten-hot pizza right out of the oven. But that was exactly the point. While it would remind the diner exactly of its namesake, it would not make you feel in the least bit full the way a slice of rich pizza does. And the visual pun of a tiny, tiny stamp of food packed with so much flavor was a great riff on the bad rap that haute cuisine has among some people: tiny portions. All of these aspects made people think about the mini-pizza they were putting in their mouths, and it made everyone laugh.

In March 2003 the James Beard Foundation released the final nominees for the restaurant and chef awards to be held in New York in May. The previous year I had been nominated for the Rising Star Chef Award, only to be beaten by Jean François Bruel, the talented protégé of Daniel Boulud. I didn't expect to win that time, but Bruel was a product of the entrenched and powerful New York empire of Boulud.

I would be lying if I wasn't disappointed, but I felt I would have my shot.

Still, it rankled me more than a little, not that I lost, but that I lost to a chef who was in my mind merely implementing the cuisine of his mentor at db Bistro Moderne. Here we were at Trio breaking our backs to try to do something completely new and original. The criteria for the award were: "A chef age thirty or younger who displays an impressive talent and who is likely to have a significant impact on the industry in years to come."

I did my best to set my ego and jealousy aside and focus my ambition squarely on creating new dishes. We were in the middle of filming a TV show for the Food Network called *Into the Fire*. They had a crew of guys filming at Trio trying to dig into our creative process. It made me aware after seeing the clips just how hard the whole team was pushing, how many ideas were coming out of our kitchen.

Going into the awards this time around I felt like we were in a better position to win. By "we" I do mean me, but recognition of this type was really for our whole kitchen and for Henry. The *Food & Wine* award raised our recognition nationally, and I felt we had a shot. Plus, most important, there were no New Yorkers on the list.

Despite my pride in our work, I was uncomfortable in the atmosphere of a big event. I wore a cheap rented tux and walked around holding a glass of champagne while deflecting any questions about Trio's food from the press or my peers. I was terrible at schmoozing and just wanted to head back to Evanston as quickly as possible. So I just smiled and tried to enjoy myself without looking nervous.

Finally it came to our category. The nominees were read, and before I realized what was happening, I was onstage with Henry slapping my back and Jean François draping the medal around my neck. I walked up to the podium, thanked Henry, the kitchen, and the front-of-house teams, and turned to walk off the stage when I spotted a tall, lanky man standing just out of sight of the crowd. He was jumping up and down like a schoolboy. As I drew closer I realized it was Thomas. He grabbed me by my shoulders, patted me on the back, and said over and over in my ear, "Congratulations. You did it." I am pretty sure he was more excited for me than I was.

He also had a better idea than I did of what such recognition could do for a chef's career.

Shortly after returning home from the Beard Awards, Angela told me she thought she might be pregnant again. I never thought I would have a family. After watching the turbulence of my parents' relationship and feeling the effects firsthand of a difficult marriage, I never wanted to assume that risk. My father had lectured me about how hard his career choice was on home life and how it forced difficult decisions and sacrifices.

I had begun to compartmentalize my life. Everything in my career was locking into place just as I had hoped, and I made it my mission to see that that didn't waver. My dedication to cooking was growing daily. And while I didn't anticipate being a father of two, I promised myself I would do my best at being a father. I kept telling myself I could do both, even though I knew the demanding circumstances surrounding the goals I had for my career would make it much more difficult.

My relationship with Angela continued to strain with the knowledge that we were having another child. Finances started becoming more of a concern, and she urged me to look for a job that would pay more money while requiring fewer hours. I immediately dismissed the notion knowing that the momentum I had now was rare.

Days would go by and we would barely speak. I would tend to my responsibilities as a father, showing Kaden how to cut the grass and shovel the sidewalk, making taking out the garbage a morning adventure, building a gauntlet of Matchbox car racecourses, and going three rounds of wrestling before my escape to work by 10:00 A.M. every day. As time went on, I stayed at Trio later and later after service, sometimes not getting home until 2:30 A.M. I was at home six hours a day and slept through most of them. Angela and I basically became roommates once again.

That compartment in my life was basically empty.

The food, however, was evolving at a rapid pace after the Beard Award. What started as a desire to break away from the model that was instilled in me at The French Laundry became an unquenchable desire to create entirely new experiences and tastes for diners. We had more ideas than we could develop, more creative urges than we could satisfy. This was a good problem to have. Our kitchen team was locked in and feeding off of each other.

As we pushed the food in new directions we began to realize that the plates, bowls, and silverware that had been used to consume food for hundreds or thousands of years did not work optimally for the food we were now creating. The "pizza" was a great conundrum. How does one serve it? You can't simply put it on a plate, and even if you did it would look absurd. And you couldn't exactly use a fork. It needed to be elevated so the guests could easily get their fingers under it. At the time, we were presenting the guests with homemade bubble gums of unusual flavors. This was brought to the guest inside a balloon that they had to pop in order to get the gum. Their experience would then be extended, casually, on the car ride home. As I looked around the kitchen to find something to serve the pizza on, I saw the pins. We decided to put the pizza on the head of a straight pin, and to put the pin in paraffin wax at the bottom of a large bowl, thus emphasizing just how small it was.

These were novel solutions that did make good use of minimal resources, but we didn't create anything truly new. They were fun, but they weren't innovative.

I turned to the Internet and started searching everything I could find on service pieces, plateware designers, silverware manufacturers, and even jewelry designers. In the span of a few hours after service I e-mailed forty-three designers and companies explaining who I was and what we were trying to accomplish at Trio.

A few days later I received my only response from a designer named Martin Kastner. He explained that he had grown up in the Czech Republic, where every eighteen-year-old male had to do a mandatory two years of military service. After completing his secondary-school studies in blacksmithing and locksmithing, Martin first trained as a paramedic, but after nine months switched to restoring the Horsovsky Tyn Castle, a Czech cultural monument. It was an opportunity for them to get a qualified person at almost no cost. Martin spent time restoring sixteenth-century armaments in a castle out in the country. For good measure, they also gave him a bunch of old padlocks—centuries old—to reverse engineer. There were no keys and he wasn't allowed to crack them open. He had to learn to think like a lock maker from the sixteenth century, hand forge a test key, and try again. He cracked most of them. In between restoring metalworks, cracking locks, and fixing old gates, he fed the bears that lived in the moat. The local circus had run out of money, and that seemed like a safe place to keep them.

When his service ended he enrolled at the Fine Arts Institute at Usti nad Labem, then went on to the Academy of Arts, Architecture and Design in Prague, where he graduated with an MFA in metal sculpture. He married an American, Lara, who was living in Prague, and returned with her to the United States, founding Crucial Detail design studio in San Diego in 1998.

Martin's response was cautious, deliberate, and inquisitive, completely in line with what I was to learn was his analytical personality. He was very interested in identifying the problems we faced in the current service lineup available to chefs, and to determine whether there were ways to find better solutions.

We started an e-mail exchange to get to know each other better, and it became apparent that we had similar goals in two entirely different disciplines. We quickly became comfortable with the process and settled on our first project, a holder for a lavender-flavored Popsicle.

Martin got to work, and a few days later sent me some sketches outlining his initial ideas. Even though Martin and I had never met in person, I could tell from these early designs that this was the start of something very exciting. The thought of having original service pieces to complement the food made me downright giddy.

His initial set of ideas was fairly mainstream and pretty much what my first idea would have been. A concept he called the "Folded Sheet" was simply a piece of stainless steel with holes bent at a strong angle, each of which would hold the handle of the Popsicle, which now looked more like a lollipop. The next, "The Caterpillar," was something akin to a bottom-weighted heat lamp, with the heavy base positioning the Popsicle vertically to prevent it from falling over. "The Shadow" was a more conceptual version of the folded sheet that used the silhouette of the Popsicle itself to create the final form. As the designs came in I could see the direction he was going. Each one was a bit more abstract, yet still cohesive. They started to meld aesthetic concerns with functionality in a way that made it hard to determine which was the priority. After every e-mail I would tell him that I loved the idea and that he should start making the piece as soon as possible, and each time he would encourage me to be patient, explaining that he had a few more ideas to flesh out. I was eager to get moving in order to have it completed for Trio's tenth anniversary celebration event we had planned in three weeks. The restaurant was hosting a giant open house that included a large tented area in the adjacent yard, and many local chefs were coming up to cook a course in honor of Henry and the restaurant's birthday. We would have a captive audience, and it would be a perfect opportunity to show the local industry where we were headed.

Martin finally sent me his finished design. In the e-mail he hinted that he'd had this idea in mind all along, but that he hadn't shared it because he thought it might be a stretch for me to accept right off the bat. "The Tripod" wasn't a Popsicle holder at all—at least not in the way I would have ever envisioned one. In fact, in many ways, it was the anti-holder, because it wasn't a drilled tray, plate, or object that grouped the sticks together.

Martin had rethought the entire idea. The sphere of frozen lavender became the locking mechanism for a set of three collapsible legs that when unfolded displayed the Popsicle four inches above the table. When the guest grabbed the three legs and squeezed them into one stick, they became the handle that the guest would use to eat the frozen tea. It was smart, witty, original, and brilliant.

Trio's budget was very tight, so I had to ask Henry for permission to wire Martin a check to get started. The total was $300 for a one-hundred-piece run, and Martin wanted a $100 deposit.

An incredibly important collaboration and friendship was born with "The Tripod."

Chefs are human, and while few want to admit it, they cook with varying degrees of enthusiasm for different people. Regulars of the restaurant, serious foodies who are enjoying their meal profusely, colleagues, and of course key journalists all get a little extra effort and a different level of gusto put into their meals. While our baseline standards were incredibly high at Trio, we did have another gear we could kick into.

We recognized that we were still climbing a tall mountain and that it was important to take a step with every person who walked into the restaurant. We were far from being in a position of complacency. The kitchen often sent out extra courses to seemingly random tables, and I would urge the front-of-house staff to alert me to any tables that seemed particularly into the experience so I could ratchet it up even more.

William Rice, a longtime supporter of Trio and an extremely influential national food writer, was coming in. Rice had eaten at Trio right before his retirement from the *Tribune,* and he subsequently wrote a feature on me for the paper. I connected with him right away. His eyes were both gentle and piercing at the same time, making him look like Sean Connery, and his dry, whip-sharp sense of humor made him incredibly fun to talk to.

I had no idea who Bill was dining with even after he introduced his friend David to me. And at that point Rice was retired, so this wasn't a meal for an article and I wasn't under the watchful eye of an active food critic. But for me this table was even more important.

My connection with Bill was strong, even though I didn't really know him as a person. I respected his open mind and appreciated that he saw promise enough in what we were trying to achieve during my early days at Trio to support it, and now to bring his friend all the way to Evanston to experience it. It was a huge compliment, and I wanted to return his respect with mine. I wanted to blow his mind.

The team created a twenty-six-course, fifteen-wine, four-hour dinner for the two friends, pulling out every stop and every new technique and presentation we had developed since his last meal. Looking for some spontaneous inspiration, I made contact with one of my favorite purveyors, Kate Lind, a woman who owns a tiny organic farm in Three Rivers, Michigan.

Kate takes a very "Summer of Love" approach to her life, and it carries over to her business. She talks to chefs directly and tells them what looks good on the farm a couple of days prior to delivery, which allows her to avoid the high-technology model of the Internet and FedEx. I would constantly bug her for obscure ingredients that I had read about in old cookbooks, and she would promise to plant or forage for them if they weren't readily available. A few weeks earlier she had reminded me that the angelica I encouraged her to grow was ready, but she explained apologetically that she only had two plants because her husband, James, had mistakenly tilled most of them under. "You know James," she said. "He gets on that tractor and starts daydreaming and the next thing you know half the field is gone."

At the time I assured her it was okay and asked her to leave them in the ground. I had no idea what I was going to do with them, and we didn't have a guest coming in who I felt was worthy of the suddenly very rare prize. Until now.

I had Kate gather a bunch of blooming horehound mint, which would become a bite-size gelée paired with lime, fresh-cut evergreens, chanterelle mushrooms, and ramps for the rabbit with evergreen vapor course. And per my instruction, she harvested the two lonely angelica plants.

After extra-early days leading up to Bill and David's dinner, many after-service brainstorming meetings about the pending meal, and consultation with Joe on the menu progression and wine pairings, I felt we were ready. It was our most ambitious menu ever. This was due not only to the number of courses but also to the risks we were taking with some of the concepts. A chocolate dessert used mustard seeds for texture like you might see poppy seeds being used in pastry preparations, and we laced the buttercream with Dijon. We paired caviar with a kola nut ice and steamed milk, while a raspberry and tapioca dessert came with a long-stem rose for the diners to smell before they ate the parfait.

But the biggest risk was the angelica. The plants arrived in pristine condition, standing upright in a cut-off gallon milk jug filled with water to keep them from wilting, the beautiful green leaves nearly as large as my open hand. They were gorgeous, and certainly even more so in my eyes because I knew the story behind them. I knew Kate had sourced the seeds and grown them specifically for me, and that these were the only two we would get from all of her efforts.

Historically the plant's hollow stems had been used as straws for cocktails, perfuming the beverage with their celery-like aroma. So it seemed natural to honor that tradition and have Bill slurp something through the cleaned-up branches. I began removing the plants from the jug with the intent of snipping away the leaves and paring them down to a single straw, when I stopped. They looked like flowers in a vase, they were alive, and they were a part of that small farm in Michigan. We needed to serve them that way. In fact, that needed to be the entire point of the course. After a brief description from the maître d' Chris Gerber, my go-to front-of-house guy, I wanted Bill and David to remove the branches from the glass vase that we would serve them in, contemplate the angelica, its history in gastronomy, and hear about Kate and her tiny farm five hours away. What I put inside for them to eat was almost irrelevant.

I settled on a baked Ashmead's Kernel Apple puree that would be piped into the hollow stem with a syringe. That was it. Nothing more. The apple flavor worked with the anise-celery notes of the angelica, and the apples were grown on Kate's farm.

The dinner went wildly well. While chatting with the men after the meal I sensed an aura of satisfaction coming from them akin to the pleasant surprise of expectations having been exceeded. As we talked, David mentioned that he wrote a weekly column for the *L.A. Times* and wanted to write about his experience. I wasn't sure what that meant exactly, but of course I was thrilled to get more national exposure, especially because it was a genuine surprise.

On October 1, 2003, Pulitzer Prize–winning writer—and unbeknownst to me, the chairman of the James Beard restaurant committee— David Shaw wrote a feature on me and Trio for the *L.A. Times*:

EVERGREEN VAPOR AND MOZZARELLA BALLOONS

And these are just two courses in what may be the most surreal dining experience in America.

I hugely underestimated the importance of David Shaw's article. It was splashed across the front page of the dining section of one of the nation's most circulated newspapers, with superlative-laced copy, color photos of the food, and two guests smelling roses while eating the raspberry dessert. And this was penned by one of the nation's most respected food journalists. It made its way to all the food forums online and likely the desk of every writer who cared about what was happening in the food world.

As I read the article, my jaw dropped at the quotes.

"Welcome to Trio, the most avant-garde restaurant in America."

"It was a truly amazing experience. What Achatz is doing in his 13-table restaurant is nothing less than redefining fine dining in this country."

"Risky and delicious."

"Every course at Trio seems as much intellectual exercise as culinary experience—as much theater as restaurant. Take our 19th course. The waiter brought to our table a large, glass vase filled with long, green, leafy angelica branches. The bottom 6 inches or so of each branch had been hollowed out—and filled with apple puree."

"But Adrià is 41. Keller is 49. Achatz is just 29, and he's still feeling his way, still experimenting, finding his own style. He's not just pushing the envelope; he's shredding it—and then re-forming it, in different shapes, with different materials and in a far more radical fashion."

I sat in the dining room in near darkness, reading the piece over and over in disbelief. In some way I felt like this sealed our fate in some strangely wonderful way. Diners and experienced food journalists were raving about what we were doing. A couple of good reviews could be chance, some accolades might be luck or good PR, but the momentum was now undeniable. More important than that was what we were accomplishing: exactly what we had set out to accomplish two and a half years earlier. We were changing what a dining experience could be.

I was excited that the sonogram showed that another boy was coming into my life. Kaden was now just over two and the thought of him having a little brother to play with gave me some comfort. I had been spending a few minutes each day combing baby-naming sites on the Internet for something I liked, but nothing stood out. I decided to grab the phone book and start paging through. I cracked the book open to the natural halfway point, which happened to be the names beginning with the letter "K." Of course in a phone book the family names are listed first, followed by the given name, and as I began to scroll I figured this might be fruitless. Names like Kane, Kasy, and Keefer clearly would not work as a given name. But as my eyes ran down the page I landed on Keller, James T. "Wow, that works," I thought to myself. I considered naming my second son after my mentor.

Would people think that was strange?

In the end it didn't matter. It was original in that it wasn't common, it honored someone that was incredibly important to me, and I liked the way it sounded.

On December 19, 2003, Keller Mitchell Achatz was born.

Trio had a small but committed group of regular diners who were anxious to see what we would create next. Because we didn't do a ton of covers, it was easy to remember a face, a name, or a phone number of a diner, even on their second or third visit. Most of these regulars were a bit older and lived in the wealthy suburbs just to the north of Evanston, while a few were from Chicago. But one couple stood out. They were younger, laughed a bit louder, and according to our staff seemed a bit more knowledgeable and passionate about the food and wine.

After their second visit, Chris Gerber came back to the kitchen with a smile on his face and said that the Kokonas party had just made a standing reservation for the first Wednesday of every month. That was a first. "Wednesday, huh? That's kinda tough." Wednesday was the first day of the Trio workweek since we were closed each Monday and Tuesday. That meant that the kitchen had zero *mise en place* ready. What's more, we made it a practice to create new dishes for repeat guests so that they wouldn't see the same concepts over and over. You really can only laugh at a great joke or anticipate a plot twist once. To us, a regular was someone that came in four or five times a year, typically on a Friday or Saturday night. The Kokonas were scheduled to come once a month, and on the day of the week that the kitchen was at its weakest.

I didn't think about it again, figuring that I would make sure their menu three weeks later would be entirely new. Except ten days later they were back.

I didn't know it then, but Nick Kokonas, a guy who had never spent a day in the restaurant business, would soon become my business partner and friend.

Like me, he was a driven only child. He would not only help build a restaurant, he would also save my life.

———————

Toasted hot dog buns with butter—that's what I ate for breakfast nearly every day between the ages of seven and fourteen. The butter had to go on the bun before it went into the toaster oven so it melted, ideally leaving brown crunchy ridges around the spot where each pad of butter had been laid. That and a glass of orange juice was pretty much it.

It was a point of fascination among my friends' parents that Nicky Kokonas, as I was known then, only ate hot dog buns for breakfast. On trips with friends up to their summer homes in Wisconsin, or skiing in Michigan, or simply on a sleepover on a weekend, I would make the faux pas of querying, "Do you have any hot dog buns?" when asked what I would prefer for breakfast. It is safe to say that I did not grow up in a home steeped in food culture.

My father had owned a green grocery on Chicago Avenue after serving in both the Army and Navy. He had worked at the shop since he was fourteen, when his father fell ill to a series of strokes, and had saved up enough over the years to make a down payment on the Royal Food Store. My mom, of Polish descent, lived in the area and frequented the butcher across the street. "I bet that man across the street is married with ten kids. And how he flirts and looks at all the ladies walking down the street, pretending to sweep!" my mom said to the butcher.

"No ma'am. He isn't married. Takes care of his mom who lives with him and his sisters. Nicest guy in the world."

My mom headed directly across the street. Walking through the store, she bought the cheapest thing she could find, a single Twinkie. And that is how she met my dad.

My dad later owned a small diner, James Lunch, in addition to the grocery. But by the time I was born, he was nearly forty-one and his work revolved around Reliable Labor, a temporary labor office that he opened with his best friend from high school, George Karkazis. I never saw him work with food, although he cooked a mean omelette on Sundays.

My mom feared food. She had phobias about all sorts of foods. Olives stank. Chili was too spicy. Sushi or Thai food or even Mexican all had major issues. These dislikes were passed on fully to me. To say I grew up as a picky eater would be an understatement. I loved pasta, but only with a simple red sauce. I ate lots of chicken, lots of steak. Potatoes in any form were acceptable. Vegetables were to be avoided, with the exception of corn. Most vegetables that I had growing up were cooked in the fashion that my mom grew up with, which meant that they were soggy, gray, and mushy. Salt was the only seasoning used. Any others had a "funny smell" or were "too spicy," according to my mom.

Her biggest phobia was cheese. Yes, cheese. According to my mom cheese is "rotten milk" and "smells awful." "When your dad brings home the feta I don't even want to open the refrigerator!" So when I attended a friend's birthday party in seventh grade and all that was offered for dinner was pizza, I asked if they had anything else.

"Why, Nick," my friend's mom said, laughing, "don't you like pizza?"

"Well, to be honest I've never tried pizza." The look on everyone's face was astounding. I was instantly embarrassed, so embarrassed that I put a slice of the pizza on my plate and pretended I was kidding. I took a bite.

"Wow, that's fantastic!"

I gobbled down four or five slices. When I got home my mom asked me about the party.

"It was great. We had the whole gym to ourselves to play basketball, then they served pizza for lunch." I knew that would get a rise out of her.

"Do you want something to eat, honey?" she asked, assuming I had not eaten the foul substance.

"No. I ate plenty there," I said. My dad shot me a look.

"You like pizza?" he asked.

"Like it? It is the single greatest thing I have ever eaten. Delicious. Why don't you guys eat pizza?"

My mom looked at my dad, and my dad looked at me and smiled. "Next time you want a pizza, Nick, just let me know."

"How about tonight?"

A small fissure in the home cracked open, and nearly every Sunday during football season my dad and I would order a pizza from our favorite local place and enjoy it for lunch during the Bears game. Very occasionally, my dad would also have a beer, something I never, ever saw him do any other time. "Beer and pizza just go together. I used to have plenty of both before you were born." And just like that, I learned that my dad loved food, all kinds of food.

My parents encouraged academic discipline over sports or any other outside activities. I went to high school at the same school that John Hughes attended and wrote about in his trilogy of now-famous 1980s movies. *Ferris Bueller's Day Off* was filmed at Glenbrook North, and yes, I was an extra and can be seen in the film. But I wasn't Ferris or Cameron in real life. I was pretty much anonymous. In 1986 I headed off to Colgate University.

"Mr. Kokonas, where is your book?"

"I'm afraid I left it at my apartment, Professor Balmuth," I answered. It was week four of my freshman year at Colgate University, and I was taking Introduction to Logic with the esteemed but highly feared Professor Jerome Balmuth.

As many upperclassmen told me, Professor Balmuth was brilliant but difficult. He was demanding one moment, belittling the next. He was Colgate's answer to the John Houseman character of Professor Kingsfield from *The Paper Chase.*

"Well, Mr. Kokonas, a lot of good it is doing you there."

"On the contrary, Professor, it appears that it is doing me some good. That is why I was able to whisper the answer to Jim, and why you immediately called on me." The class remained silent, and Jim, an upperclassman who shared with me the secrets of his fraternity brothers' notes on the class, shot me a look to let me know that he was not pleased that I had acknowledged the indiscretion.

"Mr. Kokonas, I called on you because you did not have your book." Professor Balmuth's back was to me and he was still facing the blackboard on which he had written a symbolic logic problem. He had not written my answer—despite the fact that it was correct—and he had somehow noticed that I had not put my book on my desk, despite the fact that I was one of about fifty people in class and sitting in the fourth row. "Please see me after class, Mr. Kokonas."

My heart raced and Jim lifted a finger, shaped it into the form of a gun, and pretended to shoot me dead. It was no secret that in the first few weeks Professor Balmuth wanted to separate the "wheat from the chaff, as it were" and thin the class. Fifty-plus people was a huge class at Colgate, but Intro to Logic was a requirement for many majors, from mathematics to philosophy to economics. Eight students left the first week. He had more thinning to do. I was next.

A line formed at the front of the class and Balmuth answered questions calmly one by one. Another dropped out in front of me, and when I reached the front of the line, Balmuth asked me to go to the back of the line and wait. I was toast for sure. The two people in front of me now asked a few questions about "supplemental work"—really just trying to kiss some ass—and then I sheepishly was left alone in the class.

"Professor, I am ..."

Professor Balmuth interrupted me as he threw his trademark scarf around his neck and moved a lock of hair. "Mr. Kokonas, you're a real smart-ass, huh?"

"I am, Professor. And I'm sorry if I was rude. I thought you would find it kind of funny, because, you know, you kind of are too." I couldn't believe I said that.

Betraying no emotion, no smile, he said simply, "Follow me to my office." That was it—he was going to sign some paper and have me shipped out. I walked across the quad to the small building that housed the philosophy staff, trailing a few feet behind Balmuth, who was practically jogging. I followed him up a flight of stairs and into his office. "Please close the door behind you and take a seat."

I closed the door, and as I turned around, Balmuth had a big smile on his face and his feet were up on his desk as he reclined back with his hands behind his head. "So, Mr. Kokonas, please tell me about yourself."

I was shocked. Why was he smiling? "What do you, uh, want to know, Professor?"

"Everything. Who are your parents, where do you come from, what do you intend to study at this institution? What do you do for fun? What do you find interesting, or hard, or easy, or amusing?"

I muttered through a story about my existence to that point. He listened while staring up at the ceiling away from me, occasionally letting out a "huh" or a "reaaaallly ...?" while grinning at odd moments that to me felt insignificant.

"I figure I'll study economics, because I want to go into business, with political science as a minor because my dad wants me to go to law school."

For the first time in twenty minutes Professor Balmuth looked directly at me. "No, I don't think that is such a good idea. I think you will become a philosophy major and I will be your advisor. Every student here needs an advisor when they take on a major, and I only take a few each year. I will ensure that the huge amounts of money your parents are investing in this great institution, and in you, are not wasted. You will leave here with a real education. So what else are you taking this semester? We will go through that, make necessary changes, and then talk about next semester."

I was floored. Everyone had told me to fear this man, to muddle through his class, to study harder than you thought necessary just to eke by. And now he was telling me not only what I should study, but also that he would personally help to craft my four years at Colgate. I didn't know if I should be afraid, thankful, or completely perplexed. "Well, I hadn't thought about philosophy. What can I do with a philosophy major?"

"Economists, Nick, like to call what they do a science. Political scientists put it right in their name! Ha! But neither is a science. They are both philosophy as well, but a rung or two down. Learn how to learn, Mr. Kokonas, and the rest will take care of itself."

I left his office without committing. And that night I called my dad and told him what had happened. "You know, your grandfather used to read Greek philosophy to me at night when I was a kid. He was a totally uneducated man, and really broken at that point, but he loved to read philosophy. Plato. Aristotle. It makes sense. If that's what you want to do, that's fine by me."

The next day I brought my book to Intro to Logic and Jim was surprised to see me. "What happened?" he asked.

"Uh, nothing really. He dragged me back to his office and told me that he wanted to be my advisor and that I should study philosophy."

"Really?"

"Yeah, really."

"Screw you too, Nick!" Jim was an aspiring philosophy major and wanted nothing more than to have Balmuth as his advisor. He shook his head, and didn't look at me for the rest of the class. I realized then what exactly the offer from Professor Balmuth meant. I waited in the back of the class until everyone left.

"Mr. Kokonas, can I help you?" It was as if the conversation in his office had never happened.

"Yes, Professor. I spoke to my dad last night and thought about what you said. I'm happy to accept your offer. What do I have to do now?"

"Nothing at all. I reviewed your class schedule already and everything is fine for this semester. All you have to do now is perform twice as well as nearly everyone else in this class to earn an A. I expect nothing less of my advisees."

I spent the fall of my junior year, as many Colgate students do, abroad in London. I then returned to Colgate to find that my housing situation had fallen apart and that I was back in the freshman dorms. I met a few fellow musicians and formed a band—Rare Form—and slogged through the spring semester.

When I returned for my senior year I found everyone worried about their careers or graduate school exams. I took the LSAT and did well, and I figured I would head to law school. I wrote my senior honors thesis on the philosophy of international law, and never really worried about getting into a law school or finding a job. Because I pushed hard my first two years taking extra classes and some summer school, I had a light load senior year. I spent most of my time playing in the band, hanging out, and reading for pleasure.

Then I met my wife.

I was sitting in the third row of an ethics class when I heard someone say, "Yeah, I guess my next boyfriend should be from Chicago," and then laugh. I looked up and it was a woman who was also in my philosophy of law class. She was beautiful and somehow different. She wore clothes that were a few years older than her age, but she carried it with sex appeal. When she spoke in class her statements were reasoned and clear. I saw that as an opportunity to introduce myself. "Hey, I'm from Chicago. My name is Nick."

"Dagmara," she said. "Nice to meet you." She gathered up her books and walked out the door. That was that. Total indifference.

I began to notice her around campus, and we would strike up short conversations. But she would always end them and head off. I left my sweater on the back of a chair, and she returned it to me. We knew each other, but didn't say much.

Late on a Friday night my band was playing at the campus pub, the last band of the night. Halfway through our late set I noticed Dagmara, wearing sweats and a T-shirt, being dragged in by her roommate Jen, seemingly against her will. They sat at a table in the front. Jen was staring at me the entire time in a way that made me uncomfortable, self-conscious, and really happy. As soon as I began to flirt with her, she pointed at Dagmara and mouthed something to me. I tried to find them after the show but they had left.

And then, finally, Jen found me out one night and told me, "You know, my roommate really likes you a ton. Here, come with me. She's home studying. I'll bring her a present." I thought it was a bad idea—and a terrific one. I followed Jen to their apartment and walked in to find Dagmara reading. "Hi." We were inseparable after that.

When I graduated, I couldn't imagine working in an office every day for the rest of my life. Nor could I imagine myself as a professor or academic in philosophy. I'd gotten into law school at the University of Pennsylvania, but decided to defer a year. All I wanted to do was start some business that afforded me the opportunity to work my own hours and live or die by my own decisions. My dad and I pursued an opportunity to buy a landmark Chicago diner when its ailing Greek owner had to sell, but my dad didn't want his now "educated" son to do that sort of work. The deal fell through. When it came time the following fall to head to law school, I instead bought a ticket for Japan and visited Dagmara, where she'd taken a job. We came back to the U.S. together. I never thought of law school again.

Dagmara got a job with Citibank, and I started a small business selling posters to college students at the beginning of each new semester, and to doctors' offices the rest of the time. I didn't make much money, but it wasn't bad. It was on par with what I would have made starting out in a real job. Still, it wasn't a career.

Growing up in Chicago, it's hard not to hear stories of traders. New York has investment bankers, Chicago has floor traders, a much less prestigious and much more blue-collar job. I knew a few guys from my high school who skipped college altogether, hit the pits with a small stake, and were now developing condos while I was pondering law school. I also knew more than a few traders who were once rich and were now broke. I interviewed with companies like Société Générale and Goldman Sachs, but in the end the job offers and training programs seemed too much like jobs and not enough like a life. I would have little or no control over what I learned, where I worked, or how much money I made. So I took a job on the floor of the Chicago Mercantile Exchange making minimum wage and told myself that I would find a way to become an independent trader.

Six months of clerking on the floor was an eye-opener. The Chicago trading floors are loud, Darwinian places where your educational awards mean nothing and the last trading day could be, literally, your last trading day. Just as I was about to quit and figure out how to head to law school I met a young trader who was smart, analytical, and just leaving a large trading firm to start as an independent options trader. Even though he said he didn't need an employee I begged to work for him, going so far as to offer to pay him to work. He had the knowledge I needed.

I spent seven months working side by side with Frank Serrino as he made markets in Canadian Dollar options. Then I put up my savings from the poster business and he put up the other half of the money and I started trading 1-lots in Swiss Franc options. My goal was to make about $150 to $200 per day, then grow my account slowly, start trading 2-lots, and so on.

Trading for a living gets a lot of attention in the press due to day traders, rogue options traders who can take down banks, and evil hedge-fund thieves. But floor trading as an independent is more akin to being a professional golfer, except that every time you make a bad shot you pay money to the golfer who made a good shot. It's a zero-sum game, meaning that no wealth is created or destroyed; it simply shifts risk and money between players. It serves a useful purpose to the economy in aggregate, but as an individual trader it is akin to being psychoanalyzed 24/7. If you are good, 49 percent of your decisions will be wrong. Even if you are great, something just short of a majority will be losers. It's hard not to second-guess your decisions constantly, even though doing so produces precisely the wrong feedback and outcomes.

I read everything I could get my hands on about the markets, great traders, historical economics, and most of all, personal psychology. I made sure I was the first guy in my pit every day and the last one to leave. I was hazed mercilessly because I was young, overly serious, and about 150 pounds dripping wet. And since I was the first guy in the pit who had a computer in my pocket, I was also eventually seen as a threat.

Dagmara's father is a patent attorney and was not keen on having his daughter live with, let alone marry, someone who was falling short of their intellectual capacity. But one Christmas I was invited to ski with them in Aspen, Colorado. And there a wonderful thing happened.

Dagmara's parents were both born in Latvia, and food-wise they were the polar opposite of my parents. Constant travel and cultural exploration were the norm, and new food experiences were celebrated. One night we headed to a restaurant that sounded like a nightmare to me. Krabloonik, just outside Snowmass, bills itself as "Fine Dining & Dogsledding." I didn't see how that combination could work. In addition, their seasonal menus specialized in local game meats like elk, buffalo, caribou, and wild boar. I had to be on my best behavior, but I was dreading the dinner.

There are two ways to get to the restaurant. You can ski there cross-country—or snowshoe—or drive in through a beautiful but snowy country road. We drove in, parked, and then walked down past the dog kennels, where dogs were howling wildly in the snowy evening. The log-cabin restaurant was like a set design for the Rocky Mountain lifestyle: glowing fire, thick-beamed ceilings, warm lighting.

Dagmara's father ordered a bottle of red wine and some appetizers. I glanced through the menu and realized I would have to order a steak, because it was the only thing that looked familiar. I closed the menu quickly as the appetizers arrived.

Dagmara put caribou carpaccio on my plate and I glared at her accordingly. But this, she knew, was her chance to make sure I tried something new. She gave me that look that told me I better just go along. I took a big forkful in order to slug it back with some water, but as soon as it hit my mouth I paused. It was delicious. A silky texture mixed with capers, olive oil, and balsamic gave it everything at once—sweet, salty, and savory. I took another bite. "This is delicious. Caribou, huh?"

"Try it with the wine, Nick," Dagmara's father, Tali, suggested. "It's Australian. One of my favorites."

I had never had a decent glass of wine in my life. My parents were not wine drinkers, and I'd never had any in college. I took a sip. It was literally life-changing. I had no vocabulary to describe what I was tasting, so I just said, "Wow, what is that?"

"Penfolds Bin 707 Cabernet. You like it?"

I had already finished the glass along with the caribou. When the waiter came by I ordered the wild mushroom soup, a house specialty, along with seared elk tenderloin. Dagmara assumed that I was already drunk.

Tali and I polished off a few bottles of the Penfolds and, noticing my newfound interest, he decided to up the ante and ordered a bottle of vintage Bordeaux, as well. The entire experience was like a light switch being flipped. I had no idea that food and wine could be so intriguing and delicious.

I began reading about wine the way I read about trading. It was a fascinating subject simply because it was so vast and entrenched in history. I heard about a wine auction that the Chicago Wine Company was holding on a Saturday morning in the same building where Tali worked. I thought it would be a great way to find something we had in common and to spend some one-on-one time with my future father-in-law. I invited him along and he readily accepted.

The auction took place on the coldest Saturday morning in something like twenty years. It was well below zero outside with severe wind and snow. I woke up, looked outside, and called Tali. "That's too bad, I was looking forward to it," I said.

"Nonsense. I'll pick you up in a few minutes. I have a parking space in the building. You won't even need a coat."

We arrived in the dining room of the restaurant-club in the Prudential Building to find eighty bottles of vintage wine open and four people standing in a room with 150 seats. A man from the auction company with a British accent approached us and asked if we had purchased tickets to the pre-auction wine tasting. Tali looked at me, but I shook my head. I hadn't known about it.

"Well, never mind then. This dreadful weather has kept everyone away. No sense in letting all of this go to waste, and despite how I might try, I can't drink it all myself. Come along with me; I'll show you the highlights."

We spent the next ninety minutes sampling 1982 Bordeaux, Burgundy from three decades, ports, sherries, and all manner of California cult wines that were just gaining prominence. By the time the auction started I was inebriated enough to purchase a single case of 1983 Grand-Puy-Lacoste, not great vintage, but a good one and a good value. I was hooked. And I enjoyed tremendously the opportunity to get to know Dagmara's father one-on-one.

In 1995 Dagmara and I were married.

I spent ten years trading.

I got faster and faster at making markets, of doing the math and calculations in my head, and working on models and programs for new trades and risk analysis. After two years with Frank I left with a single employee and a great friend, Jim Hansen, and together we backed ourselves with very little money and not much experience. But we were willing to outwork everyone else.

Over a period of six years we built a company by hiring what we called "corporate refugees," teaching them how to think like a trader, and then backing them with our money when they were ready. We had former lawyers, accountants, and guys from advertising working for us. What they had in common is that they were willing to work for next to nothing for a year, devote themselves completely to retooling their psychology and discipline, and then work like hell in the pits—all because they had tasted corporate life and hated it. A few years in we had fifteen employees and Jim moved back to his native San Francisco to start an office at the Pacific Coast Exchange. I also invested in a Web company—Funbrain.com—in 1997 that was being built by Mike Cirks and Paul Hudson, the programming team that had developed our risk analysis software. The Web was poised to explode, and these two were trustworthy and brilliant. We did the deal on a handshake.

I had gone in a few years from making literally minimum wage to earning nearly a million dollars a year. I had also experienced the beginnings of what could be called "trader personality disorder." The pace of the regular world seemed wildly slow, and my temper and patience grew shorter and shorter.

Then, in 1998, I reconnected with Keith Goggin, a classmate from Colgate who was now trading at the American Stock Exchange. Over the course of a year I lobbied the Merc to allow us to utilize a dedicated connection between traders at the Amex and the Merc to exchange traded funds in New York against their futures in Chicago. When we were finally given the go-ahead to do so, we were the first to have the technology and the connection, and our business exploded. In short order we merged our firms, began trading huge numbers of shares and contracts each day, and couldn't hire people fast enough. We began to make a great deal of money very quickly.

In April 1999 Dagmara and I had a son and we named him James Talis after my father and hers. Life was fantastic.

While I spent all of my time trading, Dagmara spent her early motherhood cooking. She had always loved food, and now that she spent more time at home with our son, she spent tons of time reading *Food & Wine* and *Gourmet* during his naps. I would catch the 5:35 A.M. train into the city every day and be home by 4:30. By 6:00 P.M. a gourmet meal was on the table more nights than not. Multiple courses, handmade pastas, cakes, and even homemade gelato and sorbets were on the menu every night. When I did take a vacation we would often head to Napa. James's first birthday was spent with friends in Sonoma.

By 2001 I had largely attained my goals financially and professionally. I was tired, burned-out, and increasingly unable to enjoy anything. In February my father died of cancer. It was the hardest day of my life to watch him go. Then, on September 11th—his birthday and my parents' wedding anniversary—the terrorist attacks occurred and thirty-five of our employees were scattered around lower Manhattan fleeing the scene. My priorities changed quickly after that. Trading didn't seem terribly serious or important. In early 2002, after Dagmara pointed out that I was not happy, something that I myself had failed to realize, I rather abruptly retired from my firm.

At thirty-five years old, I was in some respects back to square one. I had no idea what I was going to do with the rest of my life.

We traveled for a bit and hit many of the great restaurants in Paris—Taillevent, La Tour D'Argent, L'Arpège, and L'Ami Louis among them. We also enjoyed a fantastic meal at Don Alfonso 1890 on the Amalfi Coast. Dagmara continued to cook, and now that I had more time, I started to expand from my basic love of grilling on my Big Green Egg to learn more complex techniques. But the withdrawal from work and the adrenaline rush of trading was hard to replace.

For a while I spent time looking at other Internet companies to invest in and small private-equity deals. These were satisfying to analyze because they were small, nimble companies built by passionate people. And while I invested in a few, I wasted a great deal of time going down blind alleys. I wanted to trade again, and a friend in the hedge-fund business provided an opportunity.

Then, on a Friday afternoon, Mike from Funbrain called Dagmara and invited us to a lunch at Trio.

I had been to Trio with my in-laws for a few brunches and one dinner, both under Rick Tramanto and Shawn McClain. I had enjoyed it, but wasn't anxious to go back, especially not for a lunch on a Friday. But the Cirks had the reservation and we loved to travel and dine with them, so off we went.

At the last moment, Mary and Mike had to cancel, so Dagmara and I indulged in a guilty pleasure all by ourselves. We were practically the only people there other than the staff.

We sat down and an elegant, thin gentleman approached the table. "Can I offer you a glass of champagne, perhaps, while you look over the menu?" Dagmara and I looked at each other and giggled. It was such an odd spur-of-the-moment lunch that we decided to go all in. "Sure. Please."

"The chef does have a tasting menu the appropriate length for a lunch if you are so inclined."

"Why not?" Dagmara said.

By the time our first substantial course came we were slack-jawed. After one bite of the lamb, which was woven together almost like a rope, I motioned for the waiter. "Is everything okay?" he asked with a smile on his face. He could tell we were pleased.

"Yeah. Everything is beyond okay. Uh, who is in the kitchen?" I knew from my previous visits that something had changed significantly, and for the better.

"We got this new kid from The French Laundry, and he's blowing our minds," he said.

We were incredulous. We had been traveling far afield to eat at Michelin-starred restaurants, and yet here was this tiny restaurant ten minutes from our home.

"We should come back for dinner soon," Dagmara said to me. I agreed. We made a reservation for the following Wednesday. After that meal, Dagmara suggested we eat there the first Wednesday of every month.

Chris Gerber was overjoyed by that request. "No problem at all. It will be a pleasure to see you next month."

CHAPTER 14

Over the next six months Dagmara and I ate at Trio seven times, and I had been there an additional two or three times with business associates and friends—an excessive number of meals for this type of restaurant. Each time was a revelation, and each time at least a few new dishes hit our table. Sometimes, all eighteen or twenty courses were brand-new. We had developed a rapport with the waitstaff and with Trio's owner, Henry, and had chatted with chef Achatz on a few occasions. Every time we went to eat somewhere else it felt lesser in every respect, so we kept going back, despite the cost and the sometimes awkward feeling of being a regular at a restaurant of this type.

The food was like nothing we had ever eaten—imaginative, daring, odd, whimsical, avant-garde. But more than anything else, it was delicious. We would often comment that X or Y were the best preparation that we had ever had—"That was the best rabbit ever, period." "Yeah, but what about the short rib?"—and our ride home and conversation the next morning would be a dissection of the meal, its ingredients, and "Why the hell isn't anyone else making food like that? I mean, if I could just get the short rib as a stand-alone dish, I'd be at that restaurant every week."

We had, it seemed, become full-fledged foodies, and we passionately believed that Trio was the best restaurant that somehow no one knew about. Sure chef Achatz had won numerous accolades, but Trio was often only half-full on a weekday, was hidden inside an odd rooming house, and was in the suburbs. Tell a New Yorker or a San Franciscan, as I often did, that the best meal in America was to be had an hour outside Chicago, and the ensuing guffaws would reverberate out of the phone.

The first time we really spoke with Grant was after a particularly memorable meal. We had brought along two good friends for whom fine dining was a foreign and hostile endeavor. They had been to a few of the Temples of Gastronomy and very much enjoyed the food but highly disliked the pretense and formality of the experiences. The husband told me on the way to Trio, "Look, I get that it's good food. And I understand that it's expensive because it costs the restaurant so much to make it, etc., etc. But if I want to be treated like an asshole and then pay for it, I'll go visit my lawyer. And I usually eat a hot dog on the way home, by the way." We assured him this would be different—fun, even.

We arrived at the restaurant, a mere ten minutes from our homes, after listening to this harangue about formal dining. Greeted personally by Chris Gerber, the young and affable maître d', we were led to a table "that you have not yet had the chance to enjoy. Another view of the room." Chris was making a joke about the size of the small room and had raised his eyebrow in mock irony, but the humor was lost and The Husband shot me a look that said, "this place will be no different." A bottle of Grand Siècle was brought out to us as a gift from Henry, and the waiter asked whether or not we wanted to see the menus, despite knowing that we would say, "Whatever the kitchen wants to do is fine with us." "Off we go then," he said. The first course did little to change The Husband's mind. Pear-Eucalyptus Olive Oil was a beautiful sculpture of a bite, an *amuse* that let you know this would be a different kind of meal. But it was only a single bite. The plate was taken away, and I received The Look once again. I smiled a knowing but cautious smile.

The second course fared little better in his opinion. Michigan Brook Trout Roe with ginger, soy, and papaya was a showcase for Steve Stallard's hand-gathered caviar. We had enjoyed this roe in another preparation before, and it was shockingly good. Each egg popped with a slow push of the tongue against the roof of your mouth and let out a burst of flavor that was unrivaled in any caviar I had previously eaten. Gathered only two days before, according to our server, what it lacked in provenance it made up for in taste. Still, this was but a few small spoonfuls, and The Husband had more or less given up. He relaxed, thinking he was correct.

Then came Tempura of Rock Shrimp. Dagmara let out a little squeal of delight upon seeing and smelling the vanilla bean–skewered shrimp as they made their way to our table. This was a personal favorite of hers. Visually arresting and sitting carefully in what the staff called "the squid"—a stainless-steel base with six vertical prongs to gently grip the tempura—this was the first shot across the bow of The Husband's resistance. There is no way anyone could not like this. First of all, it was deep-fried shrimp with a bit of candied Meyer lemon and cranberry compote, hardly a challenging taste for any palate. But the genius of the dish lay in the use of the warmed vanilla bean as an aromatic handle. It is said that most men not only love the smell of vanilla, but that it has an almost aphrodisiac quality. Whatever the case, the combination was delicious and the method of eating it was anything but formal: Pick up the vanilla bean with your hand, tilt your head back, bite the shrimp off the end. The Husband liked this one, I am sure, as his only statement was, "Holy shit." We all laughed and the waiters smiled because they knew—they had seen this many times before. And they also knew what was coming next.

As the table fell into a blissful silence, four waiters quickly appeared, each carrying a long, slender plate. The first thing I saw was a giant hard-boiled egg. The waiters placed the plates before us in synchronized fashion, and three of them disappeared, leaving Scott at the end of the table. "Any guesses?"

"An ostrich egg."

"Hell, an elephant egg!"

"No. This is a new one," he paused for effect and smiled. "Balloon of Mozzarella with heirloom tomatoes, some basil puree, olive oil, sea salt, pepper. Inside the mozzarella balloon you will find tomato water, and that will serve to incorporate all of these garnishes. Enjoy." With that he left the four of us staring at this work of art on a plate, wondering how to deface it properly.

The plate was beautiful. The balloon of cheese was absurdly large, and the heirloom tomatoes—red, yellow, green zebra, brandywine—had been cut into geometric shapes that temporarily obscured their identity as tomatoes. There were green streaks of basil puree, and a pile of sea salt, itself composed of tiny pyramid-shaped crystals, sat in a far corner of the plate. I gingerly cut into the bottom half of the mozzarella balloon, surprised to find not a huge hunk of cheese, but rather a thin, indeed balloon-like, shell. The tomato water poured out and the mozzarella deflated slowly. The tomatoes were exceptionally well chilled, the basil and olive oil perfectly combined, the tomato water sweet and salty.

"This guy is a frickin' genius. Seriously." The battle for The Husband was over. And it was won with, essentially, a really fancy caprese salad. Genius indeed.

Of course, at this point in the meal we had not even gotten to anything resembling a main course. These were but the preliminaries. They were clearly designed to set the stage, to awaken not only the diners' palates but also to open their minds. Here is caviar—from Michigan. Here is a jumbo fried shrimp—with a vanilla-bean aroma. Here is a caprese salad—though you won't figure that out until tomorrow. This was my third or fourth full dinner under chef Achatz, but I was starting to understand, however faintly, his method. And it was illuminated not by reflecting on my own experience, but rather by watching a reluctant diner be won over completely. I sat there silently cheering on the kitchen, wondering what would happen next.

The meal continued for four more hours, twenty-four courses in all. The Husband did not want another bite, he assured the waiters. If he did, no doubt the kitchen would have made sure he didn't leave hungry. We were the only patrons left, and it was near midnight on a Thursday—late for suburbia. And perhaps to ensure that we would eventually leave, chef Achatz appeared from the kitchen, sauntered over to our table, put his hands on his hips, and said, "So, how did we do?"

A twenty-year-old kid cooked this? You have got to be kidding me!

We all had that reaction. Grant Achatz looked much younger than his years, and he was young to begin with—only twenty-nine. He was thin, not particularly tall, good-looking and clean-cut, but in every way—and not in a bad way—average. I suppose we were expecting a middle-aged, overweight, Hollywood casting version of a mad chef. The ladies were smitten. A waiter appeared with a glass of champagne for everyone, including Chef, and he pulled up a chair and sat with us. We all talked at once, telling him with great inebriated enthusiasm what he must have known we'd say: we loved it, it was great, how did you do that? But as the conversation became more natural he asked questions that were more probing: Why do you feel the shrimp is such a powerful course, when after all it's just fried shrimp? Were you put off by the fact that there were leaves and sticks in a bowl surrounding your food? He listened to the answers and you could see that he actually cared. Sure it was nice to get compliments, but here was a rare chance to measure his audience, to see if intent met with reaction.

I like to talk and often unintentionally dominate a conversation, and yet this time I became unusually silent. I watched him listen—it was an unusual situation, this young artist who is not only talented but also measured and smart. This was the first moment that I thought that Grant would one day soon be far from here, and that perhaps, vaguely, in some way I should be involved.

The next morning I searched the Internet for the book *Blue Trout and Black Truffles: The Peregrinations of an Epicure*, which was then out of print, found a copy on Alibris.com, and had it sent to chef Achatz as a way of saying thank you. That book began an e-mail correspondence between us.

The week before Dagmara's thirty-fourth birthday, I sent chef Achatz the following e-mail:

> Chef:
> As you know, we are coming in again next Wednesday. Sorry to come back so soon, but there is nowhere we would rather celebrate Dag's birthday.
> Incidentally, she is ethnically Latvian, speaks Japanese, and loves Thai food.
> Good Luck!
> Nick

I knew the e-mail would ruin his weekend, and I felt bad about it. There was no way he would read three disparate ethnic references and simply give us the set menu. He had five days to construct a meal for Dagmara based on those hints, and he would also have us as an audience for the first time because we had reserved the kitchen table on Henry's recommendation.

We were seated at a table that was elevated and directly across from the pass. Grant's and the sous chefs' backs were to us, but we could watch them plating the food for other guests as we arrived.

After a champagne cocktail was mixed before us, Grant turned around and came toward our table. "Hey, happy birthday, Dagmara. You guys ready?"

He had a bit of gleam in his eye and looked at me with a tilt of his head as if to say, "What, is that all you've got? Latvian with a bit of Asian?" That is a look that I have since come to know well. Instantly, I was eager to see what he had come up with. But the first course had us worried.

One of the chefs, Nathan, brought over two black perfume atomizers about the length of my forefinger and placed them before us. "Virtual Shrimp Cocktail," is all he said, until Dagmara and I looked at each other and began to laugh. "Should we spray ourselves with it? Do we smell bad?" she asked. The other chefs were all looking over their shoulders to gauge our reaction and it wasn't going well. We were laughing but we weren't…eating. We had no idea what to do. Unlike the waiters out front, the chefs didn't have the quick comebacks, and Nathan simply said, "Spray it into your mouth." Okay.

It did, of course, taste like a shrimp cocktail. The initial flavor was shrimp and tomato that lingered a bit, followed by the horseradish burn at the back of your throat. But it was ephemeral, just a mist after all. We looked at each other and thought, "Wait, this is what this guy wants to do when he has a willing audience?" I thought that maybe we, or he, had bitten off more than we could…well, not chew.

I need not have worried, of course. What was to follow was, quite simply, the best meal of my life.

On that night Dagmara and I dined not only with each other, but also with a kitchen staff that exuded passion for their jobs. I had visited other commercial kitchens and had eaten at other kitchen tables, but I had never seen anything like Achatz's kitchen. First of all, it was quiet, but not the absence-of-a-yelling-chef kind of quiet. It was nearly silent. Motions were slow and refined. No one was in a hurry. Trinna, the expediter at the head of the pass, would call out "Table 14, 2 Tour, 1 Veg Fish okay," and the team would acknowledge the order in near unison by repeating exactly what she had said. The kitchen had a melodic rhythm. Occasionally, Achatz would ask something like, "Chef, how are we on the goose?" and someone would answer, "Now, Chef." Grant would look left, move his arm 20 degrees, and there would be the goose sitting on a round metal sheet ready to be plated.

The only disruption we witnessed was when Dave Carrier actually raised his voice and shot one of the chefs a vicious look, then swung back around and asked hastily for some Darjeeling tea. We had been watching Grant pains-takingly put a plate together with tweezers for about fifteen minutes during our previous courses, and it seemed that he had just thrown away whatever it was he was working on. Clearly, something had gone wrong and it would take time to fix it. Carrier and the other chefs had swung into action, hastily concocting an unplanned course to buy Grant time.

Once replated, Grant brought over the next course. A carefully con-structed matrix of tiny minted melon balls, alternating between the green of honeydew and the orange of cantaloupe, sat beneath a semi-melted layer of prosciutto that was sliced so impossibly thin it was almost translucent. It was an absolutely gorgeous dish.

"What happened to the first one?" I asked.

"Never did this one before. It didn't work like I expected," said Grant very matter-of-factly.

The menu continued on like that. Original Achatz creations, often devoid entirely of identifiable time, place, or cultural references, interspersed with ingredients and preparations that clearly referenced Dagmara's favorite ethnic cuisines: Kumamoto Oysters with Sapporo Beer and Ginger, Geoduck Clam with Sushi Rice, and deconstructed sushi flavors with wasabi, nori, and sesame all riffed off of Japanese cuisine. Kiwi seeds with coconut and lime, a curried skate wing with mango, and charcoal grilled pineapple all hinted at Thai flavors.

But the showstopper came in the middle of the meal. Latvian sorrel soup with smoked ham hocks and quail eggs. Born and raised in America by par-ents who fled Latvia under Russian occupation, Dagmara grew up as a first-generation American: firmly rooted in the United States but with language and cultural ties to her ancestry. Placed before her at this meal, in the midst of the kitchen staff that had made it, was not just a soup but a bit of her child-hood. She laughed even as she teared up a bit. Achatz had hit the home run.

When we finished the meal I knew that no one, anywhere in the world that night, had enjoyed a better meal. Not only were we privileged to eat it but also to watch the care and craftsmanship with which it was made. So when Grant came over I told him just that. "Chef, at some point, you know, you are going to need to move on from here. If you ever decide to do that, I would like to build a restaurant with you."

"What kind of place would you want to build?" he asked.

"I am not in the restaurant business. It would be your place, your ideas, and your vision. But all I know is that there is a disconnect here between the kitchen and the front-of-house that I never realized before tonight. If you took care of that, you would have the best restaurant in the world."

"I think our service here is great," he said quietly.

"It is," I replied, "the best service anywhere. I am talking about the decor, the art, and the room. You put your food with the same quality service in the city, with design that aligns with the modernity of the food…well…" I trailed off, not wanting to seem rude.

We paid the absurdly reduced bill and left a hefty tip that we hoped would be shared with the kitchen.

I wasn't expecting that to be my last meal at Trio under chef Achatz. I also wasn't expecting the e-mail from Grant that I received a week later.

Dear Mr. Kokonas,

I very much enjoyed cooking for you and Dagmara on her birthday. I hope you both had a great time.

Chris Gerber had told me previously that you inquired about speaking to me and I had only assumed it was because you wanted to discuss business. The truth is, that happens with some regularity. I have been approached by several customers who wanted to invest in a restaurant with me. I have had some offers from other restaurants who want me to move to New York or Los Angeles to take over their restaurants. I wasn't terribly interested in either opportunity—one because I was not ready to build my own restaurant, and the other because I did not want to be fit into someone else's vision.

Last night I had a chance to watch you just as you had a chance to watch us. I noticed that you and Dagmara cared about the food and considered the technique and presentation. I admit that I listened in to your discussions intently. It was therefore not surprising when you mentioned to me that you would want to talk to me about building a restaurant.

When I asked you what kind and you answered that you had no idea . . . well, that was the perfect answer.

If you are serious I would welcome the opportunity to speak with you about my business plan. If not, no problem.

I will always welcome the opportunity to cook for you both and genuinely appreciate your support of Trio and me.

Sincerely,

Grant

I read the e-mail from Grant at 6:00 A.M., ran upstairs just as Dagmara was waking up and said, "We're going to build a restaurant with Grant!"

We scheduled a meeting at my house.

What do you cook for lunch for a world-class chef? I was far more worried about that than I was about the business at hand. After considering various intricate menus, I settled on not cooking at all—that was safest. I bought fresh honeydew melon, prosciutto di Parma, some aged Parmesan reggiano, some olives, and prepared a basic antipasti plate. At the last minute I decided to make some pasta and fresh marinara as well.

Grant strolled up my front walk, took off his peacoat to reveal a plain white T-shirt, black pants, and clogs, and shook my hand formally and with purpose. In the other hand he carried a business plan. We intended to impress each other.

He handed me a packet entitled "Business Plan for AG" and I invited him into my kitchen. I casually served up the melon and prosciutto that I had painstakingly arranged. He was quiet and reserved, sizing me up, looking over my house to see if I was the type of guy who could afford the restaurant he wanted to build.

"Do you know why four-star restaurants have tablecloths?" Grant asked me as we started into our conversation.

"I suppose it's because it feels luxurious. Fine white linens look and feel good. They are soft to the touch, beautifully made..."

Grant interrupted, "No, not really. It's because the table under the tablecloth is shitty. It's usually a piece of plywood bound to a wobbly base that is cheap and barely balanced. You may not recognize that consciously, but you know it, you can feel it."

"You know what I want?" Grant asked, not waiting for my answer. "I want beautiful tables. Bare tables. Black ones."

And so began the design process for our restaurant.

After the antipasti we retreated to my home office and sat down. I leafed through his business plan and could tell that he had spent time writing it. It was fourteen pages long, clearly organized, and well thought out. But it lacked a certain analytical rigor and was made from an online template. I was impressed with his effort, but I only put so much credence in business plans anyway.

Grant wanted to walk me through the plan, but I stopped him and said, "Look. We can get this done, I don't think it will be a problem to find the money or time or the space to do it. But I need to know that we will be friends. I need to learn more about you. If we can't be friends then I don't want to do this. The process of building this from scratch will suck at times. It will be difficult and stressful, and if we don't trust each other implicitly and see eye-to-eye, then I don't want to be involved."

For the first time since he walked in the door Grant seemed at a loss. He spoke slowly, choosing his words. "I'm not really friends with any of my coworkers. We work. We don't really hang out."

"We won't be coworkers. We'll be business partners. That's different." I could tell that he thought I was nuts, so we adjourned back to the kitchen and I heated up the pasta with marinara.

Grant sat down in my dining room and took the first bite. Looking up he asked, "Would you be terribly offended if I asked for some salt?" I realized immediately that I had forgotten to salt the marinara. None. Zero. "Not at all," I said, retreating to the kitchen to grab some sea salt. Grant looked up at me as he vigorously salted the pasta. One big pinch, then another. There was a shit eating grin on his face. He openly mocked my sauce.

Apparently my pasta lacked a certain…rigor. I smiled—the friendship part wouldn't be a problem.

"Totally bare tables?" I asked.

"Yeah. It would look really striking and different. The plates and stainless will pop against the wood. It will feel strong under your hands." Grant clearly had pictured all this in his head a thousand times. I could see that the business plan was irrelevant compared to the vision he had in his head.

"Is there a four-star restaurant anywhere with bare tables? Where do you put the silverware? What about when a water glass sweats and it goes all over the wood with nothing to absorb it?" My list of concerns was long.

We sat at my computer and did what we would do a thousand times during the course of creating our new restaurant: We consulted Google.

In this case, the quick survey was that no, there was not a top-30 restaurant in the world that had bare tables. The dew point of water could be calculated with a simple formula, and we could refrigerate water just above that temperature so that a glass would not sweat when placed on the table. Laundering fine linens for twenty-two tables, fifty weeks a year would cost approximately $42,000 annually. We could build mahogany tables for less. It all made perfect sense.

And just like that we had our first design mantra for the new restaurant—no tablecloths. More important, we could tell instantly that we spoke the same language, we enjoyed challenging each other, and we got along well.

The scariest part, for me at least, was over.

"Look, Nick. Grant is a genius, but don't put half-a-buck into a restaurant. I know people who have invested in restaurants, and they do it because they want a reservation and they get emotionally wrapped up in the romance of it. It's like a charitable donation. You will never see your money again."

I was driving to a coffee shop with Greg Callegari, the hedge-fund manager with whom I had been working for the past four months. Greg was in his late forties and ran a fund-of-funds that had a few hundred million in assets. Well dressed and relaxed in an old-world-Italian-via-New-York manner, he seemed like he should always have an espresso in one hand and a phone in the other—and he usually did. In his world, "half-a-buck" meant half a million dollars, and he gave his advice with his usual smile, shake of the head, and easygoing laugh.

"I know, I know," I replied, "but this will be different. It's not really a restaurant. It's going to be more like a performance-art theater, something that no one in this country has really done before."

"You're not helping your case." He smiled again and almost giggled. It did sound absurd when put like that. "Look, you're gonna be feeding people, right? In my book that's a restaurant. And in the real world, investors get screwed when they invest in restaurants. But that's okay; they know that going into it. They are patrons of the arts; it's an ego thing for them. They want a fancy living room where they can take clients and say they own the place, get the best table. All I'm saying is sure, help Grant out, but put in an amount of money that you can afford to lose. Tell me you're not going to put in five hundred. You don't even know the guy."

I would come to hear that a great deal. This was a rich man's folly, and while it's okay to get a tax write-off and hobnob with a great chef, it would be stupid to drop everything and build a restaurant—especially with someone you actually met for the first time a week ago.

"Greg, I don't think you understand what I'm saying. I am going to close up the fund and build this with Grant. I know how my money will be spent because I'll be the one spending it. I appreciate the risk you took in helping me start the fund, but you can tell that my heart's not in it, right?"

Greg looked at me with a smile and shrug of the shoulders. I think deep down he knew that I wasn't in love with the hedge-fund world, that I wasn't putting in an all-out effort. He had seen it all in business and wasn't easy to frazzle. "All I'm saying," he said calmly, "is to take a few days before you decide. Figure out what this guy is about. For all you know he is an addict or something. These guys—chefs—are unstable. You don't want to spend that kind of money to find out he has three kids in Mendocino and an ex-wife chasing him across the country."

"He does have two kids, and they're living with him in Evanston," I replied. "He was the sous chef at The French Laundry at twenty-two or some such shit. I've eaten all over the world and I'm telling you, he is the best right now."

"Married?"

"No. Living with her."

"See?"

"Whatever. The real reason I brought you here was to get you to invest." I looked over to him in the passenger seat and smiled a wicked, ironic smile. "I suggest half a million because this is a fantastic opportunity, but will take an amount as low as a hundred thousand should you lack vision."

I had considered Greg's objections myself. Since the e-mail from Grant and the subsequent meeting at my house, my mind raced constantly through the scenarios. Why did I want to do this? How could this fail? Hell, how could it succeed? Would it really happen?

Part of me thought that some objection would surely arise that would make doing it impossible. Part of me hoped that I could find a graceful exit before I did too much damage to Grant and his career. I searched for reasons to not get involved, and there were many. Anyone I asked, even casually, about their experience in restaurants told me tales of hardship, failure rates, and lack of profitability. I mentioned my plan to a chef I knew who owned three successful suburban restaurants, and his response was blunt: "You seem like you have a great life. Why would you want to do that to yourself?"

And yet. And yet.

These were all of the same objections I faced when I started out as a floor trader. Other traders would tell me, "You seem like a smart kid, why the hell do you want into this crazy business?" The saying on the Chicago floors was that only two out of every hundred guys break even their first year, and out of those only one out of a hundred becomes a millionaire. Usually, though, they were telling me that just as the valet brought around their Porsche. The restaurant business seemed similar—long odds, difficult hours—but with huge rewards if you succeeded. The chef who told me not to get into the business was himself now building a fourth restaurant. If the first three were so bad, why would you build another one? I never really got an answer to that question.

I left the breakfast with Greg determined to press on at least another week, to see what happened. But either way, I knew for sure I would close the start-up hedge fund. I couldn't be sure that the restaurant was a good idea, but it was clear that my trading days were, for now at least, over. And that clarity felt pretty good.

When I got home I called Grant and told him that I quit the hedge fund, and that much at least was definitely true. I did not, however, voice my hesitancy or concerns.

"Good. Because I gave notice to Henry today."

"What?" I panicked. "Even if we go through with this it's not the kind of thing you just open a month from now. I mean, we have a business plan but those are total bullshit. This could take years to put together, eighteen months at least."

"I want to be open by the fall. I think we can be open by November. Why should this take more than nine months? Anyway, I can't work at Trio while we build the restaurant, and you quit, right? So let's go."

Maybe Grant could sense that I would waver, or maybe he was just nuts. Or maybe he was bluffing. Either way, I just felt scared more than anything. Maybe Greg was right. Maybe putting that much money behind a guy you don't know is just plain stupid.

But my gut was telling me the opposite.

"We need to send out a packet to potential investors. Something sexy, not a typical business plan," I said.

"Let's send 'em food. That's what I do, after all."

"Yeah, and I'll work out the rest of the plan. Can you come by this afternoon?"

"No, I told Henry I would be here for the next two months. I owe him that. But Monday is no problem. I'll be there at ten."

That would give me the weekend to figure out a way to tell Grant that I was out. By Wednesday he could tell Henry that he wasn't going anywhere, that his deal fell through. It would only be a mild embarrassment.

But when I got home, I sat down at my computer and started writing:

AG will fulfill the culinary and aesthetic vision of chef Grant Achatz. At twenty-nine years old, chef Achatz has already received two of the most prestigious national awards available to young chefs. In 2002 he was named one of *Food & Wine*'s Top Ten Best New Chefs, and in 2003 he was awarded the James Beard Foundation's Rising Star of the Year Award. Under the direction of chef Achatz, Trio Restaurant was granted its fifth Mobil Star—an honor bestowed upon only thirteen restaurants in North America. With the establishment of AG, chef Achatz will create a restaurant experience that will be completely unique and will compete with the very best in the world. . . .

Three hours later I had a fourteen-page executive summary that told the story of Grant, the vision for the restaurant, and the plan to raise funds and search for real estate. It was all of my thoughts, all of my conversations and e-mails with Grant, distilled into an explanation of why this restaurant needed to exist. It flowed easily.

I wasn't writing it to convince investors; I was writing it to convince myself. By the end of the day I had reread the plan twenty times, and despite my better judgment I e-mailed Grant:

> Chef,
>
> Find attached the investor packet overview and revised spreadsheets. Let's talk on Monday about how to make this look aesthetically beautiful, and if we can send food, that would be pretty cool . . . but that's your department.
>   —Nick

My overall plan for raising the money for the restaurant was pretty simple: go to the people I had done business with for the past ten years and convince them that we would be building the best restaurant in the country. Just as important, I'd let them know that I was in this as a full-time gig and would personally be watching over their money.

I quickly laid out an operating structure that was both simple and effective. The restaurant would consist of three companies—the restaurant itself, an investor group, and the management company. Grant and I would be the only people who were members of all three groups and therefore had a controlling interest. But the fact that I was also the biggest investor meant that I would always have the other investors' best interests in mind when making decisions. After hearing all of the horror stories about investors getting screwed in restaurant deals, or having kick-out clauses in contracts as soon as things got good, I wanted to create a structure that rewarded investors long-term and that kept them interested in future projects.

Just as important, I would stress to Grant that we needed to keep the scope of the project small. We couldn't have a giant Bonnet stove that cost a few hundred thousand dollars. That's just a chef's ego in the kitchen—like a sports car. I called it the "dick in the kitchen." Grant was doing brilliant work at Trio with nothing fancy, and he thought we could build the place in 3,500 square feet.

I realized that if the restaurant revenue was 50 percent greater than Trio's, then that 50 percent would be almost all profit. The more I thought about it, the more I couldn't imagine it not working out like that. If Trio was in Chicago, wouldn't more people come simply because it was easier to get to? Out-of-town business travelers weren't willing to go out to Evanston, but if Trio were in downtown Chicago it would be packed, right?

Before Grant came over on Monday I decided to call Jim Hansen to let him know that I was going to be closing up the hedge fund and that we really were going to build the restaurant. I could always count on Jim for a levelheaded reaction that would be a good gauge for the more emotional responses of others. Instead, it fell squarely in line with what I'd been hearing.

"Clearly you have too much time on your hands. Chill out for a few days, then decide what you want to do." This was the advice I was getting from everyone I trusted, it seemed. And it was not what I needed to hear. Grant would be coming by in a few hours, and I wanted to appear confident and calm. Instead, my most trusted friends were telling me in every way possible to slow down. I went to the kitchen to see what Dagmara thought.

"Jim thinks I'm stupid to be doing this," I said. "Greg thinks I'm stupid to be doing this. It's your money, too. I'm talking about putting up five hundred thousand dollars on a restaurant. What do you think?"

"If you want to do this—if you need to build it—then you should build it, regardless of what anyone thinks."

"Even you?" I asked.

"I think you should build it," she said. "I think Grant is a genius. I thought that before you did, right? Who wanted to get the standing reservation at Trio?"

Grant arrived at my house at ten on the dot. He pulled up in his beat-up Ford and walked to the door looking exactly as he had at our previous meeting: wet hair, unbuttoned peacoat, white T-shirt, semi-wrinkled black pants, black chef's clogs. I opened the door as he was about to ring the bell.

"I just want to let you know that I'm freaking out about this," I blurted out. Perhaps not exactly the strategy I had planned in my head, but a very honest assessment.

Grant smiled and laughed. "That is *not* what I needed to hear right now. I am catching shit at home for quitting Trio without even knowing you. She has a point."

"Well, if we screw this up we'll both be unemployed," I said.

"Yeah, but you seem to be doing a bit better than I am," he said, laughing, gesturing at my house.

"So are we really going to do this? I mean, it feels like we don't really have a clue what to do next. I know you can run a restaurant, but can you build one?" I asked.

Grant looked at me, gave a grin, and said, "How hard can it be?" He flopped his coat on the back of one of my dining room chairs and laid out a few sheets of paper. On them were sketches of some logos for the restaurant. Another sheet had a few kitchen layout sketches, and another had some dining room layouts. "I want Martin to design the restaurant," he said, referring to the designer who worked with Trio.

I looked down at the sheets of paper and despite Grant's bravado, I was not feeling equally confident. The logo sketch looked like the doodle from the back of a high school kid's notebook. The kitchen layout had no stove at all—I guess I didn't need to worry about the Bonnet, I needed to worry that Grant wanted to invent a new stove completely. And as far as I knew, Martin was not an architect.

"Martin is the guy who designed the gadgets that the food sits on?" I asked.

"No. Martin is the guy who designed the *serviceware* for Trio. If you're going to be a big-shot restaurant owner you need to learn the lingo, Nick."

"That's great, Chef. But you need to learn what an architect does. There are things like electrical plans, plumbing, and, oh, I don't know, walls and such, that will need to be built. And these guys called 'engineers' work for the city and have to approve it all. You have to be a licensed architect to get those approvals."

"Martin can design it, then we can have an architect work out the details," Grant said. "I trust him. He's the only one who really gets what I do."

"But you'll be paying twice then—and architects charge about 15 percent of construction cost."

"Seriously? That's crazy."

"Seriously. Not to mention that I doubt any architect worth anything will want to partner with a designer who has precisely no experience building a restaurant, or anything else for that matter."

"Speaking of which," Grant said, "I want to get something clear from the beginning. This is my restaurant. I want to be the chef/owner, or I don't want to do it."

"Chef/owner it is, then. I don't really care about titles. You shouldn't either. You should care whether or not you are going to get real equity in the place, unlike most chefs who simply get the title but don't own much. As soon as our investors are paid back plus a preferred return, we jointly vest into 50 percent ownership through the management company. Plus you'll be given shares in the investor group for contributions you make during build-out, or for anything that we receive for free from manufacturers who give us something based on your reputation. I'm trying to structure this so you have real ownership, and I am doing that out of self-interest so that you don't decide to go anywhere in five years. So given all of that, we will call you the Grand Pooh-Bah or whatever the hell you want, okay? And I promise never to tell you what to send out of your kitchen, or to ever deliver a plate to a table. Deal?"

"Sounds fair. But I am chef/owner. It means something to me. It's the dream of every chef and has been mine since I was a little kid." Grant said this with real emotion.

"Okay. Chef/owner. I'm just calling you 'G' from now on," I said, laughing.

"No. Don't."

CHAPTER 15

Once we got rolling on the business plan, things flowed. Every day I would write up ideas—about the dining room, our identity, serviceware ideas for Martin, and anything else that came to mind—and e-mail them to Nick. He would send me just as many drafts regarding raising money, equity splits, cash flow projections, and build-out costs. Then we would simply comment on each other's work. It was efficient and satisfying to work in this way while still running Trio at full tilt. We sent literally dozens of messages a day.

We discussed names for the restaurant all the time. Ideas like Avant-Garde and Achatz and Grant came from Nick. But I didn't want an eponymous restaurant. I wanted a name that meant something about the philosophy of the place. Then I remembered that a cook had mentioned the word "Alinea" to me. It was that funny, backward "p" symbol that indicated a new paragraph or a new train of thought. I hastily put together a list of names in an e-mail, snuck "Alinea" in the middle, and sent it to Nick. His reply was quick: "Chef. I Googled 'Alinea,' and it's the best possible name for our restaurant. The rest of the names are okay. But that one is great. We are done."

We had a name we loved right from the beginning. We did not, however, have the most important thing—an actual building.

When I sent Nick ideas for dining room and kitchen layouts, he would simply write back, "Fantastic but largely irrelevant until we find a building. To a certain extent, what we find, and what we can afford, will dictate the design."

I didn't like the sound of that. I imagined a great blank canvas where I could create the space I wanted without limitation. I was free to think of tables that came out of walls without legs, dining spaces that could transform over the course of an evening, and a kitchen that was a series of open work surfaces flexible enough to accommodate any station at any time. Whenever I brought up such ideas, however, Nick seemed to shoot them down, and it was getting more than a bit annoying.

On a Monday morning at ten sharp Nick was out in front of my house in Evanston. He wanted to meet early, before our meeting with a broker. I got in the front seat and he handed me a set of huge maps.

"Dagmara blew these up at Kinko's. These are the neighborhoods we will likely want to locate Alinea in: Lincoln Park. Gold Coast. Michigan Avenue offshoots, maybe the gallery district in River West, maybe West Randolph Street. How well do you know Chicago?"

"I spend a hundred hours a week in a kitchen. Before that I lived in Napa, before that in Michigan."

"I thought you worked at Trotter's?" he asked.

"Yeah, for a whole eight weeks."

"Well, we're screwed then. I've lived here my whole life and I get lost five blocks from my house," he said, laughing. "Anyway, Dagmara knows I'm a directional idiot, so she gave me these maps and three highlighters—red, yellow, green. Mark the good ones in green. Pretty basic, but at least we'll have an idea of which streets might work and which won't."

"So we just drive around?"

"Yeah. Let's just drive around and see what strikes you."

We headed east toward Sheridan Road, then south at Lake Shore Drive through Rogers Park and into Chicago. The first place we landed was Lincoln Park.

"This is currently the most upscale neighborhood in Chicago. Used to be the Gold Coast over by the lake and Dearborn east of here. I guess it still is, but now all the younger families with money are building or buying around here. Everything is getting torn down and rebuilt, most of the time on multiple lots." He pointed to a massive house on a beautiful, tree-lined street. "What do you figure that costs, Chef?"

"I have no idea. Looks sweet, though. Seven fifty? A million?"

"Ha. Three and a half to four is my guess. Could be more; I can't see what kind of yard they have back there. Lots are going for eight hundred at least. No house, just the land."

"Who the hell is buying them?" I really couldn't fathom it.

"Guys like me!" He laughed at his joke.

"I'm clearly in the wrong profession."

We turned off the residential street and on to Armitage. "And there is Trotter's, G."

I hadn't been back since I left, and it all felt so different from this perspective. "Well, we can't locate around here. That would just be stupid. We can't be so close to Trotter's."

"Why not? Let's just buy out McShane's Exchange across the street from Trotter's and call the place 'Fucked' instead of Alinea."

He was waiting to deliver the punch line so I played along. "Fucked? As in we are fucked for doing this?"

"No, Chef. Fucked as in 'F-U-C-T.' Fuck You, Charlie Trotter." He wailed with laughter, practically drooling.

I smiled but tried not to laugh. "You won't hear me repeating that."

"Come on, Chef. You'll kick his ass. He's been here fifteen years. One of the best meals I ever had was at Trotter's in 1994. It opened my eyes to haute cuisine. But it hasn't changed much except to put in more tables, and that's never a good thing. Every fifteen or twenty years a new kid comes to town and takes over. You're that kid. Twenty years from now, some kid will kick your ass. It's the way of the world."

We went street by street as best we could, then hopped to a different neighborhood and did the same. By the time our meeting with the broker came around we had hit the five major areas that Nick and Dagmara had come up with, highlighted any streets with commercial properties, and had surprisingly little green on our maps. Then he pulled out another set of maps.

"My sister-in-law Anita has a demographic mapping program—

she moonlights doing maps for their brother Edgar while she's in school. She was nice enough to drop these in there. Those stars in blue are all of the three-star restaurants in Chicago according to the *Trib* and *Chicago* magazine. The red ones are the four-star restaurants. The overlays are demographic indicators like age, income, stuff like that. Those probably don't matter much for us. But with the exception of Arun's way over here, our map lines up pretty well."

We parked near the gallery district and walked up to the address listed on the e-mail printout from the broker. It was, of course, a closed restaurant.

We met the broker, Kim, out front. A tall, lanky guy with a full head of white hair, he introduced himself to us and couldn't help but look surprised. I was in my usual attire of black pants, white T-shirt, chef's clogs. Nick was in jeans and a pullover shirt.

"So, Edgar tells me you guys are building a restaurant? What kind?"

"Well, it's kind of hard to explain," Nick piped up after an uncomfortable silence. "Grant here is one of the best young chefs in the world. It will be ultrafine dining."

Kim's eyes nearly popped out of his head. You could tell he thought we had precisely no idea what we were doing. "How many seats?"

"Sixty-five," I said.

"And how big of a bar area?"

"No bar. Just sixty-five seats."

Now he was totally confused. "You definitely need a bar. That's where restaurants make all their money," he said, as if to educate us. "So it's like a bistro? You probably don't need something this big, then. Check average?"

"About a hundred and sixty five dollars."

"Per person?!" he nearly shouted. "What the hell kind of food is it? Like Trotter's?"

"Yeah," Nick looked at me and laughed. "His food is exactly like Trotter's."

We headed inside and it looked like an old nightclub. Lighting fix-tures were hanging from the ceiling by cords, and old neon signs were screwed into the wall behind a filthy bar. The space itself was large, but it was bisected by brick arches that made it look like you could at best turn it into a really cheesy Italian restaurant—the kind with a mural of old Italy painted on the wall. We headed to the basement, which looked like a catacomb.

"This would be great for a wine cellar," Kim offered. "Can you imagine those arches stacked with wine?"

"No, not really," I said. "Where's the kitchen?"

"It's over here," he said, motioning to a corner of the basement.

"Naw, I don't need to see it. No kitchens in basements. If the kitchen is in a basement, cross it off your list."

Nick and Kim looked at me for a second, and then Nick spoke up. "Grant, I bet most of these places put the kitchen in the basement so that they could put the seats on the main floor. They're just trying to maximize floor space for seating. The basements rent out at half price or less. So if the asking price is forty-five dollars per square foot, the basement might be an extra twenty dollars, maybe less. Sometimes they throw them in for free."

I paused. No one was considering me in this equation. "Look. That's great and I get that. But you have to understand; the kitchen is where I live. I spend sixteen hours a day there, sometimes more. I want it to be spacious and to be well lit, ideally with daylight. It has to be well cooled, too. Commercial kitchens are too hot and the people and the food suffer because of it. I want this kitchen to be cool. Our cooks will be happier. I will be happier. No basement kitchen."

"Okay," Nick said. "No basement kitchen." He looked at Kim. "I think you get what we're going for here, right? This is not a bis-tro, nor is it really much of a restaurant. Think of it like this: We're building a gallery that happens to have a kitchen and seating. Find us something like that, with tall ceilings but preferably not rustic or wood. We're going for modern. And basements are for storage, not people." He looked at me and made a sarcastic smile.

Kim stared at us for a second as we headed out. He definitely thought we were nuts. We didn't bother going to look at anything else that day. It was just understood that the rest of them were a waste of time.

I spent a few days driving by myself through the neighborhoods, imagining a restaurant facade in this storefront or that. Nothing seemed right. Nick trolled all of the online real estate sites and came up empty, occasionally sending me a few listings for price reference.

Then he called me and said that Kim had put together a few places that might work. So we set up another meeting on a Tuesday and met him in front of Japonais, a huge and hugely successful restaurant in the old Montgomery Ward Catalog House building, which had recently been converted to luxury apartments and upscale retail.

"They have a few really great spaces in here," Kim said when we met him. "Totally new, totally blank spaces. Just concrete floors, stubbed-out utilities, and twenty-foot ceilings."

We met the listing broker and a rep from the building and were escorted into a cavernous space with huge, round pillars. I could easily imagine a grand dining room with a huge kitchen. There was natural light front and back.

"How do you enter off the street?" I asked.

"You don't," the listing agent said. "You have to come through that part of the building that we just went through." She gestured toward the lobby area.

"Can't we just open something up over there?" I pointed to the windows that looked out over a branch of the Chicago River.

"No. The building doesn't want the foot-traffic pattern that way. Bad for the residents."

"So basically, this is inside of a mall," I said.

The building rep had clearly heard this complaint before. This was a totally workable space, but hidden inside a huge, huge building. "We are offering a sizable rent credit against build-out costs," he offered.

Kim seemed surprised that they mentioned this to us so quickly. He and the listing agent were still unsure about us. But I guessed the building rep was desperate. Nick chimed in, "What is 'sizeable,' exactly?"

"Well, that all depends on how much you intend to spend. But three hundred fifty to four hundred thousand dollars is not out of the question. And by the way, chef Achatz, I have eaten at Trio three times and it's extraordinary. I can't wait to see what you build."

This was a first. Someone recognized us and knew that we would have big ambitions. And my reputation could work to our advantage. But I didn't want to be stuck in a residential building, hidden from the street.

"Thanks very much," I said. "However, I don't think this will work, though it is a great space. I really imagine something that has a street presence, that when you think of the restaurant you think of it as a building, not inside of something else."

We headed toward the door. Nick shot me a look, and when we got in the car he said, "I completely agree that that wasn't right, Grant, but if you tell them exactly what you're thinking all the time, they'll simply stop looking for us."

This seemed incredibly stupid to me. "Really? Why? Is it so hard to make a couple of calls, dig through the MLS, and set up some meetings? Isn't that what they do?"

"Yeah, it is. But if they think we're going to say no to everything, then we won't be worth their time."

"Hell, he'll make more on one deal than I do in three months. Seems worth it to me."

"Okay. But don't be negative. Tell me what you think, but don't tell them."

"But if I don't tell him, then he won't know what I want!" This was absurd!

"You don't know what you want! You just sound wishy-washy and inexperienced."

And that much was true. We were exploring neighborhoods and

buildings and I was learning by elimination what I didn't want. But now I knew.

"Okay. Here's what I want. I want a building that is all by itself, a stand-alone structure. It needs natural light. The kitchen needs to be on the first floor, and ideally the whole thing is on one floor. So I need a one-story building on one of those streets we highlighted in green or yellow. Thirty-five hundred square feet. You know how much it needs to cost, I don't. So you deal with that part after we find it."

"I'm pretty sure that the building you just described doesn't exist on those streets. We've been up and down them a dozen times." We had been at this for a few weeks. News of my impending departure from Trio was starting to leak, and to be sure, I was itching to tell people and the press myself. Nick was constantly reminding me that this might take a year or two, when I kept insisting that we could open in six months.

We went to see two more former restaurants. One was near the Hancock building and had a submarket lease and seven years left but was asking $600,000 to buy a load of crappy tables and kitchen equipment that we would never use. The second space was three doors down from Paul Kahan's great restaurant Blackbird. The public space wasn't bad, but the kitchen reminded me of the co-op walk-in I cleaned out when I was a kid. Whoever left just walked out of the place and left things to rot. Why wouldn't the building owner clean that out before showing it to a prospective tenant? Everyone involved seemed lazy and I was growing exasperated by the process. We told Kim that neither would work and that we really, really didn't want to see any former restaurants since we didn't want to buy stuff that we wouldn't end up using.

"Well, you know what they're really selling is the liquor license, occupancy permit, and the value of the lease if it's submarket. It can take six or eight months to get a liquor license and costs, well, a lot of money. I've heard forty or fifty thousand dollars to get one these days."

I looked at Nick and he didn't seem surprised by this. We got back in my car and headed toward Lincoln Park, where there was one more space he wanted to show us, which wasn't a restaurant. When we got about halfway there I spied something across the street.

"You know, hold on a second. Pull over here. The other day I was driving around here and saw a sign hanging off a building . . . there!" I pointed at a building on Halsted Street and Nick pulled over. Kim was in the car behind us and he pulled over as well. We hopped out of the car. "What does that say?"

A sign hanging off the building read: FOR LEASE. 1,000 TO 5,000 SQ. FT. DIVISIBLE. It was indeed a stand-alone building, but it was ugly. A woman sat at a desk in the front window. "Let's go have a look?"

"Sure," Nick said, though he and Kim looked skeptical.

I knocked on the door and the woman came around to open it. "Can I help you?" she said.

"Hi, I was just driving through the area and saw your sign. We're looking for a space for a . . ." Kim cut me off.

"Hi. I'm a real estate broker representing some clients who are looking for a building in this area. If it's convenient could we come in and look around? Is the owner on premises?"

The woman paused a second and looked at the three of us skeptically. "I'm Denise Trammer and I own this building. I'm an attorney, and I lease out space to a number of small businesses—some of them may be moving." She glanced over her shoulder like she was sharing a secret. "You can come in if you want, just please don't tell any of the tenants that you're looking to rent. Some of them may be kicked out, and I don't want them to know yet."

The exchange felt really odd. First of all, here was Kim sticking himself in the middle of the situation and cutting me off. Then there was Denise, who was renting her building, but maybe not. We were supposed to pretend like we were clients of hers and talk to no one.

There was a small hallway with drapes that covered some stairs, then we turned left down another hall and saw a small travel agency in the front half and what looked like a computer drafting firm in the back. We walked quickly through the first floor, barely glancing in, and no one gave us any notice. Then we headed up a back stairway to the second floor.

Wow. The second floor was completely empty—just one big open space with a drop ceiling and those awful ceiling tiles like they have in high school. Giant bulbous skylights dotted the ceiling. We walked toward the front of the building where a bunch of computers, each with ten screens, sat on desks. Printouts and papers were strewn all over the place. A huge marlin hung on the wall.

"Trading firm," Nick said.

"That's what trading firms look like?" I asked.

"Yep." Nick peeked at the screens, still on, and smiled.

Ms. Trammer piped in, "They moved out last week, and I believe I have a tenant taking over this floor soon. Their stuff should have been out of here by now."

"I doubt that," Nick said. "No way they would leave these fired up and walk out the door, except to go to lunch. According to the P/L line at the bottom of MicroHedge they're up twenty-two thousand dollars on that position today." Nick walked casually out of the room and down the front stairs through the curtain. Surprisingly, he kept going, right out the front door. I followed him out, while Kim was left to deal with the owner.

"It's perfect," Nick said.

"You know, I was just thinking the same thing. And I have no idea why."

We grinned at each other, not knowing that the next two months of negotiations would be pure hell.

But we had found Alinea.

"What's the next step?" I asked Nick as we got back in my car. We had said nothing to Kim about loving the space and had dutifully gone through the next building that was on Armitage right near Trotter's—we'd forgotten to tell him about the "Not Near Trotter's" rule.

"I think it's time that I invite Tom Stringer and Steve Rugo to dinner at Trio," Nick suggested. "Can you arrange that for next week sometime?"

"Sure. Who are they?"

"They're the guys who are going to design the place. Steve is an architect. Tom is an interior designer. They do primarily high-end real estate, and I've worked with both of them on my home. I like them and trust them. But most of all, they know how to craft a true luxury experience."

"Wait. That website you sent me to the other day? Those homes looked like they're for old people. Beautiful, to be sure, but not modern at all," I said.

"I agree. But when I say they do the luxury home market, what I mean is that I am by far their poorest client. They're doing work on really high-end stuff. Ten million plus, that kind of thing. They'll be able to source materials, furniture, and fixtures that Martin wouldn't even know exist. We can't design every detail from scratch. Plus, ultimately, if we want to build something remarkable with good flow we'll need a supremely talented design group, and we can't afford to hire one. We've set the budget super low for what you have in your head. Alinea has to make money, but it has to look like there is no way it can."

"Agreed. So how can we afford them if all they do is really expensive builds?"

"We're going to offer them equity ownership in the best restaurant in America in exchange for their services and the ability to purchase goods at wholesale. And it's your job next week to convince them that that's possible."

"Sure. That's easy. That's what we do, Nick."

A week later we were sitting in the lush office conference room—if you could call it that, since it looked more like a fabulous living room—of Tom Stringer Design Partners with Tom and architect Steve Rugo, who came over from his office. They had eaten at Trio two days earlier, and Nick had picked up their check but hadn't attended. "I am the architect of Henry's demise," he had said. "No way I could eat there again." Nick, like everyone, loved Henry.

As usual, our counterparts were impeccably dressed, while we both looked like we just woke up.

"So tell me, Nick," Steve said. "I assume you didn't buy us dinner at Trio because you thought we under-billed you last month." He laughed heartily, and we all joined him. "No. As you probably guessed, Grant and I are going to build a restaurant together, and we'd like you to be the architect and Tom to do the interior design. This in collaboration with Martin Kastner, the designer who is working on our logos, website, and service pieces. And with us, of course."

"That sounds like a fantastic opportunity, Nick. We would love to be a part of it," Tom said immediately.

"Well, there is a catch, Tom," Nick said playfully. "We can't afford your services."

"Did you go broke in the last week, Nick?" Steve asked with a smile.

"No. But we want this to work as a business. We've found a place on Halsted Street that is residential in size. We want it to be very modern, but with a comfortable scale. I think you would both be fantastic at making that happen. But if we treat this like one of the homes you design, we can never make it work financially."

"But it isn't a home, is it?" Tom asked. "A restaurant is much more like creating a stage set. You have all of these people interacting, moving about the space: the waiters, the food carriers, and of course the patrons who literally put on costumes of a sort to go out to a dinner like that. They want to be seen. But they aren't living in it. They come for a few hours and leave. It's very much a set piece."

"And does that mean it can be done more cheaply than a home?" I asked.

"Of course," Tom answered. "But I assume you're trying to build a grand restaurant here. It will need some scale, some central themes. Too often, I think, chefs who have great food that is like art—like yours, Grant—simply strip everything else away and say 'the food is the important thing,' and you're left with a blah room. I'm thinking modern but plush and sexy."

Nick seemed encouraged by this discussion, but I was getting a bit annoyed. Who was this guy, and what did he know about my vision for my restaurant? I fell totally silent and let them talk.

"I agree," Nick said. "But all of that is moot if we can't build the whole thing at a reasonable cost. We want to spend $1.25 million all in. Soup to nuts."

"That includes things like the computers, forks, phones, kitchen, everything?" Steve asked.

"Yep. The whole thing."

"Nick, we spent almost that much building a simple chain restaurant grill on North Avenue. That's nothing for a four-star restaurant."

"I know. Which is why I am going to ask you to do the entire project in exchange for a piece of ownership. We will, of course, cover your expenses. But the rest we get free for the design, and all of the furniture, tables, lamps—anything like that—we don't pay a markup on. In fact, ideally, you would call in some favors or find the best guys who'd want to do it to be involved with the project."

Steve began to giggle. Then it went into a full laugh. "And we want to do that why, exactly?"

"Because in five years this will be the best restaurant in the country, and you will have been the architect of record. And if we do it for that cost, it will actually make money."

The fact was, Nick was always talking about a budget of $1.6 million, but I assumed he was lowballing the number to get a reaction and to account for the usual slippage.

"I see," Steve said, still laughing. But he wasn't laughing at us. Instead, it felt more like he was laughing at the audacity of the proposal—but with a sense of respect. Tom was more reserved and said nothing, and was instead doodling on a pad—apparently already thinking about high-end restaurants.

"Well, that's really all we have for now. We don't want to start the process yet and we haven't even raised any money, at least not formally. But if you're willing to look at our proposal, we're sending something out in a few days."

"Absolutely, Nick. And Grant, I have to tell you that that was the best meal of our lives. Truly. I get to travel to a lot of wonderful places, and that was just exceptional." Tom seemed genuinely moved.

We left and hopped in Nick's car. "Well, that went well, I think," he said.

"Nick, don't take this the wrong way, okay? But that did not go well. It didn't go well at all. I feel like this whole thing has slipped out of my control. I appreciate your efforts, but look, these are your people. The potential investors are your people. I'm over here by myself, and yet this is my restaurant, something I've been planning my whole life. Three weeks ago you had never thought of doing this. Now you're discussing the proper flow of customers. It's . . . well, it's kind of insulting." I didn't mean that to sound as harsh as it did. But it needed to be said. The only person I wanted designing Alinea was me. I wanted a hand in everything.

Nick paused a second, then kind of smiled. "Do you eat out much?" he asked.

"Obviously not, but that's not the point." I could see where he was going with that. "I'm in the kitchen ninety-nine percent of the time, but I still know what makes a great restaurant."

"Exactly. You have been in the kitchen for the last twenty years. Meanwhile, I've been lucky enough to eat all over the world, to travel through Europe, Asia, the U.S. To stay at great hotels with amazing service. I fully admit that I have no idea how to build a restaurant. But we will both be better off once you admit that as well. We need an architect. It doesn't have to be Rugo. Feel free to suggest someone else. You can draw the kitchen on a piece of graph paper all you want, but at some point an architect is going to need to put it in a blueprint for the City of Chicago to approve, and that guy has to be licensed. I trust not only that these guys are willing to help, but that they're more capable than you might imagine."

The rest of the car ride was a bit frosty. I think we both made our points. I wanted a hand in everything. Nick knew that I couldn't do it alone.

"So let's head to an art shop and figure some things out for the investor package," said Nick.

"Yeah, okay.

We headed to Evanston to a small store near my house and searched for papers, folios, and boxes. Then we went to the Container Store to find something to put the food in. We settled on some small vials that were sealable and didn't seem overly lablike.

We headed to Nick's house and reformatted the business plan to fit the unusual paper size—eight inches by eight inches square. I wrote a quick cover letter, and a few hours later we had our prototype investor package: a fancy brown fabric box that had a simple "alinea" symbol on the cover in a gothic-looking script. Inside the box, on the top of the lid, were five small, neatly labeled vials filled with a dehydrated five-course meal: "Dry Martini" on the left, leading all the way through a "Lamb Essence," and finally a "Powdered Crème Brûlée."

Inside were three sections: an executive summary detailing my personal history, the goals for Alinea, and a brief overview of how we intended to manage the build-out; a series of spreadsheets detailing the operation of the restaurant and the structure and payout of the investment; and a press kit consisting of reproductions of some key articles about Trio.

Nick had already spoken to every one of the potential investors personally and assured me that they were all people who would be able to contribute something beyond only money. He stressed over and over, "We only want investors who are smart and for whom this is an inconsequential investment." I had assumed we would have to find dozens of people who would each contribute $10,000. He was targeting the fewest number possible. "This entire package is unnecessary to get the investment. We could just send an e-mail. But I think this shows that we are very serious about doing something different and unusual. These guys see business plans all the time. I guarantee not one of them looked like this. But this won't get us the money. Yes, these guys are also my friends, but they'll negotiate a better rate of return. I would be disappointed if they didn't. It's critical that everyone looks at this as a business, not a restaurant."

Still, I felt all alone in a corner and had no money of my own to contribute. One frequent patron of Trio had always told me that he would invest if I ever started a restaurant. So Dr. Mark Davis, a surgeon from southern Illinois, was included in the list at my insistence.

We cleaned up our presentation and then started an assembly line on Nick's dining room table. Dagmara cut the paper down to size, Nick printed everything out, and I boxed it all up. We shipped them out that night.

"So that's it? Then we wait?" I asked.

"No. I think we follow this up with a dinner," Nick said.

"We can't do a dinner at Trio, that wouldn't be right."

"No. I'm thinking we do a dinner off-site somewhere. Sort of an introduction to the concept."

"The first Alinea dinner . . ."

"Yep. We send out an invite to anyone who comes back interested. And that's where we close it and get commitments."

I had no idea how to do such a dinner logistically. I would have to create a dozen new dishes while running Trio, and then create those outside the Trio kitchen.

"When?" I asked.

"Two weeks from now. We can do it here. In addition to the numbers we need to make everyone realize that they are part of something great, and to make sure they get to know and trust you outside the restaurant setting."

We set a date for May 4, 2004.

ALINEA INVESTORS DINNER
4th May, 2004

AMUSE

CRISPY STRAWBERRY / WASABI

DRY MARTINIS

SAUCISSON A L'AIL / APPLE / MUSTARD SEED

SPOONFUL OF BORSCHT

PUREE OF FOIE GRAS / HONEYDEW MELON SPONGE

CARROT SODA / LEMON DROPS

DUCK SKIN HUNAN STYLE

CELERY SORBET / CAVIAR

DINNER

CHILLED SOUP OF SPRING LETTUCES / BLUEBERRIES / CRÈME FRAICHE

POACHED MAINE LOBSTER / COMPLEMENTARY FLAVORS

RIBEYE OF PRIME BEEF / VARIETY OF EGGS

CRISPY CHOCOLATE / LIQUID CAKE

MINTS

Chefs Curtis Duffy and John Peters backed up their cars into Nick's driveway. "Here they are," I said.

We had already moved all of the furniture out of Nick's family room, and Dagmara helped Chris Gerber arrange a single long table down the middle of the room. Low vases filled with herbs were centerpieces that would become part of the aroma for the meal. Chairs were rented and Nick ran off on last-minute trips to Crate & Barrel for extra wine and martini glasses.

As Curtis and John started to unload the car, Nick's jaw dropped. "Holy shit. Did you guys bring all of Trio over here?" Our equipment was neatly stacked, wrapped in plastic wrap, and labeled. Nick's kitchen filled in an instant.

Though investors from New York and San Francisco couldn't make it, everyone from the Chicago area arrived—five investors and their wives, as well as Tom Stringer and Steve Rugo. We enjoyed a glass of champagne and I gave a simple toast: "I have dreamed my whole life of putting together something like this. I appreciate you all coming here today to help launch this project to build Alinea. I hope you'll enjoy this evening." I raised my glass. "To new ideas and a new train of thought."

Chris served food and occasionally Nick would run in to lend a hand. Curtis, John, and I put out the first Alinea dinner.

"Chef. It was brilliant," Nick said afterward.

"It was a mess," I said. "But the best we could do here. Was it worth it?"

"I can't imagine that this is not inevitable now, Grant."

Nick was right.

We were able to line up the investors in the weeks that followed with minor tweaking of the deal he put together. All told, $1.6 million was committed to Alinea, including $500,000 from Nick personally. It was a figure that blew my mind.

The pressure had ratcheted up. Sure, I had reconceptualized Trio, but I had never built a restaurant from scratch. It was a daunting prospect, made all the more real by the huge amount of money it would take and the faith that these people had placed in me.

Trio's last night was a riptide of emotion. I was incredibly excited to finally see the initial steps of my goal to open my own restaurant realized, and yet I was sad for the end of the current era at Trio and the dismantling of the amazing team we had created. The majority of the staff had been with me since the opening day back in 2001, and the personal bonds that had developed were the most profound of my life. A wet-behind-the-ears chef and a bunch of mismatched cooks had come together, and with sheer determination, a dose of naïveté, and a lot of true passion, created something that was both unpredictable and rare.

Three years in, we were a well-oiled machine. Everyone knew each other incredibly well. We could finish each other's sentences and, more important in the world of cooking, step in as the other was stepping out.

We had learned the dance.

On the eve before our last performance at Trio we sat in our post-service meeting like we had every night for the last three years. Of course, we all knew this was the last time we would assemble together, and while there was some time spent reminiscing, the main focus was Trio's last day.

I knew I didn't have to address it directly—everyone knew what the goal was before I said it—but I think the group wanted me to voice it.

After I went through all of my thank-yous and acknowledgments of appreciation for the years of commitment and dedication, I threw around some jokes about some of the pointiest moments that we had all shared, and then I turned serious.

"We have come this far, and what we have accomplished is amazing; we should all be very proud. We cannot let our guard down," I warned. "This is our last show—everything we've pushed for has come to this day. Keep it tight. Stay focused. The diners coming in tomorrow are expecting the best meal of their lives. We owe them that. We owe us that. Let's come in tomorrow and do exactly what we have done for the last three years." I was acting tough, like the leader that they had all come to expect, but inside I felt different.

It was important to take the next step, to take another risk. But this one felt far from risk-free. This time I had as much to lose as I did to gain.

The next day I showed up at 9:30 A.M. The night before we had identified the VIPs who were dining with us and how we wanted to give every table as many courses as possible. That made for a big prep day. Shortly after I unlocked the door the cooks started filing in. The call time was 11:00 A.M., but everyone was in and at their boards by 10:15. We had pledged to re-create some Trio signature dishes on our last night as a tribute to the restaurant, Henry, the diners, and us.

Mark Caro, an entertainment reporter for the *Chicago Tribune* who was interested in food, asked to be a fly on the wall during Trio's last night. He planned to write a feature on the transition of Trio and give a few teasers about Alinea.

He showed up at eleven on the dot, wondering why the kitchen was already humming, and I showed him around and introduced him to the staff before settling in to my prep. He stood to the side of the kitchen, observing. Every now and then he would dart in and approach me with a few questions. He was trying to dig into my emotions. I was guarded with details of Alinea, telling him point-blank that the article should be about Trio out of respect for Henry and the restaurant itself. I did, however, slip a few times and tell him things I would have never told the staff, and he quoted me: *"When I think about it, it's like when you're sitting there watching your girlfriend getting on the airplane," the chef said. "You feel it here, in the pit of your stomach."*

We intensely pushed through the prep day, planning to give each table at least three extra courses, although many of them were slotted for more. We wanted to go out with a bang.

The front of the pass was covered with a large copper sheet. Eight feet long and four feet wide, it was only visible to the guests who might be at the kitchen table, and of course to all of the staff. Every day it would oxidize to an ugly green-blue color and every night the copper was polished with a homemade paste. The recipe came from The French Laundry, and was composed of lemon juice, distilled vinegar, flour, and salt. Most of the time I would do it myself, using a green scrubby and a deli of the paste; if I was busy doing something else, David, Nate, or John did it. But each night it got done without fail, even though on many nights nobody would notice except the staff. Tonight, on Trio's last night, I made sure I had time to do it myself.

"The cooks wrapped up their prep work and, as the 5:00 P.M. opening time approached, they wiped down surfaces, swept, mopped. "You've got to start the service with a clean kitchen," Achatz said as he polished the copper siding of his work area. "Otherwise it just doesn't feel right."

And that was it. This night was so different than any other night we'd ever had at Trio. Going back to the first day, right up until this one, we were always looking forward. On a bad night we would take comfort in knowing that we always had tomorrow to get it right. Other nights we would go home knowing how in the shits we were for the next day, but tonight we had nothing, good or bad, to look forward to.

But somehow it was the perfect ending.

"Elsewhere around the dining room Saturday, Trio regulars and first-timers were experiencing their own versions of that wistful good-bye, filling the closing-night reservations slate for one of the greatest shows on plates. Back in the L-shaped kitchen, the 30-year-old Achatz and his team of a dozen chef/artists were treating the evening as just another Saturday night gig, grooving like a crack rhythm-and-blues band that has found the pocket and won't let go.

"In one typically fluid sequence, a cook set fire to a stick of cherry wood, blew out the flame and let the smoke swirl up into an overturned glass that the next cook placed over stacked medallions of smoked beef tongue—all while others dressed the plate with prime beef rib-eye, morel mushrooms and an exotic variety of lettuces and drizzled sauces."

Around 2:45 A.M. Caro walked out of the Trio kitchen. Everything was done—the last guests, Anthony Marty (aka "Yellow Truffle," as he was known on eGullet) and his party, had finished their thirty-plus-course kitchen table menu and waddled out of the building in a food and alcohol daze. The final clean-down was finished and nothing was left to do, but the staff milled about, trying to act busy, to prolong the inevitable. I swung around the corner and headed into the pastry station to see what else needed to be done, knowing that they were the last to put food out, when I ran into Carrier. As we clumsily collided, I fell back and he caught me. Before I knew it he had pulled me into a bear hug, lifting me right off the floor, and we both started to cry. John rounded the corner and fell prey to the emotional collapse, and soon Nathan and Chris joined. It was ridiculous for a bunch of ego-driven cooks—and fitting at the same time.

Trio was no more. Building Alinea would begin in earnest.

CHAPTER 16

Alinea Investor Update

October, 2004

My apologies for the delay before this first update, but as you will see below, a tremendous amount of work has been done to move Alinea toward reality.

Also, I want to put a special THANK YOU right at the top to Mike Cirks and Paul Hudson for allowing the Alinea Team to use their FBLab offices. Grant, John, and Curtis have turned the "FunBrainLab" into the "FoodBeverageLab" and made it a headquarters for their daily work. The FoodLab is also the "Cost Savings Lab," and the three chefs have spent a great deal of time sourcing everything from multiple suppliers. Ultimately, we will have a spreadsheet that documents the differences between bids, but at this point I am willing to bet that the FoodLab has paid for itself. But none of that would have been nearly as possible or efficient were it not for the amazing office provided by Mike and Paul—free. Not only is it a great work environment, but it's also a place that Grant can meet with the press in a professional and serious manner. Thanks!

THE DESIGN PROCESS

Right up there in the Let's-Give-A-Thank-You department is Steve Rugo and Tom Stringer, our architect and designer, respectively. We came to them with a silly schedule, a simple building, and lofty goals. In a very short time they have delivered a finished set of plans that will provide an exceptional environment in which to dine.

Here is the space as it looks right now. . . . *SEE FIGURE 1*

Front window on the second floor—Tom Stringer looks over the plans. *SEE FIGURE 2*

As you can see, the landlord had everything stripped out of the second floor. It is pretty much a white box. Grant, Joe Catterson, Curtis, and John taped out the plan on the floor to see how it would function from a service perspective. The blue box to the left is where the stairway will be. It will look something like this. . . . *SEE FIGURE 3*

The stairway will be manufactured from steel and will be able to support much of its own weight. It will be anchored against the back wall, top and bottom. This will make it appear as though it is floating in space. The "walkway" 1/3 of the way up was Grant's idea—and a great one. The guests will be forced to take a bit of a detour, and underfoot will be alternating granite and glass, giving them a view of the water and votives below. Framing the stairway on both sides (one is cutaway) will be draperies that extend all the way up to the second-floor ceiling. It should be a dramatic focal point of the space.

The floor plan has gone through three major iterations. Since the building is narrow and long, it was ultimately decided that the flow worked best if the guests arrived at the center of the space. In addition, we wanted to create an emotional trigger right when the guests get through the front door—a moment of "am I in the right place?"—and a walk that will heighten the tension as you approach the "real" front door. Thus, the "wedge" entry was created.

Here is the plan. . . . *SEE FIGURE 4*

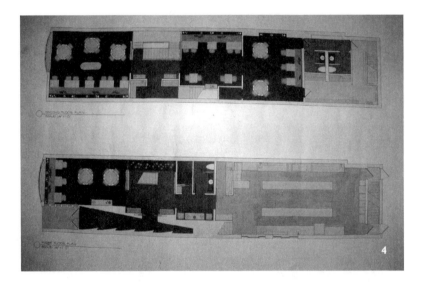

After making their way through the wedge, the guests will enter the "gallery" area, right in the middle of the restaurant. There they will be greeted, coats will be checked into the coat check (just next to the downstairs WC), and most will be led upstairs to the three dining rooms that occupy that floor.

The dining spaces are all of similar size and scale. Each will house a custom-designed and -built service table to aid in service and the wine program. In addition, the second floor houses two distinct "back-of-the-house" service areas. The first, just across from the guest staircase, is where the food servers come up from a private kitchen staircase (allowing the food service to move discreetly between the two floors). It will provide a staging area for food service to the two front dining rooms, and will house refrigeration for the wine program. The back service area will be substantial, providing service for the back dining room, but also housing full stemware-washing capabilities—minimizing the number of trips down to the kitchen washers and polishing area. Great care was taken in planning the layout so that the guests are well serviced at every table—but also so that the service can discreetly tuck things (or themselves) out of the way.

Tom has also done a great job while being presented with a formidable task: interpret Grant's vision for Alinea and make it happen. Through weekly discussions and a few blind alleys, he has found a palette that has informed his design decisions for the space. *SEE FIGURE 5*

The floors will be honed granite in the public spaces, with gray carpeting in the dining rooms. The banquettes will ap-

5

pear to be freestanding furniture and will be covered in the fabric with the circular patterns at top. The custom-made chairs (now in their third iteration) will have the black and gold pattern (second down from the top) on their back, while the inside will be a contrasting tan of a much softer material.

The banquettes will appear to be freestanding but will be anchored to the wall . . . they will obviously be longer than this picture indicates. Above them will be a shelf that supports a series of lights in glass tubes, along with flower arrangements in similar glass tubes. These are currently being designed for custom manufacture. *SEE FIGURE 6*

6

This is the first iteration of the chairs (in a generic covering). Ultimately, it will be slightly less curved at the top. They will be very comfortable . . . and look great. *SEE FIGURE 7*

Perhaps the most controversial decision design-wise was also made at the earliest stage—The tables will be beautiful and unadorned. Yes, that means no table linens. Grant has said from the beginning that he hates seeing cheap table bases at even the very best restaurants. But the decision to abandon linens altogether took a great deal of thought. What will glasses rest on; what will silverware rest on; what about

condensation or spills; what material is durable enough? Etc. etc.

In the end, Alinea will have tables that are hand-made from a tiger-maple veneer. The ends will be tapered and thick—about 3 or 4 inches—giving the table an impression of heft and sturdiness. It will be coated with 10 layers of bar-finish in a matte polish. 10 layers sounds like a lot, but you cannot see its thickness as you can on a bar-top. This will prevent chips, scratches, watermarks, etc. Martin Kastner at Crucial Detail is helping Grant to create service pieces that will hold the silverware and centerpieces. The wine flight glasses will rest on linen or custom coasters.

Most of all, the visual field of the restaurant will be striking gray carpet with beautiful light colored wood floating above it.

The bathrooms will be equally slick. The first-floor bathroom will need to be ADA-compliant, so we are somewhat limited as to how interesting we can get with the WC itself. But the second floor poses no such limits . . .

The basement will house the wine cellar (temp and humidity controlled, but fairly utilitarian for now—not a showpiece), employee bathroom, employee lockers, utilities, and a small office.

Two contractors reviewed the plans, and Steve will pick one of the two in the next week or two. Both have large operations that contain all of the trades in house, allowing for a faster build-out. Due to our aggressive schedule, he has approached them with the concept of "here are the plans and this is how much we can spend . . . can you make that happen?" Everyone is well aware of the budget constraints. Ultimately, it will be tight, but right now we think we can make it on-budget.

Part of the reason that we are optimistic is that SML Stainless in Canada has provided a great bid for the kitchen and service areas, including all refrigeration, counters, compressors, and equipment. We will not purchase the stove or the ovens from them, and we are getting the induction units for free, but everything else is coming from one shop . . . signed, sealed, delivered, and installed. This will be a top-notch and totally unique kitchen . . . and I know that both Grant and I thought that we would never be able to do it at this level.

Ultimately, I feel like we are on track in a big way to deliver what looks like a $3 million restaurant for half of that. Steve, Tom, and their respective staffs, especially Lindsay and Becky, deserve a lot of credit for making it happen.

FOOD LAB

All of this would be a nice exercise in design and business were it not for the fact that Grant can cook! Oh, and I can't . . . so please forgive any errors in the descriptions below . . . I am certain that something will be incorrect!

The Food Lab will prove to be a great commitment on the part of the investors.

The first 4–6 weeks were spent researching: purveyors, ingredients, cookbooks, specialty items, etc. In addition, the chefs sourced and developed relationships with myriad suppliers—everything from silverware to ladles to chef's coats to stemware . . . it has all been bid out to multiple suppliers. SEE FIGURE 8

Three weeks ago, the kitchen team began spending every Tuesday and Wednesday at the test kitchen—which is, unfortunately for now, at my house. While it is adequate, it is certainly not the best environment for them. Still, the alternatives proved to be too costly and we could not find an empty commercial kitchen. So until Alinea is opened, we have cleared off some shelf space, moved some of our appliances, and brought in the best blender I have ever used (everyone go online and buy a Vita-Prep blender right after you read this—you will thank me later).

Despite the limitations, Grant has made sure that the team is well prepared, and it has been an honor to watch them cook. Perhaps most surprising to me is that there are no shortcuts, so to speak . . . peeling grapes is a difficult task even for a skilled chef. But the result is . . .

Peanut Butter and Jelly. Peeled grapes, on stem, coated with peanut butter, wrapped in a super thin cut of bread, broiled for a moment, and served. Ultimately, Grant hopes to get the grape stems with a leaf still on . . . *SEE FIGURE 9*

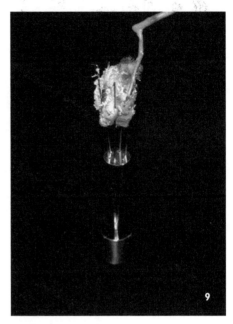

A few weekends ago the chefs were invited to the Culinary Vegetable Institute in Ohio.

The CVI produces over 650 varieties of vegetables, many of them heirloom, obscure, or otherwise unheard of. Here is chef Duffy checking out one area of the farms. *SEE FIGURE 10*

They came back en-
ergized and excited
by what they had seen
there. For example, here
is an Hoja santa leaf . . .
SEE FIGURE 11

Grant smells it be-
cause it's distinctly like
sassafras—or root beer.
Those squashes in front
of him, as well as a va-
riety of mushrooms, will
ultimately be wrapped
and cooked in the leaf,
and presented to guests.
I have not yet seen the finished dish here, and it is still under
development. But access to these types of products has whet-
ted Grant's creativity, and the lab environment helps to realize
a truly finished dish.

Another unique food product came from Terra Spices. SEE
FIGURE 12

Terra sent Grant a
series of "spray dried"
juices. These are fine
powders that when
put in the mouth turn
instantly into a pud-
ding consistency.

Grant mixed three
of them in perfect
combination—coco-
nut, banana, and pineapple—and then added cane sugar, all-
spice, a thinly sliced hot pepper, and vanilla into a glass. Next
to the glass will be a beaker with coconut water and rum. Pour

the liquid into the glass and you have a delicious Caribbean pudding . . . instantly made and incredibly smooth.

Here it is just before being mixed. *FIGURE 13*

One dish sounded perfect to me on paper—Prosciutto, Passion Fruit, Mint—and ended up tasting just as perfect. A thin, dehydrated slice of rolled prosciutto sandwiches a passion fruit sorbet and mint. *SEE FIGURE 14.*

Really more beautiful than this lousy photo, it is surprising and great. One of the nice details is the prosciutto itself. . . . Rather than a simple slice, Grant cut 15–20 slices of prosciutto and then rolled them, wrapped them tight in cellophane, froze it, and cut it crosswise on a meat cutter. Then he dehydrated the resulting slice . . . delicate, tasty, and pretty . . . *SEE FIGURE 15*

What is the offal of the vegetable world? Perhaps it is the stem of broccoli—usually cut off and discarded. Grant decided to build a dish around Poached Broccoli Stem.

Of course, first it is cooked sous-vide in butter for about one and a half hours. Then it's placed on broccoli puree. Then it's covered with a super-thin slice of brioche—pan-fried in butter. Around the plate you have an "Achatz-Packet" of smoked wild coho (?) roe wrapped in thin slices of grapefruit like little raviolis. There are also broccoli flowers, broccoli florets, and a grapefruit puree. A nice little veg dish! SEE FIGURE 16

16

Finally, one component of the venison dish that is currently being developed is venison "corned beef." The venison was salt-cured in water, salt, cinnamon, and other spices for three weeks. Then it was poached sous-vide for three hours. Then cooled. The result was tender, amazing venison "corned beef" style. This will comprise one component of a larger venison dish.

Some of what you have seen above should make it onto eGullet in the near future. Safe to say that when Alinea opens, Grant will have a whole new bag of tricks to show the world . . . and it is shaping up well.

PR

Publicity is going very well. We have retained Jenn Galdes of Grapevine Public Relations, and although she is not officially on payroll until November, she has done an amazing job already.

Grant has done interviews for *Food & Wine*, *Chicago Social*, and the *Sun-Times,* and we have scheduled for the *Chicago Tribune Magazine* and several other publications. Grant is doing two charity events: Harvest Moon (run by investor Joel Baer's wife, Jamie) coming this week, and the Museum of Contemporary Art in November. We have already been mentioned or featured in two issues of *Food & Wine*, the *Tribune*, the *Sun-Times*, *Chicago* magazine, and publications from as far away as San Diego and Cleveland. Our website has gotten press in and of itself, and has been visited over 13,000 times.

There is buzz in the Chicago press that this is the "most anticipated" or "most highly anticipated" restaurant to hit Chicago in a long time. They are already grouping Alinea with Trotter's.

IN CLOSING

I hope this update gives you a sense of where we are and where Alinea is going. There are countless items that I did not bring up but easily could have . . . but then that could fill a book.

By the next investor update we should:

Have started the build-out

Know within a few weeks our realistic opening date

Have finalized many more budget items and will present you with a line-item comparison

Have more press, more great dishes, and more good news.

As always, feel free to call with any questions or concerns.

Nick and Grant

decided that Alinea needed to be a clean break from Trio. I would ensure that the restaurant would be innovative from day one by creating an entirely new opening menu that focused on new ingredients, new techniques, and new methods of serving the food. So in the midst of the business planning, the building design, the websites and logos, there was one thing that I really was fully responsible for: the food.

We looked for a professional kitchen that we could rent three or four days a week to serve as a place to test ideas and dishes, but were unable to find anything suitable. We ended up using Nick's home kitchen. This was not an ideal situation for me or for his family, but it was all we could find. Online we spun it as our "food lab—somewhere in Chicago." It sounded exotic and sexy. In reality, John, Curtis, and I would drive out to Nick's house with boxes of ingredients, put on our chef's whites, and work until they kicked us out for the night.

It is impossible to *try* to innovate. You can't decide to turn creativity on or off. All you can do is present yourself with interesting problems and try to find solutions. Then you refine those solutions again and again. That is what we did constantly while building Alinea, and what I do as I develop new dishes.

Everything that I see, hear, and feel, I relate to food. When I go to a movie and watch the cinematography, I ask myself why the director chose that lighting, those colors, that setting, and then I imagine scenarios where we light Alinea in a similar fashion, or dress a waiter in an unusual outfit to mirror the food, or create a mood with similar dialogue. Most of these ideas are never used, but occasionally they resurface months or even years later when I least expect them to.

Once when I was working on a seafood dish for the opening menu at Alinea I decided that I wanted to create a "sponge" of sauce with flavors of the sea. The seafood sponge has obvious origins, but the reference would be subtle to the diner. It wouldn't look exactly like a sponge, it would only hint in that direction. We worked for a time on getting the flavors right, on figuring out how to make the stock set up properly to look like a sponge. That part was largely technical and simply required experimentation and time in the kitchen. What came next, however, was less linear and far more unexpected.

As I was plating the dish for the umpteenth time it occurred to me that we should include the scent of spring flowers to enhance the dish and reference to spring. Quickly, I settled on hyacinth as the flower that was needed. I had no idea why. I just knew that hyacinth flowers should surround the dish, and then we would have waiters pour hot water over them to release the scent as the diners ate. I sent John out to a florist to pick up some flowers that were as close to hyacinth as we could get this time of year, and we made the dish again, setting the bowl with food inside a larger bowl that held the flowers. Nick got a teakettle of hot water for me and I poured it over the flowers—instant spring in the middle of winter.

Everyone else looked at me quizzically. This didn't make much sense to them. But as soon as I smelled the sweetness of the shellfish along with the musk and sweetness of the flowers I was transported back to my childhood. Until that moment I had no idea why I wanted to pair this fish with flowers. But once it was all together, I remembered a day when I was twelve years old, fishing for walleye with my dad in the late spring. We would tuck in along the shore and eat lunch among the wildflowers.

Fish and flowers made sense to me not for any culinary reason, but for a sentimental one. Scent is powerfully tied to memory.

As I explored using aroma to enhance a flavor, I began to veer off course and play with ideas of place—rabbit "in the field" or frogs legs "in the woods"; and of childhood—burning oak leaves, fireside Christmas morning. I recognized that even when a diner did not have an awareness of why these pairings worked, they still stirred their emotions and enhanced their experience.

E-mail from Grant and Nick to the Alinea Investor Group:

Alinea Investor Update

January 17, 2005

FRENCH ONION SOUP

As you might expect, things are moving at a more rapid pace now that the holidays are behind us. I apologize for the delay in this update, but we have been waiting for weeks to get the final bids in from the contractors fabricating the stairway. We had redesigned some of the tectonic elements in order to reduce the costs. Now that we have these numbers, I can more accurately gauge the final costs associated with the entire development project. Bluntly put, we are behind schedule and over budget. That aside, everything else is great! And despite the sarcasm we remain confident that our design, building, and marketing efforts are succeeding beyond our expectations.

FOOD LAB—CRUCIAL DETAIL

SOUS CHEF CURTIS DUFFY

Grant, Curtis, and John have continued to refine and develop new dishes and techniques for Alinea. In addition, four kitchen days were spent creating and making dishes to be photographed for the website. The opening menus will include something similar to this:

THE 12 COURSE OR "MENU 2"

PB&J	pb&j
CRAB	dungeness crab, young coconut, cashews, mace
HEART OF PALM	hawaiian heart of palm in six sections
BROCCOLI	poached broccoli stem, grapefruit, crispy bread, roe
ORANGE	burnt orange, avocado, olive oil
TOFU	mediterranean rouget, tofu, shichimi togarashi, toasted sesame
FROG LEGS	florida frog legs, morels puffed and natural, spring lettuces, orange rind
BISON	north dakota bison, corned leg, blueberries, smoking cinnamon
HAZELNUT	hazelnut puree, granola of corn, grains, and curry
DESSERT	to be determined
CHOCOLATE	to be determined
CRÈME BRÛLÉE	dried crème brûlée

THE 30 COURSE—OR "MENU 3"

PB&J — pb&j

BITE — to be determined

ORANGE — burnt orange, avocado, olive oil

TORO — toro of bluefin tuna, ginger bloom, yuzu

TBA — to be determined

ONION — spring onion soup, gruyere, shaved bread, rue

HALIBUT — atlantic halibut, sunchokes, waterchestnuts, lilac vapor

CELERY — chinese celery, razor clams, horseradish

FROG LEGS — florida frog legs, morels natural and puffed, spring lettuces, orange rind

RADISH — radish pods, eggplant, sea beans

LAMB — to be determined

BEEF — prime ribeye of beef, A-1 flavors

HAZELNUT — hazelnut puree, granola of corn, grains, and curry

PROSCIUTTO — prosciutto., passionfruit, calamint

FOIE GRAS — shattered foie gras, dandelion greens and flowers, mustard

TRANSITIONAL — to be determined

MELON — honeydew melon, cucumber, yogurt, mastic

SHELLFISH — prince edward island shellfish sponge, fennel, pear, licorice

FOUR FLAVORS — sweet, salty, bitter, acidic

CRAB — dungeness crab, parsnips, young coconut, cashews

BROCCOLI — poached broccoli stem, grapefruit, crispy bread, roe

ARTICHOKE — braised artichoke, liquid truffle, garlic, parsley

TOFU — mediterranean rouget, tofu, shichimi togarashi, toasted sesame

BISON — north dakota bison, corned leg, blueberries, smoking cinnamon

CHEESE — to be determined

BACON — bacon, butterscotch, apple

TROPICAL — instant tropical pudding

DESSERT — to be determined

DESSERT — to be determined

CHOCOLATE — to be determined

CRÈME BRÛLÉE — dried crème brûlée

20

THIS IS THE WAY THE MENUS WILL BE PRESENTED ON OUR WEBSITE.

The size of the circles, or "flavor markers," indicate the size of the course, and their left-to-right orientation corresponds to how sweet or savory the course is. The menus in the restaurant look as they do above, but each element is printed on a

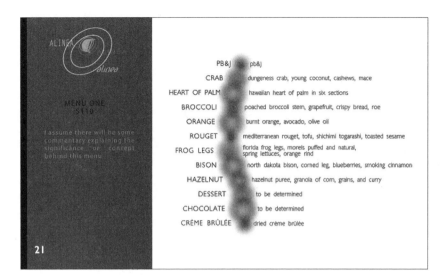

ALINEA
alinea

MENU ONE
$110

I assume there will be some
commentary explaining the
significance or concept
behind this menu

PB&J	pb&j
CRAB	dungeness crab, young coconut, cashews, mace
HEART OF PALM	hawaiian heart of palm in six sections
BROCCOLI	poached broccoli stem, grapefruit, crispy bread, roe
ORANGE	burnt orange, avocado, olive oil
ROUGET	mediterranean rouget, tofu, shichimi togarashi, toasted sesame
FROG LEGS	florida frog legs, morels puffed and natural, spring lettuces, orange rind
BISON	north dakota bison, corned leg, blueberries, smoking cinnamon
HAZELNUT	hazelnut puree, granola of corn, grains, and curry
DESSERT	to be determined
CHOCOLATE	to be determined
CRÈME BRÛLÉE	dried crème brûlée

21

separate piece of vellum. So, for example, the flavor circles are on the first piece of vellum, on the next page is the basic item "Bacon" and on the third page down is the description "bacon, butterscotch, apple." The three menus are tabbed and simply labeled "one" "two" "three"—with no mention of degustation, or chef's menu, etc. The entire package is bound by a single piece of stainless steel on the left. Martin did a great job with this, and ultimately we hope to reflect the menu with a large art piece in the stair area based on the same appearance of the flavor circles in glass and light.

HAZELNUT YOGURT, CURRY SAFFRON, FREEZE-DRIED CORN IN EDIBLE TUBE

22

HONEYDEW, CUCUMBER, MASTIC

23

24

Martin Kastner continues to create collateral material and design service pieces. The menus and wine list are done and they are interesting, elegant, functional, and fit very well with the overall aesthetic of the restaurant. In addition, Martin has created a cork presenter (see below) and several prototypes for new pieces. We have also settled on an art-piece concept that he is creating for the end of the entrance hall. Called "the swarm" in concept, it will be a kinetic piece that greets diners at the end of the long entrance wedge.

THIS WILL APPEAR ON OUR WEBSITE.

Finally, Achatz LLC has put Joe Catterson, our GM, on payroll early. Joe is beginning to work four days a week interviewing potential staff, helping to create the employee manual, choosing and sourcing service pieces, and researching potential POS systems. Joe is also returning calls and e-mails from patrons requesting reservations. The investor group does not absorb Joe's payroll costs.

"JOE, LOOK NATURAL!"

25

INTERIOR DESIGN

The interior design budget was originally estimated at $175k. Currently, the actual cost is roughly $189k. Given that the decorative lighting budget is included in these numbers, I feel good about how much we are getting for the money. Tom has done an excellent job of sourcing furniture, then redesigning it and having it made at more modest prices.

For example, our first two prototypes for the custom tables were of generally poor quality with a bad base, ugly finish, and just didn't look luxurious. This is the most recent iteration. *SEE FIGURE 27*

The table is mahogany and mahogany veneer. We are making adjustments to the size of the top and the material of the base to create more leg room. But the look and feel is amazing. A room full of these will look very elegant, especially when set with stainless steel accents, china, stemware, etc. *SEE FIGURE 28*

In addition, that is our fifth prototype chair. The only change from this to the final chair is that we are sloping the back an

extra inch to increase the lumbar support. The chairs have been ordered and are in production. *SEE FIGURE 29*

The contrast of the chair materials is not as pronounced in person as it is in this picture. The back is black and tan houndstooth in a material that looks like silk, but in fact is a

highly durable (500k double rubs) material that can be washed with soap and water. The chairs are costing, all in, roundly $400 each—which is an incredible price/quality ratio given the junk we looked at for more money.

We have ordered 50+ silk accent pillows in four different materials that will alternate seasonally.

The LED lighting system is in production. It will consist of 50+ tubes varying in width and height from 6" diameter and 3 feet high to 16" diameter and nearly 8 feet high. These will be supported by a hidden system behind the banquettes in each dining room and will be placed in groups of three. The color and intensity of the light can then be computer controlled and varied throughout the year, or even subtly throughout the evening. For example, you could program them to change from light green to pale orange over the course of five hours.

The banquettes will be in a solid black material that feels like velour or velvet. The neat thing is that the material has the color bound to each fiber before it is woven at the molecular level . . . and therefore even though it is black and very soft, it can be scrubbed with soap or even bleach without the color fading.

Finally, we have eliminated for budget and design reasons the mechanical doors between the kitchen and the front of the house on the first floor. Instead, that entire wall will consist of glass panels akin to the ones used for the front entrance stairway. Since this does not border any dining room, we have decided to eliminate the kitchen door altogether, giving guests a glimpse into the kitchen from the front gallery, the coat room area, and the first floor restroom. It should be very dramatic.

SCHEDULE, PERMITS, INSPECTIONS

We were finally able to pay for our liquor license, which means that the 45-day mandatory posting period began on January 14th. That is very good news. All of the local investors who have already been contacted are going on the 24th for fingerprinting. We should have the conditional permit in hand well before necessary.

The schedule appears to look something like this:

- 1st week of March—Conditional Liquor License Granted
- End of March—Construction finished
- First week of April—Carpets installed, furniture placed, art hung
- Next 1–2 weeks—Buffer period for permits, liquor task force, COO and health inspection
- Concurrently—Kitchen staff and front-of-house training
- First week of May—Investors and creative team dinner. 1–2 friends' dinners.

COST SAVINGS

In the midst of an update that will ultimately ask for a greater commitment from investors it may seem odd to mention cost savings! But we have received some good news on that front lately.

First, Ermenegildo Zegna USA has notified us that they do indeed wish to move forward and work with us on cross marketing. Zegna will be presenting three options to us next Monday, but at the very least we will be assured to save significant money and our staff will be wearing truly elegant suits. Basically, we will be able to buy all of their suits at wholesale, and Grant will get a seasonal line

of clothing for free. I will send another e-mail to you all when we confirm the details of their offer. And thanks to Zegna customer and Alinea investor Dr. Mark Davis for making the introduction—you must have bought a lot of suits there, Mark!

Second, as promised, CookTek has delivered a set of induction burners for free. We signed no agreement to market for them, though we will feature them on our website and will be testing their products. I am sure they will make mention of it in their corporate literature, which is fine by us, so long as they do so respectfully. *SEE FIGURE 30*

LOTS OF INDUCTION BTU'S

PolyScience has been a real find. Not only have they lent us without charge various laboratory-quality water baths that we will use in the Alinea kitchen, but also Philip Preston, their CEO, has designed and manufactured the coldplate or anti-griddle to Grant's specifications. Basically, it cools a griddle to –40 Celsius, enabling Grant to create unique textures with various foods. He is a great resource for us and will no doubt aid Grant in creating new cooking methods and techniques for the Alinea kitchen.

COLDPLATE IS FREEZING PUREED MANGO WITH CRÈME FRAÎCHE DOLLOPS. SEE FIGURE 31

31

Alinea Investor Update
April 10, 2005

THE WINE PROGRAM—AND A NEW INVESTOR

As many of you know, we had dinner last month with Roy Welland. Roy is the owner of Cru restaurant in New York (recently nominated for the James Beard Best New Restaurant Award). In addition, Roy has put together what can only be described as one of the premier wine collections of the world. He and his wine director Robert Bohr have agreed to consign an amazing list of fine and rare wines to Alinea. Robert has spent a great deal of time and effort constructing an offering that will immediately have an impact on the Chicago fine dining scene, and will put Alinea alongside the best Chicago has to offer. Coupled with Joe Catterson's uncanny ability to craft wine flights, and his ability with our allotted budget to round out the list with fine American wines and unique allocations that he is getting locally, we will have a truly spectacular wine experience available to our patrons.

Since we need to raise more money, it seemed equitable to offer Roy the opportunity to invest in Alinea. In addition to aligning his interests with ours, Roy is a highly successful entrepreneur in a variety of disciplines—he will certainly be an asset to the Alinea Investor Group. Investor Keith Goggin has done business with Roy on the floor of the American Stock Exchange for years and has during that time expressed to Nick his high opinion of Roy and his character.

Roy has accepted our invitation to invest in Alinea, and wishes to contribute 10 percent of the total raise. Of course, such an addition is subject to your approval, and we ask that you e-mail me such approval as soon as possible. Also, we ask that our investors keep the provenance of the wine completely private— for many reasons, we do not wish to disclose how or where we acquired such a collection, especially since this has been a well-kept secret and is sure to surprise many patrons and the press.

Welcome Mr. Welland—and thanks Keith for the concept and introduction.

CONSTRUCTION

Construction is moving apace now and nearly every day brings major changes.

We passed all of our rough-out inspections a few weeks ago.

The entire interior is now insulated and dry walled, and this, quite obviously, has really given shape to the rooms. The entire restaurant is taped, mudded, sanded, primed and ready for tile and final paint. The kitchen tile is complete . . . and the entire kitchen will be installed by SML starting tomorrow. By this time next week, the kitchen should be completely done! It was quite a sight to see it all coming in off the 18-wheeler this morning at 8 a.m. *SEE FIGURE 32*

THE NORTH WALL OF THE KITCHEN IS NEARLY COMPLETE.

THE DOWNSTAIRS DINING ROOM TAKES SHAPE. PART OF THE STAIRWAY (UNPAINTED) CAN BE SEEN AT RIGHT. SEE FIGURE 33 Right now we are pressing very hard to be finished with everything by April 22nd. This will allow us a short (!) window of time to have the inspections and the liquor task force through prior to opening. I have spoken to the city about this dilemma and they appear to be willing to help. It will not be easy to make it, but everyone involved, from the architect to the designer to the contractor, are taking the attitude that there is no other choice. Crews are working extended shifts seven days a week to make it in time. As always, we will know better as time goes by, but for now, we are optimistic and sticking to our schedule.

RESERVATIONS

We continue to receive phone calls every day for bookings in May and June. We are still a month from opening and May is filling up very well. Every Saturday and nearly every Friday in May are booked to capacity—about 1,000 guests for the month. The media frenzy is about to begin, which will solidify the remaining positions open. Below is a list of press that will land before the opening.

1. Chicago Tribune "Aroma in Cuisine" cover story in good eating section.
2. Chicago Tribune April 15th story about deadlines "last chance to make your Alinea reservation now if you want a table"
3. Chicago Tribune cover page feature in the "Tempo" section.
4. Chicago Tribune friday "Dining" section "Chefs Cooking For Other Chefs"
5. Chicago Tribune friday "Dining" section "The Alinea Time-line"
6. Chicago Magazine "Alinea Opening" written by Phil Vettel
7. Where Magazine cover of Spring Dining Issue
8. Met Home Design 100 Issue "#66 . . . Restaurant to go to"
9. Metropolis Feature on Martin/Alinea Service Pieces

10. RES—Sweden, high-end travel magazine (similar to Travel + Leisure)
11. Arena Magazine UK-based men's-interest mag (similar to GQ)
12. Playboy short feature on Alinea's opening
13. Bon Appétit story on Alinea and Moto using technology
14. Nation's Restaurant News feature on Alex Stupak (pastry chef)
15. Travel + Leisure small paragraph on where to go in Chicago
16. Food Arts small pieces on Alinea's opening
17. BusinessWeek small piece on opening of Alinea.

Soon after opening we have some major hits lined up:

1. Gourmet feature on Martin/Alinea Service pieces.
2. Gourmet feature on Alinea (acclaimed writer Bill Rice has come out of retirement to write this feature)
3. NY Times' Melissa Clark is dining at the restaurant on opening night.
4. Michael Ruhlman has devoted an entire chapter to me in his upcoming sequel to *The Soul of a Chef* to be released in the fall.
5. Acclaimed NYC photographer Alan "Battman" Batt's book series.
6. Food & Wine magazine story on technology in professional kitchens.
7. Wine Spectator editor dining at restaurant on June 18th

As you can see, Alinea will consistently be in the public eye over the next six months. As we all know, this will dramatically help put people in the seats. The latter list does not include the inevitable reviews from the *Tribune*, *Chicago* magazine, *CS*, *North Shore*, *Chicago Reader*, *Newcity*, and the *Sun-Times*.

PREVIEW NIGHTS

The preview nights are still scheduled for Saturday, April 29th and Sunday, April 30th. There have been some questions as to who is invited to these nights and if investors can bring guests.

These nights are a chance for the Alinea staff to simulate a normal service night. As such, they are critical to polishing the kitchen and front-of-house staff's training prior to opening to the public. Just as a normal night, you will be assigned a reservation time, and, since we have so many groups of two, we will also group some folks together into 4-tops and sixes. As it stands now, just with investors, their spouses, and those individuals who have contributed to the design of Alinea, or have graciously provided goods or services as partners of the restaurant (Zegna, CookTek, PolyScience), we are at 42 people per night. Therefore, we will not be able to accommodate any guests on these nights.

We will be having an investors-only champagne toast late Friday night prior to the preview nights. This will occur after the Alinea staff goes home . . . and hopefully things are in good enough shape that we are able to host a small gathering this evening. We look forward to giving you the personal and in-depth tour of the restaurant at that time.

We have intentionally undersold the first week of operations (in case we don't make the deadline, and because of the desire to put on a superb face to press the *NY Times, Tribune,* and *Bon Appétit*—all of whom are dining at Alinea in the first two days). Therefore, if you are coming from out of town and wish to have a guest fly in, we will be able to accommodate a limited number of reservations on Thursday and Friday of opening week. Please let us know.

Finally, we were looking back over some papers from early in this process and found the Investor's Dinner Menu from last year. The date: May 4th, 2004. One year to the date!

THE BEGINNING . . .

We expect that this will be the final formal investor update. Nearly one year has gone by since most of us gathered at Nick's house to embark on the "new train of thought." While much has been accomplished during that time, we understand that we are just now approaching the beginning of Alinea, the restaurant. We genuinely thank each of you for your financial support, confidence, and assistance that has gone well beyond money. Each of our investors has contributed ideas, time, expertise, and goods that have gone beyond the role of an investor. We intend to remember and honor those contributions.

Thank You,
Grant Achatz
Nick Kokonas

The painting was finished, the drapes hung, and the furniture delivery truck was coming up to the front door, followed shortly behind by Tom Stringer. A small army of men carried in the table bases, wrapped tops, service pieces, lamps, and chairs.

Up until this moment we had no idea what Alinea would look like. Certainly we imagined it in our minds; we had seen and approved each of the designs one by one. But we really didn't know.

Quickly the tops got screwed into place, the chairs were unwrapped and laid out, and Tom was putting the perfect crease in each of the forty-two (down from "fifty-plus" for budget reasons) pillows that decorated the banquettes. As night fell, the room took on a glow from the LED tube lights and the scene was set. I looked over at Grant and he was shaking his head.

He was standing alone in the upstairs dining room near the window looking across at the stairway and the other rooms. I approached him. "What do you think?"

"It's beautiful. Everything I hoped and yet very different in some ways. They did a great job...and I gave them so much shit," he said, laughing. "It looks great."

I pulled out a chair and we sat down at newly numbered Table 25 and rubbed the armrests the way you would the first time you hold on to the steering wheel of a new car. "How does it feel?" I asked.

"I don't know," Grant said as he looked around. "It feels...just...surreal. Like this can't exist."

"Congrats. Now you get to start doing what you know how to do. And I will fade away."

Grant looked at me. "I have been thinking about that, actually. I want you around after we open. No one else knows the goals here, the ins and outs of this place and the ideas. What are you going to do once we open?"

"I'm not going anywhere," I laughed. "That was all just bullshit to make you feel okay with me."

We stood up, laughed, Grant slapped me on the back, and we headed downstairs to lock up.

Tomorrow was a big day.

The health inspector came on May 1 and told Grant and me that everything was perfect, except we needed baseboard moldings in the basement to prevent pests from going back and forth between rooms. Our foreman, John Lincoln, refused to force his people to stay overnight, so I grabbed a cook who I had never met before, headed to Home Depot, bought some vinyl baseboards, caulk, and glue and headed to the basement at 8:00 P.M. We spent all night measuring, cutting, and installing the baseboards so the inspector could be back first thing in the morning. It was the basement, a nonpublic space, so it didn't need to look great—at least not for now. For good measure, we finished up laying the ceramic tile as well. There was no point in driving home to go to sleep for an hour or two.

When John came in the next morning carrying a bunch of vinyl base, I let him know that it was unnecessary. "You can take that back out to the truck. It's done and the inspector will be here in an hour."

"How? Who did it?" he asked.

"I did, John. That's how you get shit done. You stay up all night and do it." I was tired, hungry, and pissed off. But it now looked like we would open on time.

The liquor license inspectors came on May 3, and I was feeling pretty smug. Hardly any restaurant in Chicago opens on time, and none of them open with a liquor license in place.

I had sat in City Hall for hours and hours, waiting to meet with the appropriate clerks to personally file the paperwork. Everyone told me to hire a lawyer and an expediter who "knew City Hall." After interviewing a few of them I didn't feel like there was any special difficulty in the actual filings, it was just about access.

So I figured I would get everything together in a really organized fashion and then simply wait it out. I told the secretary that I was her new friend who would be sitting there waiting to see someone. She encouraged me to simply leave the paperwork there and it would be filed appropriately. But I figured it would just sit on a stack. So I spent a few days working on my laptop while sitting in the waiting room. Every time I left to get lunch or a snack I offered to bring something back for the ladies behind the counter. Eventually they started saying, "Sure, honey." I knew I was set.

After a few days of waiting, I was finally able to sit down with a stern, overworked processor who was literally buried behind two huge stacks of license applications. She did not look happy to see me. "You know, you can hire an attorney to do this for you. It's the best way. If you can't afford one, then there are city agencies that can help."

"I do know all of that. I'm here today personally because I want you to know how critical it is that we get a liquor license by May 1st. We could open without one like everyone else does, but we're aiming far higher than that."

I told her the full story of Alinea. She ate a sandwich. I was now a pleasant diversion, a crazy guy who was building a restaurant who thought it was going to be great. I finished up. "All I want you to do is review what I have here, right now. Then I can make any corrections necessary and it skips that first stack. Then I hand it right back to you, we know it's correct, and you can send it on its way right now."

She smiled and stuck her hand out. Everything was neatly subdivided in an accordion-fold legal folder. She grabbed a red pen and went through it all. She asked questions, made a few notations, and handed it back to me. "You can work over there," she said, motioning to an empty desk in the corner.

An hour later, all of the information that was incorrect or problematic had been fixed. She looked it back over, grabbed three stamps and an ink pad, and started stamping like crazy. She handed it back to me. "You gotta go file it at the State building. Pay the county money here first, though."

Everything was filed in time for the inspectors to be cajoled into show-ing up the day before we opened. They walked through the restaurant, jaws dropped. "Where's the bar?" they asked.

"We don't have a bar. Just wine service and some spirits as part of the menu or perhaps an after-dinner drink," I said.

"Fancy shit, huh?" They looked at each other and laughed. It felt more like a tour of the restaurant than an inspection, but once we had everything we needed, I sent someone off to get the actual license.

It felt like a coup. I was told over and over again that "no one opens with a liquor license." We never had a contingency plan. We joked that we would hand out bottles across the street as people pulled up, but really, we just knew that somehow we would make it happen. "MIH" was our mantra.

One by one the inspectors came, and one by one we got the stamps needed for our occupancy placard. I thought we were done when we got a knock at the front door.

"Buildings," was all the man said as he rushed past me in the front hall. He was short and wide, in jeans and work boots. He had a wallet on a chain and a big inspection badge hanging around his neck.

"Hey, nice to meet you. I'm Nick Kokonas. What are you here to inspect?" I really thought we had crossed everyone off the list. I had no idea who this guy was or what he was doing there.

"I need the plans for the building. I literally just got back from Florida. Vacation. I am not happy to be here, but they rushed me over. Give me your plans, please."

"Okay. One second." I went to the basement and gathered up the master set of blueprints and handed them over. "Do you mind if I follow you around?" I asked.

"Do whatever you want."

He started walking through the restaurant quickly, pointing at the ceiling, then at a door, without saying anything. He headed upstairs, toward the back dining room, and said, "This is a storage room? Ha!"

The City of Chicago counts every fourteen inches of banquette as a "seat," or a person. No one could believe we only intended on seating fifty people upstairs. So we had to make the back dining room temporarily into a "storage room" and put fire doors back there. As soon as the inspectors left, of course, we were going to pull them off and had already designed a cap that looked like a fancy molding to hide the mounts. We even signed an affidavit stating that we only wanted an occupancy of fifty upstairs, even though according to the city's math we could get one for one hundred. This guy saw through that ruse, because it was clear that we intended to operate that room as a dining room. There was fancy carpeting and a built-in service station. He made a note on his pad.

"Where are the third and fourth means of egress?" he asked.

I led him to our back staircase. "This is fucking steep!" He pulled out a tape measure and sized up the treads. I was ready for this one.

"That is a preexisting, nonconforming staircase," I said with confidence.

"What did you do, tear the whole place down except for this one staircase?"

"Yes, basically. All of this has been approved by the city inspectors and we have had every other inspection necessary. All the stamps are on there," I said, pointing to the blueprints that were getting crushed under his arm.

"I really don't care. There is no way you are opening in two days. No way. You don't have a fourth means of egress, you don't have emergency lighting, that stairway back there is a joke, and I am wildly curious how the hell you got these plans approved with all of that." He started heading down the stairs and out the front door. I ran ahead of him and stopped him.

"Look. This is a span-concrete construction, a b-3–rated fire building. We only need three means of egress. The emergency lighting is some fancy shit that retracts into the ceiling. We didn't want it to look bad. Please, take a moment and go inside and I can explain your objections. Do you like espresso? I think you need a double." He softened, considered the coffee, and headed back inside. I found Grant busy in the kitchen training some cooks. "Come here, now. We are fucked. This guy from Buildings is a crazy man and was about to head to City Hall with our set of stamped plans. Call Rugo. Call our attorney. Get them over here immediately."

I ran upstairs, grabbed a waiter I hadn't yet met, and ordered him to make a double espresso, pronto. I led the inspector to a table in the upstairs front dining room and asked him for the blueprints, which he reluctantly gave to me. I opened them up on the table.

"Hi. Let me reintroduce myself. I am Nick Kokonas. For the past year, almost to the day, building this restaurant has been my life's work, twenty-four hours a day. There is a young chef downstairs who has been working toward this day since he was a kid, literally. Now I know none of that matters if we have something that is not to code or is dangerous. But I assure you that is not the case."

He had calmed down and I was able to walk him through the plans, starting with the demolition plan that showed clearly that the back stairs were preexisting. Then I went through the approvals from the city for the special emergency lighting, the fire rating of the floors and cinder walls, the type of drywall we used, and the lowered occupancy permit. "You mean you fought to get a lower occupancy?" he asked. "No one does that."

"This is not a normal restaurant. As I said, this is going to be a very unique place."

A sudden look of awareness crossed his face. "Hey, what did you say the name of this place was again? And your name?"

I told him.

"Shit. I know who you are. You're friends with Bobby Meltzer, right? This is that fancy place he was telling me about." The espresso arrived, and right behind it came our architectural team and lawyer, who had rushed over. I waved them off subtly to go away. I was pouring sweat but trying to look calm.

"Yeah, it is. We did everything right here, I swear. It's not a typical build-out, but it is to commercial grade and it's well hidden by intent. We wanted it to look like an old brownstone that has been here forever, but it was originally built as a crappy Mexican restaurant in 1989. Please, take your time and go back through after you look over the blueprints. But enjoy your espresso first."

"I just have one question," he said.

"Okay, shoot."

"How long after I leave do those fire doors come off back there," he said, laughing.

"Ten minutes, tops." I smiled. "But we will be well under the occupancy, I assure you." I knew then that we were all set.

An hour later we had our last stamp. I sent someone to go get the occupancy placards, walked downstairs to the front dining room, stretched out on the banquette, and went to sleep.

The staff of Alinea gathered together for the first time. I asked everyone to form a semicircle in the kitchen and I stood between the passes in the middle. It was the moment. We were four days from opening night. Some of the staff were people I had worked with for the past four years. Others I was seeing for just the second time.

Everyone grew silent. I took a long pause before addressing them, gathering my emotions and thoughts.

"I grew up in St. Clair, Michigan, flipping eggs at my parents' diner. It was all I loved to do growing up. It became who I am. And at some point, for a reason I don't even know, I began to dream that one day I would own my own restaurant. And eventually I began to dream even bigger, that one day, by the time I was thirty, I would own a restaurant and it would become a great one. The best in the country, maybe the best in the world.

"My thirtieth birthday was a week or so ago. So I missed that goal by a bit." Everyone let out a bit of a laugh.

"You have all arrived here in the past few weeks, and Joe Catterson has done a great job of letting you know what to expect here. But there is more to it than that. That is just the start.

"What you see here started with a conversation over a year ago. Nick Kokonas, that guy over there, and I met and started to work on this. Curtis Duffy and John Peters joined us in working on this every day for the past eight months. Joe, our GM and wine director, has put together a great group of people. It has been a real push to get this done in time and make it as amazing as it is—you can still hear the pounding downstairs. We killed ourselves to get this done on time.

"But all of that is meaningless. Our goal here, together, is to make this the best restaurant in the country. I know what it means to work at a place like that, and I saw what it takes firsthand when I was at The French Laundry. I want Alinea to be better than that. I demand that Alinea become better than that.

"Anyone here who is not on that program should leave now. This is not a restaurant, or a paycheck, or just your job. This is our statement, our measure of what we can be.

"This is my dream. I am lucky enough to have a shot at it. And it will require all of us working together in a singular fashion to pull it off.

"Thank you for joining me. Alinea means a new beginning and a new train of thought. Let's keep that in mind as we start tomorrow."

I paused and everyone clapped. I saw Joe Ziomek, one of our long-time waiters from Trio, looking at me with emotion. Nick, who was sitting on the pass next to me, legs dangling down, was slack-jawed.

"I should add that I owe a great deal of thanks to Nick for having the faith in me to make this happen. He quit his job, put up a ton of money, and has killed himself over the past few months to help get this built. Nick, do you want to say something?"

He was incapable of speaking. He had lost nearly fifteen pounds in the past two months, was exhausted, and was not even expecting the whole staff to gather that day. But it is really rare when he has nothing to say. The man likes to talk.

"I. Well. I simply know that this is, well, it's going to be great." He was choked up and waved his hands saying he was done.

No one said anything else.

The two "friends and family" nights had gone well. Or well enough.

I sat down with Dagmara and friends each night and ate through the twenty-five-course Tour menu one evening and the twelve-course Tasting the next. Both took forever. Waits between courses were so long that at one point I feigned going to the bathroom simply to peek into the kitchen to see what was going on. Grant was working frantically at plating food and simultaneously directing cooks on other courses. It looked far more chaotic than I expected.

The food was good, but not at Trio's level. A few of the servers were spot-on—they were veterans who had worked with Grant for years. Others had a style that was completely off, either too formal or too casual. Many were making amateur mistakes: serving across a diner, placing the forks and knives on the "pillow" serving piece the wrong way, or missing a wine pour before the food was coming.

After the second preview night I hung around until everyone had left and sat with Grant. "Chef, it felt rough out there," I offered up cautiously.

"Yeah, ya think?" he said, half laughing, half exasperated. He went on to explain that it took years to get Trio to the place it was. "We've been at this now three days. No one knows what they're doing yet. Half of the dishes are being plated wrong. It's going to be rough for a while. That's why we're limiting reservations. Exactly what I've been saying all along."

Demand to dine at Alinea in our opening month was crazy. We only had two phone lines set up and they were both jammed constantly. I was answering calls during the day and telling people that we were booked, but when I looked at our reservation sheet I could see that we had tons of room. Grant had notes that popped up on the screen reading "Limit to 45" and "Limit to 40" and occasionally "Limit to 52." None of it made sense to me at the time. But after sitting down to dinner I could tell that neither the kitchen nor the front of the house was ready.

But May 4, 2005, was upon us.

We were being very public with the development of every aspect of the restaurant, and because of our postings online the world had a front-row seat to the risks we were taking with the project. There was no denying that no restaurant had ever put so much out there to create something so conceptually different in this country, especially right out of the gate. And with that came the speculation.

Food & Wine stated in a profile that Alinea was the new best restaurant in the country—and that was two months before we even opened. Conversely, people posting on food forums predicted we would close after two months, failing miserably.

The day had finally come, the construction was just finished, and boxes of food were whittled, pureed, foamed, gelled, and simmered down to tiny components of intricate dishes. The energy was high. I had a ton to be nervous about. Not only was this the first day of Alinea, but it was also make-or-break time.

Gourmet magazine sent in a writer named Tom Vanderbilt to pen a feature specifically on the presentation of the food, focusing mainly on Martin and the Crucial Detail pieces. Michael Ruhlman was dining to gather the final material for his book *The Reach of a Chef*. The dining rooms were filled with super-foodies with giant cameras in hand ready to capture every detail of the experience. For some it was a race to see who could get the most comprehensive report about the restaurant posted on the Internet and into print first. For others it was about documenting something important. Regardless of the future of Alinea, and more fittingly because of the seemingly unpredictable nature of it, everyone could not wait to step into the hallway, be seated at the bare wood tables, and taste the food that had captured so much attention before a single meal was served.

Even the *New York Times*.

Two months earlier, Melissa Clark from the *New York Times* had called and requested a table for opening night. When I spoke to her on the phone she explained she had tried to secure a table via the reservation line but was told we were full. She went on to say that she was in town visiting her cousin Edward and really wanted to try Alinea. I cleared a table that we had blocked in order to keep the reservations modest in an effort to maintain quality. It was the *New York Times* after all, and Melissa was quite nice.

Chris Gerber nervously asked if I was ready. The kitchen was on fire with activity. People were scrubbing the stainless countertops, others were vacuuming the black rugs, and yet others were still frantically preparing their *mise en place* for the night's service.

"No," I said angrily. "Does it look like we're ready?"

"I know it's only five twenty, Chef . . . but . . . but there are at least ten people waiting at the front door. I have to unlock it; it's raining out there."

"Fine. Open the fucking door."

I whirled around while my eyes scanned the kitchen to access our status and to find Curtis or John.

"You hear that!" I yelled to the team. "The door is open. We have guests in the house. Are you READY?"

Some answered by calling back, "Yes, Chef!" But it was not in unison, and it was not everyone.

I turned to Curtis. "This is going to be rough. We need to carry this." He simply looked at me and nodded.

The family and friends dinners had been less than stellar, but I expected them to be. And while I knew we were going to be far from perfect tonight, I also knew that we had to be far better than any other restaurant's opening night. Or at least that was the expectation I shared with the guests who had watched us practice, train, and document for the last six months online.

Joe had created a reservation template that spread the diners evenly throughout the evening, making it manageable for the staff to process the load. That plan failed immediately when the line started to form outside the locked door. People were showing up an hour early for their reservations, and what should have been a smooth buildup turned into a smackdown as soon as Chris flicked the dead bolt on the front door.

I told Chris and Joe to try and slow the speed that the tickets came into the kitchen by stalling certain tables, but there was only so much they could do. The people were here, and they wanted to see the show.

Every couple of minutes I was interrupted. Nick would swing through and ask how it was going, Ruhlman was in the kitchen taking notes and asking questions, and known Trio guests like Anthony Marty wanted to say hi and offer congratulations. Because Melissa had booked the reservation under her name and was not a critic and therefore had no reason to be anonymous, I told Joe and Chris to bring her into the kitchen before the meal so I could meet her and say hello.

In between pickups I kept glancing at the door, knowing she was going to arrive at any moment. Out of the corner of my eye I saw Chris walking a woman into the kitchen. She was by herself.

I walked over to the corner of the kitchen to find Michael in friendly conversation with the woman.

"Chef, do you know Melissa?" he said.

I introduced myself, trying to act as calm as possible, but I was listening to the sounds behind me to determine how the service was going. After some small talk about the opening I asked where her cousin was.

"Oh, he must have had to use the bathroom," she said, turning around to see if she could spot him. I glanced at the foyer with her to see Chris chatting with a man in the shadows.

Michael sensed that I wanted to get back to the plates, so he gave me the out.

"Chef, you better get back in there, it's opening night," he said with a firm nod.

Press demand for opening night was crazy. It seemed that nearly every food magazine in the country wanted to send someone out. But as important as the press was to us, we wanted regular patrons in there as well—otherwise, the whole thing would feel like a press preview. Grant wanted to severely limit reservations on opening night to about thirty-five people, but he didn't want the restaurant to seem completely empty. So I was reluctantly scheduled to sit down at 6:30 at a 6-top with two investors and their wives. We were the table that didn't really matter in terms of pacing and mistakes.

Grant gathered the staff, and I saw once again why he was so successful. He talked about execution, excellence, and our goals. He let everyone know who the press was and why Michael Ruhlman being in the house this night was so significant, and he thanked all of the key managers for doing so much in such a short time. The staff was ready to run through a brick wall by the time the doors opened at 5:30.

When the front door opened I heard Chris Gerber say, "Welcome." I watched from the front dining room as the electronic doors opened and the first diner, Sean Brock, walked a few feet past them, disoriented, then moved back toward the actual entrance, laughed, and came in with a look of wonder. "That worked perfectly!" I thought.

I greeted guests as they arrived and then made myself scarce—I had never worked in a restaurant in my life, and I didn't have the faintest idea what I was supposed to do. I looked up at Grant as I headed toward the basement office to wait for my reservation time. He grabbed my arm. "In fifteen minutes I want you to go into the teens and make sure they're putting the silver down right," he said. "Don't correct them there. Just make sure it's being done right."

"I thought I wasn't supposed to set foot in the dining room," I said.

"Gerber's my eyes and ears. You, you're something different."

Grant was calm. Diners were spaced out twenty minutes apart on the sheet, but everyone was arriving early. And that included Melissa Clark from the *Times*.

I called Dagmara, Jim, and Joel and told them to move our reservation back to eight just to give the kitchen some time. And then I moved from room to room and watched. Everything was new to these diners, and their faces were beaming. Anthony Marty was constantly taking digital pictures. Our servers moved at a slower, steadier speed. Things were going well.

When Dagmara arrived, I met her in the front hall, gave her a kiss, and suddenly made the transition from a worker to a diner. It was an odd transition, and I realized at that moment that Alinea, for me, would never be like Trio. I would never be able to enjoy a meal of Grant's again. Instead, I'd be working. I reluctantly headed upstairs.

All I could do the entire dinner was listen to the other tables and to watch and gauge their reactions. But my back was to most of the dining room, and directly behind me was Melissa Clark and her guest. Michael Ruhlman was motioning to Dagmara to get my attention, and when I glanced over my shoulder at him, eating as a single diner a few tables down from Melissa, he called me over.

"Is everything okay, Michael?"

"Yeah, it's great, Nick," he said as he grabbed my tie to pull me in very close, "but I thought you might want to tell Grant that the guy eating with Melissa Clark is Frank Bruni." Bruni was the head dining critic for the *New York Times*. This didn't make any sense.

"Are you sure?" I asked.

"You should go tell him now," was all he said.

I walked back over to my table to eat the course that was just presented so as not to draw attention. It was a bison dish served with beets, with smoking cinnamon sticks below it. One of the cooks had once showed Grant a glass Crate & Barrel candleholder, and this provided inspiration for the plating. Four small indentations originally designed to hold tea candles now held the bison, and burning sticks of cinnamon were placed below in a long, cylindrical hollow bottom. I wolfed down the food as quickly as possible and excused myself to the restroom. Then I ran down our back service staircase into the kitchen and up to Grant.

"What's up?" he said, seeming far more like his usual self.

"That guy with Melissa Clark is Frank Bruni."

Grant stopped plating and looked at me. "Are you sure?"

"Yeah. Ruhlman told me. He seemed certain."

"Well, that's just great." Grant turned and began plating again with a shrug of his shoulders. I stood waiting for him to say something more but he was done. So I walked back up to the table, worried.

A week to the day after we opened, on May 11, 2005, the *New York Times* dining section had a huge picture of what they referred to as "A sandwich, of sorts, at Alinea in Chicago, a passion-fruit sponge rests between swirls of dehydrated prosciutto." I was ecstatic to be getting such a huge article. Until I read the first few paragraphs:

OF THE MANY WAYS RESTAURANTS HAVE EXPRESSED THEIR APPRECIATION FOR BISON, NONE IS QUITE LIKE ALINEA'S.

The dish might well be called Reefer Mammal. Or Stoned on the Range. Ribbons of bison meat filled egg-size indentations in the surface of a horizontal glass tube, the hollow interior of which contained burning sticks of cinnamon. Smoke seeped from the open ends of the tube, infusing the air and summoning associations well beyond the gustatory.

"This whole thing is like a bong," said a server.

The next of nearly twenty-five courses, a strip of partially dehydrated, butterscotch-coated bacon, arrived dangling like a Wallenda from a teensy trapeze. My friend and I were instructed to yank it from the wire with our fingers, a maneuver with a crumbly coda. She felt sure that a shard of hers had gone missing. She later found it—inside one of her pumps.

Those first few paragraphs were horrifying. It said nothing of the four-star service we were aiming for, the elegant rooms, or the sensual aspects of the food.

The rest of the article was a take on how a few restaurants in the country, including minibar, Moto, wd~50, and Avenues, were exploring molecular gastronomy. The title was, "Sci-Fi Cooking Tries Dealing With Reality." As I read it I began to panic. There were mentions of Graham Elliot Bowles using Pop Rocks and Altoids in his food. Words like "gimmickry" and "mad scientist" littered the article. These were precisely the comparisons we were trying to avoid.

And then I got to the inevitable quote from Charlie Trotter.

"If it's truly valid, I'll be delighted to have this conversation with you in two years." He went on to call it "child's play" and, to paraphrase philosopher Jeremy Bentham, explained that "I want to make sure our young colleagues are not literally producing something that is merely nonsense upon stilts."

"FUCT, indeed!" I thought. I was pissed off. I wasn't a chef, or even part of the industry, but I would never, ever publicly flog someone who is taking such a huge business risk in my industry and putting their heart and soul into it. In sports that's called a "locker-room quote": you pin it up on the wall of the locker room to get your team amped up to kick the other team's ass. In my mind I had already fired up the laminator so I could put that up on the wall of our employee changing room. I picked up the phone to call Grant. He didn't answer. I called four more times. No answer. I drove to Alinea.

I found Grant standing at the pass looking at the article. He had clearly read it twenty times. He was beside himself and angry.

"Chef," I said, "that is huge coverage for a restaurant on its first day. And while a ton of it is awful and they lumped us together with chefs that are doing something completely different, in the end Bruni came around and hedged himself. Look:

> But at its best, Alinea was spectacular, sometimes in utterly traditional ways. What made those frogs' legs memorable was not their moody habitat but their succulence.
>
> And sometimes Alinea was spectacular precisely because

it dared to be so different. Mr. Achatz puréed foie gras and molded it into a thin, hollow cylinder, which he then filled with a sweetened rhubarb foam and served cool. The temperature, texture and architecture of the dish turned the emphatic wallop of the liver into an ethereal whisper."

Grant looked at me and his eyes were on fire. "Dude, you have no fucking idea what you're talking about. Do you know how many times the *New York Times* dining critic reviews restaurants outside of New York? Never. Never at Trio. Once at The French Laundry, and it made the place. This was our shot. What the fuck was he doing reviewing us on the first night? Who does that? And all that crap about Pop Rocks and Altoids, and, and…Trotter! What the fuck is that?"

I tried to answer, but Grant stormed off to the front dining room. I had to agree. When the *Times* photographer came in, we had high hopes that Melissa was going to do a puff piece on our opening. But we didn't expect an overview of avant-garde cuisine in America, with Alinea at its center, penned by Bruni. Grant came back in.

"And you know what? Trotter has never once eaten my food. Never once. He had reservations at Trio a few times and canceled every time. How can he say that?"

"Well," I offered up, "perhaps the *New York Times* hasn't featured him much despite his success, and he's simply jealous. Or he's threatened. You won't be part of the old-boys club until they're forced to admit you. Then they'll come running."

Grant stormed off again.

And then the e-mails and phone calls started pouring in.

Friends who I hadn't spoken with in years e-mailed me from California, Colorado, New York City, even Colgate. All of the e-mails were the same: Is that your restaurant in the *New York Times*? Amazing pictures. Great article. I can't wait to try it. Congratulations.

I forwarded all of the e-mails to Grant, along with a note that read, "I guess people just look at the pretty pictures and don't mind Bison Bongs. And the phones are ringing like crazy."

Grant was already back to work. There would be no convincing him that the *New York Times* article wasn't a disaster. But he realized better than I did that Trotter was right about one thing: Alinea would be a marathon, not a sprint.

I arrived at the restaurant around noon. We had been open only a few weeks, but already my role was diminishing. I felt more in the way during service than I felt needed, and the final construction elements that were cobbled together in order to open on time had been tightened up. For the moment, there wasn't much for me to do, so I turned my attention to seeing how the business was progressing. Our primary concern until now was the push to get open. Now it was time to focus on making Alinea a business.

I set up my laptop in the front dining room and poached some Wi-Fi from our neighbors. A man, about fifty, abruptly entered the room, seeming agitated and rushed. Wearing a gray suit, a bit rumpled, he looked like he was going to sell me something, so I didn't introduce myself.

"Can I help you?" I asked.

"I'm here to see Grant."

"Do you have an appointment? Is he expecting you?"

Grant appeared quickly from the kitchen, stepped between me and the salesman, and led the man upstairs. I went back to the task of building a spreadsheet to track our daily sales and forgot about the exchange.

After an hour had passed I had a few questions regarding how detailed Grant wanted to track food inventory, so I headed back to the kitchen. He wasn't there.

I could rarely get an hour with Grant alone since he was simply too busy tweaking the menu and trying to put out fires. I figured it was a reporter, not a salesman, who had cornered him, and he was unable to get away. So I went upstairs with the pretense of grabbing Grant for a phone call.

He was seated facing the stairway at Table 25. The man's back was to me, and as soon as Grant saw me arrive at the top of the stairs he shot me a look that told me to back off. I gestured with a shrug, "What's going on?" and got nothing in return. This was serious. The city? Another inspector? If that were the case then certainly he would call me in. An attorney, perhaps.

I went back downstairs and sat behind my laptop, but I couldn't work. I was concerned that something odd was going on up there. Another fifteen or twenty minutes passed before Grant came down, shook the man's hand formally, and turned toward the kitchen. The man headed for the front door. Never shy, I stepped in front of him and introduced myself.

"Hello, I'm Grant's partner in Alinea, Nick Kokonas."

The man smiled broadly at me, grabbed my hand with a genuinely crushing, aggressive handshake, and said, "Good to meet you, Nick. I'm Grant Achatz."

It took me a few moments to process that. Grant Achatz?

"You mean Grant Achatz, Sr.?" I mumbled.

"Well, not senior really," he said, finally releasing my hand after having thoroughly proven that he was far stronger than I. "But I am his dad."

I looked toward the kitchen, caught Grant's eye—he was watching the exchange—and he just shook his head and let out a small laugh.

"Mr. Achatz, I'm really glad you came by today. Pretty amazing what your son built here, huh?"

"I suspect he had some help. I'm eating here tonight…it should be …"

"—you're eating here?" I interrupted.

"If it's okay with you, yes."

"Of course it's okay. It's more than okay, I'm happy to have you." I tried not to sound shocked, but it wasn't working. "I think you'll be amazed how wonderful it is. Your son is a truly gifted chef. You must be very proud of him." I said this more as a suggestion than a question.

Grant Achatz, Sr., turned and walked out the front door. I stood for a second and thought, "How long has Grant known that his dad was coming here, and why had he never mentioned it to me?"

"So that's your dad, huh?"

"Yep. He looks older, but that's him all right."

"Did you know he was coming by?"

"Yeah, he's eating here tonight."

Grant said that so matter-of-factly that I was offended. To me, after not seeing your dad for seven years, this constitutes real news. "You didn't tell me," I said.

Grant looked at me as if to say, "Why would you care?"

"I think it's a great thing that he came by. Whatever's happened, life is short and he's your father. I would kill to have my dad walk through that door right now and see this. I know it's not the same, but you'll feel better about things in the long run. I'm glad he's eating here tonight. You're going to blow his mind."

"He won't like it. Not really. Whatever."

CHAPTER 19

Nearly every culinary magazine in the United States and most major newspapers wanted to cover Alinea beyond simply mentioning its food or decor. Profiles of Grant began to proliferate, but increasingly, other than the local papers, we were becoming wary of letting some national critics in. The kinks were still being worked out, and the New York Times article taught us that reviews of the restaurant were great, but associating ourselves with the broader movement in what the press termed "molecular gastronomy" could backfire. We were willing to wait for profiles that singled us out.

Grant explained his theory to me, and I in turn let our publicist Jenn Galdes know that we would, for a short time, be taking a hiatus from any further press coverage and instead remain focused on the online forums and emergent blogs, media vehicles that would allow us to showcase the unique experience that Alinea provided and that were increasingly becoming the go-to place for customers who wanted to research restaurants and read reviews. This is the last thing a publicist wants to hear, so she kept pushing. Time after time we said no, insisting instead that we wanted to wait for the truly big hits that could make a difference in Alinea's long-term worldwide reputation.

This seemed absurd by almost any standard. Restaurants normally kill for any PR, and it was true that the New York Times article did far more good than harm for our business and reputation. But Grant was adamant about controlling the flow this early in the game.

Then Jenn called me and said, "Grant doesn't want to let John Mariani in. I can't tell you how stupid that is. He does the national list of the Twenty Best New Restaurants every year for Esquire. You guys are a shoo-in, right? You'll probably get the number-one spot. He wants to come in next Friday. I have a reservation at the ready and Grant wants me to cancel it. I'm not sure how I can do that. I haven't come up with a viable excuse yet."

Grant did indeed cancel the reservation. But later Mariani was back in town and Grant was convinced to let him in. The only opening we had on short notice, however, was at 5:30, when the doors opened. Grant would be preparing our smaller menu for him, not only to get him out the door in time for the reservations that we already had booked, but also because after extensive research and reading Mariani's reviews for years, Grant knew full well that the man was not a fan of anything resembling molecular gastronomy.

While I didn't typically spend much time at the restaurant during service, I made sure to be there as Mariani arrived with Jenn. I greeted him warmly and walked him back to the kitchen to say hello to Grant. He looked at me and said, "I haven't eaten dinner this early since I was a child."

I didn't quite catch what he meant. "Pardon me?" I said.

"Don't you think it's a bit early to be eating in a civilized fashion?" he glared at me.

"Well, this is all we could do on short notice without kicking someone out. Just think of it as a late lunch and I am sure you'll be okay." I smiled warmly and was met with a half grin.

He shook Grant's hand stiffly and was led upstairs. I told Grant what he had said. Grant looked at me. "Jenn's an idiot for bringing him here. He'll hate it even if he loves it. It was a mistake to let him come. He couldn't write anything positive without changing his opinion in twenty previous articles." He shook his head and went back to cooking.

I went downstairs and killed time for an hour and a half, then headed upstairs to check on their table. When I got there, Jenn had a forced smile on her face and was raising her eyebrow at me. "Mr. Mariani, how is everything tonight?"

"It's interesting. What do you call that thing that you served the, uh, what was it on it," he said, looking at Jenn, who of course had no idea which course he was referring to. It was then that he started going back through his notes, which were, to my horror, written on our wine list.

Martin had crafted four wine lists for us since we couldn't find a binder that we felt fit our quality and aesthetic considerations. So he created four sets of steel bands with custom-made screws and fittings, then made the Excel spreadsheet template that would place the margins just right. Since we only had twenty tables and they were staggered seatings, and since most of our customers chose our wine-pairings program, four wine lists were enough. But just barely enough. And now one of them was about to walk out the door.

"Mr. Mariani, perhaps I can bring you a notebook to use?" I asked.

Jenn glared at me, and I back at her. Mariani ignored me completely and kept writing. I was appalled and getting angry. Critic or no critic, this was simply rude and entitled behavior. I walked away before saying anything further, headed down to Grant, and said, "You were right."

"Why, what'd he say?"

"He's using our wine list as a personal notebook."

We sent a check to the table that was promptly paid. Jenn couldn't believe we did that, and clearly thought it was another strike against us. Our attitude is that reviewers pay for their meals or else the review is biased. We had never comped a member of the press or any bloggers, nor did we intend to.

John Mariani walked out the front door of Alinea that night carrying our wine list and a handmade, one-of-four stainless-steel binders.

On August 18, 2005, the first major critical review of Alinea was to be printed.

Online at eGullet, from 10:05 on opening night, the reviews and page views poured in. Chef Sean Brock wrote, "We were the first table sat at Alinea on opening day.... Alinea will change the way people look at restaurants forever. I can't even imagine what this restaurant's future will hold." Yellow Truffle posted pictures that were better than our promotional shots. He analyzed the menu construction and visual design, and even created a spreadsheet of wait times between courses versus bite size. These obsessive reviews ensured that the foodies of the world and anyone who Googled "Alinea review" would read firsthand accounts from diners about their experiences.

More important, the national and international press could quickly gauge our daily changes to the menu, the evolution of the food and service, and the reaction of patrons. This real-time access to a restaurant and constant reviewing was a new phenomenon, and we were among the first to not only embrace it but to encourage it. A great deal of the interest drummed up about Alinea in the mainstream press mirrored directly the phrases, comments, and thoughts that these forum-posters created. We started playing a game where we would post something in a forum and see how long it took for the mainstream press to pick up the story. It usually took less than a week.

Still, in 2005 the "food blog" as we know it today did not yet exist, and these forums were the provinces of mostly hard-core foodies. A bad review in the *Chicago Tribune*—which for us was anything less than four stars—would be crippling to our business and our goals.

Grant was adamant about trying to spot Phil Vettel, the head critic of the *Tribune*, knowing he would be in soon after opening and likely several more times before he wrote a review. The goal was for there to be no more surprises like the Bruni fiasco on opening night. Reservation books were scoured for odd-sounding aliases, common phone exchanges, and bogus credit cards for confirmation. Every single reservation name was Googled. Headshots of every major and minor critic in the United States were posted in the office. Grant personally watched every diner come in. Anyone who seemed a bit too interested in minor details or spent time jotting notes regularly was suspected of being a critic.

The *Trib* covered Alinea's opening with a very positive "preview" that asked whether any restaurant could live up to the preopening hype, and then answered its own question with an emphatic yes, and then some. But until the official review comes out, you never know. There is a tendency among critics to want to give a restaurant something to strive for, room to improve. So a great restaurant opening will often get three and a half stars rather than four out of the gate.

I was in southwest Michigan for a family trip with friends when we suspected the *Trib* review would be in the paper. I couldn't contain myself, so I woke up early, drove to the market and got there before the newspapers were delivered. When the stack finally arrived shortly after seven, it didn't take me long to realize the review would be four stars—there was a box on the cover of the paper directing you to a four-star review in the dining section. I flipped the paper open and the entire dining section page was filled with photos and a giant headline: Alinea Plays to Perfection.

From the first line to the last it was more of a love letter than a review. I skimmed it quickly and then got to the last paragraph:

> It seems silly to suggest that a three-month-old res-
> taurant has matured, but that's the sense I get from
> Alinea these days. The restaurant has lost the jittery

> atmosphere of its early weeks and has mellowed into
> a calm, self-assured and highly polished operation.
> Alinea has found its rhythm, and what a spectacular
> rhythm it is.

I quickly bought five copies, sat down in my car, and read it again and again. I was overjoyed not only because my efforts had paid off, but also because this is the review that Grant had been waiting for his whole life. His restaurant, the restaurant he built and owned and created, had joined the elite in Chicago. I picked up the phone to call him, knowing he would still be sleeping.

"I got the paper, Grant," I said. "It's not good. It's fantastic." I read the review to him and described just how much real estate they gave us. His reaction was muted.

"Awesome. That's great," he said sleepily. "I'll talk to you later." It was a curious reaction, but one that I came to realize meant that his goals were much, much bigger.

This was only the necessary first step.

When the *Esquire* Top 20 New Restaurants of 2005 list finally came out, it wasn't a surprise that we weren't included. Nor was it a surprise that Mariani managed to get in a dig at us.

> Chicago is presently in the sensationalist grip of a few
> hocus-pocus chefs trying to make headlines based on
> things like burning incense next to a dish of venison
> and forcing desserts into squeeze tubes—a total mis-
> understanding of the experimental cuisine of Spain's
> Ferran Adrià.

That inaccurate nugget—we never used any incense—was tucked into his review of a restaurant named Butter that would fail quickly and close permanently within two years. While Butter proved to be less than stellar, its talented chef Ryan Poli went on to open Perennial with the BoKa Restaurant Group, our neighbors next to Alinea.

We were livid about the treatment in *Esquire* for about a day. We wondered to ourselves how well Mr. Mariani knew chef Adrià's cuisine, and we bitched about our inability to say no to him when we knew it was the right thing to do.

And then a shit-storm with Mariani at the center hit the Internet and was picked up by the *L.A. Times*. Mariani was accused of getting complimentary meals, making demands upon restaurants, and having his travel expenses paid for by visitor bureaus and groups of restaurants. He dismissed the accusations, but the damage was done, raising doubts about the *Esquire* list and the selections made, as well as ethical considerations regarding the reviews.

The Internet played a huge role in the controversy, and by not being included on the list, Alinea benefited more than if it had been. In many people's eyes, exclusion of a few restaurants in the Chicago area lent credence to the complaints. And the fact that we were online posting up our business plan six months before we opened put us squarely on the side of the interested public.

The Mariani flap made me all the more excited when I found out that Jeffrey Steingarten was coming to dinner. I loved his writing and his surliness and was confident that he would see through the exotic presentations straight through to the flavor and technique. But I also knew he would try to ruffle our feathers.

Shortly after he sat down I headed to his table and greeted him with unabashed enthusiasm. "Mr. Steingarten, it's not a stretch to say that one of the reasons that this restaurant got built is because I love your writing and it helped me understand and love food."

"Jesus, I am so sorry," he deadpanned. "Listen, is snow going to begin falling from the ceiling or something? Because I expect some strange stuff here tonight," he said, and smiled at his joke. "Call me Jeffrey."

"Jeffrey, if you want snow I am sure we can arrange it. But that would be an odd and tacky request," I replied. "Enjoy your meal, snow or no." He was laughing, which was good, so I left quickly. When I came back two hours later he was about sixteen courses in and had his napkin tucked somewhere near his chin. He patted the banquette next to him and I sat down awkwardly.

"Nick, I don't say this often, but Grant is just a genius. How did you know? I must have written well." He giggled at me.

I explained how I met Grant and how I simply helped to facilitate things and that our staff was just drinking the Kool-Aid and loving the place. It felt fantastic to see someone whose food writing I respected so much really understanding the whole place.

We knew that when he returned to New York he would begin spreading the word there.

Alinea settled into a steady pace over the first year as we expanded reservations to full capacity. The restaurant was booked solid except for January, when Chicago turns into a tundra and tourists and business travelers smartly stay away. It was nothing like running Trio—it was like my days at the Laundry.

Alinea made money every month in our first year. It was, on every level, a success. My home life, however, was a different story.

Before Kaden was even born I had made the decision to not run out and get married, despite the pregnancy. Marriage was a difficult subject for me. I watched the relationship my parents had growing up. I had until recently completely rebuffed my father. I knew that I didn't want to have that sort of relationship with my sons and I wanted to do everything in my power to set an example for them and to engender trust.

But I was very adamant about not getting married.

Angela and I had two wonderful children, and she kept the home together in a fairly tight fashion. She was a dedicated mom who spent nearly every minute of every day tending to the boys. I was, of course, working nearly all of my waking hours at Alinea. I was not a great father in that I was largely absent five days a week working sixteen-hour days, but I made every effort I could muster when I was there. But I was a terrible spouse. I had no emotional time for Angela, and in many ways my feelings vacillated between appreciation and, well, something else.

While Alinea was being built and had just opened I could defer any talk of marriage by shrugging my shoulders and simply saying, "When?" I had no schedule other than wake up, go to work, come home, go to sleep. The restaurant was always in my head, and there were really no days off, no moments off.

As our relationship continued to struggle and disagreements became more frequent I chose to shut down rather than argue. Silence, after all, was the path of least resistance.

In the midst of a tiff in which Angela confronted me about getting married and I tried to change the subject, she marched to the refrigerator, where we had a calendar that helped us remember things like birthday parties, doctors' appointments, and when I would get paid. She grabbed a red Sharpie and drew a large red "X" through a square cell that marked a date.

"Here," she said loud enough so that I would hear her from the other room. "If you don't ask me to marry you by that date, I am leaving . . . with the boys."

I knew we weren't meant to be together, and the kids had been the glue holding the relationship together before Kaden was even born. But over time our interactions grew worse, and what started out as trying to do the right thing for everyone turned into the opposite. But the thought of her taking the boys back to California or Arkansas, where she grew up, was devastating to me.

I wanted desperately to do the right thing for the kids, so I did what I thought was right. I waited until the day before the crossed-out date on the calendar and—ringless and begrudgingly—asked her to marry me.

The wedding was scheduled for March, when Alinea was in its slow season, and Mark Davis, the doctor who had invested in Alinea, generously offered up a house in Napa that was part of a vacation club he belonged to for the wedding site. After I told Thomas that we were getting married—a TFL alumni engagement, no less—he offered to cook for the reception, which Angela arranged to have at Silverado Vineyards, where she once worked. Once everything was set, I asked Nick if he would preside over the ceremony.

"You want me to marry you guys? I'm not exactly a minister," he said.

In California it was easy to get an online certificate, and it was completely legal. "Come on. You would do a great job and I'm not exactly religious. And I don't want some old justice of the peace." He agreed and got a kick out of it.

Two days before the wedding, Angela and I went to the Napa County Courthouse to get our wedding certificate. As we approached the building she turned to me, knowingly, and said, "Well, are you ready?" My stride slowed to a stop. "Here's your out—you don't have to do it," she said. I knew at that point, as I did months previous, that this wasn't really the case, and resumed walking to the front door of the building.

When the date finally came we gathered with around forty family members and friends in a stunning mansion in Napa. Nick and Mark took me out, and Dagmara and Angela went to dinner at Bouchon before meeting the guys at Pancha's, the only bar in Yountville. Nick was intent on making sure I had some sort of bachelor-party experience and began ordering shots for everyone. I didn't want to drink.

I began to panic. Was I doing the right thing? Clearly I knew that Angela and I didn't belong together, but was this the best thing to do for the boys? Instead of this being the happiest day of my life, I was instead asking myself how I let it come to this. The answer, of course, was that I had invested no time or thought in my personal relationships. My waking time and my dreams were of restaurants and food and my career. And now I was getting married to someone who I did not know well enough and who I did not honestly love.

I sat looking at the pool table and thinking about my time at the Laundry and the great nights we would have here blowing off steam. As I did, I started to shut down completely. Nick came by. "G, don't take it so hard," he said. "An ass-kicking on the pool table is nothing to get upset about." I shook my head.

"I'm just not feeling well. I'm going to bed."

"Nonsense. I will allow no such thing," he said. "Here. Have another shot of tequila and try to forget you're getting married tomorrow."

"That's just it. Exactly," I said. "I thought I was doing the right thing, Nick, given the circumstances, but now I'm not even sure that's the case."

Nick tried to calm me down and told me that everyone has jitters. But I think he knew that my situation was different. We returned to our pool game and didn't say much.

The next day I got married.

One of Angela's friends from Napa was a hairdresser, and when she arrived she decided to redo Angela's hair and makeup, which had been done earlier that day in a salon. This delayed the start of the wedding by nearly an hour and did nothing for my nerves. Meanwhile, Nick, sensing my complete state of distress, offered to put me on the next plane back to Chicago. Mark backed him up. It was clear to them that I was making a mistake. But I stayed.

Nick kept the ceremony short and sweet and did a fine job as a stand-in minister. Within fifteen minutes, we were married. My panic didn't subside.

Everyone headed over to Silverado, where I arrived to find Thomas in the kitchen personally cooking a full French Laundry meal for my wedding. It was, needless to say, not your typical wedding fare. I felt incredibly guilty about putting him through so much trouble. "Nonsense!" he said.

When we returned home Angela could tell that I had shut down, and that I regretted my decision. I was barely able to speak most of the time, and I couldn't articulate what was going on in my head. But she knew, and it became the source of constant tension.

When I returned to work I found myself staying later and getting up earlier just to avoid the conversation that we would inevitably end up having. People at work could tell I was different too. Wedding gifts from other chefs and restaurants were piling up in our downstairs office, unopened.

Three weeks after returning from Napa, while monotonously trimming a hundred branches of rosemary for a version of the centerpiece that would adorn the table and ultimately become an aromatic component to a lamb course, my mind began to wander. It became very clear that in order to have the best possible relationship with my two sons I would need to leave the very house they lived in. It seemed counterintuitive, but right in that moment it was undeniably clear. Two days later I moved out, and six months later, we were officially divorced.

CHAPTER 20

The amount of media, both print and Web-based, that was covering Alinea was amazing, and we were fortunate to get it—many other restaurants would have killed for it. But I wasn't content. In order for me to achieve my goal we needed the silver bullet. One of the most influential food writers in the country had to put a giant stamp of approval on our cooking by heaping tons of praise and superlatives on Alinea in a highly regarded print medium. Only a handful of writers have that power, and we clearly missed our shot with Bruni and the *Times*. That left Ruth Reichl.

I had watched firsthand how powerful her voice was when she crowned The French Laundry "the most exciting place to eat in America" in a feature for the *Times*. Since I personally helped create that specific meal, it gave me confidence that she would see both the connection to the food that excited her back then, the evolution of that base, and the originality of what we were doing at Alinea. Having been open now for seven months, I felt we were ready for her.

I asked Nick if he thought it would be okay to e-mail her personally and invite her to come to the restaurant. This confused him. "Why would it be bad? What's wrong with that? In fact, if you write the e-mail well I bet she'll find it refreshing to be getting a personal note from the chef rather then being pitched by a publicist." I tried to explain to him that most chefs go through PR channels to sway journalists into their restaurants, and that e-mailing her myself may seem too forward, cocky, or even arrogant. Or it might even challenge some sort of ethics thing. He assured me it would be fine. I e-mailed Michael Ruhlman, figuring he would have her current contact info, and to test the waters with him to see if he thought I was off my rocker for asking her in.

Michael responded with her work e-mail at Condé Nast and a bit of caution. He didn't try to talk me out of contacting her, but simply asked if I felt we were really ready to have her in. He gently recalled the Bruni thing and politely reminded me that Alinea had only been open for seven months, not seven years. After service that night I sat down and wrote:

> Dear Ms. Reichl:
>
> I hope this finds you well. I hope you don't mind that I'm reaching out to you; I received your e-mail address from Michael Ruhlman. I am writing to invite you to dine at Alinea, but first I'd like to tell you a story.
>
> You likely don't know it, but I was in the kitchen working the garde manger station the night you dined at The French Laundry back in 1998, the dinner that you later wrote about in the *Times*, and that subsequently led you to proclaim the Laundry as the most exciting restaurant in America. I first-hand saw the energy that came from your table being in the restaurant that night, and I witnessed Thomas in a way that I never had before.
>
> Because of the way that meal resonated with you, the playfulness, the flavors, and the execution, I think you would very much enjoy Alinea. The experience is very different than The French Laundry; in many ways it is a present-day version of it, but yet very much our own vision and expression of creativity. Please accept my invitation to dine at Alinea.
>
> I would love to show you what we are doing here in Chicago.
> Sincerely,
> Grant Achatz

After completing the e-mail draft I saved it and returned to working on the spring menu. I didn't feel completely right about sending it off yet, so I decided to sleep on it. If I felt good about it the next morning, I told myself I would let it fly. And so I did.

I was peeling sweet potatoes for a new tempura course that I had been working on when Joe came walking toward me with a grin on his face. Joe is not one to smile much, especially in the morning, but he was clearly smitten with something and was looking forward to telling me.

"Good morning, Chef. I know you don't enjoy having large parties in the restaurant, but we got a request today for one that I thought might interest you. A woman from *Gourmet* called and wanted a table for fourteen. She claimed Ruth was going to be in the party, apparently a bunch of them are in town for some type of event."

Jesus.

We hated large groups, so much so that we made it our policy to try to avoid booking them except on the rare occasion that we were slow due to the post–New Year's Eve season. Fourteen was our absolute maximum size. It fit comfortably into our downstairs dining room, but it was stressful on the kitchen and service. The nature of the Alinea experience does not lend itself to big parties.

But we couldn't say no. "Do you think she'll really be in the party, or is this a marketing event that is trying to leverage her name to get a party booked?" He shook his head. The call came in from New York, caller ID said it was Condé Nast, and the girl made it a point to say Ms. Reichl would be dining.

"We have to do it then."

"Okay. I'll block the downstairs room. Do you want me to handle it as per normal? Take a thirty percent deposit at booking, etc.?"

"Yes," I replied. "Standard procedures."

"Any price breaks, or quote them the normal room charge, etc.?" Joe asked, just to be sure.

"Same as always," I replied.

I was excited but freaking out at the same time. Apparently my e-mail had put a bug in her ear about Alinea, or maybe it was just a coincidence. But either way she was coming—as a 14-top! Jesus.

I immediately walked over to Alex Stupak, our pastry chef, and told him the party was booked.

"Fourteen? Fourteen? How can we do a perfect dinner of our food for a fourteen-top?" he exclaimed.

"I'm not sure, but we have a few weeks to figure it out."

We engineered a menu that was the best representation of what the kitchen had to offer and what we thought we could produce for a 14-top on a busy night. We had to consider everything. Not only the output of the kitchen and service, but things like whether we had enough serviceware to accommodate a 14-top along with a normal service. Sure, we had around thirty of every piece, but we had to assume that many of those would be in use at the exact moment we needed them to fulfill the *Gourmet* party. If we had thirty specially designed pieces from Crucial Detail in inventory but twenty were sitting on tables when we needed to pick up the fourteen VIPs, we would be in trouble.

We knew this would be a very different type of dinner than it would be if Ruth were to come in with a smaller group. Would they be talking business? Would many of the diners have special requests? Would all of them even be into food? Typically when a food writer comes in, the reaction of the chef is to shove as much food down their throat as humanly possible. In this case I intentionally held back. I knew this was a different animal, and I suspected at some point, despite how much she clearly loves food, she must get sick of being force-fed. I knew if we did it right she would return, and I knew the limitations of Alinea. It was my goal to make every course we sent perfect. Quality over quantity.

The dinner went incredibly well. Ruth did in fact show up, and we served the 14-top a seventeen-course meal that we paced impressively. The ticket came in the kitchen at 8:13 and the last course walked at 10:54. The anticipation for her arrival had been building for days prior, and the team was incredibly fired up. In the staff meetings leading up to the dinner I had explained to the team the backstory of the article she wrote for the *Times* about The French Laundry, and how much I respected her. They knew we needed to not only perform perfectly, but also to do it under less then ideal circumstances.

After the last course left the kitchen, I walked over to Alex in the pastry station and shook his hand.

"What do you think?" he asked.

"Given the circumstances, I don't think it could have gone better." He raised an eyebrow, smirked, and shook his head. A few minutes later Ruth Reichl was standing in the kitchen. She didn't say much, and I was of course a bit timid about engaging her. Standing at the end of the kitchen she watched the cooks still in full swing of a busy service with a seemingly permanent smile on her face. I didn't know what to think. Surely she has seen dozens of kitchens, many of them the best in the world, but somehow she had a curious and pleased calmness on her face. It was like she didn't know what was happening, but somehow loved it.

We chatted briefly and I thanked her for coming. After she turned and left the building Joe came up to me and asked what she had said. "Not much, Joe—and I think that's a good thing."

At that point I hurried up and waited. And waited.

Several weeks went by, and I started second-guessing my gut feeling on how much she enjoyed the meal until I got word that her assistant had called to book a second reservation. The requested date was a month away, but Alinea was going through some growing pains. Alex had given notice, and along with him his second in command of pastry, Jordan Kahn. This was a bit of a blow for me, because Alex had been a huge creative force at Alinea since day one. Ruth's pending reservation was for August 25; Alex was leaving at the end of July.

I met with the team of sous chefs and we jointly made the decision to not hire another pastry chef. Alex's desserts were a perfect fit for the style of cooking we were doing, and I couldn't think of another person who would make a seamless transition. John Shields, one of the sous chefs, offered to move off the hot line and oversee the pastry station.

Ruth made a reservation for a follow-up visit. That told me something good was going on. The second visit was for two people, and they requested the Tour menu. I remembered back in 2001 that *Gourmet* had put out a restaurant issue that contained their ranking of the fifty best restaurants in the country, but I didn't know they only did the list every five years.

Ruth arrived with *Gourmet*'s senior editor, John Willoughby. Joe escorted the two into the kitchen for a quick hello. The team slowed their rapid pace, and sous chef Curtis Duffy flicked off the exhaust hood, rendering the kitchen absolutely silent. After a nervous greeting, I thanked them for coming, and they were then led upstairs to their table. At that moment, it was as though someone had turned an old-school movie projector back on—the kitchen exploded with action and sound. I instructed all the cooks, the running staff, and the expediter that I wanted to see every plate for her table on the way out and on the way back. The phrase "coming and going" was born. If the chef is looking at all of your plates on the way out and after they're cleared, you've achieved the ultimate VIP status. I knew I would likely plate most of her food myself, but this was a simple way to make sure that nothing got past me if I happened to be working other tables. I sent a message up to the dining room to bring the captain down to the kitchen. Peter Koludov, the bald Bulgarian who had waited on me when I was trying out for my job at Trio, and who had subsequently come to Alinea when we opened, was running the team in her room.

"Peter, this has to be perfect, I mean perfect. We have been doing this together now for four years, you know what has to happen. I want to see everything that comes off that table. Everything. Glasses, silverware, napkins. And I want to know which of them it came from. And tell everyone to tell me immediately if she makes any comments to you. Anything, even the color of the walls."

"Yes, Chef."

Moments later the ticket came in the kitchen. I grabbed it from the front waiter's hand.

Order in: two Super Soigne Tours.

Typically the expediter would call the orders out. Without breaking rhythm the team shouted back to me.

"Two Super Soigne Tours, Chef!"

Goose bumps ran up my arm.

They smiled after taking bites, laughed at Peter's jokes, and engaged the team throughout their twenty-seven courses over four hours. Every plate came back clean, and all reports were that they were having a great time.

After the meal they came downstairs and into the kitchen to say good-bye. I asked them the same question I ask every guest that I meet after their meal.

"So, how did we do?"

Ruth stood there looking at me with a giant smile on her face and did not say a word.

"Chef, you have Ruth Reichl on line two," one of the reservationists whispered to me as I peeled asparagus.

I walked to the host area and saw the light for line two blinking; I grabbed the handle and pushed the button.

After exchanging greetings she spoke up. I was wildly and unexpectedly nervous.

"Grant, I don't know if you know this, but every five years *Gourmet* does a restaurant issue where we rank the fifty best restaurants in the country." I told her I recalled seeing it back in 2001, and remembered that Chez Panisse came in at number one and the Laundry at three.

"Well, the issue will come out this October, and I wanted to call you personally and tell you that we have chosen Alinea to be on the list." She paused for dramatic effect. "At number one."

I was speechless. Dumbfounded. Ecstatic. Every good emotion one can imagine, all at once. After trying to gather my thoughts, I thanked her profusely. I don't even remember hanging up. I'm not sure if I said good-bye.

I immediately called Nick.

"Dude. So remember how Ruth came in?"

"Of course."

"I just got off the phone with her. Turns out they are putting out a list of the country's fifty best restaurants in the October issue." I took a play out of her book and paused. "Alinea is number-fucking-one dude. Number one."

I immediately went downstairs and penned a thank-you e-mail to Ruth and sent it off the next day.

> Ms. Reichl:
>
> It has been a day now, and your phone call has settled in. I hope I conveyed my excitement properly, but I suspect I was too surprised to do so. As I said to you before, I truly believed you would enjoy Alinea, but I never expected to receive such an honor.
>
> Two days before we opened Alinea I addressed the entire staff. I told them anything less than being the best in the country would not be good enough for us. Thankfully the majority of the people that were present to hear that speech are still at the restaurant. It will be a true pleasure for me tomorrow when we gather as a staff, open some champagne, and I have the opportunity to thank them all for helping me achieve a goal I have had for ten years. And more importantly, we individually, and as a team, can bask in the accomplishment . . . if only for a few minutes before the front door opens, and we are reminded of the responsibility we have.
>
> Best,
>
> Grant

I was sitting in my home office reading e-mails when my cell rang with Grant's familiar ring-tone. "Hey Chef, what's up."

When he finally got to the punch line I quite literally jumped in the air. "Number one? Are you sure?" I whooped and yelled and swore when Grant confirmed what I was hearing. "That is huge, Chef. Just huge. I can't believe it. I mean, top ten would be an honor, right? Number one is insane. Do you know anyone else on the list?"

"Nope. That's it. Just that we are number one."

I really couldn't believe it. That was a ballsy move and would definitely be controversial. I could see putting Alinea top five if they wanted to make a statement, but number one seemed, quite frankly, not possible.

We had very specifically stated that we wanted Ruth Reichl to declare that Alinea was number one in the United States just as she did, essentially, for The French Laundry. But that seemed like an unattainable goal, the kind you set out there as a benchmark that you will likely never reach. Alinea was only eighteen months old.

I was also keenly aware that achieving goals very quickly could produce unexpected emotional results. It happened to me in my trading career, and I immediately thought that the aftereffects of the listing could, ironically, be detrimental to Grant's well-being.

"Chef, I don't want to sound negative, but this is too soon."

"What? You're nuts. Can't you let me enjoy the moment? What is wrong with you?"

I explained that I very much wanted him to enjoy the moment and that I was on my way down to celebrate with him and the staff. "Still, you need to guard against a letdown. You just achieved a major goal of yours. Alinea, your restaurant, listed at number one in the country is something you have always wanted. It is still a young restaurant and financially we are just getting rolling. I am worried about you, frankly. I want this to happen, but in some ways it is too soon. You just have to trust me on this."

He clearly thought I was crazy, so I dropped it for then. "Okay. Whatever. Look, I am going to go to the bank and withdraw ten thousand dollars. I think we need to give our entire staff a cash bonus. Nothing says thank you like money, Chef." I drew up a quick spreadsheet and divided out the money by the number of days an employee had been with us, including during our build-out. Even staff members that had been hired a week before got something. Several came up to me and told me that they had worked years in other top restaurants without so much as a thank-you. Grant told Joe and he ordered up a huge bottle of champagne.

The staff was summoned to the front dining room, and they could tell it was good news by the fifty champagne glasses being filled. As always, Grant gave a genuinely inspirational speech, then turned it over to me to hand out the money.

"Let's remember what got us to this point," I said. "We have to keep embracing the vision of Grant to constantly change and reinvent Alinea. However, for a moment, let's just drink."

Most people think that the constant evolution of Alinea's cuisine is the result of one person—me—being struck by original ideas at every moment of the day, even when I sleep. Some diners speculate aloud while visiting the kitchen after their meal, wondering how we come up with the food. Sometimes that happens, but it's very rare. Most of the time the ever-changing menu, the tireless pursuit of being constantly new, is the result of hard work.

The Grind.

In the kitchen we often refer to "The Push." In our world, the push is the exact opposite force of the grind. You have to push to overcome the tendency to grind to a halt. It is a willful act.

It used to be that the next idea started late at night after all the cooks had gone home, the kitchen was clean, and the orders for the next day were called in. I would grab my laptop, some notebook paper, and a few key cookbooks that I use for ingredient referencing and hunker down in the dimly lit dining room. The staff always joked to the guests seated at Table 14 that they were sitting at my desk, and it was true.

When we were building Alinea, Tom Stringer asked quizzically while glancing over the blueprints, "Grant, where's your office? I don't see it on here."

I laughed, pointed to the 900-square-foot kitchen and said, "Right there, Tom. If I'm behind a desk somewhere, I'm in the wrong place." From 2:00 A.M. until around 4:00 I read the notes that I had jotted down on c-fold towels throughout the prep day, scan restaurant websites and food forums, and stare at a list of seasonal ingredients that we planned to focus on for the upcoming menu change. Occasionally, when I was really excited about an idea, I walked back into the kitchen and started to work out the idea right then. At 3:00 A.M. Some of my most personally fulfilling dishes came from being aware of my surroundings and recalling instances in a day that I somehow, in the moment, related to food.

And so, after the *Gourmet* edition came out and the news flashed Alinea as number one, I took Nick's constant haranguing to heart.

I would not lose The Push to The Grind.

One particular night we had very rough service. It was one of those times when absolutely nothing went right. In the midst of trying to push out a large pickup of lamb, one of our purveyors, Kate Lind of Sustainable Greens, walked in the back door right on schedule. Every week she drives the five hours to Chicago with a van filled with fruits, lettuces, herbs, and vegetables that were picked that morning; and every week she walks in while the kitchen is at full speed. If it were anyone else I would send them away to come back at a more convenient time, but after all this time, Kate was part of our family.

I turned and smiled at her as she plunked down a flat of red raspberries on the counter. The very moment the sweet, roselike perfume wafted in my nose I heard the shattering of multiple wineglasses hitting the cement floor. Breaking anything in the Alinea kitchen is a big no-no, but breaking glass is a mortal sin. A front-of-house team member was carrying a tray full of glasses through the busy kitchen. He ducked and dodged as a few of his team members hurriedly moved food out to waiting diners and cooks quickly moved from one task to the next. As he spun to avoid a collision, the tray tilted and sent the wineglasses crashing to the floor. The kitchen went silent, and everyone looked at me to see what I would I do. I slowly closed my eyes, pursed my lips tightly together, and turned to the sound. The cooks knew what kind of night we were having. I was being very vocal with them—in other words, I was kind of yelling—and Kate's delivery broke any rhythm that we might have been getting back.

The back waiter who had dropped the glasses was shielded from a verbal lashing by Kate's presence. I simply opened my eyes, looked at him, and pointed to the back door. He knew what that meant and seemed to be thankful for this quiet dismissal. He put his head down and walked out.

Three hours later, alone in the downstairs dining room, I put my head down on the table for a second to rest. I was beat. I was already almost seventeen hours into that day and more than seventy hours into the week. And it was only day four. I was forcing myself to work on the fall menu—it had to be done—but I just couldn't focus. As my mind drifted and I started to recall the day and where we went wrong, I remembered the wineglasses breaking, and I smelled raspberries. And just like that it happens. Raspberries that are fragile like fine glassware, maybe even clear like stained glass. They smelled like roses, so we'll pair them with roses. I walked back into the kitchen, pulled the tray of raspberries from the cooler, and looked at them.

"How the hell do I do that?" I thought to myself.

The idea was the easy part—it practically landed right in my lap. Now I had to figure out how to actually make it, and then how to serve it. The rush of excitement that the good idea produces started to fade after I realized it was almost 4:00 A.M. and I needed to at least get some concepts down on paper for the next day so the team would have a starting point. I pulled the various pectins, starches, and hydrocolloids out from the spice cabinet, then e-mailed Martin the idea so he could get a jump on a service piece for the raspberry course, in case we actually figured it out.

In a conversation with Anthony Bourdain, he asked me why I took this road. He noted that it was clear to him that I was a good cook from my connection with Thomas at The French Laundry, the meal that I helped cook for him while I was there, and his friend Michael Ruhlman's opinion of me in his books.

"Man, I mean, I think you're a genius, but you're being sort of stupid by taking the hard road, no?" Bourdain laughed in my direction. "Surely you could cook great French food, or contemporary

American food without killing yourself to reinvent the wheel. What's up with that? Why do it?"

I looked at him for a second, sighed, and shook my head.

"I don't know, it's just what I do. And . . . in some ways it controls you. One thing leads to another and to another."

It was a terrible answer. The reply itself was true, but my lack of explanation made me pissed at myself for not articulating it after I walked away. Bourdain threw me the lob and I didn't swing. A lot of people criticize the type of food we do at Alinea. Many don't even know what we do, others don't understand it, and some think it's bullshit. Here I had the chance to explain "the why" to a guy that not only liked to talk and has the ability to reach many people, but who stands on the opposite side of the philosophical fence.

All of my life I was surrounded by success. My parents owned their own restaurant before they were thirty years old, and despite their relationship and personal issues it provided for them very well. Through their generosity it gave me a springboard. I was exposed to Trotter's pursuit of excellence and his standing at the top of the U.S. dining scene. I watched Thomas grow into an international culinary giant who will undoubtedly be heralded as one of the greatest American chefs ever. The whole time I wanted to be as good as all of them. I knew the only way to come close to that was to do something different; otherwise, I would always be in their shadows.

Once I made the decision to do something different there was no going back.

And now, after the accolades poured in, the work just continued. The Grind.

Alinea was less than two years old. We had a ton left to prove.

I had attended a few culinary congresses that were popular in Spain over the previous couple of years, starting with one in Barcelona when I was at Trio, and then a couple in San Sebastián after Alinea was up and running. I always found these events enjoyable. It's never bad to travel to Europe, especially Spain, and professionally it was a chance to meet some of the world's greatest chefs and gain inspiration from their cuisine and restaurants.

Held every winter in Madrid, Madrid Fusion is one of the largest and most highly regarded events of this type in the world. Chefs fly in from as far as Brazil and Japan to take the stage and show their peers their innovations. In January 2007 I decided to take sous chefs John Shields and Curtis Duffy with me to Madrid Fusion.

During the four-day-long event the congress is generous enough to organize a series of dinners for the presenting chefs in various restaurants in Madrid. These dinners were a chance to connect on a personal level with the media, the sponsors, and the host chefs.

Toward the end of the congress, John, Curtis, and I decided to go to the last of the organized dinners. When we arrived we were seated with a group of American journalists and chefs that included Joyce Goldstein. I immediately found myself engaged in conversation with Joyce as she told stories of cooking "back in the day." I was fascinated by her tales of Alice Waters and Judy Rodgers and the origin of what would become known as California Cuisine. It was way better than any history gastronomy class that I had attended at the CIA. I barely noticed Curtis and John hovering around the table next to us in between courses. As the meal was winding down, John literally pulled me out of my chair and away from Joyce.

"Dude, what are you doing? You should hear these amazing stories she's telling over here."

"Yeah, well, read it in a book," he said with a smile. "There are some people over here I think you should meet."

As I approached the table I recognized a woman with whom I was all too familiar: Antoinette Bruno, the CEO and editor in chief of the culinary webzine StarChefs.com. Antoinette and I had had a bit of a run-in during StarChefs' rising-star award search in 2005. She had approached us about coming to the restaurant for a tasting, which after the Mariani incident translated to "free meal" in my mind. I hadn't really heard of StarChefs at that point, and her personality was, well, let's just say demanding. She wanted to come in during off-hours, eat tasting or reduced-size portions, and take pictures. This is not what we did. We politely declined, and she insisted. We declined again and she insisted. And then I turned it over to Nick to be the bad cop.

Nick explained to Antoinette that we didn't feel like I should be positioned for a rising-star award from StarChefs since *Food & Wine* had given me one of their ten Best New Chef awards more than three years earlier, the James Beard Foundation had given me their rising-star award in 2003, and I had won countless local awards. Just for good measure, he quoted the *New York Times* in a September 2005 article: "Astonishingly self-assured at 31, he will be, I believe, the next great American chef, up there with Trotter and the French Laundry's Thomas Keller."

Losing his patience with the assertive Bruno, he simply said, "Grant's star has already risen, you missed the upswing, and we're looking for bigger things." Nick then went on to diplomatically suggest our pastry chef Alex Stupak, which she willingly accepted.

I had no real interest in chatting with her, and I was about to walk away from the group when I heard John say, "Chef, this is Heather."

I turned to see an attractive young woman with long wavy brunette hair and sleek glasses standing with her hand extended ready to shake mine.

After the introduction we pulled some empty chairs from a nearby table over and the four of us sat down. Antoinette said hello, and I couldn't help but feel a little uncomfortable. It wasn't that I disliked her or had any bad feelings toward her or StarChefs, but the way things had gone down, it wasn't exactly like being reunited with a long-lost friend. Nevertheless, that was two years ago, we were in Spain, and all of us had had a few drinks by this point in the evening. Will Blunt, Antoinette's partner in StarChefs who I had met a few months earlier while I was cooking at Trotter's nineteenth-anniversary dinner, was at the table as well. As we started talking about that event, he asked if I would be willing to do an interview and submit a recipe of one of the courses that I had prepared at Trotter's. After some good conversation about food and the industry, the group decided we didn't want the night to end just yet and opted to go out for some Cava. One bottle turned into several, and before I knew it I found myself in a tiny dive bar in Madrid watching John and Will go head-to-head in a Jameson consumption contest.

After our late-night foray into the streets of Madrid, Heather and I went back to my room and stayed awake talking until the sun came up. Heather and Will headed for the airport a few hours later, while my group stayed for another night. I tried to talk her into changing her flight and staying an extra day, with no luck.

When I woke up the next morning, I immediately went to my computer, found the StarChefs website, and tried to locate Heather's e-mail address. I wanted to talk to her more. Again, no luck—it wasn't listed. I decided to e-mail Will when I returned from Spain to get it.

It turned out I didn't need to. A couple of days after returning home Heather e-mailed. She explained that Will had assigned her to talk to me about the tempura shrimp served on a vanilla bean that we had contributed to the Trotter dinner.

"Thank you, Will," I thought to myself.

We bounced some subtly flirtatious e-mails back and forth, and after our time together in Spain and our conversation about the Trotter article, I knew I definitely wanted to see her again. Our e-mail exchanges soon gave way to much more efficient g-chats. I hinted about coming to New York to visit her, and she made it clear that she wanted to eat at Alinea in the near future. In March, a couple of months after we met abroad and countless chat sessions, she stopped in Chicago on her way to a cheese tasting in Wisconsin.

Heather ate at Alinea with her friend Alina—yes, just one letter off—who was working at *Gourmet* in the marketing department. The meal sealed the fate of our relationship. She told me that the emotionally charged meal was the best of her life. To my good fortune, I was able to impress her with creativity, passion, and delicious food, and the fact that she not only understood those things but enjoyed them made me even more attracted to her.

The conversations increased over the next couple of months, and when I was invited to fly to London to attend the World's 50 Best Restaurants awards ceremony put on by *Restaurant Magazine,* I asked her to come with me. I knew the invitation was way over the top for how well we knew each other, but I figured it would be exciting and fun for both of us. After a bit of deliberation she declined. So I told her that given the fact that she was not going to fly to London with me on a whim, I would change my flight plans and travel from London directly to New York and lay over for a day or two. She didn't know it, but I had a plan. Our birthdays were only three days apart. If I came back directly after the awards we could meet in New York and celebrate. I made the flight changes and booked a reservation at Per Se.

I decided to stay two days in New York, arriving on April 26, one day after my thirty-third birthday. After reaching the hotel I immediately went out and bought three giant handfuls of deep purple calla lilies, one of her favorites, to fill the room and ordered up a bottle of champagne on ice for when we returned from dinner. Our first night we decided to go to Mas, a restaurant owned by Galen Zamarra. Galen was good friends with Keith, and I had met him when Keith brought him to Trio once before. I arrived early and incredibly nervous, grabbed a seat at the bar, and waited for Heather to arrive from work. An infatuated night in Spain was one thing, and the subsequent chatting online was another, but reorganizing my international flight itinerary with the sole purpose of spending time with this woman took things to a different level.

Shortly after she arrived and the first glass of champagne disappeared my nerves subsided. Things were as natural in person as they were over the phone.

The next night we went to Per Se. I knew what to expect, but I was excited for Heather to experience the perfection and creativity. The maître d' welcomed us and showed us to the kitchen so we could say hello to chef Benno. Settling into our table, clearly the best one in the house—it was close to the fireplace and offered sweeping views of the entire room and Central Park—I heard a familiar voice from behind.

"Welcome to Per Se, Chef."

I turned my head slightly to confirm my suspicion—it was Michael Minello. Michael started as a commis on my first tour of the Laundry and quickly became one of the people in the brigade that "got it." Chef, Eric, and I quickly took a liking to his quick wit, sense of humor, and most important, his cooking ability. He stayed on and worked his way through many of the stations before deciding to slow the pace of life down a bit and transition to the front of the house. When Per Se opened in 2004, he was part of the opening dining-room team, and he's been there ever since, having risen in the interim to the position of captain. I stood to shake his hand and give him a hug. It was great to see him. After I introduced Heather he confirmed any allergies and dislikes, subtly inserting some inside jokes from our time together cooking, and told us that the sommelier would be over shortly to sort out our wine plan.

After pouring glasses of Grand Siècle and confirming that we did in fact want to let him pair the wines with the courses he slyly re-marked, "Good choice—we have some special bottles open for you, and it turns out we had a Grand Cru Burgundy tasting with a few DRC's at lunch here today, and sadly some of the bottles still have wine in them."

What a shame, Heather and I said in unison.

The meal was the most emotional I had ever had in my life. Part of it was the excitement of the circumstances—the spontaneous change of plans to come and see Heather—while another part of it was nostal-gia: tasting flavor memories that were some of the most prominent and important in my life, like the cornet, oysters and pearls, and coffee and doughnuts. And of course, I had begun to recognize that I could very well be falling in love.

It was great to see Heather experience some of my favorite bites of all time. Chef Benno had crafted a menu that was both familiar and altogether new, dishes like Quail in a Jar, Degustation of Kona Kampa-chi, and Shad Roe Porridge were new and exhilarating, and the wines poured were incredible. At one point midmeal the sommelier poured us each a glass of DRC Montrachet, giving Heather the 1979 and my-self the 1982. We sat savoring the wine for fifteen minutes after the matching course had been cleared. The aromas and flavors of those two wines are burned into my memory forever.

Six hours of amazing food, stellar wines, flawless service, and staring into each other's eyes was coming to an end as we nibbled on the final *mignardise*. By all accounts we were thinking how the dinner was perfect, that nothing was amiss, when one of the bulbs in one of the giant floor lamps flickered out. We looked at each other and smiled. Well, I guess the night wasn't perfect after all, I said jokingly. Before she could agree Michael glided over to the light, raised his arm to the bulb, and snapped his fingers. The light popped back on. He slowly turned to face us and with a slight smirk gave a wink. We laughed in astonishment. In fact, the night was more than perfect. It was magical.

After the Per Se weekend Heather and I started making it a priority to see each other frequently. Within four days I found myself back in New York for the James Beard Awards, where I was nominated for Best Chef Midwest. After I won the award, a large group that included some of Heather's friends, Nick, Martin and his wife, Lara, and sous chefs Curtis, Jeff Pikus, and John Shields celebrated with drinks and conversation at Employees Only. I told Heather at that point that we should make an effort to see each other every ten days or so; we could take turns flying to each other's city. A pattern emerged, and the Jet-Blue frequent-flyer points started adding up quickly. Slightly more than a month later I flew to San Francisco—where she was working on the StarChefs rising-star event—to meet her for a weekend.

We strolled through the farmers' market and collected provisions for a romantic picnic at Point Reyes, and later that night raced down the coast to an amazing meal at Chez Panisse. Everything was going perfectly, we were truly in love, I was starting to reap the rewards of years of hard work, but something was bothering me. My tongue had become very sore, and I had begun to use gum as a shield to prevent my teeth and tongue from touching. Heather noticed it while we lay in bed the morning after Chez Panisse.

"Do you always sleep with gum in your mouth?"

I was a bit embarrassed, but I tried to explain to her how I had made repeated trips to the dentist only for them to tell me I was biting my tongue at night. They prescribed me a mouth guard, which I normally use, but I figured the gum would be a suitable substitute in this situation. I told her I was sure it was nothing, that I was planning to go back to the dentist when I got home and have them try to file my teeth down on that side—it might just be a sharp spot.

After the San Francisco weekend I was confident that I was in love with Heather and that I was about to enter the world of a long-distance relationship. Our early days together were a whirlwind of spontaneity and excitement that any romance novel would envy. We continued to fly back and forth—sometimes for less than twenty-four hours—just to see each other. Nick thought I was completely nuts.

"Dude, you think you don't have enough going on? Running the best restaurant in the country, being a father, and now getting into a relationship with a girl who lives in New York—are you nuts? You're a glutton for punishment, and lack of sleep, apparently."

I couldn't argue with the logic. It certainly didn't make sense from a time perspective. I was logging ninety- to one-hundred-hour weeks at work and then spending my days off with Kaden and Keller; throwing this relationship into the mix was in fact crazy, but completely necessary.

We planned for Heather to fly to Chicago over the Fourth of July weekend to meet the boys. Alina had started seeing Pikus, and she decided to come with Heather to Chicago. We all decided it would be fun to prepare an elaborate dinner at Alinea together. In the weeks leading up to the weekend, the four of us exchanged e-mails about the menu and who would prepare what. We decided on the following menu:

FOIE GRAS MOUSSE WITH PX GEL AND TOAST

SURF CLAM SASHIMI WITH FRESH CORIANDER SEEDS AND LIME

BUCATINI ALLA AMATRICIANA

STRIPED BASS WITH WHITE ASPARAGUS, PEAS AND THYME

RIB EYE OF WAGYU WITH RED WINE REDUCTION AND POTATOES

VANILLA ICE CREAM SUNDAES

Having the entire Alinea kitchen to cook in on a day the restaurant is closed is a beautiful thing. But sharing this experience with these people was amazing. We all pulled out cutting boards, poured some Krug, and casually chatted while we prepared a feast. It was one of the best cooking moments of my life.

Meanwhile I was in extreme pain.

Since leaving San Francisco, the sensitivity in my tongue had worsened to the point where I could barely eat. The pain was excruciating. With the gum and a good dose of champagne I figured I could get by without it looking obvious, and I did pretty well. I was getting up frequently, ducking into the bathroom and applying a generous layer of oral gel toothache cream to my tongue. This only proved to give temporary relief; after I returned to the table and started to eat the next course the antiseptic qualities of the cream were rinsed away and the pain returned. But I had to eat this food; I didn't want to ruin everyone's evening by letting them know I was hurting.

The next day Heather and I took Kaden and Keller to North Avenue Beach. I was nervous about how Heather would react to them. Up until this point she had only seen me as the older, successful well-known chef who was flying around the world. In a way I had a dual identity: energetic chef most of the time, followed by providing father some of the time. I wondered how that would make this beautiful, ambitious young woman feel. The boys took to her right away, and before you knew it the three of them were engaged in a full-on seaweed war. She gave Keller a piggyback ride most of the walk home, and then played Wii and drew on pieces of scrap paper into the evening. It seemed to me that the day had gone well—I even had to talk her into letting me put them to bed so we could have some alone time.

PART 3

LIFE, ON THE LINE

walked into the Alinea kitchen and saw Grant for the first time in a few days. He looked really sick—his hair was matted down and his eyes were hollow. He was gaunt.

"Chef, you look really sick. What's up?"

He pulled me by my sleeve into the polishing room adjoining the kitchen. "Remember when I told you about that thing on my tongue? Well, a few weeks ago it started hurting again, but this time really bad. It got to the point where I couldn't eat. So I went to the dentist again and she insisted that I'm biting my tongue at night. I know I'm not biting my tongue."

He looked ill overall, like it wasn't just a mouth problem. All I could think of was VD.

"Dude, I am guessing that perhaps your little jaunt in Spain left you with a gift that keeps on giving," I said with a laugh.

"No. Come on. Seriously. This has been going on for a while. Remember? I told you about it before, but then it went away. Now there's a little area that hurts like you wouldn't believe if my tooth rubs against it." He removed a wad of gum from his mouth that he had been using as a buffer between the spot and his teeth. "I have to keep gum in there or I can't talk."

He seemed almost panicked, or as close to panic as I had ever seen him.

"Let me see it," I said.

"No. I'm not going to show you my tongue."

"Come on. What's the big deal? Let me see it."

He opened his mouth and carefully stuck out his tongue, then grabbed the tip with his fingers and rolled it to one side. I felt odd standing in an alcove of the Alinea kitchen looking in his mouth, but once I saw his tongue I could tell something was wrong. There was a small white area surrounded by a highly inflamed circle, and his tongue seemed misshapen and swollen. It did indeed look painful. I had no idea what it was, but it didn't look normal. I figured he had an infection of some kind and told him he should go to the doctor the next day.

"I have been to the dentist three times in the last six months."

"No. Go to an oral surgeon. Just call the nearest one and go."

The oral surgeon asked me to open my mouth. Because I couldn't talk at this point I had typed up a letter detailing the problems and handed it to the receptionist upon arrival. The letter said:

> *Due to my increased difficulty in talking I figured this would be the best way to fully and efficiently convey what has been going on.*
>
> *In early 2004 I noticed a very small white dot on the side of my tongue. When it came in contact with my teeth while speaking or eating it was painful. It was sensitive to spicy foods and temperatures. It slowly increased in size and floated in and out of bothering me. Six months later I decided to go get it checked out and went to an oral surgeon in Evanston. He did a biopsy that came back clean. The soreness persisted and eventually started to become a bit of a furrow in the side of my tongue. There were periods of time that it didn't bother me at all, fluctuating with periods of extreme soreness. But even at its worst it was annoying but tolerable.*
>
> *However, two weeks ago I woke up and it was extremely sore. When I looked in the mirror I could literally see the imprint of my bottom teeth deeply imbedded in my tongue. At the same time my left gland started to swell. The nighttime clenching continued and my tongue continued to be very sore. I went to the dentist to see if she could file some of the sharper edges off of my bottom teeth; she then fitted me for a night guard. It was for the top teeth and it proved ineffective. I have been fitted for a bottom guard that should be ready in a few days.*

Last week my tongue became so sore that I couldn't talk with-out buffering my tongue from my teeth with a piece of gum. About four days ago the tongue began to swell near the tip at one of the points that always showed the most aggressive imprints from the grinding. It is now that swelling location that is making eating and talking impossible. Sleeping is difficult as well. The enlarged point is very sensitive. At its worst two days ago, the pain was intense and seemed to travel to my ears, throat, and even the side of my face. Also the last day or so I noticed a lot of saliva, quite thick, although this seems to have lessened as of today.

I have gone through one 10-day cycle of amoxicillin about three weeks ago along with a chlohexidine gluconate rinse, a viscous lidocaine solution, and a fluocinonide ointment. I just started another round of amoxicillin two days ago.

Obviously not being able to eat, sleep, or talk is a big prob-lem. But for me especially anything involving my tongue comes as a great concern due to my profession as a chef. I am due to present a lecture in NYC this Thursday, and as you might ex-pect was hoping to get this under control in time to keep that appointment . . . eating would be nice, too, although weight loss is appreciated.

I opened my mouth, he looked in, and his mood changed in-stantly. "I'm going to want to take a biopsy of that," he said. He didn't look at me as he left the room and returned quickly with two more doctors.

He explained how the biopsy would work. The doctors looked at each other and one said, "Make sure you take a good sample."

As opposed to what?

He took a healthy slice of the area and despite the anesthetic I nearly flew out of the chair. But it was over that quickly. He explained that it would be sent to a lab and that he'd have results in a week to ten days.

I still didn't know quite what he was testing for. "What kind of test is it?" I asked.

"We are testing to see if the tissue is cancerous." He began packing up. It seemed like the exam was over. I was waiting for him to do something else, or to prescribe some antibiotics or something. But that was the extent of it.

"And that's it? Nothing else to do?"

"Not right now. We'll see what the test results say. In the meantime I'm giving you a prescription for some pain medication."

I left the office feeling very uneasy. If there was a chance that the test result *wasn't* cancer, shouldn't he be trying to figure out what else it could be?

I headed back toward Alinea and called Nick on my cell. "Hey. I went to the oral surgeon. The guy freaked me out. Took a biopsy and that was it."

"Well, that's what you went there for, right? Did he say anything else?"

"No. Not really. That's why I'm worried."

A few days went by and we heard nothing. The pressure of the uncertainty clearly weighed on Grant and was reinforced by the constant pain in his mouth.

I decided to call the oral surgeon's office to try to get the results of the biopsy more quickly. Grant was nervous, to say the least, and neither of us had a good feeling about the outcome.

A woman answered the phone.

"Hi. My name is Nick Kokonas and I'm the business partner of one of your patients who recently had a biopsy. He was told that he would have to wait seven to ten days for the results. I was wondering if there is any way we can pay the lab to expedite the analysis."

She was confused by this question. "This biopsy was performed on you?" she asked.

"No ma'am. It was performed on Grant Achatz. He is a chef at a nearby restaurant named Alinea. Have you heard of it?"

"No."

That was too bad. I was going to use that angle. I pressed on, "Well, he's

Courtesy of Lara Kastner

- *Left:* Candy cap mushroom ice cream with spun muscovado sugar and BLiS maple syrup, presented on Crucial Detail's "antenna" service piece

- *Below:* With Dagmara and Nick on opening night

Courtesy of the author

- In the kitchen at Alinea

- Hot potato, cold potato

- Heart of palm, from the
  opening Alinea menu

Pheasant, shallot, cider gel, burning oak leaves

Wild turbot with hyacinth vapor

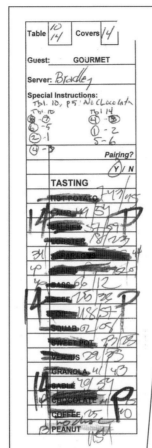

- *Right:* 14-top ticket for *Gourmet* magazine

- *Far Right:* Ruth Reichl 2-top dinner

- *Below:* Design meeting with Martin Kastner, two days before diagnosis

- *Above:* First day of chemo treatment, working on the Alinea book

- *Right:* After my boys shaved my head into a Mohawk

- *Above:* Cooking
  with Heather at
  her parents' home,
  midtreatment

  - *Below:* Post surgery to
    remove my lymphs

- *Above:* Fishing with the
  boys…"tough as a worm"

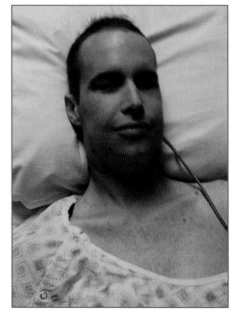

• With Heather at the James Beard Awards for Outstanding Chef

• Eating dinner at le Musee restaurant in Sapporo, Japan

a world-famous chef. His restaurant was named the number-one restaurant in the country by *Gourmet* magazine. Number one. He is in tremendous pain and is having a very difficult time eating, let alone performing his job. And frankly, ten days seems like a long time to have a potential cancer diagnosis hanging over your head. If there is anything at all we can do to speed up the lab results it would be hugely appreciated."

She really wasn't following any of this, it seemed. "So, he's a chef, he can't eat, he's in pain. Has he seen the doctor?"

I grew frustrated. "Look. I need to speak with someone there that deals with the lab. It is critical that we get these results very soon. Is there someone else I can speak with?"

"Please hold."

A few minutes went by and I could feel my blood pressure rising. Thankfully, someone came to the phone who was on top of things. I repeated my entreaty.

"Well, the doctor can request the results more quickly in emergency situations."

"Great. Have him do that, please. Grant is in a great deal of pain, his livelihood depends on his palate, and frankly he's freaking out a bit. I really would appreciate anything you can do to expedite this on his behalf."

She promised to do her best.

I called Grant and relayed the conversation. "You know, it feels a bit better today, actually," he said. "Maybe it's nothing."

The next morning the oral surgeon's office called me.

"We have your biopsy results and the doctor would like you to come in first thing tomorrow morning. Can you make it at nine thirty?"

"No. Not really," I replied. Ideally, I would be asleep at 9:30 in the morning, since I was leaving Alinea these days at around 3:00 A.M. and getting to sleep closer to four. We were implementing a series of menu changes, and the kitchen was struggling to keep up. "Can you just tell me the results over the phone?"

"No, sir, I'm sorry. I'm not allowed to do that. Only the doctor can give you the results."

"Well, can you have him call me, please?"

"No, sir. The doctor needs to see you at nine thirty A.M. tomorrow. He will give you the results then."

My blood ran cold. I knew.

Negative results, I figured, were good news that could easily be communicated over the phone. You get a strep test, they call you to tell you that it's negative.

"Okay. I'll be there." I hung up the phone and immediately dialed Nick. "Hey. The office called me and said they got the results. But they'll only tell me the results in the office and want me to come in first thing tomorrow morning. That can't be good."

"I am sure it's just a formality," Nick said. "Or maybe they want you to come in because they want to see if it's changed at all, or to prescribe medication or something. Even if the result is negative, they still have to figure out what is wrong."

He was right, but not convincing. "I don't know. Think about it. If it were negative, why wouldn't they just tell me?"

"Who knows? Insurance reasons, the fact that she's just a secretary, or maybe the doctor is just on the golf course today and she didn't read the results. Speaking of which, I'm leaving for Michigan tonight to play in a tournament up there. I should cancel and come with you. What time is your appointment?"

"Nine thirty. But don't come. I'll give you a buzz from the office when I hear. We're probably nervous over nothing."

I headed up to Lost Dunes Golf Club in Bridgman, Michigan, the next morning.

I was going to go up a night early before the tournament and get in a round and relax in one of the cabins, but I decided to wait and see if Grant changed his mind and wanted me to come along to the appointment. When I didn't hear from him, I figured he didn't want me around, so I woke up at six, picked up a buddy of mine, and drove the two hours from Chicago to the course. It felt like an odd thing to do, but at the same time a doctor's visit is a private thing and I could tell that while Grant was thankful for my help in getting the results quickly, he wanted to go on his own.

I told my friend Bruce that I would likely be distracted due to my concern over Grant's situation. "Does he smoke?" he asked.

"No. Never had a cigarette ever, he claims."

"He's got something, but it's not likely to be cancer. He's like thirty years old or something, right?"

Lost Dunes is a small, gorgeous private club, and that weekend's tournament was the annual member-guest event, which drew a field of 120 or so golfers. I was, to say the least, nervous and distracted. Despite the prohibition against cell phones, mine was on "vibrate" and was sitting in my pocket. There was nothing I could do but wait.

Our first competitors would be member Chris Morrow, a fine golfer and all-around great guy, and a guest of his visiting from Florida named Andy Fox, also a single-digit handicapper. As far as distractions went, this was my favorite one in the world—match-play golf.

I went over to say good morning and to introduce Bruce. Chris and I had met once or twice, but only in the context of events like this one. He shook my hand, then called Andy over to say hello.

I noticed right away that Andy had something wrong with his face, something missing. I couldn't quite pinpoint what it was, but then he turned and I could tell that he was missing half of his jaw. He wore a goatee and spoke normally, so it wasn't obvious. But it was definitely not all there. A scar traced down his esophagus on the same side, making his neck thinner than usual. My first thought was that he had been in a fire.

We chatted for a bit about the course and the impending match. Andy had a ton of energy and spoke in rapid-fire sentences. He was thin and fit and clearly in good shape for a guy in his forties. I felt instantly comfortable with him in a way that golfers who love the game and have played their whole lives do when they meet a passionate competitor. You see someone roll a putt and you can tell what kind of person he is.

"Hey, Andy. What happened to your face?" I asked. I said it in an offhanded way as I struck a putt, but I wasn't worried about offending him. I could tell he was a confident person.

"Oh this?" he said with a smile. "Cancer. I should be dead. But I'm a ten-year survivor, and I'm about to kick your ass all over this golf course."

Then it hit me.

The man standing in front of me on this course had the same cancer that Grant was about to be diagnosed with. I lost my composure and Andy could sense it right away. The coincidence was insane. I could only stare at the ground.

Andy put his hand on my shoulder and said, "Hey. Don't worry. You didn't offend me. I've been living with this for a long time now. Life is great."

"Andy, it's not that," I said as I led him to a corner of the busy practice green. "My good friend had a biopsy a few days ago. He's going to the doctor in about an hour to hear the results. I should be there with him."

As I explained the situation to him, I could tell that he thought it didn't sound great.

Our tee time was coming up. Chris and Bruce came over toward us and we headed toward the first tee. Andy must have told Chris about the situation because Chris's mood grew sullen. I realized that Grant's appointment started half an hour ago, but there was no message. I excused myself to duck into the trees to make a quick call, then dialed Grant's number.

He answered on the second ring.

"Hey. Did they see you yet?"

"Yeah, I'm talking to the doctor now."

"What did he say?"

"It's cancer."

Silence.

"What kind? What else?"

"I don't know. He's right here. You talk to him." He sounded truly shaken.

The doctor introduced himself and then relayed the news to me: "It's squamous cell carcinoma. It's a serious cancer. At this point I don't know any more than that. I'm referring him to a specialist, an ENT at Masonic who's also an oncologist. He'll be able to do the actual diagnosis."

"Is this like skin cancer? Can you just remove the tumor in-office?"

"It's impossible for me to tell with certainty. But I have to say that this seems serious. When he showed me his tongue, I knew. It was obvious. He needs to go right away."

"Thank you, Doctor. Can you put Grant back on?"

Grant came to the phone and mocked a cheery "Helloooooo."

"Well, that sucks," I said. "But we don't know much yet. I know a few people who have skin cancer and it's been no big deal—the kind of thing they cut out then monitor over time. Just make that appointment with the ENT and I'll be down there in two hours. Okay?"

"Yeah. I already made the appointment for Monday. Stay up there. I'm going to the restaurant—we have ninety-eight booked tonight with forty Tours." He was referring to the large number of customers we had coming in that night for dinner and the intricate "Chef's Tour" menu that had been requested ahead of time.

"Grant. Don't worry about that."

"What am I supposed to do, go home and die?"

"Good point. I'll see you at Alinea."

"What for? Stay up there. I need some time to myself anyway. I need to think."

I hung up the phone and looked over at the first tee to see Bruce, Chris, and Andy watching me. I headed over directly to Andy. "Well?" he said.

"It's cancer. Squamous cell carcinoma." Tears began to well up in my eyes and I was trembling. I had a hard time keeping it together.

Andy grabbed both of my shoulders and looked me square in the eye when I lifted my head. "It's going to be fine," he said. "Look at me. I'm here. He can beat this."

I hit my tee shot down the center of the fairway. I walked alone the first few holes, thinking, "This cannot be happening." Then I spent the rest of the match with Andy, asking him about his ordeal and his treatment. It sounded like pure hell.

But Andy was here playing golf.

I left the oral surgeon's office in a daze.

Cancer.

I had no profound thoughts; I just wandered toward my car and marveled that everything seemed so normal. Even my tongue wasn't hurting that day.

I drove to Alinea, parked behind the restaurant, and entered through the kitchen door. The place was already humming with chefs who had come in early to get ahead on their prep.

I walked over to my station, grabbed a cutting board, and started turning artichokes. I had plenty of time to lose myself in the prep. I was like a zombie.

I thought of Kaden and Keller. I thought about what I would tell my mom. I looked around at all of the employees and worried about them.

And then I turned more artichokes. Slowly, methodically, I pressed through the day.

Three o'clock staff meeting. Introduced the new dishes. Choked down a bit of food at 4:00 P.M. staff meal. 4:30 cleanup. 5:30 doors open.

Ninety-eight guests with forty Tours. One thousand eight hundred seventy dishes to go out.

I thought to myself that I did not want to leave Alinea that night.

I thought I might just stay there until the next morning.

My third nine-hole match concluded that day at nearly 7:00 P.M. I played remarkably well, considering that I didn't think about golf for a second. The caddie would hand me a club, I would look at the target and hit the ball. I genuinely didn't care. It was a state of golf I had been trying to achieve my whole life: complete dispassion.

I walked the course thinking about my dad and his life and death. I thought about my mom's struggle over the past few months and whether or not I had made the right decision in giving the go-ahead for her brain surgery. I thought about the cruel irony that the best young chef in the world had tongue cancer and what that meant. I fought back tears for all of those things that day.

I explained to Bruce that I was going to head back to Alinea and skip the dinner that night. "For sure, Nick. Go ahead."

I arrived at the restaurant at 10:00 P.M. I had to remind myself before I walked in the kitchen door that no one there knew yet. I had to compose myself. I took a deep breath, opened the door, and looked in.

There was Grant at the pass plating a dozen dishes at once with five chefs gathered around him. The kitchen was cranking. He is still here, still alive, I reminded myself. I was calmed by the normality of it all.

I walked up to Grant. "Hey. How's it going?"

He turned his head, gave a smile and a raised eyebrow, and said, "Fantastic! What are you doing here? I thought you had a golf tournament to play."

"Yeah, well. I thought I'd drive down and say hi."

He looked good, but I must have looked like shit. "Are you hungry?" he asked.

I never ate Alinea food during service, and Grant never offered to cook for me. I found myself saying, "Actually, yes," despite my better judgment.

Grant called out, "Curtis, do we have any of that duck breast left over?"

"Yes, Chef. My station, third shelf in the back."

Grant walked over to the flattop, grabbed a pan, and made a perfectly cooked duck breast. He then heated up morels, stock, and some garnishes from other dishes while slicing up the breast. He put it all in an oversized, shallow bowl, and as if on cue, Curtis reached over and ad-libbed some freeze-dried peas, micro greens, sea salt, and my favorite, Thai long pepper. They did this in a few minutes right in the middle of a crushing service. The dish looked worthy of the best French restaurants in the world.

I was dumbfounded. "Why is it that I can't get that down the street at some French bistro? If we opened a place that did that we would kill 'em."

"Eh. It's easy 'cause we do everything right," Grant replied. "The stock. The mushrooms. No one does it like that. You know that. Boring though, right? Where's the challenge in that?" He smiled and handed me the plate.

I took it to the downstairs office, snapped a picture with my phone, locked the door, ate my duck, and tried to remain calm.

It was delicious. Just perfect.

And so terribly sad.

E-mail to the investors of Alinea:

Gentlemen,

I am truly sorry to report that Grant has been diagnosed with squamous cell carcinoma of the tongue.

For the last few weeks, and going back even further, his tongue has been bothering him. He went to a dentist a while back and was told it was a result of biting or grinding against his teeth at night while he was sleeping. The pain progressed last week to the point that he could not eat. He returned to a dentist, then the emergency room, and finally, to an oral surgeon last Monday who took a biopsy. Unfortunately, the biopsy came back positive on Friday.

At this point we do not know if the cancer has metastasized beyond the point of the tumor. He has an appointment tomorrow with a specialist and will certainly be getting more tests and eventually treatment.

Right now, the primary concern, by a large measure, is Grant's treatment and recovery from this disease. However, we do not at this point want to alert the press, so please keep this news as private as possible. Once we have a firm diagnosis we will plan a course of action for Alinea and for Grant professionally.

I know that this is going to be a complete shock to you all as it was to me, and of course to Grant. He knows that he has our full support, and if any of you have any questions or have personal experience with someone who has had treatment for cancer in the head or neck, please contact me.

Regards,

Nick

CHAPTER 22

The ENT snaked a camera down my throat. Nick looked up at the video screen above me and said something about my profound ability to deep throat. He was trying to relieve the tension, but this wasn't the tense part. As fast as it was in, it was out again, and the doctor told me that my voice box looked clear. He examined my tongue and my neck with his hands, then asked me to wait in his office across the hall. Nick and I went in there, found two seats next to each other, and looked at one another.

"Seems okay," Nick said.

"Yeah. Good that my voice box was clean. What do you think they'll do?"

We could hear the nurses shuffling around outside, asking some other appointments if they could wait a bit longer. It was a tiny room, barely big enough for three or four people, and it had the generic feeling of a doctor's office that was seldom used—an office supply desk tucked in a corner, a couple of posters on the wall detailing a cutaway of the head and neck, uncomfortable seats. We sat there waiting. And waiting. We probably waited for about twenty minutes, although it felt like a very long twenty minutes. And the room was so small . . . too small for even just the two of us. The whole time we could hear them clearing through other patients and gathering up a couple of interns. Finally, the door opened and the doctor entered with two interns who barely looked old enough to drive. I noticed that they wouldn't look me in the eye.

I feigned a smile.

The doctor had to steady himself before he spoke. Not good, I thought. Then he spoke quietly. "You know already that you have cancer. I'm sorry to tell you that it's a late stage, and that it's probably metastasized into your lymph nodes—certainly, at least, on your left side. It covers most of your tongue—or most of the visible part of your tongue. It may have bisected the midline, which I can't tell without an . . ."

At that point his voice drifted out. I understood what he was saying and didn't need to hear more. My expression didn't change, but I began to sweat and feel cold. I rejoined the conversation when Nick asked a question about treatment. I heard something about replacing my tongue with a muscle from my arm, and asked quickly, "Will I be able to taste?"

"No. It will not be a tongue, it will be a muscle that with therapy will allow you some limited speech and perhaps the ability to swallow and eat."

I was gone again. I steeled my chin by biting hard. And then Nick spoke: "Doctor, I don't think we're going to accomplish all of that today . . . perhaps it's best that we leave now."

The doctor protested, "Sir, this is very serious and I think . . ." Nick interrupted and looked at me. "I understand how serious this is, Doctor, and we'll do what we need to do—on another day." With this the doctor wrote some names on a piece of paper, gave me a prescription for serious painkillers, and we left his office.

It was a nice summer day, and we did exactly what needed to be done at that point: We headed across the street, at 11:30 A.M., to a Mexican dive bar and ordered a pitcher of strong margaritas.

We had to tell the staff at Alinea what was going on. A few people knew that Chef was not well—anyone could see that. But suddenly he was missing work at odd hours, and then he flew to New York with no notice. This was highly unusual, and everyone could tell that something was up. Some people might have thought that we were planning to open out there, because when I asked Joe to call an all-staff meeting for 3:00 P.M. in the upstairs dining room—"the 20's"—there was, at first, an air of excitement.

I pulled Joe aside. "Grant is sick."

"Yeah. I figured that; he doesn't look well at all," Joe said calmly, as usual. "Really sick?"

"Joe, I don't want to tell anyone else right now because I think it's important that it comes from Grant himself, but he's spending the day tomorrow at Sloan-Kettering. He has stage-four cancer in his tongue, and it's spread to his lymph system."

Joe looked at me with only a slight giveaway of the horror of it all. "That bad? *That* bad?"

"Yes, it's that bad. It's terrible. He's completely screwed. They are talking about removing his tongue and part of his jaw, most of his neck. Then chemo, then radiation."

Joe looked at me for a long moment but said nothing. "I'll get the staff together at three."

"Thanks."

At 2:30 I got my laptop and called Grant on iChat. We thought it would be good for the staff to see him, to know that he was still functioning, still walking and talking. "Hey. How's it going out there?" I asked.

"It's going. I'm at Heather's place."

"Cool. You know what you're going to say to them?"

"Yeah, I'm all set, I think."

"Okay . . . I'll ping you at about five to three."

The front-of-house staff gathered up their side work—folding napkins and de-linting the chairs and banquettes—and sat down. The entire kitchen staff, all twenty-six chefs, came up the back stairs and before entering the dining room took off their clogs and lined them all up neatly in a row.

My laptop sat on the beautiful black service table in the middle of the dining room. Joe was up front looking glumly at me. I avoided making eye contact with anyone, and at this point, everyone could see something was wrong. I had never addressed an all-staff meeting; usually it was Grant.

I pinged Grant on iChat and nothing happened. The wireless was new and was having issues, so I logged in again and got a sketchy connection, with his voice cutting in and out. He called my cell.

"What's up with the connection?"

"Everyone's here, Grant, but it just isn't working right. Let me get a phone in here."

We struggled for fifteen minutes to find a cord long enough to bring in a speakerphone. I was getting impatient and was worried how this would all go down. Grant kept calling my cell, and I kept ignoring it. Finally, I just yelled out, "Everyone downstairs to the front dining room." The room—"the teens"—is designed to hold sixteen diners. We had fifty-six people standing along the back wall, perching on tables, and a bunch of the chefs sitting cross-legged in a semicircle around a small black Panasonic speakerphone. I called Grant.

"Hello?"

"Grant, sorry. I have everyone here. We're crammed into the teens around a speakerphone."

"What the hell?" he said, laughing. Everyone laughed. But everyone also sensed that this was important and different. Not to mention a bit absurd. Some people were staring at the phone. Others were just looking around, wondering how they would catch up in time for service.

"Okay. So I want to first recognize chef Curtis Duffy. Curtis spent time at Trotter's, then came over to work with me at Trio. He, along with John Peters, was the chef that helped me build the original Alinea menu, worked on the food lab, sourced everything, and has been invaluable in what we have done along the way. As you may know, he will be moving on to take a job that will allow him to spend more time with his new baby and his wife. On behalf of everyone at Alinea, we owe him a debt of gratitude for all that he has done.

"Chef Jeff Pikus will be taking over as chef de cuisine. Jeff has also been with me since the Trio days, and in fact pretty much started his culinary career there. He is tremendously dedicated and hardworking, and I am certain the kitchen will not slow down at all under chef Pikus."

I thought to myself, "What the hell is he doing?" He's trying to make this sound like a normal meeting, but meanwhile everyone is looking at me wondering why the hell they're staring at a phone that they can barely hear, listening to routine—albeit big—changes in the kitchen.

"Next, I want to welcome chef..." Grant continued on, welcoming the stages who were visiting from Europe for the week and apologizing that he could not be there to greet them personally. This wasn't moving along very quickly.

"I want to take some time to talk about menu changes that we were going to put in place this week but will move to next week...." He was losing the crowd. People were literally looking at their phones, or folding the napkins without listening at all. Grant finally paused for a few breaths. We were nearly thirty minutes into the call.

"I suppose you're wondering why I asked everyone to be here today, why I'm talking to you through a telephone. Of course, I wanted to talk to you via the video so you could see that I'm here and fine, but that didn't work out.

"Anyway, three years ago I noticed a small spot on my tongue. It was nothing. I went to the dentist, they took a biopsy, and it came back clean. But it never really went away." Everyone was listening now; the mood changed instantly. He continued, "About a year ago it started bothering me again, but who has time for these things...." He continued on, telling the story. By now some people were starting to tear up, to cover their hands over their mouths, hiding their dropped jaws.

"After meeting with the doctors at Masonic, Nick did his magic and pulled some strings and got me into Sloan-Kettering tomorrow. We know at this point that I have cancer, squamous cell carcinoma, on my tongue. It's not good, in fact it's stage four. But I'm seeking the best care possible and want to assure you of one thing ... really just this one thing: Alinea will continue on being the best. It has to. If there is one thing you can do for me it is this: keep doing your jobs, keep Alinea there for me, keep this dream that I had, that we all share, alive. At some point I'm not going to be able to be there, but I want to know—I need to know—that it will be there for me when I get back, okay?"

There was dead silence in the room. It was palpable. Nearly sixty people were in shock; a few quietly cried. Employees who were hired two days earlier and had never even met Grant didn't know how to act at all—they had just walked into a shit-storm. Nathan Klingbail, a chef who was with Grant at Trio, then worked at Schwa, and then recently came to Alinea, looked up at me, mouthed the word "Sorry," and ran out the back door of the restaurant.

"Is everyone still there?" Grant said after a long minute of silence. "Does anyone have any questions?"

No one said a word. I piped up, "Grant, we're all here and everyone has heard the news. I'm sure that I'm speaking on behalf of the whole staff when

I tell you that we intend to redouble our efforts to make sure that Alinea is better than ever. And of course you'll be back here in a few days."

"Well that's all I've got. Again, thanks to Curtis for his years of dedicated service. I'll check in with the doctors here tomorrow—they're supposed to be the best in the world—and will be back in a few days." With that, he hung up.

Everyone's eyes turned to me. I didn't know what to say. "Obviously, the situation is not good. In fact, I'm not going to lie, it's really bad."

"Could he die?" someone asked.

"It is in fact more likely than not. And so far the recommended treatment is gruesome. We are going to decide what to tell the press, but until we hear from Sloan we don't want to say anything. So I ask you for now to keep this as quiet as possible." I waited a few moments, but nobody said anything. With that I left the room. I simply couldn't say anything else. I was watching the death not only of a man, but of his life's work.

I walked outside to get some air, only to find Nathan in the alley. He looked up at me with tears streaming down his face. "Nate," was all I could muster. I walked over to him and he turned away. "You think I haven't cried over this, Nate?"

"I'm really sorry," he said. "I'm not very good with this kind of thing."

"Who is, Nate?" I gave him a hug. He wiped his eyes with his chef's towel, thanked me, and strode back into the Alinea kitchen to go back to work.

I arrived at Heather's apartment in New York early in the week and we spent the better part of it eating our way through New York. I was limited to soft and wet foods that were easy to chew and that slid down my throat with minimal effort. But we managed to have fun on our tour. I wasn't sure what the Sloan appointment would hold for me so I figured I should spend as much time as possible doing what I love before seeing the surgeon.

"What do you want to do for dinner tonight?" she asked one afternoon. "Do you want to cook for us?"

Most people would think that was a strange request, but she

knew that I was staring down the Sloan appointment the following morning with a great deal of anxiety. "Yeah, I do. Perfect." If there was one thing that could take my mind off of a 7:00 A.M. visit at a major cancer hospital it would be cooking a five-course meal for seven people. I had four hours to run to Whole Foods for groceries and to cook. It would be a unique challenge, because I could only eat soft foods.

Heather arrived home a few hours later to find me just starting the potato gnocchi dough for the fourth course. She gave me a big, long hug, turned off the heavy metal music I was playing through her stereo from my iPod, and rolled up her sleeves.

"The tomatoes looked nice, so I figured I would do some gnocchi and basil."

"Awesome. I love gnocchi."

"Yeah, plus it's soft and that's about all I can handle these days. Thomas showed me how to make these when I first got there. You have to work fast or else the dough begins to soften and becomes difficult to shape. When I first started making them they were this size," I said, pointing to one I had just made as a demo that was the size of a typical gnocchi, "but then we had the idea to make them the size of arborio rice. So I would roll them tiny, like this."

"No way."

"Yep. It took forever to get the amount we needed. We used them for a truffled gnocchi risotto that garnished a salmon chop. It's pretty funny when I think about that now—chops made from fish, risotto made from gnocchi, ice-cream cones with salmon tartar inside, dishes called 'Tongue and Cheek.' Makes sense that we play with food at Alinea."

I continued to roll out dozens of the tiny gnocchi.

"I remember all of us sitting around at the end of service one day after Thomas, Stephen Durfee, Richard Blais, and I went to Hawaii for an event in 1998. Thomas was excited by some of the indigenous ingredients, like moi and fresh hearts of palm, so he sourced the products to use back at the Laundry. We were working on a dish for the vegetable menu and were focusing on the fresh palm. Mark Hopper mentioned that when you push out the center the remaining piece looks like marrowbone. Someone else thought out loud about filling the center of it, so that it looks like marrow. Mark got excited and said, "Yeah. We can make a filling out of marrow beans. Get it?"

A new dish was born, from a pun based on an inside joke. But it worked.

I finished up the gnocchi and started explaining to Heather the rest of the menu. I wanted to roast some baby beets and serve them with shaved fennel and orange segments. I had also bought some hazelnuts, avocado, and tarragon to incorporate and thought about doing a hazelnut oil and BLiS sherry vinegar dressing. Then I wanted to confit eggplant in a ton of garlic and olive oil, adding mint and pine nuts, too. "Uh, how many courses are you making, Grant?"

"Well, I want to stay busy. I made some Southeast Asian–inspired soup too—coconut milk, ginger, basil, lemongrass, fish sauce, that sort of thing. For dessert I was thinking of spice-roasted peaches with vanilla ice cream. Something simple like that. Oh. And I also made a cocktail base—Watermelon-Hendricks-Hibiscus. It's in the freezer."

"Man, you *have* been busy."

I was happy among her friends—cooking, sharing a meal, and getting to know them. It felt normal. But everyone knew why I was in town, and given the booze and wine someone had the courage to ask, "So, why spend the eve of what is surely one of the most important days of your life cooking for us?"

"You know, it's what I do. It just makes me really happy. That's all there is to it."

Heather and I walked into the waiting room of Memorial Sloan-Kettering to find Keith Goggin already there, sitting on the edge of a couch staring at the floor. He stood up as we approached him, his face expressionless and with no evidence of the boyish grin that is normally present. Keith is one of the investors in Alinea and lives in Manhattan. He and Nick went to college together, then years later discovered that they were both working as traders. They began collaborating on some long-distance projects, and when one grew into quite a big deal, they merged their firms. Keith got us the hookup at Sloan on short notice, and Nick suggested it would be useful to have Keith along, since Nick was going to stay in Chicago to seek out the best treatment options there. "He's really, really smart, analytical, logical, and when he needs to be, dispassionate. It'll be good to get his opinion." I couldn't argue with that.

I introduced Keith to Heather, and he perked up when he realized that I wasn't going to keel over. We walked down the hallway to the carbon-copy examination room, where Keith and Heather sat in the two metal folding chairs against the wall while I made my way to the patient chair. We didn't chat much as we waited for the doctor to come in, and the silence was as awkward as it was inevitable. Keith asked me if there was anything I wanted him to ask the doctors as he pulled out a typewritten piece of paper from his pocket. He had come prepared. "Not off the top of my head," I told him. "Let's see what he has to say first."

I had been through this once already when Nick and I visited Masonic. I knew what was coming, although I hoped somehow it would be different. But I was really more concerned this time about Heather. How would she react to what the doctor was about to say? I knew she would keep it together—that wasn't my fear—but the thought of her sitting there while the doctor told me that they wanted to split my jaw in half, take out my tongue, and then a few months later I might very well die was . . . unsettling. I felt bad for her.

The doctor finally walked in carrying some papers and a CD of my scan results from the previous day.

"Hello, my name is Bhuvanesh Singh. You must be Grant? How are you doing?"

"That's a pretty stupid question to ask," I thought. I paused, cocked my head sideways a bit and deadpanned, "You tell me, Doctor." We all chuckled uneasily.

For a moment, I let hope creep back in.

Then Dr. Singh started to speak.

"I have the results from your PET scan. The one piece of good news, if there is one, is that the cancer has not metastasized to your lungs or brain. However, it has found its way into both sides of your neck." This was not a surprise, as the other doctors had predicted that it had invaded my lymph nodes. As he said this, he began to feel my neck, below my ears, and under my arms. Then he pulled out the latex gloves, put them on, and asked me to open my mouth.

Having someone's hand in your mouth is never a pleasant thing, but when your tongue is 80 percent tumor, it is agonizing. Tumor tissue is firmer than regular tissue, so Dr. Singh used pressure to determine the size, shape, and texture of the tumor. He took steady notes, indicating density so he could track any changes. Since the cancer had engulfed the majority of my visible tongue, it was difficult to find where the tumor ended until he had his hand pushed firmly down my throat.

He sat back, snapped the gloves off, and looked at the three of us. Keith was the first to speak. "Well?"

"It is as we expected from looking at your scans. The cancer has been very invasive. I cannot feel where the tumor ends as we move from the oral tongue to the base. You cannot wait, cannot delay, this needs to be treated immediately."

"And what do you recommend for treatment?" Heather asked.

"We will remove most of the oral tongue, the lymph nodes in both sides of your neck, and I would like to take a portion of your lower jaw, to be safe." Just like that.

Keith lowered his head for a moment, then he snapped back. "Well, Doctor, let me take a second to tell you who this guy Grant is. He is a world-famous chef. His restaurant was named the best in America by *Gourmet* magazine. His tongue is his livelihood and his passion. You can't just cut it out."

The doctor paused for a moment, stared at me for a second, then did a double take. Clearly, by the way he was looking at me, he didn't think it was possible that I was a chef, let alone a good one.

He turned back toward Keith and said firmly, "It doesn't matter who . . . he . . . is. This is about life and death. If he doesn't get this treatment within a couple of weeks he will be dead in a matter of months. Period."

"What is the survival rate after this type of treatment?" Heather asked. She fired out the one we were all thinking. I guess I didn't need to worry about her.

"Around fifty percent. Maybe sixty percent for two-year survival," the doctor answered.

I hadn't said a word since the doctor began his examination, letting Heather and Keith ask the questions, but now I had to speak up.

"Wait a minute. You're telling me that even if you rip out my tongue, chances are good that I will die within the next year or two? What is my quality of life? Can I eat or swallow?"

"Unlikely."

"Can I talk?"

"Not really. With therapy you might . . ."

"The tongue will be reconstructed, right?" interjected Heather.

"Yes. Typically we take tissue from the arm or leg and fashion a tongue from it. But it is not a tongue, obviously, and speech will be severely compromised."

The doctor then proceeded to imitate what a patient would sound like. The noises tumbling out of his mouth were unrecognizable as speech.

Heather closed her eyes. Keith, always upbeat, always chipper, was deflated. "Well, quite simply, that is not going to happen. I'm not going to get that surgery."

"You don't understand. If you do nothing, the tumor will grow rapidly. It will be impossible to eat anyway. It will block your ability to breath. It will take your life in a matter of months. You must drop everything now, have surgery, and hope it saves your life."

"Are there any other options for treatment? Any at all. Anything."

"No. No good ones. This is what you must do."

The elevator ride down took three hours, or so it felt. The walk outside took another hour. I gathered the courage to look at Keith and Heather, let out a sigh, and said, "Well, there you go." I smiled, but just for a moment.

Heather wrapped her arms around me.

"What are we doing for dinner tonight?" I asked. "Let's go somewhere great."

They looked at me oddly at first, then understood. "Can you eat?" she asked. Heather had noticed that lately she did most of the eating and I did mostly grazing. I hadn't had a proper big meal in weeks.

"I'll pump myself full of Vicodin and I'll get through it. I want to eat."

"How about drinking some crazy wines tonight? Charlene and I would love to take you and Heather out. I can call Roy and we'll head to Cru and pop some silly bottles, stuff you've never even seen before." I looked from Keith to Heather, waiting for the nonverbal okay, got it, and smiled.

"That would be great, Keith. Life is short, apparently," I said with a laugh. "Might as well enjoy it." They didn't smile. I looked at Keith. "I don't think I'm going to get the surgery, Keith. Would you do it if you were me?

Keith spoke slowly, "I . . . I just don't know."

Keith called me at my place of refuge, the golf course.

I had been up until three that morning reading research abstracts on alternative treatments. I had long ago committed to playing a four-ball match-play tournament with a good friend, and had spent the preceding five hours walking the course, thinking about what to do. I was biding time mentally until I heard from Keith about the Sloan visit. Maybe they knew something that Masonic didn't. Anyway, there was nothing I could do.

Of course, when you don't care about the outcome of something you perform your best. I didn't think of golf all day except for those three seconds when I hit the ball. We placed second in the tournament and I sank a clutch twenty-foot putt to do so, in a playoff, with a hundred people watching. Apparently a complete mental breakdown was what I needed to get rid of the yips. This dispassionate golfer theory was really starting to take hold of me. Things around me were awful, but my golf game was at an all-time high.

The phone rang, and I headed for the parking lot to talk.

"Hey," Keith said. Over the preceding ten years, about a year of my life had been spent on the phone with Keith, talking shop and trading war stories (or any other tale he felt like spinning). Keith loved telling stories, and he did so with relish. He always started with "Hey," and then, before I could answer, would just launch right into it. Today, however, there was a "Hey" and a long silence.

"What did they say?" I finally asked.

I thought we had lost the connection. "You there?"

"Yeah. Ohhhhh." Long pause. Deep inhale of breath. "You know, it just isn't good. It isn't good at all. I mean, he's fucked."

Instantly, I knew that Sloan had said the same thing.

"How is Grant?"

"He's taking this remarkably well, or else he's incredibly good at hiding his emotions. Or maybe he didn't really get it, or believe it. I don't know. But we need to figure out a way to move him out here. You need to convince him to do the surgery. We can get an apartment for him near Sloan, get a twenty-four-hour nurse, have great food delivered. I'm sure the chefs of New York will be happy to cook for him. It will suck, but it won't suck as much as if he were in a hospital all day, every day."

"Move him to New York? I mean, is the treatment there going to be any different? His support system is here. Alinea is here. He won't want to move away."

"Well, he might not even have the surgery, he says. It was awful, Nick. I've never been in a room like that. It's just tragic."

I had never heard Keith talk like that. I'd watched him lose a million dollars on a trade and not flinch because he had made the right decision given the information. Here, there weren't many mathematical angles, and logic did not apply.

"So, where is he now?" I asked.

"He's with Heather. Charlene and I are going to take them out to dinner at Cru. He wanted to go out to a crazy dinner while he could."

"God, that's fucking depressing."

"Well, what would you do? Might as well enjoy yourself while you can. He might never taste again."

We hung up. I felt that awful emptiness of despair set in. I straightened my tie, wiped my eyes, and walked around the back of the clubhouse for the awards ceremony. Around me, a few hundred people had changed into evening wear and were having drinks, waiting for the food to be served.

I waded in, found Dagmara, stared at her for a moment, and shook my head.

It was a little past 10:00 A.M. by the time we got back downtown to Heather's apartment. We had dropped Keith in midtown and decided to go home, take a nap, then head back out later in the day for lunch and maybe a museum visit before meeting Keith and Charlene for dinner.

Heather let her cat out the window leading to the roof of the adjoining building. She and her roommates used the roof like a balcony, though it wasn't really intended for that purpose. We headed out onto the roof as well. I wanted to have the conversation that I'd been dreading and avoiding. But now, after the Sloan visit, there was no more waiting.

"I'm sorry I had to put you through that," I said.

"I wanted to go. I'm here for you through this," she said.

"Thanks. But it's not fair that you should be. I mean, we've only been seeing each other for two months, and long-distance, at that."

I continued, telling her that depending on what I decided in terms of treatment she needed to be honest with herself and with me. I felt extremely guilty and self-absorbed to be putting a twenty-four-year-old woman through something as difficult as disfiguring surgeries, radical lifestyle changes, and of course the very real possibility of death.

Our relationship thus far revolved around food. We loved eating, drinking, and cooking together. And there was the likelihood that I could no longer do those things in the near future. I couldn't see why she would be interested in maintaining a brand-new relationship through such a time—I wanted to give her my permission to leave. After all, what kind of person would walk away? I wanted to push her away, for her own good.

"Let's be honest, this is going to change my life in such drastic ways that I will no longer be the person you know. I've been lucky to have an amazing career so far, and it's likely that I would have gone on to great success. I can't see that happening now. I have to imagine that affects the way you feel. Sure there is love and devotion and all of that, but there is also the truth of wanting to find someone you are proud of and someone who can contribute to the life you want for yourself, both physically and financially. Nobody wants to inherit a burden, and clearly that is what I am about to become."

Tears began to well up in her eyes. "What are you going to do?"

"My whole life has been chasing this one goal. I have invested everything I have into it. I have dismissed relationships for it. I have sacrificed many aspects of what other people consider a normal life. I can't let that go. It's who I am. That is my identity, and if the surgeons rip that from me, then my spirit is done and I'm no good to anyone. Not me, not you, not Alinea, not my boys. And what about them? How does this affect them? They'll have a dad who can't talk about life with them, who looks funny. He can't eat with them. I worry that I'll become bitter after I lose the restaurant and my career. They are so young, and they couldn't possibly understand that it might be better for them if I'm gone. Best to go now so they can forget. Their memories . . . well, they won't remember me. Maybe Angela will marry someone and they'll always think of that other person as their dad. Maybe that's best for them."

With that, I lost it.

After gathering our composure and promising each other that we were done crying, we decided to keep our plans and head to the Metropolitan Museum of Art before dinner. Heather wanted to take me to see the "Frank Stella: Painting into Architecture" exhibit, and there was no sense in wasting the day agonizing over the harsh reality I was faced with. Shortly after we arrived at the Met I saw an old woman pushing an elderly man in a wheelchair. I am not sure if it was the sight of longevity that did me in, knowing that my own life was in question, or the idea of having someone as a caretaker, but suddenly I was overcome with emotion. I dropped Heather's hand and briskly walked away. She knew where my head was and didn't follow me. I stood in a corner of the museum for twenty minutes while I corralled my thoughts and emotions. When I rejoined Heather, we wordlessly hugged, joined hands, and continued up to the rooftop sculpture garden to take photos of the skyline. Heather never asked what triggered my crash, and I chose not to explain. I had it together for the time being and didn't want to lose it again.

After sitting in Central Park for a bit we made our way to Cru. I knew in order to get any food down I would need some Vicodin chased by some wine. My mouth was killing me from the exam at Sloan, and while I was never one for drugs, let alone a cocktail of painkillers and alcohol, it was hard to argue against it.

We arrived at the restaurant to find Keith and Charlene sitting at the bar paging through the wine book. I noticed that they had glasses of rose champagne in front of them. "What are you starting us out with?" I asked.

"I hope you don't mind that I took the liberty of ordering some bubbles for us," Keith replied.

We laughed at the absurdity of celebrating. Heather and I pulled up some stools, and Robert Bohr, the wine director at Cru, appeared with two glasses and the bottle of 1996 Dom Pérignon Rose. "Some champagne for you both, Chef?" Robert asked while extending his hand to greet me.

"That sounds perfect, Robert."

Keith slid the wine book toward us and said, "Have at it, Grant."

The wine list at Cru is not a list. It is indeed a book, or rather two large volumes—one for whites and one for reds. It is heavy, comprehensive, and several hundred pages long.

"Keith, I have no idea where to start, seriously," I said. I got the sense that Keith dined here with frequency and knew the list well. I also suspected that he had prepped the staff about the circumstances. The elephant in the room, of course, was that this was a sort of last supper, a blowout dinner while I could still barely manage one. "Go ahead, Keith. I'm sure you know better than I do."

"I have a few ideas," Keith said, grinning. Robert escorted us to our table and topped off our glasses of champagne.

"Have you made any decisions, Keith?"

"In fact, I have," Keith said coyly. "Let's start with the '90 Meursault-Genevrieres from Jobard, then some Henri Jayer wines. How about the '78 Vosne-Romanée 'Beaumonts' and the '90 'Cros Parantoux.'"

Robert looked down at Keith with a raised eyebrow and a giant smile on his face. I leaned over to Heather and said, "Holy shit."

Keith and Charlene did a great job of keeping the conversation far away from all things cancer. The food started coming and didn't stop the entire evening. A rapid-fire succession of delicious courses and endless glasses of world-class wines were the distraction I needed. But from time to time, the pain in my mouth would bring me back to reality.

Desserts came and chef Shea Gallante appeared to say hello.

The grand meal was over, and I walked out thinking that it could be my last great dinner.

was more or less certain that I was going to die fairly soon. I couldn't wrap my head around the idea of having my tongue and jaw removed, but I could somehow accept death. While I didn't express these thoughts, both Heather and Nick clearly knew what I was thinking because they kept encouraging me to press on regardless of how unacceptable the treatment options were. Surgery wasn't great, they would say, but they insisted I was worth more than the sum of my parts. I wasn't so sure.

I returned from New York feeling reasonably well physically, but emotionally destroyed. Sloan was the pinnacle of American cancer treatment, so I lost all hope when the doctors laid out my dismal options. The doctor had said, quite simply, that if I didn't follow his course of treatment, I would die a painful death within six months.

When Heather and I landed at O'Hare I got a call from Nick, who informed me that Dr. Pelzer of Northwestern University was leaving his family vacation early to see me the next morning.

A few days earlier I had received an e-mail from Roger Ebert, the esteemed movie critic and writer at the *Chicago Sun-Times*. Ebert had suffered from cancer of the salivary glands and had gone through difficult years of treatment similar to those that were being recommended to me. The note read: "Dr. Pelzer is a kind, wonderful person. I trust him with my life, literally. I feel safe around him." Additionally, he was kind enough to e-mail Dr. Pelzer on my behalf. I, however, didn't see the point in going, but I agreed to go.

We arrived early the next morning, and Nick walked up to the reception desk to check me in. The secretary looked puzzled and said

Dr. Pelzer was on vacation. Nick explained that he was, in fact, coming in this morning to see Grant, and this confused her even more. "That seems impossible. He's in Colorado."

The receptionist finally figured out that Dr. Pelzer had not yet left for Colorado and was just a room over. He came out in street clothes and led us into an examination room. In his midfifties, a bit shy and quiet, Dr. Pelzer didn't seem happy to be there, but he quickly explained why. "They all think I left a few days ago," he said. "Otherwise, they squeeze in appointments like this one." He chuckled and shook his head. I liked him immediately.

He gave me a quick examination, pulling and prodding on my very sore tongue, then took off his gloves, leaned back and gave a quick sigh. He seemed every bit the quiet, caring gentleman that Ebert described. "What did Sloan tell you?"

I relayed their diagnosis and told him what treatment they had recommended. At this point, I hoped and expected that he would disagree. Unlike the doctor at Sloan, Dr. Pelzer had a quiet confidence devoid of ego. I was hopeful that I would receive a different prognosis and a different recommendation for treatment. He paused a moment to reflect and looked at me square in the eye. "I'm afraid that what they told you is largely correct, although I never would have put it to you quite that way."

The air left the room. Again, my hopes were destroyed, though this time I didn't have as far to fall and so I merely shook my head a bit.

"What pain medication are you taking?" he asked. "You must be in a great deal of pain." I told him I was taking some Vicodin—actually, I was eating them like candy. He looked at me in disbelief. "These tumors are amazingly painful—one of the most painful cancers there is. So many nerve endings there. I'm going to write you a prescription for a patch that you put on your arm. It's fairly narcotic, so I wouldn't recommend driving much if you feel spacey from it. But it will relieve the pain and you'll be able to eat again."

I was incredibly thankful for this, but Nick was impatient and incredulous. Our last great hope was recommending, essentially, palliative treatment. "Doctor. Look, we understand the situation," he said. "But he's thirty-two years old, he tastes for a living, and really lives to taste. Is surgery really the only treatment? That just seems impossible. Given Grant's priorities and career, there must be something. I've read about other treatments and protocols." Nick was desperate for an alternative solution.

Dr. Pelzer used a model skull to describe the physiology of the disease. He was thorough, scientific, and engaging despite the macabre subject matter. He discussed in detail the aspects of the type of cancer cells that had invaded my tongue. And he got into specifics that were all too graphic . . . how it would be easier to cut my jaw in half vertically and then open it up side-to-side and have access to the whole tongue to remove the cancerous tissue. How it was critical to remove it all, plus an area around it for "margin." He would want to perform a radical neck dissection, and having watched the YouTube video that Nick sent me—he was thorough and unflinching in his research—I was terrified.

Then Dr. Pelzer, somewhat unexpectedly, as a way of wrapping up the description of the procedure said, "That is what I would do. That is what I have done for the last twenty years. But I bet Everett Vokes would tell you something very different. I don't know which is better; we can't know. But if it were me, my family, my friend, I would recommend the surgery I described. It's not pretty and it's destructive and painful, but it gives you the best chance to live. I would recommend the surgery and I would do it personally and with the greatest care. But if it's right for you, I can't say. That's up to you alone to decide."

Roger Ebert was right. This is a doctor who cared deeply about his profession and patients. Clearly he thought his methodology was best, but there was a slight chink in the armor of certitude, a concession that treating cancer is often as much art as science. And while I tried to absorb what he had just said, Nick quickly asked, "Vokes is at Chicago, right? Can you call him for us? I've tried to get in there and haven't heard back."

Dr. Pelzer recommended we see his radiation oncologist in the afternoon and promised he would give Dr. Vokes a call on my behalf. He wrote me several prescriptions for more pain medication, called over to Northwestern to book the afternoon appointment, and shook my hand. Somehow I felt a bit better.

We left the office and Googled Walgreens on our phones to find the nearest pharmacy. We walked through the city, getting lost along the way just as we did when we were building Alinea. At the first pharmacy they looked quizzically at my prescription and said, "We don't carry that sort of thing here," and recommended another nearby pharmacy. We chuckled at the thought that they think we must be addicts. I looked terrible—tired, unshaven, and I could barely speak. Nick was an emotional wreck, and though he never lost his cool at the appointments or with me, I could tell his anger and sadness were sitting just below the surface.

We walked for a while without saying a word. It was a perfect, crisp day—unusual for this time of year—and we were only a few blocks from the lake. At a corner, we waited for the light to change and Nick grabbed my arm suddenly and said, "Look, I don't want to have this conversation with you but there are certain things that you should deal with now while we can—before surgery." He kept talking about the surgery as if it were inevitable. "You need to get your life in order. You need to tell me what you want me to do for your kids. We have a policy on you for Alinea, and I'm sure a portion of that can be set aside for them—the investors are behind you, they're good people, and they're not concerned about the finances of Alinea. You need to write a will. I know you don't have much, but you don't want it in probate. That's a shit-show and lawyers will get whatever you do have. And you need to tell me what you want me to do with Alinea."

"With Alinea? What would you do with it anyway?"

"I don't know. We could keep it open, doing the recipes and menus in your honor. I don't want the place for me. We could give it to chef Keller. I don't know. I just want to know what you want me to do with it."

I smiled at him and said, "Why in the world would I give a fuck what you do with Alinea? If you have sole say in the matter, then that means I'm dead. Enjoy yourself, man. Do whatever you want."

Somehow, we both found this unbelievably funny. We laughed out loud . . . looked at each other and laughed some more. We missed the light. We laughed at our idiocy and my misfortune.

We laughed because it wouldn't be at all cool to cry.

I helped Dagmara put the kids to bed and went and sat in our den, staring at the wall. I had been totally withdrawn for months, beginning with my mom's stroke and continuing right through Grant's diagnosis. I internalized it all, except when I was short-tempered, rude, and generally not great to be around.

Dagmara sat down next to me. "You know, people survive cancer all the time. Think of all the women we know who have gone through hell with breast cancer and have come through it okay. You're doing everything you can, and he's a tough guy."

I told her about the diagnosis at length and the hundreds of pages of abstracts on head and neck cancer I had sorted through on the Internet. Her father had provided me with data and patents on anti-angiogenesis drugs, and I sifted through the American Cancer Society website for hours looking for clinical trials or some other hope of alternative treatment. I looked at her and said, "Yes, dammit, I know it's not a death sentence. It's worse than that. It's a disfigurement sentence. The Grant that we know will cease to exist in a few weeks, and I'm sorry, but that is just tragic. And after everything with my mom, I'm just not certain that he isn't right."

"Right about what?"

"That he might be better off not fighting."

She paused and looked at me and hugged me. She could see I was struggling. I pushed her away for a second and she thought I was angry, but instead I pulled out my phone and showed her the picture of the duck dish he had made that night. "Look at this. When I came back from Michigan that night he made me duck."

I lost it completely. I started sobbing uncontrollably as Dagmara looked at me.

Then she hugged me again and let me be alone. And I determined that it would be the first and last time I let that happen. From here on out, we were moving forward.

I had told my parents and the staff at Alinea. We had seen three doctors at three different hospitals. Nick was reaching out to pretty much anyone who might know something or someone to see if there was another treatment option. At some point, my story was going to leak to the press. "A Top Chef Has Tongue Cancer" is a man-bites-dog kind of headline. It would definitely make the papers.

Nick and I were alone in the front dining room of Alinea trying to decide what to do. We had a long talk about scheduling the surgery. The more set I became on doing nothing, the more Nick turned the conversation to Alinea.

"What do you want to do regarding the press? I think it's going to leak out soon enough. There is no way that our entire staff keeps silent on this, let alone all of the doctors and friends we've called. I think we should draft a very simple press release and send it off to a few key food writers."

"Fine. Do it," I said.

"What do you want to say?" he asked.

"Say I have cancer and am going to die, but will be working here in the meantime."

Nick went off to the computer in the basement. I sat looking around at the dining room for a minute, then grabbed the clipboard to see what the reservations looked like for that evening. A few minutes later he returned. "I wrote something up. I figure, keep it short and to the point. Do you want to read it?"

"Absolutely," I said.

It read:

I want to personally report that I have been very recently diagnosed with an advanced stage of squamous cell carcinoma of the mouth. I have consulted several prominent physicians and will likely begin aggressive treatment within the next few weeks. I remain, and will remain, actively and optimistically engaged in operations at Alinea to the largest extent possible. Alinea will continue to perform at the level people have come to expect from us—I insist on that. I have received amazing support from friends, family, and everyone who has thus far been told of the disease, and I look forward to a full, cancer-free, recovery.

"That's fine. I want to send out a few of these personally first. I was thinking that writers like Penny Pollack, Phil Vettel, Ruth Reichl, and Pete Wells need to see this come from my e-mail address. Then send it to Jenn Galdes and let her put it out to everyone else." I was reluctant to tell the world. I knew that once I told everyone it would be real.

I called Jenn, our publicist, from my car and let her know that Grant had sent off the press release. "He wanted to do it personally," I said.

"Makes sense. There is going to be a storm of inquiries. What do you want me to do?" she asked.

"Nothing. That's the statement in full for now. Except, well, if you get a call from someone prominent, just give them my cell number. I don't want them bothering Grant."

Five minutes later my phone rang. I recognized the number as coming from the *Chicago Tribune*, since they all start with 312-222. I figured it was Mark Caro, who penned the article about Trio's last night and whom I now hired to work on the Alinea cookbook based on that piece.

"Hello, this is Nick."

"Nick, hello. This is Phil Vettel from the *Chicago Tribune*."

"Wow. That was fast," I thought.

"I'm sorry to bother you on what is obviously a difficult day, but I was hoping to ask you a few questions. And of course I wanted to convey to Grant just how concerned we all are for his well-being and recovery."

"Thanks. Sure. Whatever you need."

Phil Vettel was the head dining critic of the *Tribune*, and I wasn't surprised he was calling.

"Well, can you tell me more about the cancer? I've done a little research, and if he has an advanced stage of squamous cell cancer that's a difficult prognosis, right?"

I chose my words very carefully, something I would do over and over that day with a number of people in the media. I focused on the positive: Grant was getting the best possible consultation from the best doctors around the country; Alinea was busy and he was fully engaged; we expect that he will beat this.

All of the reporters sounded upset. All of them offered personal well-wishes. But they all pressed me: "What if?"

"What if he loses his tongue?"

About the third time a similar hypothetical entered the conversation I slipped. "Well, if that does happen, then it would be a Shakespearean tragedy. The irony is not lost on Chef. Still, we're not concentrating on that, and I'm sure that if anyone could overcome such a thing it would be him."

"What irony is that, Nick?"

"Well, it would be no different than a painter losing his sight, right?"

I woke up the next morning to the sound of the *Chicago Tribune* hitting my nightstand. Dagmara had it folded in half and dropped it on the table. I saw, on the front page, the article announcing Grant's cancer. And I immediately saw my name. " 'It's Shakespearean,' said Nick Kokonas, Achatz's friend and co-owner of Alinea. 'This is like a painter whose eyes are taken from him.' "

I recoiled in horror. That was not what Grant needed to hear. "Brilliant," was all I got from Dagmara, with a roll of her eyes.

My phone rang a minute later. It was Grant.

"Shakespearean? I guess you're the one who needs some media training!" he said, laughing. "That's just great. Why don't you come by and poke out my eyeballs while you're at it."

I felt terrible, but was glad that he knew how the media worked.

"Front page, though. Front page," I said. "I think we finally have our angle for Oprah."

Grant laughed. I still felt terrible.

"Grant. Wake up. I just got a call from the University of Chicago, the guy I've been trying to reach. They can see you immediately. Call me."

I rolled over and saw the text message from Nick on my phone. I had no desire to go to another doctor. I felt like shit. The painkillers made me tired as hell, I could barely open my mouth, I'd barely eaten in days, and I had run out of options. I had been given a clear directive: Cut out your tongue as soon as possible.

I thought long and hard about what the doctors had all said. They weren't saying, "We'll cut out your tongue and then you'll be fine." Instead, removing my tongue was only the beginning. Chemo would follow, then years of therapy—if I lived that long. The quality of life seemed low at best, while the odds of dying anyway were very high.

And despite everyone's encouragement it was unlikely that I could be a great chef. Or perhaps I could, but would I want to be? Would I want to be surrounded by food that I could never eat?

I didn't want to live without my identity. And I didn't have the energy or desire to create a new Grant Achatz.

"Hey," I said when I called Nick. "Thanks, but I'm not going. What are they going to say that's any different? We went to Sloan-Kettering and we saw Ebert's guy. I'm sure Ebert and the whole staff of the paper were searching the world for the best doctor. They both said the same thing. I'm going back to sleep."

"Get dressed. I'm picking you up in thirty minutes. I'll drag your ass out of bed if I have to."

We drove south toward the University of Chicago hospital along the lake. The sun was bright and the lake looked beautiful. I had never been to U of C before, and was surprised that a gothic-style university existed on Chicago's South Side.

"You know, Grant, there is something magical about this place. If I could go back to school, this is where I would go. It's filled with intellectually curious people. I read Dr. Vokes's studies, and his statistics and conclusions were consistent and logical. I know nothing about the hospital, but I'm hoping it's like the rest of the place."

"Whatever it is, this is the last one. Then I have to decide. I already have, actually."

"Fair enough."

We parked and found our way to the reception area of the oncology center. Nick walked up to the desk to check me in, but before he could do so another woman approached from the hall and walked directly to me. "Chef Achatz, I'm glad you could make it this morning. Dr. Vokes saw the article in the *Tribune* and then we realized that your friend had called here already. So we reached out to get you in as soon as possible. Dr. Vokes is confident he can help and is anxious to meet you."

We followed her to an exam room where she asked me a few questions about my insurance and I filled out a few forms. Dr. Vokes came in with two younger doctors.

Tall, angular, with cropped thinning hair and an unidentifiable European accent, Dr. Vokes introduced himself. "Hi, Grant, I'm Everett Vokes. I'm glad that we were able to find you so quickly. It is important that we sort this out as quickly as possible. I understand from what I could gather that you have an advanced case. But we will look that over right away. I have also taken the liberty of calling Sloan-Kettering and Northwestern to get copies of your scans, with your permission, of course." Vokes spoke slowly but confidently, and began to put on some rubber gloves. He realized that he hadn't introduced himself to Nick and said hello and waved since he already had the gloves on.

"Grant, or should I call you Chef? If you could come over here and sit down, I'll give you a brief exam. I assume it's okay for Nick to stay?"

"Just call me Grant. Nick is the guy who dragged me here today against my will. He can stay," I said, laughing.

"Okay, then. Why did he have to drag you? Are you not feeling well?" Dr. Vokes asked this with childlike simplicity.

"You know, Doctor, he does have cancer," Nick said. Everyone smiled.

"I meant, are you feeling different or unusually unwell compared to how you were feeling, say, a week ago?"

"No. I just didn't really see the point of coming."

"Well, let us be the judge of that. I think you might be surprised. So, then. Open your mouth as wide as possible. This will not feel great but I will take care."

Dr. Vokes gently pulled the tip of my tongue out and over to get a good look. The pain was excruciating, but he acted slowly and methodically. In a minute he was done.

"Well, it is as they said. You have a late-stage cancer in your tongue and probably in the lymph nodes on the side of your neck. I will have to see the scans to know more, but I can tell you a little bit about what we do here."

Dr. Vokes went on to explain that while the standard of treatment over the last twenty years put surgery first, the clinical trial under their guidance had reversed the process, putting chemotherapy first.

"We intend to shrink the tumor with a series of chemotherapies, including the use of cetuximab followed by aggressive targeted radiation. Our goal is not just the eradication of the tumor, but limiting the occurrence of metastasizing after eradication of the localized area and overall preservation of the organ whenever possible."

"That sounds like you're saying that you don't want to cut off my tongue," I said.

"Indeed. I most definitely do not wish to cut out your tongue. We try to balance quality of life with preservation of life. The two should go hand in hand. But if the treatment is not working then certainly we will look to surgery as an option to save your life. We do not sacrifice one for the other. But I also believe that we do not have to. Our method works better and saves more lives while saving organs."

This was unbelievable to hear. No other doctor had even considered this, and yet it made so much sense to me. I looked over at Nick.

"My father-in-law is a patent lawyer who does a lot of pharma work and he steered me towards Erbitux," Nick said. "In his words, 'when it works, it really works' and . . .'"

Dr. Vokes interrupted Nick, "Yes, that's right. When it is effective in an individual, for whatever reason, it significantly reduces the size and scope of the tumors."

"So, in reading everything," Nick skipped ahead, "the argument against doing this type of protocol is that it turns the tissue to mush, not the technical term, and if the tumor remains the necessary surgery becomes difficult or, well, really difficult."

"Yes, that is true. But we have a great team here and we do a very targeted radiation to try to preserve as much of the surrounding tissue as possible. It could very well be that Grant is not responsive to the treatment, in which case we revert to a standard treatment. But a majority of people are responsive and the resulting surgery, if any, is less than it would have been, which preserves the organ."

"And your survival rates?" Nick asked.

"Unpublished at this point, but we are nearly inverting the previous rates."

Nick was beaming.

"So why is it that everyone everywhere else we've been has told us the opposite? Why is it that you're the only ones embracing this?"

Clearly this made Dr. Vokes a bit uncomfortable, like he knew the answer but didn't want to be so blunt. Thankfully, two other members of his team—the surgeon, Dr. Elizabeth Blair, and the radiation oncologist, Dr. Daniel Haraf—had entered the room.

"Someone needs to be the smartest guy in the room, I guess," said Dr. Haraf.

We all laughed at that.

Dr. Blair explained that unlike many surgeons, she believed that the ideal situation was one where she never had to operate on a patient. Sure, she wouldn't publish new techniques, but her patients would be alive. Dr. Haraf had a morbid sense of humor as he described the radiation protocol. "Basically, we target it exactly to the spot of the tumor using a computer model of your head in 3D. That said, I'm the guy that makes you so sick that you'll want to die. But ideally you won't."

I instantly liked the team. It's hard to describe. It's not just that they were saying what I wanted to hear—that I had a chance of living and that if I lived I would keep my tongue—but that they embraced the idea of doing something new, something different, something better.

"You know, I've been waiting to hear this, and now I'm a bit wary. We named our restaurant 'Alinea,' which means a 'new train of thought.' We strive for new and better and different. And still, I'm thinking that you guys are either really smart or really crazy."

"Let's hope smart," Haraf said. "But there is nothing wrong with a little crazy, too."

The doctors left for a few minutes so we could talk it over and see if we had any questions. The most amazing part was that because it was a clinical trial, the university paid for any nonstandard treatment. The only toss-up was the double-blind study regarding the amount of radiation and whether or not it was inpatient with a three-week stay in the hospital, or outpatient and five days per week.

"What do you think?" I asked Nick. "I can't see a reason not to do this. What choice do I have?"

"I think we're home, Grant. These are good people."

CHAPTER 24

Chef Keller reached out to me and asked if it was a good idea to throw a party for Grant and a few close friends. "A blowout dinner somewhere."

Of course, his heart was in the right place. He had called Grant several times, and I knew that Grant was downplaying the gravity of the situation. I wrestled with what to do. Should I e-mail chef Keller and tell him the whole story? Or would that be betraying a trust I had with Grant? Ultimately I decided to write Thomas a detailed e-mail, running through our entire experience yet trying to remain as objective as possible. I let him know about the daunting prognosis, the disappointing doctor visits, and yet the hope we had for Dr. Vokes's course of treatment. After all, he cared so much that he deserved to know the full extent of what Grant was going through. I also knew how proud he'd be to know what a strong leader he still was at the restaurant, and how much his support of Grant meant to him. I welcomed any questions he had and offered him a place to stay if he wanted to visit, as I suspected he no doubt would.

I couldn't help but feel that I was writing a letter not to a mentor of Grant's, but to another member of our family, even as I felt that I was betraying a bit of trust that Grant had placed in me.

Nick called to say he was arriving in a few minutes to pick me up for my first chemo treatment. I got dressed, and oddly I felt better than I had in months. I was wearing two morphine patches on my arm, so I was definitely feeling no pain. Because of that I ate well, slept great, and, despite the fact that I was pumped full of narcotics, I wasn't in the least bit tired. I was amazingly clearheaded.

Three days earlier I was convincing myself to avoid surgery and simply die. Then we met with the team at U of C and suddenly I was entering treatment. I really had no idea whether this was the right decision, but it was the only course of action I had.

It felt great to actually be doing something, to fight this in some way. It felt great to have a chance.

I hopped in Nick's car and we headed south down Lake Shore Drive.

"You ready?" he asked.

"Yeah. I feel good," I said.

"I bet you do—you're toasty!" he said and laughed. "Keep a few of those patches around for the crew, just in case we get sick of dealing with you."

"Naw. It won't be that bad. I'm ready for it."

"Dude. Get steely. Get steely. I watched my dad go through mild chemo, and it sucked. It won't be bad at first, but it'll get there."

"Thanks for the encouragement," I said and laughed. But I knew what he was talking about. I was, of course, terrified. "What is chemo, anyway? What do they do?"

Nick looked at me like I was out of my mind. "Are you fucking kidding me? You didn't look this shit up?"

"Nope. I started to look at the stuff on the Web and it just freaked me out—the surgeries, guys with no necks—fuck that. That's why I keep you around."

"Well, it really is nothing, procedurally speaking. A slow IV drip into your veins of highly toxic shit that tries to poison the cancer cells. It generally does a good job of that, but the problem is, it kills a lot of good cells, too. So basically, it slowly kills you from the inside out, hopefully killing every single cancerous cell while leaving the rest of you intact enough so that you can recover and live. But today, all I expect that will happen is that you'll sit there for a few hours with a needle in your arm and then go home."

"Really? That's it? We can work on the book. I brought my laptop."

We arrived at the medical center without getting lost. Small miracles already.

A nurse said, "Well, hello, Mr. Achatz. Welcome. I'll take you up there, but first we'll take some vitals. This will be routine. Every time you come in, more or less, we'll take your weight, blood pressure, temperature, sometimes a blood sample—just to make sure you're progressing along okay and getting everything you need nutritionally. We also mix the chemo to your weight each time so we know you're getting just the right amount. So we'll do this, then you'll wait over there while the lab mixes up the potion. Sometimes it's quick, sometimes it takes a long time, depending on the hour of the day and how busy we are. They do their best to be quick, but with this sort of thing you kinda want to get it right, right?"

Damn, she was cheery.

Soon enough, we were led to a large room that was bisected in the middle by a nurses' station. All along the outside were a series of curtained-off enclosures, the kind you see in an emergency room. Along one wall there were glassed-in versions of the same. I got the feeling you didn't want to end up in one of those. It was all brightly lit with a buzzing staff. It all seemed so normal.

As we walked along the line of stalls I could see the people sitting there, IV's standing on poles behind them, reading magazines, sleeping. No one looked too terribly sick, but I couldn't help thinking to myself: All of these people have cancer.

I looked at Nick, and I could tell he was thinking the same thing. In fact, he looked more fearful than I felt.

We came to the second-to-last little stall, and I was told to sit in what looked like a firm-backed La-Z-Boy. Nick perched on a stool. He was looking kind of grim.

"What's up?" I asked.

He looked up and forced a smile, but I could tell something was bothering him. "Nothing," he said. He was lying.

He paused a second and could tell that he wasn't fooling me. "Last time I was in one of these places was with my dad," he said. "I went with him once or twice. We talked about life and such, but it was depressing. Neither of us wanted to talk like that, so we just talked about business and stuff. He eventually told me not to bother coming—that he would like to read or sleep. I should have gone more."

"So let's talk business, let's work on the book. I want to bang this out and get it done."

A nurse arrived before I could pull out my laptop. She was perky as well. "They must force themselves to be like that," I thought.

"We're almost all set here. My name is Peggy and I'll be here most days. If you need anything at all, just holler. Today's your first treatment, right? So you know what to expect?"

"Not really," I answered. "I signed up for this two days ago."

She seemed surprised by that but continued, "Well, basically, you're going to sit here while we give you the dosage of whatever you need on that particular visit. Ninety-nine percent of the time we hook you up, you wait and do whatever you want, and that's that. Just ring us when it's almost gone, but we usually know how long it takes. If you feel dry, hot, cold, whatever, you let us know—even if it seems like nothing. Okay? Since today is your first treatment with Erbitux we're going to make sure you don't have an allergic reaction of any kind."

"Like what?"

"Well, a small minority of people have a violent reaction to it and we have to discontinue it. Nothing life-threatening or anything, I swear." Big, reassuring smile. "Just a nasty rash, fever, that sort of thing. If you make it five minutes without it, you're good for the three hours."

I had no idea how long these treatments would last. I figured I would go in, get a few shots, a few X-rays, and move along. This slow drip was going to kill me with boredom more than anything else.

With that she flipped the little switch on the drip and the first drops of chemo hit my bloodstream.

"How does it feel?" Nick deadpanned.

"Boring."

Chemotherapy sessions were every Tuesday. I would get up early and try to arrive at the hospital by seven. The chemo chairs were first come, first served, and if I made it in on the first round it significantly reduced my time at the hospital.

I would settle in, get hooked up, and immediately pull out my computer to start working on the cookbook or talk online with Heather or Nick. At some point during each treatment Dr. Vokes would stop by to see how I was doing and answer any questions I had. Typically these were just casual conversations; the nitty-gritty medical discussions were left for my weekly exams. But a couple of weeks into my treatment, he wanted to see how I was progressing.

The thing was, I felt better than I had in months. I thought it was possible that the drugs were working already. It was easier to eat, easier to talk. I felt odd telling him that, thinking it was all in my head.

"It's possible, Grant. Here, follow me."

Dr. Vokes led me out into the hall and into an examination room. "Let's have a look."

He felt my tongue slowly, and quietly repeated, "This is good, Grant. This is good. You're responding well to the Erbitux. A very good sign."

I was ecstatic. I thanked him and walked outside as a sense of calm washed over me. I felt like I could eat again, like I had a window on life. I hopped in the car and decided that a quick trip to New York was in order. Later that night I IM'd Heather to suggest the trip. She must have been thinking the same thing, because she quickly suggested Gramercy Tavern.

Heather: just saying hi
wanna go to gramercy on sunday night?
4:55 PM **me**: I do ...but I just don't know what I'll be able to eat
me: I just had some soup
Heather: i don't think that'll be a problem
me: tried to eat some with some chunks. it went over so so
Heather: no chunks will be involved
4:56 PM **Heather**: you know mike anthony's dad was

diagnosed w/ a stage 4 tumor in the base of his tongue about
8 years ago?
4:57 PM he got surgery, and is now totally healthy

We decided to make it happen. Earlier in the month I had exchanged e-mails with Thomas and he suggested I let him know when I
was next in NYC. So before we left I texted him and asked if he was in
town, suggesting that he and Laura Cunningham join us at Gramercy.
They were arriving the night we were dining, so they agreed to join
us at the end of the meal for dessert and some wine.

We were seated at our table and greeted by chef Michael Anthony. I thanked him profusely for making special preparations that I
could eat and let out the bombshell that Thomas Keller would likely
join us for dessert if his flight wasn't delayed.

The meal was perfect. Mike engineered it with a firsthand understanding of my limitations. Going in I was afraid it would be composed of liquefied courses, and while I would not have complained,
I was feeling better and wanted to push the boundaries in an effort
to feel normal, at least for a night. I needn't have worried. To the
untrained eye the meal would have looked entirely normal. Perfectly
cooked trout was served with sunchoke puree and pickled shallots.
Chilled pea soup surrounded a dignified mound of moist, dressed crab
meat, and handmade pasta came coated in a silky sauce.

Just as we were finishing our final savory course Thomas and
Laura walked in. They spotted me and could not hide their shock that
I looked like myself. I introduced them to Heather, and Thomas im-
mediately commented on how healthy I looked.

"What, Chef? You thought you were coming to see an invalid? I
feel great actually, best I have in weeks."

I filled them in on my treatment and the story of finding the U of
C. The mood was emotional—it was the first time they were hearing it
from me directly. I told them about telling the staff, and Nick's take on
the reaction in the room. Then Thomas asked me how long I intended
to work at Alinea.

"All the way through, Chef."

He smiled at me and nodded his head. He wasn't surprised.

I couldn't decide how and when I should tell the kids about my cancer. I thought about not telling them at all, but Nick and Heather urged me to be as honest as possible. They were so young that I knew that they couldn't fully understand the facts of illness and death, but I also knew that my physical state would gradually deteriorate even under the best of outcomes. There would be no hiding it.

I made a point of spending more time with them than I usually did. One afternoon after a morning chemo treatment the three of us were deep into a Wii tennis tournament when I decided to pause the game and tell them. I stood up, turned off the TV and sat them on the couch. Keller started to whine and Kaden looked up at me with a puzzled look, wondering why he was being punished.

"Hey, guys, Dad needs to talk to you about something." The boys could tell my tone was serious and Keller quit his tantrum and Kaden sat up straight. I knelt down on the floor between them and put my hands on their legs.

"I'm sick, boys."

Kaden interrupted, "Is that all, Dad? Can we play now?"

"No, bud. I need to tell you this. I have an illness that is very serious. It's called cancer and it is in my tongue and neck. Do you know what cancer is?"

The question was directed at Kaden. At almost six years old, I thought he might have heard the word before, either at school or on TV. Keller was only three and a half and I knew that he had no idea. He looked over my shoulder at the TV, clearly hoping that I would turn it back on soon.

"It's a thing in your body, like a bump," Kaden said.

"Yeah, kinda like that. There are many different kinds of cancer, and all of them are bad for you. I have a lot of it in my body right now, and so I need to take some really strong medicine to get rid of it. But the medicine is going to make me really sick too."

Kaden thought that was odd. Why would medicine make you sick? "What if it doesn't go away?" he asked.

I didn't want to tell them that I could die. There seemed no point in doing that. I skipped over the morbid details for now and kept things simple. "I'm going to look different for a while, guys. I'll probably lose a bunch of weight, get a nasty, pimply rash, and my hair will fall out." They found that part funny.

I didn't know what else to say. I fought back tears and tried to project love over my fear. "Do you guys have any questions?"

Keller shot back immediately, "Nope!" I smiled at them, gave them a hug, and flipped the Wii tennis back on.

The next day I decided to take them out fishing. During the summer months I tried to get them out one day a week, just like I used to go with my dad or uncle. We had fun exploring the different baits that we could cull from the Alinea kitchen. Cheddar cheese, shrimp, bacon, and baby octopus were some of the favorites. I taught Kaden how to cast, and he was to the point where he could do it on his own.

We headed out to the lagoons in the northern suburbs and I set Kaden up. Keller disappeared for a moment. When I went to see what he was up to, he was throwing handfuls of the shrimp I had brought into the water, giggling all the while.

"Dude, what are you doing?"

"Feeding the fish, Dad. Look, they're coming right to the top. We can catch them now."

Out of bait and only ten minutes into our fishing trip, we packed up our stuff and headed to a nearby gas station to buy some night crawlers. Returning back to our spot I got Kaden set up again with a bobber and a hook. I instructed him to get a worm from the container and bring it over. He returned with a huge one.

"If you're going to fish, guys, you have to learn to hook the worm yourself. Watch."

I grabbed the worm and began to thread it on the hook. The worm thrashed about in my hand and finally succumbed. Both boys were mesmerized. I handed the rod to Kaden and pointed to where he should cast. He fired the rig into the water, spun the crank to lock the wheel, and stood quietly.

I was about to start getting Keller's pole set up when Kaden spoke up over his shoulder. "Hey, Dad—do you think the hook hurts the worm?"

"Nah. You can cut them right in half and they still live. Want to see?"

"No thanks, Dad."

A few seconds of silence passed, and then Kaden spoke up again. "Dad. Can worms get cancer?"

I froze. I instantly knew that their worry and understanding far surpassed my expectations. The news of my cancer was all over the newspapers and the TV. It was unavoidable even for a six-year-old.

"I suppose they can. But I doubt it would hurt them. Look how tough they are." I motioned to the worm I was hooking on Keller's pole.

He paused for a minute and I thought he was going to drop the subject. Then he said, "Yeah. But you're pretty tough, too, Dad. It's not going to kill you."

My heart sank. I grabbed him, put him in a headlock, and gave him a noogie with some underarm tickling.

"Yup. I'm as tough as a worm."

Heather and I were seeing each other seven to ten days a month, taking turns making the commute from Chicago to New York. I planned a two-day trip to see her before she went to Bethesda, Maryland, to visit her family. I had not yet met her parents, but I could sense she wanted me to come along. I was incredibly apprehensive. After all, I was nine years older than her, had two sons from a previous relationship, and, oh yeah, stage-four cancer. That was a good amount of baggage to bring into any relationship, and no parent could be happy that his or her daughter was bringing that guy home. Despite that, I suggested I stay an extra day and head down with her to see them.

We pulled up to the curb and got out of the cab to see her parents, sister, and grandmother excitedly squeezing through the doorway all at once to come out and greet us. Her mother hugged us both simultaneously and all of my fears about not being accepted vanished.

After the general introductions and small talk, Heather and I got right to work. Dinner, of course, was the plan. We quickly dispatched Doug, her stepfather, on a shopping mission while we started kneading pasta dough and making a marinade for the fish he was picking up. Her mother set the table on the back patio, lit candles, and gathered basil, oregano, and rosemary from the garden.

We banged out dinner in record time, all the while sipping wine and chatting with her family: fresh pasta with tomatoes, garlic, and herbs; scallops grilled over rosemary branches; grilled bass marinated in orange juice and herbs. Heather roasted some grapes with Pedro Ximenez to spoon over Greek yogurt for dessert. As we sat on the back porch eating by candlelight in the peaceful summer night, Chicago and cancer felt far away.

Thomas and Laura had commented on my normal appearance during our meal at Gramercy a few weeks earlier, and I had even felt bold enough to tell Nick and Heather that I thought maybe, just maybe, the drugs wouldn't affect me at all. Nick told me I was delusional. He was always trying to prepare me, but I thought he was wrong. Turns out, he was right.

After dinner Heather and I laid down on the couch, unable to do much more since we were stuffed. She was rubbing my back and running her fingers through my hair as we chatted with her mom when she stopped and I heard her say, "Uh, oh."

I turned to see her staring at her hand. It was full of light red hair. The drugs were starting to take full effect. My cells were starting to divide more slowly, to die off.

I returned home the next day and decided I had to shave my head. My hair was pouring out of my head in a steady stream and even a slight breeze would leave a blanket of hair on my shoulders. I couldn't risk it coming out in the food while I worked. Facing the inevitable, I decided to try to have fun with it.

With Kaden and Keller flanking me on the couch while we watched *Dirty Jobs* on the Discovery Channel, I asked them if they wanted to do something crazy. Of course they said yes, so I encouraged them to pull out my hair. Keller was the first to take me up on my offer. With a devilish look he pinched a small amount between his thumb and index finger and tugged. He winced, anticipating my reaction to what he thought was a painful act. He didn't even notice the hair between his fingers.

"Holy cow, Dad, look at your hair!" Kaden shouted, pointing at the clump in Keller's hand. "Can I try?"

The boys took turns yanking hair from my head, each grasp becoming larger and larger as they laughed hysterically. They could only reach the sides, right above my ears, so after a few minutes I got up and looked in the mirror. I had the start of a Mohawk. Perfect. I figured I would take it a step further and surprise the Alinea staff with a cleanly shaven hawk. That was more than a bit out of character for me, but perfectly in character for many of them. The boys helped me shave the sides and back as best as we could and then we walked over to a cheap chain barbershop to have them clean it up.

When I sat in the chair and removed my baseball cap the hairstylist recoiled visibly. "I told them they could give me a trim," I said, pointing to the boys, "but they didn't do such a good job." The guys howled with laughter as she tightened up our handiwork. I slapped my cap back on and returned home. I snapped a pic of myself with my phone and e-mailed it to Nick. The phone rang ten seconds later. "You look like a serial killer. Psycho, man. Love it," he said.

I walked into Alinea the next day with a full-on Mohawk. For me it was a simple attempt to lighten a serious situation and put the team at ease. Of course at this point, everyone knew I had cancer and was undergoing treatment, but this was the first time the side effects of treatment made it obvious that something was happening to me. The staff responded in an act of solidarity and either shaved their heads or crafted Mohawks of their own. Sommelier Scott Norman, an employee I'd worked with since Trio—and who himself is without kidneys and has been through countless surgeries—Mohawked his goatee, since he already had a shaved head. We may have looked nuts to our high-end customers, but I had never felt a tighter bond in the restaurant.

Each fall StarChefs.com holds the largest culinary industry conference in the United States, bringing the top names in food to New York for three days to share ideas and socialize. Heather worked for StarChefs, and she persuaded me to take part in the conference that year. The planning for these events happens months in advance, and I was scheduled to give a demonstration on the main stage. But after my diagnosis, Heather let the organizers know that I wouldn't be participating. In addition to being preoccupied with my predicament, my doctors had also asked that I not plan any travel, just in case. I had participated in many of these types of events around the world and always found it challenging to decide what to show my colleagues. The audiences consisted of the leading names in the industry, and the goal is to show a totally original concept that would blow everyone's mind. Once I was officially removed from the docket, I joked to Heather that I was completely at ease now that I didn't have to rack my brain for a brilliant idea to show the industry. Cancer was a terrific excuse for mediocrity. But the reality was that I wanted desperately to go and prove that I was still alive, still working, still creating food. And I also wanted to show support for Heather's efforts in producing this event.

My body was in steady and rapid decline at this point, and I hadn't even started radiation yet. A rash resembling pubescent acne began to cover my face and arms, my skin was dry and cracking, and I was temporarily sporting a Mohawk on my way toward baldness. Going to work in this condition was uncomplicated. I spent sixteen hours a day around the same group of fifty people. They knew me well and they viewed me as the same chef I was before I got cancer. The staff worked harder than ever to maintain standards, even while it must have been hard on them to look at me as a daily reminder of their own mortality. But they didn't show it. Alinea was the most comfortable place for me to be every day, because I had exactly the kind of support I needed.

I didn't, however, want to embarrass Heather or myself. I looked terrible. Heather had last seen me prior to shaving my head—when I still looked fairly normal. Over the subsequent ten days the shit had hit the fan. The rash had come on strong, I had lost ten pounds, and my head was now completely shaven. For the first time, I looked like a cancer patient. She knew I wanted to come to the conference and encouraged me to attend, but I worried she would freak out when she saw me.

The nausea was near constant now and my energy was waning as well, but I decided nonetheless to go. Heather was moderating a panel called "From Kitchen to Cookbook" with Jeffrey Steingarten, publishers Ann Bramson and Will Scwalbe, and literary agent Lisa Queen. I was invited to join the discussion. I needed to prove to myself and the culinary world that I was still relevant.

I arrived at Seven World Trade Center and called Heather so she could come out and meet me. She greeted me in the lobby with a giant hug and kiss, burying her face in my shoulder to try to hide her sudden tears at seeing me look so frail and sick. Then she grabbed my hand and led me up the elevator into the mass of people milling about on the conference floor. Most people didn't recognize me, and I was incredibly self-conscious. I couldn't believe Heather wanted to be seen showing affection toward me looking like I did. It gave me strength to press through.

The panel was scheduled just after I arrived, so I jumped right in. I'm sure at least part of the crowd had no idea who I was until Heather introduced me. I kept a bottle of water by my side and hoped my voice wouldn't give out. I did reasonably well and even managed to crack a few jokes and earn a few real laughs from the audience. After the discussion, a few of the attendees came up and asked for photos with me.

Other chefs greeted me throughout the night with a hug and a pat on the back, followed by conversation as usual. Everyone went out of his or her way to act as though nothing was different, but not in a way so as to not acknowledge the elephant in the room. Ultimately, I was grateful to them. I even agreed to join in as a judge on a "Best Pacojet Dish" competition, even though I know some people wondered if I could even taste.

At this point, taste was not an issue.

had dreaded the chemo because I had heard about all of the nasty side effects. The reality was that I was in far better shape after twelve weeks of Erbitux and traditional cancer therapy drugs than I was before I started the treatment. Yes, I had a case of acne that would rival that of any adolescent, as well as some issues with basic human functioning (some of the drugs make a bowel movement nearly impossible). But the tumor had shrunk, the morphine patches on my arm controlled the pain, and I was able to speak and eat better than I had in months. I felt like it was working—and I was told by doctors that I was responding well—so emotionally I was on a high.

Then came the radiation.

I was told from the beginning by everyone on the medical team that they were going to "take me low"—almost kill me—while trying to rid me of the cancer. This included weeks of intensive targeted radiation treatment on my tongue, jaw, and neck that would burn the inside of my mouth and throat like a severe sunburn. The skin covering my tongue and throat would peel off like wrapping paper, taking with it my taste buds. Of all of the side effects of treatment, this is what I feared the most. If I couldn't taste, could I really be a chef?

I knew that the most important aspect of what I did came from within, not the ability to taste or evaluate the completed dishes. After all, I had a team of more than twenty highly trained chefs in the kitchen, some of whom had been with me for more than six years. During their time with me I had trained their palates to mirror mine through the constant adjusting and tweaking of the dishes they presented to me for final approval. I basically brainwashed them into tasting exactly as I did, and now I had no choice but to believe that they had been paying attention.

I drove myself to my first radiation treatment. A group of Chicago chefs and restaurants had offered to pool together some money to hire a driver to take me to treatments, and while that was an amazing offer from our community, I did not want to be seen as a victim. So I decided to drive myself as long as that was possible. Occasionally I would find it necessary to pull to the side of the road, vomit, and then drive on. But I had driven myself to all but the very first chemo treatment, so I planned to do the same for the radiation sessions.

A few weeks earlier I had been fitted for a harness to secure my head to the table during the radiation. This would prevent me from moving during the treatment and spare the areas of my head and neck that didn't need the radiation and subsequent savage burning that the beams produced. Dr. Haraf asked me at the time, "Are you claustrophobic?" I replied, "No, I don't think so," although I wondered what he had in mind. He laughed and replied, "Well, by the end of this we'll know for sure!" I guess if your job is to benevolently burn people from the inside out you develop a unique sense of humor. I smiled but didn't laugh. I had no idea what he was talking about.

At my first appointment, Dr. Haraf and an assistant came in with the fiberglass harness, which was crafted to my exact dimensions and resembled the head restraint that kept Hannibal Lecter from, well, eating someone. It was intimidating and scary, but not claustrophobia inducing. Instead, I was far more scared that the radiation would hurt as it was being applied. But that fear was unfounded, and the treatment lasted less than thirty minutes. I got up, walked out as I had come in, and drove back to Alinea. One down, sixty-three to go.

I settled into a routine. I would wake up in the morning, try to force down some food, a protein drink, some Ensure, and head to Alinea to make my presence felt. Then I would send off a few e-mails about the book to Martin, the designer, or Lara, the photographer, then head to radiation. For a few weeks I deluded myself into believing that it wouldn't be so bad. But then the scariest moment came.

The third week into my treatment I drove back to Alinea on a Friday afternoon. It was a typical night for us with eighty-eight confirmed reservations, thirty-eight of which were for the twenty-six-course Tour menu. Doing the math, that means that 1,688 dishes would need to leave the kitchen in the span of about seven hours. Three new dishes were hitting the menu that night, and a chef was visiting us from Spain. I arrived to find the kitchen humming, but not totally in sync.

At this point, the effects of the radiation were minimal. A light burn on the outside of my skin had begun to form, and I could feel a constant dull pain in my mouth again. Eating began to hurt more, but it was tolerable given the amount of painkillers I was on. As soon as I arrived at my station, right in the middle of the line, a *chef de partie* came up with a beige-colored sauce on a spoon. "Chef, is this what you were looking for?" he asked. This happens continuously whenever we introduce a new dish. We refine and refine until the recipe and plating are second nature, tasting constantly along the way. I grabbed the spoon, put it in my mouth, swished it around, and winced slightly from the pain. But that was not the issue—I was used to the pain by then. I looked at the chef, checked his face to make sure it was not some sort of joke, and then grabbed another spoon and took a second taste out of the pot. I called over to sous chef Dave Beran, and said, "Chef, give this a taste and tell me what you think." A few on the line noticed and worried briefly that something was amiss. He hurried over, tasted it, shrugged, and said, "Seems fine to me. Maybe a bit more salt." I shrugged, tossed the spoon into the *bain-marie*, and said, "Seems perfect to me."

But mentally, I was panicking. My mind raced at a million miles an hour. I grabbed five tasting spoons, walked over as casually as possible to the stove and randomly tasted a few of the sauces simmering there. Nothing. I grabbed a pinch of salt, put it directly on my tongue, and it tasted—no, felt—like slowly dissolving sand. And just like that my sense of taste was gone. I had no idea how to react, other than to try to hide it from the kitchen staff, at least for the time being. I called together the sous chefs in the front dining room and said, "As I go through this treatment, I'm going to need to begin relying more on you guys to taste the nuances in the food." Dave looked at me and knew the truth. He had seen it in my eyes. I couldn't taste, and he knew it.

I walked back to my station and continued to prepare for the evening. Would everything be okay tonight? How would I know if it were off? For the first time since the treatment started I was genuinely scared.

And the hard part had not even begun.

Alinea was hanging together. Chef Pikus and the core group of sous chefs had absorbed the initial blow and were putting out the same quality that Grant demanded. New dishes were being introduced, and on a nightly basis diners would finish their meals, come down to the kitchen, and be shocked to see chef Achatz standing at the pass. He didn't often come over to greet them and ask about their meals—he could barely talk—but he was there, standing and working. More than a few teared up at the sight.

"It's just so fantastic and so sad at the same time," one woman said to me as she gripped my arm. "Please tell him it was a wonderful experience and that we are all praying for his recovery."

I heard this over and over, and yet I still did not believe the food could be the same. An entirely new fall menu was conceived at a time when Grant could barely eat and executed while he could not taste. I made a reservation to come in and eat, something that I rarely did.

Grant knew why I was there, even though I claimed that I just felt like going out to dinner.

The meal was different. It was certainly Alinea-like in its appearance, but it was richer, more earthy, and more decadent. Nothing was too out there or too challenging. And everything, but everything, was fantastically delicious. It was, quite simply, the best food I had ever eaten at Alinea. I was shocked.

When I got down to the kitchen I walked up to Grant and smiled. "Sorry. I guess I should have known."

I hadn't heard him speak in a few days, but he looked at me and said, "You know, we know what we're doing here."

We both laughed. "Well, you must have been keeping those up your sleeve for a rainy day. It was like French Laundry meets Alinea. Completely safe but visually unique. A brilliant move. No one could not like that."

I e-mailed everyone involved with the cookbook that night to set up a meeting for the next afternoon. We'd put our plans on hold, not knowing how Grant's treatment would affect his ability to work. But it seemed that it was possible to move forward after all.

Mark Caro, Martin, Lara, and I sat down at the "rock and roll" table in the back dining room—so-called because for some reason that is where all the famous musicians have sat at Alinea.

None of them had seen Grant in a few weeks, and the changes were huge. He had lost a substantial amount of weight, his face was pockmarked with pimples and burned from the radiation, and he was largely bald. His lips were bright white from the lotion he slathered on to keep them from bleeding, and he had to coat his mouth with gelled painkillers just to drink water, let alone talk.

"What are we here for?" Mark asked. "I mean, you told us to hold off for a while."

I explained that while the book was a priority for Grant, it wasn't a priority for me. I wanted to make sure he kept his focus on his treatment and health first and Alinea second. The book could wait or not happen at all. But I wasn't entirely honest with Grant about where I'd left things with the rest of the team. I'd told him that they were proceeding with the writing and design, when in fact I'd confided to them that I thought it was unlikely that the book would happen that year. I didn't want them spending their time on something that wouldn't come to fruition; it wouldn't be fair to them.

We sat down at the table and Grant joined us. Nobody said anything. Grant looked around. "So, what's everyone been doing? Nothing?"

Mark tried to dip a toe into the conversation. "Grant, we're all concerned about you and your health, and it seems that the book can wait. I'm working on writing, but obviously we haven't had the chance to talk and connect over the past month or so."

Grant looked at Martin, who shrugged his shoulders a bit. Lara couldn't photograph anything that wasn't being made in the kitchen, so it seemed as though she was probably off the hook. But Grant didn't see it that way.

"Who has cancer here, me or you guys? Why hasn't anyone done anything? This is pathetic. We'll never get this done at this rate. I don't understand it. If you don't want to do the book, tell me and I'll find someone else to do it."

With that he stood up and walked downstairs back to the kitchen. I apologized to everyone for allowing the meeting to take place. I should have known this was going to happen. I headed downstairs.

Grant didn't want to talk to me, but I pulled him aside. "Look, just because you have cancer doesn't give you the right to be an asshole. They're concerned about you. This doesn't just affect you; it affects everyone around you—Martin, Lara, the kitchen, me, your mom, your kids. None of us have cancer, but it's still an emotionally trying time. I'm the one who told them not to do anything. I didn't want to waste their time. I didn't expect that you'd still be in the kitchen working. Now that I see I was wrong we can get going. Put together a shooting schedule and I'll make sure we get Lara in here to photograph every day if necessary. But don't yell at them. Yell at me."

Grant was annoyed and having none of it. "We need to get the book done," was all he said. What was unspoken and understood was that this was his legacy now, not just a book.

He wanted to document everything before he died.

My mother took the train from Michigan to stay with me during the hardest part of my treatment. Until now, I had tried to keep her away, and I'd done a reasonable job of taking care of myself. I was proud that I had made it this far. But she called and told me she was coming down whether I liked it or not.

I thought that having her there would mean more stress, not less. It wasn't that she was bad at caring for me; in fact it was the opposite, to a fault. My apartment had never been cleaner since she started mopping the floors, cleaning the bathrooms, and washing my bedding every day. I just didn't want to accept her help. It made me feel as though I was reverting to my childhood, and it made my deteriorating physical situation all the more real. There she was, sitting on my couch thinking of things to clean, so nervous, scared, and upset that she was unable to sit naturally. I felt guilty. Nobody wants to be the cause of their mother's suffering.

It was late October and the radiation sessions had been bumped up to twice a day. I was burned badly then, singed bright red from my upper lip down to my lower neck. My skin was leathery and stretched taut, and if I turned my head too quickly or too far it would simply crack and bleed.

My mom came with me one day as I went through a five-hour chemo session followed by the second radiation treatment of the day. I explained to her that it was a waste of time, but she sat quietly with me, looking glum.

I knew I was in trouble when we headed in to the routine follow-up appointment at the end of the day. I had triple-layered my shirts, tucked my cell phone in my back pocket, and left my shoes on hoping to pick up a few ounces as I stepped on the scale. The nurse tapped the counter balance to the left until the needle started to float. I looked up. One twenty-nine. Shit. The nurse shot me a look of disapproval and shook her head.

Dr. Vokes entered the room with my chart and introduced himself to my mom in his characteristically warm, confident way. Throughout the treatment he had an incredibly calming effect on me. He always had an aura of assurance no matter what the circumstances were.

"Well, Grant, you seem to have forgotten our little deal," he said. "Have you been eating?"

I had a ploy all worked out, but before I could say anything my mom cut me off. "Tell him the truth, Grant." Her tone was angry and sympathetic at the same time. The tone only a mother can pull off. I told Dr. Vokes that it had been tough, but I was feeling better and would start to eat.

The doctors had warned me of dramatic weight loss and its consequences. Most head and neck cancer patients end up with a feeding tube at some point in their treatment, since normal ingestion becomes impossible. I began the treatments at 172 pounds and was told that when I reached 140 I had to do whatever possible to maintain that weight. I fought against the thought of the tube not because I was afraid of it, but because it was a point of pride. But there was no denying the scale no matter how hard I tried to convince them that it was a different, miscalibrated scale and I was wearing fewer clothes. The pain of eating was not the only thing preventing me from getting enough food. I could taste nothing. Eating had gone from embodying every possible emotion for me to only one: loss. I was reminded at every meal that I could not taste, could not cook, could not be a chef. It was mental agony.

"Give me three days and I promise I'll bring it up over one thirty."

My mother then reminded me that I couldn't even drink water without throwing up. She began suggesting to Dr. Vokes to give me a feeding tube. I was getting more and more annoyed with her and simply stood up, grabbed my coat, and told Dr. Vokes that I would be over 130 in three days. He agreed to give me the chance as long as I went to a nutritionist.

I was fairly well versed in removing texture from pretty much any food. That was not the problem. I couldn't eat anything without vomiting five minutes later. I thought it was absurd to see a nutritionist. But I went.

Her intentions were good and most people would have found her suggestions helpful, but I was a special case and she knew it. She began by apologizing. "I can't believe I'm telling you how to manipulate food." The irony of the situation was obviously not lost on her, which made the meeting more bearable.

She asked me about my eating habits and my estimation of my daily caloric intake. I explained that eating was impossible and even liquids would not stay down. She kept pushing for a caloric value.

The truth was that I was getting less than 200 calories per day. I was diluting apple juice fifty-fifty with water because the straight juice was too acidic for my scorched mouth. It felt like I was drinking habanero juice. I managed to get down eight ounces a day a few sips at a time. Once she heard that she realized that solid foods were out, so she began describing how to liquefy and supplement ordinary foods. I was polite as she recited some of her go-to's until she got to the third one. "You can puree canned chicken soup in a blender with some water, but just warm—anything hot would be like getting into a hot bath with a sunburn."

That was it for the nutritionist. I stood up, thanked her for her help, and went to find my mom in the waiting room. Canned chicken soup wasn't on my repertoire even if I was indeed dying, and the thought of it pureed and lukewarm made my stomach twist. No thanks.

As we headed to the parking garage I joked to my mom that it was a good thing I was there to drive her home. She didn't laugh. She was helpless and panicking, and my attitude was not helping matters.

The IV fluids hit my bloodstream to hydrate me, and I knew it would be a battle to get home before the urge to vomit hit me. I hoped I could make it all the way home, and I drove hard on northbound Lake Shore Drive. We had made it to Navy Pier, about the midpoint of the trip, when I began to lose the fight. I looked toward the shoulder, and traffic prevented me from pulling over, so I grabbed one of the strategically placed large plastic cups I kept in the console, placed it under my mouth, eased off the accelerator, and vomited into the cup. I just kept driving. This was normal. My mom was horrified.

We arrived home at five to find that the burn masks I had ordered on the Internet had arrived. I was pretty excited to try these out, so I went upstairs and applied them to my face, hoping they would ease the pain. My mom took her spot on the couch. With my face wrapped in bandages I plunked down next to her and we sat in silence for what felt like hours.

It was a Thursday at 5:30 P.M., and I realized that the first guests were arriving at Alinea while I sat on my couch covered in bandages feeling like death and my mother periodically began to sob next to me. My mind raced between dark, amplified thoughts of my own death to worries about the mundane. Every thought was a disaster and was working over my emotions like a pro fighter hitting me with body shots, wearing me down.

I hope they remember to order roe from Stallard.

Will the regular tables be disappointed that I'm not there?

Do they need me tonight?

I love fall. I wonder if this will be my last fall.

Will Heather stay with me if they cut out my tongue? It's not fair to her.

This treatment won't work. It will come back. This is all for shit.

What will the boys do after I die? What will they become?

Nick will know what to do for the funeral.

I felt my mom's hand come to rest on my forearm. I looked up and she was looking at me and tears were running down her cheeks. "Why is she crying?" I wondered. Then she reached up with her other hand and wiped the tears from my face with a tissue.

Guess I started it.

"What's wrong, honey?"

I couldn't respond. I just sat there shaking my head, my emotions hindering any chance of articulation. I tried, but my sobbing choked off the words. It's a good thing I couldn't tell her what I was thinking:

I look like a fucking Martian.

I can't taste, talk, or swallow.

I am too young to die.

The restaurant was doing fine. Chef Pikus grew immensely as the responsibility for day-to-day operations shifted firmly to his shoulders. Grant's hours slowly diminished as the radiation took its toll. I would walk in to see Pikus, head down, working at a frantic pace. "How's it going, Chef?"

"It's going," he grunted at me with a weak smile. But I knew he was killing himself to make it happen, each and every day.

Suddenly, though, without really noticing at first, Grant wasn't there. I knew he was at a low point, and while I would have wanted to be pampered, he wanted to be alone. Still, I didn't get any e-mails from him, and he wasn't online or logged into his e-mail account. I occasionally got a few words: "Feel like shit, can't eat, puking, sweating." If he wasn't at the restaurant at all and wasn't checking in, I knew it must be bad.

I e-mailed to ask what I could do to help, if there was anything I could bring him. I heard back two days later, "No, thanks."

Finally I couldn't take it any longer and drove by his apartment and rang the bell. After a few minutes he came to the door and I was horrified by his appearance. He waved a hand at me but said nothing, and did not offer to let me in.

"Hey. I came by to see if I could bring you some soup or help you wash up or something." I was reaching for something to do, knowing that nothing was possible or desired. I really just wanted to see if he was alive. He shook his head at me.

I told him I would leave him alone and it was good to know he was surviving. "Another week," was all I could muster, referring to his few remaining treatments. "Just another week."

He shut the door and I got back in the car and drove to Alinea. Dave came over and asked if I'd seen Grant.

"Yeah, I saw him. He looks good," I lied.

walked into the treatment room for the last time and sized up the linear accelerator, the official name for the machine that administered the radiation. I removed my shirt and turned to the counter where the techs kept my custom-fitted mouthpiece. It was designed to position my tongue for accurate radiation exposure, not for comfort. I forced my mouth open and slid it in. The smell of blood instantly reached my nose. I couldn't taste it, but I knew it was there. The tech entered the room and greeted me for the second time that day. "All right, last time, eh?"

I shook my head in agreement as I laid down on the platform. They strapped my head in, stepped out of the room, and the machine hummed to a start. "Yep. Last fucking time," I thought to myself.

I had made it.

After the machine ground to a halt and they freed me from the harness, I sat up and began to gather my things. "Do you want these?"

I turned and saw the attendant holding my head harness and mouth guard. I shook my head no and then garbled, "I won't need those again." She explained that some people liked to keep them for posterity. I wanted nothing more than to forget about the whole thing. I looked horrible, but I was still vertical. The treatment protocol had taken me to physical and mental lows that I didn't know existed, but I was relieved that regardless of the outcome—whether I lived or died—this ordeal was over.

I walked across the hall, hopped up on the table, and was greeted by Dr. Haraf for my exit exam. As was always the case, he started with a few jokes as he ran me through the standard series of tests, opening my mouth as wide as possible and turning my neck from side to side. He felt under my chin and the sides of my neck, checking the severity of the muscular atrophy caused by the radiation.

I avoided conversation as much as possible, pausing to reformulate answers to his questions in the fewest number of words. The inside of my mouth was completely raw and my body was producing mucus to protect my open sores.

"Carry-over cooking, just like a prime rib getting pulled from the oven," Haraf joked. He explained that even though I had made it through the last of the radiation treatments, the process of cellular degradation would continue for a few weeks. It would get worse before it got better. "I told you it would be miserable, and I didn't lie. But you took it like a champ, much better than most." I smiled at him. Somehow Dr. Haraf always made me smile despite the horror I faced. His humor always spoke to me directly. He referred to the radiation machine as his Fry Daddy and talked about eating beef tongue as he prodded my own tongue, feeling for any remnants of a tumor. "Feels good," he said. "I can feel one tiny spot in the back, but it's likely just scar tissue. When Blair cuts you open in a month she'll know for sure. But it looks good."

I had gone through countless hours of chemo over the past four months, and then faced down radiation twice a day for six weeks. I spent the majority of that time pulling fourteen-hour days at Alinea, acting as normally as was possible. And yet I still didn't know if it was all worth it. Did it work? Was the cancer gone?

Indications were promising, and all of the doctors agreed that the tumor seemed to have vanished based on physical exams and CT scans. But they cautiously warned that the scans were only accurate to one millimeter. That was about a thousand cells, and any one of those could be malignant and eventually a cause for reoccurrence: one would grow to two, then four, then millions. The biopsy would give a good indication of the primary tumor site, but that would be a whole month from now. The drugs and radiation would continue to do their job for another two weeks, and after that my tissue would need time to heal before surgery. No judgment could be made until then.

My health started improving incrementally. Slowly, without noticing any day-to-day improvement, my body began to heal. Week to week, I would notice small changes. I flew to Heather's parents' house for Thanksgiving and cooked a giant, traditional feast. I even managed to get down some mashed potatoes after dousing them heavily with gravy. But I still couldn't taste a thing, and each meal increased my panic that this might be a permanent condition. I seasoned the food by memory and by feeling the salt between my fingers.

By early December I was back in the Alinea kitchen at almost full speed. Surprisingly, my energy was increasing despite the fact that I was still not eating much in the way of solid food. I often texted Heather at 8:30 A.M., when I was heading in to work early to shoot pictures of the Alinea book and create new dishes. It felt amazing to be back. We scheduled the Alinea holiday party for the first week in December so I could attend prior to my surgery. I even had a head covered with fuzzy hair.

Dr. Blair explained that the team wanted her to perform a selective neck dissection to remove the majority of the lymph node chain on my left side and a more limited excision of the nodes on my right. This would increase the chances of eradicating any remaining cancerous tissue. The surgery was scheduled for December 13, 2007, exactly five months to the day after I found out I had cancer.

During a phone conversation a few days before the surgery, I asked Dr. Blair about recovery time and reminded her of my plans to fly to Washington with Heather for Christmas, then celebrate my recovery in St. Barts shortly thereafter while Alinea was on its winter break.

"Okay, then," she said. "I guess we're not going to staple you shut—those will set off the metal detectors in the airport for sure. I'll stitch you up as pretty as I can. You do realize, however, that you will be incredibly swollen and sore. And there will be a drain tube hanging out of the back of your neck, by the way."

Dr. Blair went on to explain that she was going to be as gentle as possible, but that the surgery would have its own set of side effects. Most notably would be giant chipmunk cheeks and a swollen neck from the lack of natural "drainage" that the lymph system normally facilitates. "We're taking that plumbing out, so it will take a while for the fluids to find a new route. In the meantime, it'll build up a bit, and that's why we have to insert the drain tube. If all goes well, we can remove it in about five days, but your movement will be very limited."

She spoke nonchalantly about what sounded like a transformation from E.T. to Frankenstein Chef. Just when I was beginning to feel more normal, the emotional roller coaster was beginning anew.

They had, of course, warned me about all of this, but I had put it out of my mind. The surgery battered my newfound optimism in a way I didn't expect. I was once again scared of a new set of unknown challenges—and the answer to whether this was all worth doing.

The surgery was set for 7:00 A.M. My alarm went off at 5:20 and I peeked outside to see the car service I had arranged already waiting outside. As I got dressed, Heather wished me luck, then hugged me forcefully and wouldn't let go. She was scared too. I jokingly told her that it was unlikely I would die on the operating table after surviving the rest of it. The irony would be too great. I tucked her back into bed and walked outside.

Al, the driver who had taken me to some treatments when I couldn't drive myself, was familiar with the details of my story and had witnessed firsthand my physical decline. "This is it, Al," I said as I slid into the backseat. "They're going to cut me open, pull half of my neck out, and figure out if they cured me." He was typically a chatty guy, but this statement silenced him for the entire ride to the hospital. As we got off Lake Shore Drive he finally spoke.

"You're going to be all right, Grant. Since the first time I met you I could sense something different. You are a lucky guy, oddly enough. It isn't your time."

With these words I picked my head up and our eyes met in the rearview mirror for a second. I pursed my lips and nodded, hoping Al was clairvoyant.

Dr. Klock, the anesthesiologist who I was reluctantly getting to know, briefed me on the drugs he was going to give me and confirmed that I had no known allergies. We passed the time waiting for Dr. Blair by chatting about his experiences dining at Alinea with his brother, who was a chef. "Good to know he liked it," I thought.

The curtain flew open and a smiling Dr. Blair walked over and held my hand. "Okay, kiddo, you ready for this? Before you know it you'll be on a beach in St. Barts." They each grabbed a side of the gurney and wheeled me to the OR.

"Count backward from ten," I heard Dr. Klock say, and I was out.

I felt some rustling of the covers over me and I started to dream that my boys were jumping on me while I was in bed. Slowly the noises became clearer and I could make out adult voices.

"Grant? Are you awake? Can you open your eyes?"

The room at first seemed black and white and full of moving shadows, but it slowly became clearer and colors began to appear. Dr. Blair's voice registered, and as my eyes flickered open I remembered where I was and why I was there. "Can you speak to me?" she asked once my eyes opened.

"How did it go?" I tried to say, but the words wouldn't form. She knew what I was asking.

She leaned over me while grasping my hand and whispered into my ear, "It's clean. It looks good, Chef."

I went into the recovery room and Grant was awake. I was shocked that the skinny guy who was wheeled into surgery suddenly looked like he had gained thirty pounds. He was swollen, bloodied, and had a tube hanging out of the back of his head. But he was aware. And the ordeal was over. He headed home the next morning.

Three days later I walked into the Alinea kitchen to see Grant standing at his station with the tube still hanging out of his head. I was fairly shocked to see him, though not surprised. "Hey, Skeletor," I said, grabbing his elbow while he worked, "you think the health department thinks it's a good idea to be working with a head drain in?"

He smiled at me as best he could. I stood at the end of the kitchen and noticed that Pikus was smiling for the first time in a month and the rest of the crew was working vigorously.

When I came back to the restaurant at 10:30 that night I knew Grant would still be there, working. I drove back just to make sure he left. I knew no one else would tell him to go get some sleep. As I walked up to him he looked up at me and raised his eyebrow. "I'm leaving in five minutes," he garbled.

"Good. Welcome home."

I didn't attend the James Beard Awards. I was emotionally spent and couldn't imagine sitting there hoping Grant would win Best Chef in America. Once he did, the usual press hit, but I was not expecting to see any more news about Grant's ordeal or subsequent honor in the local papers nearly a week later. I woke up, made coffee, and out of habit opened to the editorial section of the *Chicago Tribune*. There it was—the top editorial of the day: "The Taste of Triumph," along with a color picture of a pleased Grant.

I read the piece, smiled, and put down the paper. It felt like closure, the whole of it. The Beard Award for Outstanding Chef was great, but now this summed it all up.

I called Grant. I knew he would still be sleeping, but this was cool. In my mind, this was the best article about Alinea or Grant ever written.

"Hey."

"Sorry to wake you. I assume you haven't heard about the *Trib* yet?"

"No. I am, as you might imagine, sleeping."

"Well, you're the top editorial—a wonderful piece. Can I read it to you?"

"Sure," he said half asleep.

I put the phone on speaker and read aloud:

The Taste of Triumph.

The ¶ has long been used by editors and English teachers to mark the start of a new paragraph. Called an alinea, the symbol connotes a break from the previous chain of thought—a new chapter.

Alinea is the name that celebrated chef Grant Achatz chose for the Lincoln Park restaurant he opened in 2005. It was a fitting choice. Achatz, who serves both a tasting and a tour—offering each guest at least a dozen courses—reinvents his menu, rewriting his customers' dining experience each season. In May 2005 *Tribune* restaurant critic Phil Vettel said, "Alinea is the most exciting restaurant debut Chicago has seen in—well, maybe ever." In 2006, *Gourmet* magazine named Alinea the best restaurant in the country. In 2007, it was named the 36th best restaurant in the world by *Restaurant Magazine*. In 2008, it jumped to 21st.

Sunday night marked the most momentous paragraph in Alinea's already famous story. Achatz, at age 34, won the James Beard Award—think Oscars for kitchen whizzes—as the top chef in the United States. This was another victory for the restaurant scene in Chicago—considered by many foodies as the most innovative and inventive dining city in the country. And it was remarkable affirmation for Achatz's perseverance and pluck. Achatz is the third Chicago chef—after Charlie Trotter and Rick Bayless—to take home the prize.

And it's safe to say he is the only one, in the history of the award, to have managed the feat after losing his sense of taste.

In June 2007, Achatz was diagnosed with stage IV tongue cancer. That's as bad as it gets—there is no stage V. Several doctors told him the only way to deal with the disease would be to cut out three-quarters of his tongue. That has been the treatment protocol for four decades. His ability to speak properly would be compromised. His ability to swallow might disappear. And his ability to taste? It would be gone.

The man whom *Gourmet* editor Ruth Reichl credited with redefining the American restaurant decided to do the same for the treatment of tongue cancer. Achatz enrolled in a clinical trial at the University of Chicago that began with chemotherapy. Radiation followed. By October, his sense of taste had vanished. Still, he worked. He dreamed up new dishes. He experimented with ingredients. And he relied on his sous chefs to calibrate the flavors and finalize the balance of dishes he couldn't taste.

Many people have firsthand knowledge of the physical and emotional struggle with cancer, particularly with an advanced cancer. We'd venture that many people who have never unfurled a napkin at Alinea are cheering Grant Achatz.

His cancer has not reappeared. His sense of taste is slowly recovering, though it may never completely return. His triumph—well, there are many ways to savor that.

"That's amazing, right? And on the editorial page too. Top of the page."

"Great."

"Grant. This is not the food section. This is where the real news goes. That is a hugely inspirational piece."

"Cool. Is that a big deal?"

I laughed to myself for a second and thought about it. "No. You know, Grant, relatively speaking, it's not really a big deal at all. Go back to sleep. I'll catch up to you later."

"I'll be at Alinea by noon."

# EPILOGUE

The James Beard Award for Best Chef in the United States was indeed a turning point. And for a few days it sustained me. But like all such awards and recognitions, the adrenaline rush was fleeting, the ego boost decidedly temporary.

There is no doubt that the award and resulting press revitalized Alinea. Bookings went up, and the demand for me at speaking engagements soared. The news seeped out that I was alive, and better still, that I had beaten the odds. I was downright "inspirational." I was asked to cook at private dinners around the country, and even on a Gulfstream for a major studio executive—price no object. But I didn't do any of them. Five months after being declared "cancer-free" I was still very much living with cancer and the aftereffects of having my cells killed from the inside out. I could barely swallow, still couldn't taste, and basic human functions were a daily trial.

So when the rush of the award was over, the work of running Alinea came back to the fore. The restaurant had survived, even thrived, in my absence. I learned that my team had taken to heart my leadership and entreaties. At first this was all uplifting and remarkable. But what I was not prepared for was normalcy.

A few months after I returned, it dawned on me that things were back to normal. I was declared cancer-free, and I told everyone that the treatment had worked. But I didn't believe it myself. The doctors didn't use the term "cancer-free," because the grain of the scans only goes down to one millimeter. That's small, but it can contain plenty of cancer. If even a single cell metastasized anywhere in my body, one becomes two becomes four becomes four hundred million pretty quickly. I understood that math all too well.

Everyone around me was relieved. We plugged away at finishing up the Alinea book, the restaurant was full, patrons mentioned the cancer and my struggle but it was a victory, not a funeral. While I knew that everyone wished me well, their positive attitude was grating. I felt like shit physically and mentally. Didn't they know how sick I still was? Didn't they know that most of the time these types of cancers reoccur and patients die quickly thereafter? Didn't they know that while I cooked their meal I slathered lidocaine solution in my mouth and forced down a small bowl of soup and a vanilla milkshake with protein powder, nearly choking every time I had to swallow? Not to mention that I still couldn't taste.

During the treatment it was easy for me to stay engaged, play the part of the positive thinker, the can-do guy. Six months later I was pissed off, tired, and withdrawn. And it began to affect my personal relationships.

In the kitchen I was unusually quiet. I usually keep to myself and try to lead by example, but now I just put my head down and tried to get through the days. I could feel the staff fracturing. They had put so much into running the restaurant while I was dying that they had a hard time dealing with me now that I was alive. The cooks were tentative around me, unsure how to act. That just pissed me off more.

I would go a week or more without speaking to Nick. We would do shoots for the Alinea book, compile recipes, and he would look at the results and comment or make edits in an e-mail chain, but he wouldn't call me. I knew he came by Alinea because checks were signed and spreadsheets were sent to me, but he studiously avoided me, or simply walked through the kitchen and said, "Hi, Chef" as though he were greeting an intern. What the hell was his problem? Why was he tired and disengaged?

Then, one day after repeatedly reworking a course under my direction, chef Pikus simply told me, "I can't do this anymore." I picked my head up only for a second, just long enough to look him in the eye and muster a matter-of-fact "okay." He slammed his hands into the back door, sending it flying, and walked out. I put my head back down and started working on the dish as he had left it so it would be ready for service that night.

Jeff held this place together while I was on my back, and now a relatively straightforward dish prep sent him off. His always intense, introspective psyche had had enough. Did he crack or did I? Fuck him. He just walked out. I wouldn't do that; I wouldn't burn that bridge, I thought to myself. Instead of chasing after him, discussing things, figuring out what went wrong, I just blamed him. As far as I was concerned at that moment, Jeff no longer existed.

While I hit points during the radiation that were spectacularly low, I rarely if ever felt sorry for myself. But months later I did. I questioned whether or not I could be a chef. Can I do this? Can I keep making food if I can't taste? What if my taste doesn't come back? Then I'm a charlatan, a faker. Alinea has won enough awards, enough stars. I am beat.

For the first time in my life I wanted to quit.

I wanted desperately to leave and see what else was out there. Alinea was my home, and now it felt like a trap. Could I really do this for another ten years, another twenty? I could take those high-end private cooking gigs and make more money working fifteen days a year than I do working three hundred.

Oprah called. Nick was right. The cancer thing, if you live through it, is perfect fodder for *Oprah*. We got the irony and had a laugh when the call came in. Still, I felt a profound sense of responsibility to go on there and tell my story, to tell other people who suffer from this insidious disease that there are alternatives to hacking apart your tongue and neck. That they shouldn't take no for an answer. But when I actually filmed the show, sitting in the greenroom with Heather and Nick, I didn't feel the rush anymore. A year earlier I would have killed to be on *Oprah,* to talk about my food, to make the case for my cuisine and restaurant in front of her huge audience. Instead I just sat there and poured a half pint of cream into my coffee to cool it down and fatten myself up.

Slowly, though, I began to realize that I hadn't died.

I kept waking up and the same people were there supporting me, working beside me, pushing me along. I spoke with my dad more frequently. Heather didn't go anywhere. She stayed beside me, and that meant a ton. Martin and Lara pulled all-nighters for weeks to complete the Alinea book, even traveling to China to oversee the printing personally. In the end, it was better than we could have hoped for at the beginning. I'm not sure any of us felt vindicated by our decision to create it in-house. We just felt relieved that it got finished.

Nick started talking about what to do next. That's his role. He doesn't work shifts at Alinea, but he tries to see around the corners. And so we started fielding requests for restaurants in New York and Las Vegas. And I got the urge to go bigger, to prove I was alive. And that began to consume me.

We headed to New York to look at sites and did the same thing there that we did in Chicago. The difference this time around was that we were a known entity and Keith was in New York and had pre-scouted a number of locations. The third place we looked at was just perfect.

All of the super high-end restaurants in New York are uptown. This was in SoHo, a great contrast. It was a beautiful vintage building with vaulted ceilings and, amazingly enough, an entire back area that was almost a conservatory. The kitchen, if placed in the back, would have glass on three sides, one of them being the ceiling. This was unheard of in Manhattan. The owners were two older gentlemen who were well aware of Alinea and wanted nothing more than to see us put a four-star restaurant in there. I was ecstatic. After the long search and awful negotiations for Alinea, this seemed too good to be true. Keith was beaming. "I told you guys. This is fantastic, right?"

We were being trailed that day by the writer D.T. Max, who was working on a profile for the *New Yorker*. It was hard not to be enthused. I talked to him about my goals, about how my taste was slowly coming back. Nick had reiterated to me over and over again that there were two magazines in the world that had truly great writing, and the

New Yorker was, in his opinion, one of them. While it may not have had the biggest circulation, it did, perhaps, have the most influential.

My ambitions were returning.

Nick was unusually quiet. Really quiet. And when we got back to the hotel he looked at me and said, "Why the hell do you want to build a restaurant in New York when you can barely function and still can't taste?" He had been the one pushing, and now he was disengaging again. It seemed that his earlier enthusiasm had been fake—something to keep me motivated—but now that it was a distinct possibility, his real thoughts became evident. And that just ticked me off.

I told him that my taste was coming back, slowly for sure, but definitely. And of course every chef would want to own a restaurant in New York. New York and Paris are the dining capitals of the world. People go out to eat in New York at 11:00 P.M. We would kill it there.

"It's about your ego, then," he said. "It doesn't get us anything. And with all due respect, who's going to put up the money at this point? Everyone is enthusiastic now, but will they write a check for a guy who just survived stage IVb cancer and can't get an insurance policy? Do you think the landlords will give us an out-clause on that?"

"So we never build another restaurant?" I said rhetorically, getting angry.

"We might. But only after you're healed. You need to take care of yourself. You can fake it with others, but I see the case of lidocaine you packed. I know what you can taste, and I know why you want to do this. But it's a loser, even if you assume we do it right. And right now, we can't do it right."

"So you don't want to do it?"

"It isn't about 'want.' I get the desire. I came to this city as a trader when we were riding high and it was a blast. My ego was every bit of yours. But no matter what we do here, we lose. If the restaurant here is better than Alinea, then our flagship suffers. If the New York place is worse than Alinea, then obviously that's a failure. If we do the same thing, well, that's a loser, too. Those are the three possibilities, and I know you don't want to come here to build a three-star concept. So it's a lose-lose-lose, existentially, as those are the only possibilities— same, better, or worse."

He was making sense and pissing me off at the same time.

We got back to Chicago and Nick made virtually no effort to move things along. I realized quickly that he had no intention of putting together a New York restaurant. Every time I brought it up he turned the focus to the book. "Let's just get the book out, Grant. Better opportunities will come along."

Nick talked to Keith, who was disappointed. He expressed surprise that the investors seemed willing to invest, that the Vegas developers kept calling too. Maybe he knew too much, or maybe he had just lost faith a bit.

Either way, I began to feel that he was in my way.

The New York and Vegas deals fell to the side. We explored them, and each time we came to the conclusion that they weren't right. I wanted to push, to move on, but on some level I agreed. We should be getting something more, something better. But nothing came along that we were genuinely excited by. Odd TV shows based on *American Idol* but with cooking, restaurants in Dubai, and endorsement deals for pans were all shot down.

I arrived at the University of Chicago at the one-year mark of my remission and got the full body scan and physical exam. I still weighed less than 145 pounds, but the scans were clean. And six months later, at eighteen months, they were clean too.

The Alinea book came out and we did events in New York and Chicago. Nick also called Thomas and asked him if he would do a series of dinners with me. One at Per Se, then at Alinea, and then finishing at The French Laundry. The planning and dynamics of the dinners were difficult, the costs astronomical, and the press was not terribly kind given the economy and the $1,500 per ticket price—on which we barely broke even. But Nick's heart was in the right place. He simply wanted to force me and Thomas to cook together again after

I nearly died, to get a moment to reflect on our relationship as mentor and apprentice. The dinners went off well. We had pizza in the Alinea kitchen after service, Nick and Thomas shared a bottle of cheap pinot, and at TFL the whole staff got In-N-Out burgers. It all felt like family.

The book sold very well and introduced our cuisine to thousands of people who would otherwise have missed it. Martin was recognized with a Communications Arts award for the design, a huge honor—especially considering it was his first book—and *Alinea* won a James Beard Award, beating out the likes of *Under Pressure* by Thomas, who was gracious to invite us to what would have been his victory dinner at Per Se with the entire team that made his book. As always, he was as excited for me as he would have been for himself.

My taste buds came back in waves. First I could suddenly taste sweet. Then it would retreat and salty would come back. Then I would get a wave of savory, meaty taste that would be fleeting but real. I would rush into the kitchen, grab a tasting spoon, and go down the line to see what worked and what didn't. It was an amazing education to get these building blocks one at a time. Finally, on a trip to L.A. to meet with some TV producers for a documentary, Nick and I ate at Spago after literally bumping into Sherry Yard, the longtime Spago pastry chef, on the street. She dragged us in against our will. I was eating more, but couldn't fathom making it through a tasting menu. We slid past Don Johnson at the bar and were given the best table in the house. I looked at Nick and said, "I hope you're hungry, because anything with a sharp edge or a spice is going in your mouth."

But suddenly I could taste. A few things hurt if I chewed in the wrong spot, but the flavors were amazing. I had been afraid to venture too far from safe foods, but now I could see that I had been too conservative. Nick started blind-tasting me to see if I could really taste—who else would do that?—and sure enough, I was batting a thousand. The TV show and the documentary never panned out, but the trip was worth it for that meal.

I was back.

It's hard to take the long view when you have cancer. From the moment I understood the diagnosis until well after my treatment ended the concept of a "future" did not exist for me. Planning long term gave way to making sure I was enjoying myself more in the moment.

Time with Kaden and Keller became special. I never had a talk with them where I told them I thought I was going to die or that the odds were I wouldn't make it to forty. I just spent my Mondays and Tuesdays with them doing the things that I valued with my dad when I was a kid. Those times felt better than before.

Work, however, felt different. If I wasn't building toward a future, then pushing hard in the kitchen, creating new dishes and techniques, seemed less rewarding, pointless even. And building a new restaurant began to seem foolish.

Nick had always encouraged me to invest for the long term. I enjoyed spending money even when I didn't have it, and I never focused on savings or planning. Nick always stressed ownership over our business and intellectual property, forgoing money up front on projects like the book in order to keep control and make more in the long run. While I always agreed with the logic of that strategy and appreciated his efforts, it seemed now that I had made the wrong bet.

And yet, I kept waking up. I kept making small, imperceptible gains. My weight slowly returned and along with it my strength and stamina. There were a few days when I felt normal—or what my doctors called my "new normal." I wasn't what I once was, but I also wasn't thinking about my health during the day.

I was just living. And it felt great.

At some point I stopped worrying about what I was going to do next and started enjoying myself again. Heather moved from New York to Chicago and we began spending real time together. I planned more trips and accepted more speaking engagements and cooking demonstrations, not for the money but for the opportunity to see the world and be inspired again by new ideas, art, and food.

As I stopped worrying about the future, I actually began to believe that I might have one.

Another offer from Vegas came just after the economic meltdown. It seemed an odd time to be getting such an offer, but as real estate was being pulled from the developers to the banks, the banks were looking to finish the projects. Once again, we spent time putting a proposal together and looking at the deal. It would have been good money. But once again, it just didn't feel right. We couldn't answer the question, "Why should we build a restaurant in Vegas other than for the money?"

In May 2010 I traveled to London for the World's 50 Best Restaurants awards. Alinea moved up to number seven in the world, but even more significantly was named the Best Restaurant in North America. When we received that ranking from *Gourmet,* it felt amazing to us, but ultimately did not impact our business as significantly as we had expected. It was not reported in other magazines and newspapers, and while we would cite it to the press as one of our biggest achievements, it would rarely get mentioned. Somehow, this was completely different. The day after the awards newspapers all over the United States hailed Alinea as the "Best Restaurant in America." People began calling the restaurant telling us that our website was down. Nick texted me in London: "Servers crashed. Fifty thousand requests for our site in the last hour! Phones off the hook."

When I returned to Chicago Nick and I sat down and had a long talk. Now he was itching to do something nearly as much as I was. Alinea was rolling like never before, the book was in its fourth printing, and my health was less of a concern. He mentioned the duck breast I cooked for him on the day I was diagnosed with cancer.

"Chef, I am telling you, people want to see you cook 'normal' food. It would be a great story as well to have you show your chops. No one except me ever gets to see that."

I thought it sounded boring. "Okay. So after I cook a duck breast and a few steaks, then what? What drives the restaurant?" Alinea is about constant innovation, of searching for the new and the better and the interesting. I had come to realize that I enjoyed that search more than the execution of the restaurant itself.

"Well, after we do that, why not just do an Italian menu for a while?" he said without thinking. "Then, when you get tired of that, just do something totally off the wall—Vietnamese food."

"Naw. That's impossible. You can't retool a restaurant and a kitchen like that all the time. As soon as you get rolling on a menu you stop it and start again? And who shows up not knowing what they're going to get?"

"You do realize that you just described Alinea, right?" Nick said with a smile. "Impossible is a good thing. That means that no one else has probably done this. I'm telling you it would be fantastic to get you and the crew doing a French menu one season and a Thai menu the next. People would show up for that. The goal would be, let's be the best Italian restaurant in Chicago for three months, then the best Chinese restaurant. It would be audacious, difficult, and fun as hell. Plus we'd get to do research trips!"

Quietly, we started searching for real estate and going back through the plans that we had created as proposals for other developments. Among them was a plan for a lounge for the Trump building in Chicago. As we found real estate that didn't fit a restaurant, I started pushing for the lounge. Cocktail development is an area that I hadn't explored much but where I could see the possibility for innovation on par with what we had done at Alinea. Plus, the food concepts wouldn't fight with Alinea—the two wouldn't be compared.

One deal was almost signed for the lounge and details began leaking out in the press—apparently, the building owner wanted to drum up business for his other empty spots next door. But just as I was digging into how to arrange a drink-kitchen there, Nick called me. "I found a better spot just down the street. And guess what? It's actually two spots. We can do both."

"Both? As in, the restaurant and the lounge?"

"Yeah," he said. "I think it works even better." He explained the lease structure and the space. I drove over and was surprised by how well it could work physically.

"You ready?" I asked.

"Yeah. I think we both are."

The next day Nick sent me an overview of the project, which was just like the one we had sent to investors in Alinea. He likes to say that every great restaurant has a great story behind it, and it's important to articulate that story. It began:

"Next Restaurant will explore the great cuisines of the world.

Whereas Alinea is about constant innovation, Next will be about constant exploration. Each season, Next will strive to be the best restaurant serving a world-cuisine in Chicago . . . the best French restaurant, then the best Italian, then the best Mexican."

I read it and called him up. "I was thinking that we not only do a cuisine like 'French' but that we get really specific. Paris, the Loire Valley, Burgundy—they all have different cuisines. And then I thought, just like the Escoffier course at Alinea, we put a time on it. Paris, 1925." Once I said that, I knew we had it. Everyone would immediately understand what we were doing there. It is one thing to say we are serving French food this season. It is another to say Rome, 1948 when you're inevitably asked, "What kind of food is it?" Nick loved the idea.

"And this time, Chef, we're doing the ticket thing. I'm telling you, it'll be revolutionary because we can price it so low at off-peak times."

"But what do we call the place? It should be about travel or places or maps, right?"

"What do you mean? The name is in the e-mail I sent you," he said. So I looked again and saw "Next." I had thought it was just a placeholder, as in, "Our next restaurant will be . . . ," and at first I didn't like it. But it did answer the question of the changing menu and constant exploration. It was about what's next. I told Nick that I got it but that we could find something better. He said, "No. It's not really just about that."

He was right.

For a long time I had worried about what was coming next. Then for a short time that felt very long, I didn't think I had a future.

Now every time I was asked, "What's Next?" I could finally enjoy coming up with the answer.

Not a bad reminder.

AFTERWORD

Since *Life, on the Line* first came out in March 2011, we have received hundreds of letters, e-mails, and even visits from people who are suffering from head and neck cancer. The outreach has been truly overwhelming, and we receive correspondence every week—much of it from people who are young, who don't smoke or drink, and who have lived very clean, healthy lives. Nearly all of them face a prognosis that is grim at best. They write to say "Help" or "Thank you for the inspiration" or to just tell us their story; to have someone to share it with who understands the pain and emotions. Each person's story is genuinely heartbreaking, real, and compelling.

Some of them read our book shortly after they learn of their illness, and become proactive about seeking the most modern and innovative treatments. The vast majority, however, are already undergoing a traditional protocol of surgery followed by chemotherapy and radiation. For some, of course, that was the right line of treatment and there would have been no other choice. Many, though, simply didn't have enough information to explore every possibility and have undergone surgeries that are irreparable and devastating to their quality of life.

Over the past several months, we have given talks at cancer centers and treatment facilities, worked with charities that promote proactive cancer screening, and have raised hundreds of thousands of dollars for the University of Chicago's cancer research center by hosting dinners at Alinea. It is impossible to NOT want to help these wonderful doctors and caregivers in their work. And every week we answer dozens of e-mails, calls, and questions from patients. It is the best part of having the *Life, on the Line* story published.

Owning a world-class restaurant is great. The awards and accolades feed the ego. The money is starting to be good. The hard and creative work is life-affirming. But nothing we do is more important than helping get the message out that new, innovative, and organ-preserving treatments are available for this terrible disease. The temptation for anyone is simply to go back to living a life where one doesn't think about that awful chapter. The constant requests from readers for more information make that not only impossible but also truly undesirable.

Alinea is a small business run by a small group of people.

Next to the restaurant we have a tiny office in the coach house, which is overrun with chefs using the galley-style residential kitchen to handle overflow prep. During the summer this year, it more resembled a greenhouse than a proper office. For our interactive salad course, hundreds of lettuce plants were brought in from a farm each week, and grew among the desks. Joe Catterson's office in the back overflows with wine samples and employment reports. A closet-size office on the first floor houses our rotovaps, and normally has two or three people working on computers.

Building Next seemed like it would be an easier task than building Alinea. We had, after all, done it once, and things turned out well. But anyone who has done even a small home remodeling project knows that construction rarely goes smoothly. And building a restaurant is less about the construction than the conception.

Once we found a suitable space, we pulled in the same design team that crafted Alinea—Tom Stringer for interior design, Steve Rugo as architect, and of course Martin Kastner. The discussion began by describing the philosophy of the restaurant and came down to a single line: "Alinea is about innovation; Next is about exploration." That was the core philosophy and design edict.

The Aviary, though, was harder to encapsulate in a single thought. Doing so, we feel, is very important to any business. It is the equivalent of the "elevator pitch" for a business plan or the "Jaws with claws" movie pitch. While the overall concept must have complexity, it must also be simple enough at its center for people to grasp immediately. In turn, this pitch becomes the foundation of our PR. Like a political campaign or a rock band that has to keep playing its hits, we stay on message and repeat the tagline over and over—then build the story from there.

The Aviary sprung from a business plan we did for the Trump building in Chicago. The Trump family had approached us about doing the restaurant and lounge for their Chicago venture. Ultimately, we decided not to work on the project, but we couldn't get the idea of doing a hotel lounge out of our heads. There is so much wrong with many of them: slow service, uninspired drinks, food that doesn't work with the atmosphere or even fit on the tiny tables. We wanted to create a lounge where the drinks and service were crafted with the same care that we give to food and the dining experience at Alinea. This would mean that a traditional "bartender" would not exist. Instead, a team of chefs would be organized just as they are in a high-end kitchen. And from that thought came the core philosophy: The Aviary is a restaurant for cocktails.

This is when creating a restaurant or two is just plain fun. A group of creative people get together and a wellspring of ideas begins to flow. Once it is announced to the public, there is no turning back. A restaurant will, in the end, exist. But until it is announced it is just talk, even if a lease is about to be signed. We had to throw ourselves under the bus, so to speak, in a big way and force ourselves to make decisions.

We decided that the James Beard Foundation Awards would be a great place and time to announce the new restaurant. And like Alinea, we decided to make the announcement with a "trailer." We imagined a plane that flew from city to city, morphing its shape as it traveled through time. Martin Kastner had the idea of including a Solari board—the old train station information boards that make that wonderful clickety-clack noise as they update information, a wonderful hybrid of the mechanical and the digital. Martin spent two weeks animating the scene in an homage to Indiana Jones maps. Then we had the idea to contact one of the bloggers who was cooking his way through the Alinea cookbook—and just happened to be a digital artist for Weta Digital studios in New Zealand. Allen Hemberger jumped at the chance to help, as he was about to move from New Zealand to San Francisco to join Pixar, and had a bit of time. A few days later we had amazing digital clouds and a fully rendered future-scene of Hong Kong 2036 right out of *Blade Runner*.

The main issue of contention prior to the announcement was the idea that we would sell tickets to the restaurant rather than take reservations. And in the trailer, the line "Tickets—yes, tickets—go on sale soon" came up right at the end.

Alinea is booked months in advance and typically has a wait list of 50–100 names per night. The reality, though, is that on any given night a table remains empty. One or two parties call every night with a last minute cancellation, despite the fact that we make every effort to confirm the reservation and have a policy of charging $100 per person if the table is canceled with less than forty-eight hours' notice and cannot be rebooked. A small but vocal minority of patrons simply do not understand that despite the long wait list it is often impossible for us to contact people an hour before we open and have them commit to such a long, formal meal. The other issue is that people often have a couple drop out of a larger table of four or six. Now we have an opportunity to book an extra 2-top but nowhere to put them, as we are seating a party of four at the table of six they reserved. It is easy to see that with two or three of these situations every night, it is the equivalent of 5 percent or more of our potential revenue walking out the door. Unlike an airline, we can't simply overbook and offer up a dining voucher. With restaurant margins as tight as they are, even at an expensive restaurant like Alinea, these cancellations can make or break us.

So we had long mulled the idea of selling tickets, only to be told by both our own staff and others in the industry that it was a terrible idea. We repeatedly heard that no one would prepay for a meal they could not cancel.

Still, much of the rest of the world manages to book events with tickets. Theaters, sporting events, concerts, and even dinner theaters sell nonrefundable but fully transferable tickets. Doing so would completely change the economics of our restaurant. We would know ahead of time exactly how many people would be attending. The incidents of no-shows or late cancellations would be greatly reduced or eliminated—people could just give the tickets away to friends if something came up. And tables of two, four, and six would be filled exactly to that number. We could safely offer an amazing four-star experience at a reduced cost to the public, knowing that our revenue could be predicted with near certainty.

We kept the "Tickets—yes, tickets" in the trailer, posted it on the Web, and couldn't wait to make the announcement. But we had no idea what exactly we were going to build or how we could possibly sell tickets.

As the Beard Awards wound down, we began telling the press about the Next trailer and concept. Since we hadn't yet signed the lease, raised money from investors, or designed the restaurant, details beyond that were "secret." It felt like jumping out of a plane knowing that you would have to pull the parachute on the way down. Once in the air, it was going to happen. By the next morning, thirty-five hundred people had registered their e-mails to be notified when tickets went on sale. By the end of the week, we had nearly eight thousand prospective customers. Questions from the press about the menus came from as far away as Brazil because we included "São Paulo 1968" as one of the potential menus. In reality, we had quickly come up with a list of ideas for menus, none of which were concrete. The pressure built steadily and the expectations were higher than we wanted or needed.

The design for Next was dictated primarily by the narrow shape of the room and the concept. We needed a space that was neutral enough to serve any cuisine but still resonate with the concept. Discussions kept returning to the idea of travel and a point of embarking on a trip. Much of the excitement in travel is bound up in the expectation of a journey. We discarded the obvious references, such as suitcases and signage, and began to focus on the architectural details common to classic train stations, airports, and seaports—and stories of travel ranging from Gulliver to Jonah and the Whale. Many of these places contained steel framing that worked like an exoskeleton for the larger structure. Slowly, a morphed steel "truss" began to form in our designs as a literal and figurative backbone to the restaurant.

The Aviary, again, was more difficult. Having done away with a traditional bar in favor of a drink kitchen, we had to decide how people would be seated, what sort of tables we would offer, and what the social experience would be. Tom Stringer created a layout whereby the seating areas had high-backed, curved booths that would create privacy while seated, but allow guests to still "see and be seen" by everyone around them. We imagined it to be a high-end, futuristic hotel lounge minus the hotel.

The point of greatest contention in building any restaurant is the clear trade-off between guest comfort, luxury, and revenue. Quite simply, the number of seats often dictates restaurant design. For Alinea we threw that out the window. For Next and The Aviary, we started by trying to make them more economically viable and thus have a greater seating capacity.

We began with a check average—$40 for The Aviary and $80 for Next—and worked backward to how many covers we would need to do per night to make them work as a business, then how many seats we would need to do that many covers. The answer was something near ninety for Next and 125 for The Aviary. Both seemed doable, as the previous businesses that occupied the spaces—a mid-line Italian restaurant and a bar—had capacities far greater than those numbers. But then we began planning the kitchens.

It is difficult—no, impossible—to own a restaurant like Alinea, where every resource is available to our chefs and front-of-house team, then intentionally exclude those tools from a new restaurant. As we began designing the kitchens, sketches came from Dave Beran and

Craig Schoettler—the chefs chosen to run the Next and The Aviary kitchens—that not only included everything in the Alinea kitchen but actually improved upon the deficiencies. Why wouldn't we want to make Next and The Aviary *better* than Alinea if we had the chance? How could we ask chefs or servers or sommeliers to work at Next if it was somehow a step down from Alinea? Saying it was "different from Alinea"—although true—remained a hollow excuse to put commerce in front of quality.

Quickly, the notion that we would run a more bistro-like restaurant with Next or that The Aviary would not be groundbreaking in its kitchen design went away. Seating charts began to shrink to something very much Alinea-like, and the kitchen at Next expanded to include not only a mini-Alinea kitchen on the main floor, but also a one-of-a-kind drink kitchen that might be impossible to manufacture and a prep kitchen in the basement. At every step along the way, the argument was won for quality over covers. The designers deleted tables and started drawing more kitchens.

One of the few things that reality food television programs portray correctly is the construction of any restaurant. It is a frustrating, stress-inducing, costly process that simply cannot go smoothly. The producers of these shows do not need to ply the cast with booze and sleep-deprivation; drama will occur naturally.

The construction of Next and The Aviary took nearly eight months, and any naïve notions that it would be easier than building Alinea, or that we "knew what we were doing," were quickly dispelled. Each project has its own snafus, missed deadlines, deadbeat subcontractors, and contradictory city codes. Here's just one example.

The kitchen designs for Next and The Aviary took their cues directly from the Alinea kitchen. While Next's main kitchen is about a third smaller than Alinea's, we added a basement prep kitchen to handle The Aviary's food and morning prep for Next, and, of course, we had The Aviary's bar kitchen as well. In total it was about 60 percent more total kitchen space and fabrication than Alinea.

And then there was The Aviary's pass. The entire premise of The

Aviary is to remove the bartender from service. You wouldn't go into an Italian restaurant, walk into the kitchen, and order a veal chop, a stuffed rigatoni, and a plate of pasta directly from the chef. Nor would that chef then be charged with making all three disparate plates while washing the serviceware, finding the *mise en place*, and chatting with you about your ex-wife. Sure, in some respects the traditional bar arrangement is great. But for highly conceptual and crafted cocktails that would be delivered in a timely fashion, the arrangement is just silly.

So we designed a large, angled kitchen pass that included five drink stations—one for each drink chef in the kitchen. At each station, a curved well would hold all of the liquor, ice, citrus, and other ingredients the chef would need for five or six cocktails. Orders would then be split among the chefs by an expediter, just as they are in a high-end kitchen. All of the drawers beneath the counter would be either refrigerated or freezers. At the opposite side, sixteen drawers, fit exactly to the size of dish racks, would hold all of the glassware. The head chef would pull a glass out and put it in front of the appropriate chef, and that chef would know what drink was ordered simply by the type of glass.

The problem was that no such kitchen ever had been built before, and there was a question as to how to fabricate and weld the curved wells. We were quoted a price of more than $70,000 for this single piece of equipment. Negotiated as part of the larger contract, we got the pricing down, but with a catch: the delivery, installation, and payment needed to be made before December 31, 2010. That meant we had to ask our general contractor to have all of his subs work overtime during the holiday season to get the kitchens in shape for installation. Plumbing, electrical, refrigeration lines, and concrete curbs needed to be in place before the delivery. What we saved in negotiating the discount on the equipment manufacturing we spent on overtime hours, quick-set concrete, and expedited permits.

And then on December 22 we received a call telling us that the kitchen would be delivered sometime in late February. And The Aviary's bar pass? Sometime in April—if all of the refrigeration could be figured out. It became clear that the engineering of the pass—let alone its fabrication, due to be delivered in a week—had not yet even begun.

That is how it is building a restaurant. Some component somewhere—perhaps the contractor, lighting fixtures, banquette installation, fabric for the pillows, specialized mirrors, the metal for the "cage" in front of The Aviary kitchen, or, likely, all of these—will have issues. But you cajole, beg, pay extra, or don't pay at all, and you find a way to get it built to standards. For every difficult contractor there are those heroic workers that spend three straight days working to meet an inspection deadline.

Just as the design and construction for Next and The Aviary moved in a more upscale direction, so too did the opening menu for Next. Originally conceived as "Paris 1912" and a bistro style of food, discussions moved more and more towards Escoffier. If we did bistro-style food, how would that have been indicative of 1912 versus 2011? It is largely the same. However, Escoffier—the father of modern cooking—could provide some truly antique and transformative dishes, and we need only look back slightly further to 1900–1906.

All of the chefs became immediately more excited by recreating and interpreting this more-refined cuisine. Not only was it more in line with what we do at Alinea and more challenging, it was also something that simply could not be found at nearly any other restaurant in the world. As we moved closer to the opening, we decided to invite some friends and family to the first test dinner for the newly named "Paris 1906" menu. We also invited a few key members of the press and blogosphere.

The process of creating any menu for Next or Alinea is not linear or smooth or ever exactly finished. We take ideas, try them in the kitchen, taste the results, discuss it among a small group of people we trust, then go back and modify—and repeat the process again and again. At some point we find just the right combination of recipe and presentation. Or we run out of time.

The first formal serving of the Paris 1906 menu was, however, very much a work in progress. Some of the dishes were being plated for the first time. It was a tense moment, made more so by the presence of the press. The meal went fairly well until the Puree Palestine, a sunchoke soup, was served.

Immediately, a few diners at the table took a taste, put their spoons down after a few polite sips, and looked around. A few others dutifully finished it but clearly didn't enjoy it. And a few others gobbled it down. Then the conversation started:

"It tastes flat."

"Right. It's not just flat. It tastes like I am eating straight fat."

"That's exactly the point," Nick said. "Where would you get something like that nowadays? Nowhere. All the French restaurants have converted to a healthier style. The whole point is that this is unfiltered French food. You should go home and wake up in a sweat at 3:00 A.M. thinking you might vomit from all the richness."

"Who wants to eat like that?"

At that point, Grant, who had been listening from just outside the dining room, came in. He was not pleased that this argument was happening in front of the press. "So should we just omit salt? Because none of the Escoffier recipes call for salt. Should we just hand press the soup through a sieve? Because Escoffier didn't have a blender. Should we add some acid, or just leave it to taste totally flat without vibrancy?" It wasn't a discussion in his mind. You can't serve "bad" soup. Period.

"It could be that the vegetables were transported in salt back then as a desiccant. Or were pickled," Nick offered up, stating what had already been suggested at the table by others. But Grant was hearing none of it.

"We could do that. But we're not opening a museum, are we?"

About two weeks before the opening, we gathered together with our programmer, Brian Tucker, who was hard at work refining the ticket-sales software. At this point we had nearly 20,000 names on an opt-in e-mail list asking to be notified when tickets went on sale. For the season, we had around 2,000 tables for sale. We expected it would take a week or so to sell most of the tables, then the rest would be sold closer to the actual date of dining. Skeptics in the press and the industry remained, and while we had our internal doubts there was no reason why we couldn't just go back to taking normal reservations if it didn't work.

Still, we had much vested in the ticket system. All of our economic forecasts were based on the idea that we would sell tickets in even numbers and have a predictable cash flow. Servers and chefs would be paid as if they worked for a firm in any other type of industry— earning a salary, benefits, and a periodic bonus based on their own performance and the success of the company.

Brian presented a system that was in wire-frame form. The hard work had been done. The database underlying the system was robust, the layout of the daily "book" was elegant, and the variable pricing was easy to input and adjust. But graphically it looked like something only an engineer could love.

While we were engaged in trying to get the final construction finished and get everyone from the city through for final inspections, Martin was called in to redo the graphic elements of the ticket system. This appeared to be a simple job, but everything for every user is generated in real time. The part that the customer sees needed to be completely rebuilt both from a design and programming standpoint.

Three days before our scheduled opening we had not sold a single ticket. Load testing of the system confirmed that we could handle a significant amount of traffic. But the real world presents all sorts of issues that a simulation cannot anticipate. And then two days before opening we found a major bug. If two customers made just the right series of clicks at the same time, we could double-sell a single table. This was a catastrophic failure and a nightmare. Imagine twenty customers showing up for each table.

Panic set in. Concurrent with the training of the staff, the unpacking of hundreds of boxes of supplies, the inspections, and the test dinners, we had to retool a major piece of software almost overnight.

Working on no sleep for several days, we finally found the bug and Brian began to fix it. Clearly, there would be no time for testing. At midnight on opening day we uploaded the new code to the servers. Normally, propagating a website so that people around the world can see it, takes a few hours. Sometimes it takes a few days.

This time it was agonizingly slow.

By 10:00 A.M. on opening night we had not sold a ticket, and the website could be seen only sporadically, even on our own machines. Brian and Martin, and both of us, had not slept in nearly three days. We couldn't think straight.

Phone calls went back and forth. "We should start taking reservations via Facebook."

"No. We should do an extra friends and family dinner."

"Screw it. Just flip the switch and turn it on."

We sent out the e-mail to the first 2,000 people on the list. Some of them will see the website, we thought; some won't, but it will be random, which isn't all bad.

Then, of course, there was the question of whether or not the software would even work correctly. To say that we were nervous about the whole process was an understatement. *Businessweek*, *Fast Company*, and *The New York Times* had covered the ticket concept. We had, we felt, one shot to sell tickets to a restaurant, and if it didn't work well it would be a failure.

A Facebook page that was hastily set up a few weeks before became our information portal since it was, of course, stable and working. We described the DNS issues on there and told people that we were doing our best to correct the problem.

Slowly, the patrons who received the first e-mails, though frustrated at the slow speed of the website, began buying tickets. Quickly, opening night sold out.

Then we released the next few thousand names on the list. And again, a huge percentage of those people, far in excess of what we had projected, logged into the system and began buying tickets.

Complaints came in through e-mail and Facebook that the system was terrible. And they were right. But tables were not being double-booked—the nightmare scenario—and the transactions were being processed correctly.

We had released 60 percent of all of the available tables for the season—1,220 tables in total. Within six hours, all were sold.

Arriving back at Next we looked at each other and shrugged.

This is totally nuts.

The Aviary opening was delayed for three weeks. The push to build Next, find and train staff for both places, create the menus and drinks, all while running Alinea, proved to be too much. We had experience running one restaurant well. We were in over our heads trying to open two more at once.

It was an agonizing and fiscally costly decision, but ultimately the correct one. We held eight friends and family nights at The Aviary before we finally opened the doors to the public. We wanted to be certain that it was as ready as Next.

When we finally announced a firm opening, we had customers camping outside the front door the night before as if we were about to sell the iPhone 5. By noon on opening night, a line stretched down the block.

Over the past five months, Next and The Aviary have garnered press and accolades throughout the world. Grant was named to *Time*'s 100 Most Influential People in the World list. Next received both four-stars and three-stars from the *Chicago Tribune* for the Paris 1906 menu and the Tour of Thailand menu that followed. It seems we will get re-reviewed every time we create a new menu. Each will be analyzed, debated, and put under a microscope, only to be ditched in a few months for whatever we decide to explore next. Our Tour of Thailand menu sold out in a few hours. Childhood, on a new server system with much-improved software, sold out even faster.

In a few weeks, the new Michelin Guide comes out. It is hoped that Alinea, having garnered 3-stars last year, continues on that path. But nothing is for certain.

Five nights per week, fifty-one weeks per year, 156 employees get to work to create an experience for 420 people—eighty diners at Alinea, 120 at Next, and 220 patrons at the The Aviary and the Office. All of those people arrive with the hope that their perception of dining will be changed, that Alinea, Next, and The Aviary will exceed their lofty expectations. Every night we try to make that happen. Much of the time we succeed.

From our side it all feels more fragile than you might imagine. Just like Broadway, the show must always go on. During the massive snowstorm in Chicago in February 2011, which stranded more than 1,500 cars on Lake Shore Drive, we walked over to Alinea to call the customers personally and let them know that we could not get food deliveries that day and would be forced to close for the first time ever. We walked into a kitchen where our entire prep team, at 7:30 A.M., had been figuring out how to make a twenty-course meal happen with minimal supplies. Every one of them had walked to work at 6:00 A.M., since all forms of transport were shut down, some from as far as 5 miles away, in waist-deep snow. It was an amazing, tangible display of the dedication our employees give to us every day.

And yet, we keep pushing because it does feel like it can all unravel in a moment. One bad dish, one uninspired menu, one poorly crafted drink could sink it. We read the reviews and the blogs and the Facebook posts and analyze the experience from the other side each day. We genuinely worry about the restaurants, the brand, and our reputation constantly.

We are terrible at enjoying ourselves and what we have created with these restaurants. We always tell each other to relax a bit, to settle down and realize what has already been accomplished. But that never works.

We're always looking forward. Next year's plans include: 1. El Bulli menu. 2. Alinea redux/reframe. 3. The Aviary book. 4. #!*% Yeah: Ramen. 5. Three or more eBooks.

And so, life on the line goes onward, chaotically, without sleep and with all of the challenges of running what is now a mid-size company. We keep throwing new ideas out there, just to dare each other and our teams to make it happen.

We are fortunate to still have the chance to do any of it. And for that we are genuinely thankful.

—Grant and Nick, November 2011

INDEX

E

Ebert, Roger, 334, 336, 342
education, 18, 27–30
egg station, 3–4
eGullet, 150–52, 217, 230, 272
elBulli, 63, 101–3, 103–4, 119, 127, 146
El Poblet, 151
Elysian Fields Farm, 113, 117, 152
Erbitux, 344, 351, 360
Ermenegildo Zegna USA, 243, 249
Esquire, 270, 274–75

F

Ferris Bueller's Day Off, 167
Fine Arts Institute, 157
fish stations, 87
Fleur de Lys, 132
Food Arts, 248
food critics and reviews. *See also specific individuals and publications*
  Alinea reviews, 247–48, 262–67, 270–76, 284–85, 287, 295, 377–79
  French Laundry reviews, 83–85, 86, 266, 281, 282, 284–85, 287–88
  and Grant's cancer diagnosis, 340–41
  Grant's resistance to, 270–73
  La Jota winery article, 94–95
  Trio reviews, 107, 127, 141–45, 162–63, 215–16
Food Lab, 218, 225–30, 232–34
Food Network, 154
Food & Wine
  and Alinea opening, 248
  and Alinea proposal, 192
  awards to Grant, 148, 150, 154, 295
  and Dagmara Kokonas, 176
  La Jota winery article, 94–95
  profile of Alinea, 259
  and public relations for Alinea, 231
Food & Wine Classic, 148–50
Fox, Andy, 311–13
The French Laundry
  copper polish recipe, 216
  dinner series with Grant, 384–85
  Grant's decision to leave, 103–9
  Grant's first days at, 72–73
  Grant's new dishes at, 99–100
  Grant's training at, 73–75, 75–77, 82–85
  and Grant's Trio position, 122
  Grant's tryout at, 60–61, 61–66
  and Grant's wedding, 277
  indigenous Hawaiian ingredients, 323
  Keller's training at, 75–77
  as model for Grant's cooking, 120, 127, 132, 133–35, 156, 257
  organizational changes, 98
  reviews of, 59, 83–85, 86, 266, 281–82, 284–85, 287–88
  and sous chef position, 73, 78, 96–97, 98, 107, 120
The French Laundry Cookbook (Keller), 86
Funbrain.com, 175, 177, 218

G

Galdes, Jenn, 231, 270–72, 340
Gallante, Shea, 333
game meats, 34, 173
Gand, Gale, 106, 107, 126
garde manger stations, 63, 78, 82, 88, 131, 282
Georges Blanc, 52–56
Gerber, Chris
  and Alinea investor dinner, 212–14